**MEHL, Dieter.** The Middle English romances of the thirteenth and fourteenth centuries. Barnes & Noble, 1969. 300p bibl 71-379186. 7.50

*CHOICE*     *FEB. '71*

*Language & Literature*

*English & American*

PR
321
M49

English ed.
(1969)
Routledge
& K Paul.

Definitely fills a gap on undergraduate library shelves, providing a comprehensive, readable study surveying the most important English romances of the later Middle Ages. Mehl does not claim "completeness" for his study, but for undergraduate reading purposes, we surely find here God's plenty: discussions of four Breton lays, 17 "shorter" romances, nine "homiletic" romances, five "longer" romances, and six works classified as "novels in verse." Introductory chapters give well documented, compact discussions of the historical, social and literary milieus which produced the English romance, a genre Mehl considers (for literary as well as social reasons) to be in a class apart from earlier continental romances. His discussion of the problem of classification moves on to artistic considerations engendered by questions of length, purpose, and form; classification by earlier scholars, notably R. S. Loomis (rev. ed., 1959) or J. B. Severs (1967, o.p.) tends toward the "sources and analogues" type of manual, rather than literary criticism as such. Mehl discusses each romance separately as an individual work of art; e.g. "Sir Gawain and the green knight" rates 14 thoughtful pages. A new category which Mehl devises is the "homiletic

*Continued*

**MEHL**

*CHOICE*     *FEB. '71*

*Language & Literature*

*English & American*

romance," in which plot is subordinated to a moral and religious theme; he discusses nine such romances. Appendix on existing manuscripts of the English romances; useful and up-to-date bibliography; extraordinary, full bibliographical notes; index. Recommended.

# THE MIDDLE ENGLISH ROMANCES
## OF THE THIRTEENTH AND
## FOURTEENTH CENTURIES

# THE MIDDLE
# ENGLISH ROMANCES
## OF THE
# THIRTEENTH AND
# FOURTEENTH CENTURIES

by

Dieter Mehl

*Professor of English at the University of Bonn*

Routledge & Kegan Paul

LONDON

*First published 1967 under the title*
Die mittelenglischen Romanzen des 13. und 14. Jahrhunderts
© *1967 Carl Winter, Universitätsverlag, Heidelberg*
*First English language edition published 1968*
*by Routledge & Kegan Paul Limited*
*Broadway House, 68–74 Carter Lane*
*London, E.C.4*

*Printed in Great Britain*
*by Butler and Tanner Ltd*
*Frome and London*

© *Dieter Mehl 1968*

*SBN 7100 6240 0*

Owing to production
delays this book was
published in 1969

# CONTENTS

v

# PREFACE

A book on Middle English Romances hardly needs an apology. Much valuable work has been done on individual poems in recent years, but the few general surveys of the romances do not, on the whole, seem to have taken much account of the genre as a whole, and it is generally agreed that a fresh look is needed. In this study I propose to consider the romances rather as a characteristically English type of narrative poem than as inferior copies of French models and I attempt a new classification. Though I have tried to make full use of all previous scholarly work in the field, I have not aimed at completeness and certainly not at superseding the indispensable manuals of Laura A. Hibbard and J. E. Wells (J. B. Severs). Without these, any study of the romances would be a much more difficult undertaking. I am aware that much of what I have said will not be new to specialists, but I hope that I have succeeded in placing some of it in a new context and in suggesting some fresh lines of approach. I have, therefore, dealt rather briefly with source-problems, but have tried to select a fair number of typical and particularly interesting romances and in each case endeavoured to discuss those elements that seem most relevant for a better understanding of the poem in question.

Since one of the assumptions of this book is that the term *romance*, as applied to about a hundred Middle English narrative poems, does not really have any precise and useful meaning, I toyed with the idea of doing without it altogether; but scholars on the whole know what they mean when they talk about romances, and it seemed more sensible to keep the term as a rather loose, but practical label which has to be defined afresh for each work.

I am deeply grateful to Professor Wolfgang Clemen for much helpful encouragement and advice. Professor Walter F. Schirmer, who himself has worked on this subject for many more years than I, very generously placed some of his notes on the romances at my disposal. I should also like to thank Professor Karl Heinz

vii

Göller (University of Regensburg) and Dr. Beatrice White (West-field College, London) for their kind interest and useful advice and the University of Munich and the British Council for travel grants.

My wife has been of invaluable help in producing the revised and expanded English version of this book which was originally published in German by Carl Winter Universitätsverlag, Heidelberg. It is to her that my greatest thanks are due.

All quotations in the text are taken from the editions listed in the bibliography. I have, however, not indicated where italics or parentheses (for conjectural letters) or capital þ and ȝ are used in the editions.

D.M.

*University of Bonn*

# ABBREVIATIONS

| | |
|---|---|
| *Archiv* | *Archiv für das Studium der neueren Sprachen und Literaturen* |
| EETS, ES | Early English Text Society, Extra Series |
| *ELH* | *A Journal of English Literary History* |
| *GRM* | *Germanisch-Romanische Monatsschrift* (NF = Neue Folge) |
| *JEGP* | *Journal of English and Germanic Philology* |
| *MLN* | *Modern Language Notes* |
| *MLR* | *Modern Language Review* |
| *MP* | *Modern Philology* |
| *PMLA* | *Publications of the Modern Language Association of America* |
| *RES* | *Review of English Studies* |
| *SP* | *Studies in Philology* |

# 1

## INTRODUCTION: THE MIDDLE ENGLISH ROMANCES

Since English medieval literature was first seriously studied, scholars have been in the habit of separating a certain group of narratives from the vast assortment of Middle English verse, and bracketing them together as *romances*. It seems rather strange that unlike most literary terms this particularly vague one has hardly ever been seriously questioned, although it has so far not proved especially helpful and says very little about the form or even the subject of the works it is usually applied to.

To the scholars of the nineteenth century, when medieval studies reached their first climax, the common denominator was, of course, the subject-matter of the romances. As the English poems were mainly approached by way of the French romances and *chansons de geste*, it was taken for granted that the same criteria could be applied to both, and that the English romances were only derivatives of the French—and very inferior ones at that. Thus, George Ellis, whose collection of *Specimens of Early English Metrical Romances* was one of the most influential works on the subject,[1] seems to have been interested almost exclusively in the content of these poems, as his prose abstracts suggest. His classification of the romances according to 'matters' has been adopted by most scholars up to the present day.[2] The individual character and literary form of the English romances seem to have concerned him very little. Since then, most of the romances have been compared wherever possible with their French sources in some detail;[3] but such comparisons, consisting for the most part only of lists of differences and parallels, were used mainly to prove the migrations of certain stories and motifs or to illustrate cultural differences between the two countries. It has become a critical commonplace to allow the English romances a certain freshness, charming simplicity and

I

native vigour, but to dismiss most of them as inferior translations or imitations. It is worth asking, however, whether the English romances are no more than mere translations and whether, in addressing a completely different audience, the English authors did not create a new literary type that should be judged by other standards than the French 'originals'. A brief review of the historical situation may serve to illustrate this.

## THE HISTORICAL CONTEXT

The English romances were, practically without exception, written very much later than their counterparts in French and German. The flourishing of the romances, in France and Germany, had by the fourteenth century given way to clearly derivative productions, while at the same time new forms and conventions were being created. It was only then, however, that in England the old romances were taken up again and newly adapted to suit changed tastes. To talk about imitation and decline is hardly appropriate here. The classic form of the courtly novel that had evolved in France, only provided a very vague model for the English adapters and they did not succeed in creating new and exemplary literary genres as did the German poets of the twelfth and early thirteenth centuries. Even Chaucer is no exception here; his work only reflects the great variety of literary forms in Middle English, and one could use *The Canterbury Tales* to illustrate almost every type of Middle English narrative poetry.[4] He seems to have been attracted by the idea that he could turn his hand to any kind of tale, from Saints' legends to courtly novels, from edifying *exempla* to ribald *fabliaux*, and each time excel his predecessors or, indeed, parody them. If one could at all claim for him that he developed his own favourite genre, this would have to be defined as a short and yet leisurely narrative whose individuality lies in the manner of telling the story, rather than in its subject-matter. This variety of form and subject is almost the only thing Chaucer's tales have in common with the romances, if we except agreements in smaller details of subject and style.[5] His poetry is, needless to say, highly sophisticated and courtly which can only be said of very few romances.

This astonishing variety of literary types and the failure to produce something like a 'classic' genre[6] can at least partly be explained by reference to the social and political background. We shall have to ask for what audiences, by whom, and under what external conditions the romances were written. As these questions have been discussed before in some detail, a few general remarks will suffice.

It is on the whole admitted that English knighthood never achieved the same exclusive and creative unity as it did in France and even in Germany.[7] Wherever something like a distinctly courtly environment grew up in England, it was very dependent on French models, an off-shoot of French ideas of chivalry, French even in language, and lacking native strength and individuality. During the last decades it has become evident that in Norman England, especially under Henry II, there was far more literary activity than had previously been supposed, and important works of literature and scholarship were produced,[8] but it can be said even of the first centuries after the conquest, that courtly society and culture was less exclusive than on the continent. The influence of Chrétien de Troyes, for instance, was not very far-reaching, and even during the twelfth century the Anglo-Norman poet Hue de Rotelande portrays chivalry and courtly ceremony with a certain degree of detached irony.[9] This applies even more to the thirteenth and fourteenth centuries, the period in which most of the extant English romances were probably written. At that period we have even less reason to assume that there was a closed courtly body in society, portraying and idealizing itself in fiction, at least not in English. Instead, many of the knights took a far more active part in the more pedestrian and sober work of administration than on the continent and proved to be very useful though perhaps less glamorous members of feudal society. Thus even the most faithful translation of some French or Anglo-Norman courtly romance would be addressed to a completely different audience from that of the original and would delight the hearers (if at all) for very different reasons.

The centres of courtly life in England, too, were different from those in France and Germany. There were, to be sure, a number of smaller feudal households, castles and estates of barons and lower aristocracy throughout the country, and, of course, the Court of the English King; but they never played the same important part in the cultural life of the nation as did the French Court and some of the more prosperous households of princes and dukes in France and Germany, where often a highly sophisticated court-life and an amazing literary productivity developed. In England, with only a few exceptions, artificial courtly ceremonies and literary cliques remained on a more modest scale. Most of the social occasions, on which minstrels performed and, possibly, romances were read, appear to have differed considerably from the exclusive aristocratic festivities on the continent. The detailed descriptions of such courtly entertainments in many romances, if they had not been omitted altogether in the English versions, must have impressed the listeners mainly by their unreal, fairy-tale-like character, which was not at all the intention of the original poets. As far as their courtly background is concerned, the English romances were for the most part far more removed from actuality and from the day-to-day experience of the audience than the French. But the majority of them did not attempt to imitate the French romances in this respect anyway and reflected fairly accurately the profound changes in social conditions.

It is also typical that the tournament, a particularly characteristic form of chivalric self-realization and entertainment, never attained the same degree of popularity in England as it did on the continent.[10] Tournaments were, of course, frequently held and well attended, but they rarely displayed the splendour and formality of the French tournaments, nor were they as widely accepted. For political and religious reasons they were in perpetual danger of prohibition, often confined to certain times and places. When, especially under Edward III, they were more keenly supported and promoted, they must have already had a distinctly archaic and even nostalgic atmosphere.

The same can indeed be said for most English chivalry of the fourteenth century. The same period that saw the emergence of the English romances, also saw the steady decline of the knight, who had been such an essential part of courtly society. Just as the knight's armour began to prove useless and obsolete during the French wars, the courtly etiquette likewise seemed to become outmoded. Where it was kept alive artificially, as was the case all over Europe, it bore no significant relation to life and had only the charm of antiquity.[11] This is why, from the beginning, the English romances were fairy-tales, stories from a distant past, 'of eldirs, þat byfore vs were' (*Sir Ysumbras*, l.2). With very few exceptions, they were not an immediate confrontation with the present. They did

4

not aim at a faithful representation of present-day reality, but, as will be seen, at the illustration of moral truths by way of an exemplary story. They are, for the most part, homiletic in intention rather than courtly and topical. Even *Sir Gawain and the Green Knight*, where courtly decorum plays such an important part, is basically not a poem about chivalry, and its real meaning has not much in common with the courtly literature of France.[12] Probably, the actual manner of the knight's existence as it would appear to contemporaries, is to be met not so much in the descriptions of the Round Table and the adventures of Arthur's knights, as in the fates of the impoverished warriors, like Amadace, Launfal and Ysumbras.

Another important fact in considering the position of the knight in English society, is that the divisions between the classes were, on the whole, less rigorous than on the continent. Most sources suggest that as early as the Middle Ages there was closer contact between the aristocracy and the 'citizen', between town and country, between the King and his subjects. Thus, for instance, hardly any towns (with the possible exception of London) grew up cut off from the country, with an independent and exclusive life of their own, as in France, Italy and, to a lesser extent, in Germany. The reasons for this difference probably lie in the political history of the country as well as in the character of its people and do not concern us here. It is, however, evident that English literature was deeply influenced by these factors. One minor instance is perhaps the particular popularity of tales in which the King in disguise comes into direct contact with some of his subjects; the narrator's sympathy is always clearly on the side of the bluff citizen who treats his sovereign with very little respect and is richly rewarded in the end.[13]

The history of English as a language considered suitable for literature also has to be briefly discussed.[14] It is well known that during the early Middle Ages the overwhelming majority of literary works produced in England were written either in Latin or in French. If this important fact is neglected, as is often the case, a completely false impression of the true state of literature and scholarship during the twelfth and thirteenth centuries is created by the poor literary output in English. Modern research has made it seem likely that the use of English was far more widespread than had often been assumed. It remains true, however, that for the more ambitious poets before Chaucer, English was only a second-rate literary medium. The often quoted statements we find in some romances and historical works about the relative importance of the English and the French languages seem to point towards two conclusions. They prove that English was spreading fast during the fourteenth century, while the use of French declined, even in aristocratic circles:

> Freynsche vse þis gentilman,
> Ac euerich Inglische Inglische can;
> Mani noble ich haue yseiʒe,
> þat no Freynsche couþe seye:
>
> (*Arthour and Merlin*, ll. 23–6)

On the other hand, a large part of the literature in English seems to have been written at first with a certain amount of condescension, and many of the romances address themselves to *lewed men*.[15] However, the situation appears to have changed rapidly in the course of the century; an adequate command of French could be assumed less and less among the upper classes, and the circle of those who preferred writings in English widened steadily. I feel sure that collections like the Vernon Ms., where *lewed men* are addressed several times, and the Auchinleck Ms. were not just intended for the lowest classes, but appealed as much to the more educated who preferred to listen to stories written in English, even though they may not have been prepared to admit it. It is important to note that with the increasing quantity of writings in English the output of literature written in French declined. Most of the English romances were written at a time when even a large proportion of the upper classes was no longer able or willing to read the originals, and the period of Anglo-Norman literature slowly came to an end.[16] It can therefore be assumed that these English poems were directed at a much wider audience than is often believed and did not just satisfy the common people's appetite for cheap entertainment. With Chaucer, of course, English became the chief literary medium, and this was also the time when most of the romance-versions that have come down to us were written. Something like a new beginning can also be seen in the lyrical poetry of the time. Here, too, we find French influence rapidly declining in the second half of the fourteenth century and a more independent style beginning to emerge.[17]

## AUTHORS AND AUDIENCES

The questions of authorship and of the composition of the audience addressed by the romances are closely related. As they are better discussed individually for each poem, I shall confine myself here to a few general remarks.

For a long time it was assumed as a proven fact that most of the romances were composed by wandering minstrels who recited them at public festivities and in market-places to an audience consisting mainly of farmers and craftsmen. This theory, which can still be met with in histories of literature, has, however, been shown to be rather questionable and to be based on very slender evidence.[18]

It is not even certain that most of these poems were ever recited by minstrels. We have quite a number of informative records about the activities of the minstrels or 'gleemen'.[19] We know that they played an important part at the royal court where a number of them were regularly employed; that wandering minstrels were an important means of communication and of spreading information of various kinds; and that they often made a nuisance of themselves by their begging and importunity so that special laws were proclaimed against them. Their social status and, probably, their literary abilities, varied considerably according to whether they were regularly employed at court or wandering about the country living from hand to mouth. Evidently, they were entertainers in the widest sense. They were good for any sport to while away the time: jokes, magic, little performances of all kinds, and, above all, music. The words 'minstrelsy' and 'minstrel' seem to have referred almost always to instrumental music and those performing it. But very few records suggest that they recited extensive stories of a literary character, let alone wrote them.[20]

The debate about minstrels has often been confused by widely differing conceptions of what a minstrel really was; very often the picture was rather a romantic one. The label 'minstrel' sometimes became a last resort whenever scholars could not agree about the authorship of a poem and 'oral composition' was suspected. A sober examination of the sources—the frequent mention of minstrels in the romances has of course only very limited value as historical evidence—will bring home the fact that we still know very little about the minstrels, and what we know does not justify our ascribing to them a substantial part of the extant Middle English poems, unless we count among the minstrels all those amateurs who, apart from their usual occupations as clergymen, monks, civil servants or scribes, busied themselves with the translation, copying and dissemination of poetry.

It is to the poems themselves then, that we must turn for information about their origin. At first sight they seem to support the 'minstrel theory'. Thus, the majority of the romances begin with a direct address to the audience, with a prayer or with an exhortation to listen quietly. Many formulas which keep appearing in these poems seek to establish some contact between the author (or reciter) and his audience and make it quite clear that these poems are meant to be heard, not to be read in silence. It hardly needs emphasizing, however, that this is true of practically all medieval literature, of lyrics, chronicles, legends and verse novels alike, so that it provides no clue as to the authorship of the romances.[21] Many of the clichés often associated with the minstrels are, moreover, not confined to the romances. Collections of such tags often give a misleading impression because they take only a limited number of poems into account.[22] One can, however, easily discover that many legends, chronicles and didactic poems begin likewise by addressing an audience, often in exactly the same words as some romances. If one were to ascribe all these poems to minstrels, the minstrels' repertory would have had to be much more comprehensive than anyone has ever claimed.[23] Even the *Gawain*-poet, who certainly was not a minstrel, uses such tags, and of course Chaucer employs them frequently, sometimes without any alteration, occasionally to achieve some particular narrative effect.[24] Often these tags were taken over from the foreign sources, in which case they prove nothing about the manner of recitation in England.[25] It cannot be denied that they may have had their origin in an oral tradition, but they were subsequently embodied in the written versions and imitated by the translators. In most Middle English poems they are a purely literary convention, designed to create an atmosphere of lively recitation, and they were probably in the majority of cases read out from the manuscript rather than improvised.

This applies particularly to the longer works, like *Guy of Warwick* or the *Laud Troy Book* which could hardly have been recited *in extenso* by wandering minstrels. It seems far more reasonable to assume that such novels in verse were read aloud from a manuscript, sometimes, perhaps, by a professional entertainer, but more often by some member of the household to whom the manuscript belonged. The minstrel-tags were thus a feature of the style of verse literature. They may occasionally have been added or altered by the reciter, but for the most part they were inserted by the poet or scribe who, while composing the poem, had before his eyes the situation in which it would be read aloud.

Another fact often quoted in support of the 'minstrel theory' is the frequent mention of minstrels and their performances in the romances. We also often find descriptions of generous rewards received by the minstrels, but this is hardly proof of minstrel-authorship. The performances of minstrels were evidently an important part of any aristocratic festivity, and the generosity of the host only reflected the splendour and success of the entertainment. To include the minstrels in descriptions of courtly celebrations was a general literary practice and is even recommended in Geoffroi de Vinsauf's *Poetria Nova*[26] as a kind of embellishment of style. I do not wish to deny that there may often have been some connection between such descriptions and the occasions on which they were recited; probably many romances were composed and recited by persons who were dependent on the good-will and liberality of their master or some patron, but it would be wrong to conclude from this that the romances must have been written by minstrels.

It is also very doubtful whether many of the manuscripts that have come down to us were written especially for minstrels and were carried about by them on their wanderings, although there may be a few cases where this can be assumed.[27] It seems likely that some minstrels, either by careful reading and memorizing or by oral transmission, collected popular stories and retold them when occasion arose with a good deal of improvisation. Such versions, however, could hardly have been like those that were finally written down in some comparatively careful collection, but were probably much shorter and clumsier. Only a very few minstrels could have been in a position to acquire manuscript collections for their own use.

Many of the extant versions of Middle English romances were probably produced—as Mrs. L. H. Loomis has established in the case of the Auchinleck Ms.—in 'bookshops' where authors (and scribes) had before them a book containing some version of the story they were about to retell (either in English or in French),[28] or else some collection of tales out of which they composed a new romance. The possibility that minstrels had some share in the process or that some scribes also acted as entertainers can, of course, not be ruled out; nor can it be denied that many of those scribes just turned out haphazard, patched-up collections of tags, ready-made rhyming couplets, half-stanzas and motifs gleaned from some other romance. Moreover, it would be unwise to make a cut-and-dried distinction between 'oral' and 'literary' composition. The processes of copying, translating, and adapting were on the whole far less 'literary' than the modern reader might easily imagine. They left ample room for improvisation, the use of clichés and other features which we tend to associate with oral composition. Thus we can find in many romances striking instances of an oral formulaic technique, as A. C. Baugh has demonstrated in his excellent study of 'Improvisation in the Middle English Romance'. Nevertheless, the extant romances appear to be for the most part 'literary' creations, composed with some care at the desk, not just memorized reproductions of some improvised recital by wandering minstrels. It seems necessary to emphasize this fact because the minstrel theory in its cruder form—still not quite extinct—tends to obscure the close connections between the romances and other types of Middle English literature.

These connections become very clear when we turn to the manuscripts. Thus, we have in Middle English hardly any purely 'secular' manuscripts or collections of romances to compare with those of France and Germany.[29] Nearly all romances have survived in large collections containing for the most part religious and didactic literature. In many cases the close relationship between the romances and the other items is also suggested by the language and style of the poems.

In the course of our survey we shall often have to emphasize that many of the romances have just as much in common with some legends or chronicles as they have with each other. This fact, too, seems to suggest that often they were produced by the same authors or adaptors; in the case of the *Gawain*-poet this has long been taken for granted, though, admittedly, *Sir Gawain and the Green Knight* is not a very representative example of Middle English romance.

In many cases it has to be assumed that certain collections and the versions they contain were produced at the special request of some interested patron. The fifteenth century provides many examples of such literary patronage on a small scale, of which the Pastons are perhaps the best known,[30] but from the fourteenth century, too, we have records of it, such as Gower's poetry, the romance of *William of Palerne*, and, possibly, *Arthour and Merlin*. Although a great deal of information on this question is still lacking, there is a strong probability that the compilation of manuscripts to order, and the establishment of stationers and bookshops for the commercial distribution of literature were steadily increasing during the fourteenth century. In other words, the production of Middle English writings was far more 'literary' and professional than is often believed. On the other hand, there are only very few arguments in favour of minstrel-collections, i.e. manuscripts written specially for minstrels and carried around by them. The mixed contents of most manuscripts rather suggest some domestic circle where reading aloud was a regular practice, or the individual taste of some patron who had an anthology compiled for his own use. From the form of the manuscripts, their provenance and their contents one can sometimes draw tentative conclusions as to the composition of the audience. It may have been a more urbane and bourgeois assembly, as in the case of the Auchinleck Ms., or an aristocratic household in the provinces (*Gawain* Ms.).[31]

It can safely be said of most of the authors of Middle English romances that they were not painstakingly careful artists with a very marked feeling of their own importance. Chaucer, Gower and possibly Langland, were among the first English poets with a distinct personality which they also consciously expressed in their works.[32] The romance-authors, however, were not of that kind, not even, as far as we can judge, the *Gawain*-poet. Only very rarely do we find what we might call a distinctively individual style, something like the unmistakable Chaucerian tone of voice. Such qualities were obviously little in demand. As with the collections of Saints' legends or the mystery plays, the authors of all but very few romances have left us guessing as to their own personal character. Consequently, most Middle English poetry is anonymous, whereas many names of Anglo-Norman poets are known to us. This anonymity, however, should not be confused with the truly 'impersonal' origins of folk-songs and (possibly) heroic epics as the romantics saw them; it points rather to the obscurity of the scribe and adapter who considered his task to be fulfilled when he had copied out (or, in copying, produced) a new version of some known fable.[33] Only very few of them had the ambition (which one might have expected of the minstrels) to leave their name behind or to impress their personality on their poems. Thus, most of the romances are not carefully worked-out artistic creations, and a close analysis of form and structure, such as has produced illuminating results in the case of Chaucer's poetry, would not be of much value. It would be easy to over-interpret these poems, to discover individuality and originality where nothing but convention, or the accidental nature of transmission, was at work. Again, *Sir Gawain and the Green Knight* is an exception. Its unusually neat structure is certainly evidence of a definite poetic purpose.

The results of any closer enquiry into the question of authorship would probably be just as varied and elusive as the poems themselves are. Only in a few cases is the minstrel theory at all helpful, most of all, perhaps, in the case of such mutilated and watered-down poems as *Sir Tristrem*.[34] For the most part, however, the origin of the romances has to be imagined as a rather more literary process, a process which could range from the careless hack-writer patching some tale together out of any motif and tag he could think of, to the educated poet, well versed in courtly as well as in religious matters, who left us *Sir Gawain and the Green Knight*.

All this does not, of course, help us to differentiate the romances from the legends and chronicles as a distinct literary genre. Just as collections of romances alone were very rare in Middle English, the exclusive romance-writer was probably an exception, and most romances were written by authors who spent the best part of their time writing or adapting works of a very different kind. This applies to the compilers of the Auchinleck Ms. as well as to the *Gawain*-poet, if indeed he was also the author of the other works generally attributed to him. The close relationship between secular and religious literature in the Middle Ages is again evident here and has to be constantly borne in mind when studying the romances. It also makes it clear that the romances, like the legends and *exempla*, belong to a more popular kind of literature and are not addressed to the few initiated like Gottfried von Strassburg's *Tristan und Isolde*, but to a much wider audience.

The audience of the romances did not, I am sure, consist of the 'common people' only, the sort of people Chaucer's Pardoner means when he says, 'For lewed peple loven tales olde';[35] of these classes we know only very little, but they were probably content with far humbler productions than *Athelston* or *Havelok*. It is more likely that such romances were addressed to the large number of fairly well educated people who were not perfectly at ease with French, and who thought, like John of Trevisa, that English was the natural means of expression for all those born in England.[36] That the romances were written to be recited in taverns and market-places, as is sometimes believed, is certainly a romantic fiction. At least the versions that have come down to us seem to count on listeners who could sit still for an hour or so and who would know something about the great cycles of stories—people such as might naturally gather in some wealthy household. To judge from the manuscripts, the men who collected romances were often also greatly interested in English history, Saints' legends, and all kinds of religious instruction. The popular character of the romances, generally taken for granted by scholars, therefore implies above all that they catered for people of wide interests and from many walks of life, but it does not mean that they were only designed for the illiterate. Closer examination reveals that more erudition and craftsmanship went into them than the modern reader, misled by a superficial interpretation of Chaucer's *Sir Thopas*, is prepared to look for. The manuscripts suggest, however, that by the end of the fourteenth century the more discriminating and cosmopolitan readers began to turn to a more sophisticated and exclusive kind of poetry of which Chaucer and Gower were the chief exponents.

## DEFINITION OF THE ROMANCES

After what has been said, it might reasonably be asked what justification there is for treating so many different poems under one heading. There is no need here to enter into a fundamental discussion of the nature of romance. Most studies of that kind— like so many definitions of tragedy—suffer from a desire to cover too great a variety of works.[37] A definition of the romances that hoped to include the English poems, the French courtly novels or even the romances written by Walter Scott and Southey would contribute very little to an understanding of the Middle English poems. In using any label for a literary genre it is more profitable to apply it to some definite period and define it accordingly. Even a comparison with French or German poems handling the same stories has only a limited usefulness. In England, the historical and social context is completely different, as has been noted, and the processes of translation, adaptation and imitation led to new types which often have very little in common with their sources. *Sir Perceval of Gales* and the alliterative *Morte Arthure*, for instance, are unlike anything that could possibly have served as a model for them. This can be said of most English romances. Often, and this is sometimes overlooked, it is just as important to note what they have actually taken over from their 'sources' as to see what they have left out.

I shall therefore primarily try to define the position of the romances in Middle English literature and their relationship to other types of narrative poetry, and to see whether it is possible to draw exact lines of demarcation between these types. It will be seen that many of the definitions usually suggested are only very vague and do not apply to all the romances.

W. P. Ker, in his stimulating and influential book *Epic and Romance*, tried to establish a fundamental difference between these two genres.[38] He gives excellent examples—taken mostly from French literature, however—of the gradual disappearance of the epic and the emergence of a new type of narrative poetry which lays more emphasis on plot and incident, namely, the romances. In England, on the other hand, the development was quite different. The epic (if one can call *Beowulf* an epic) was not supplanted by another literary genre; it died out for other reasons, reasons connected probably with the political and social history of the Anglo-Saxons. The romance, subsequently imported from France, was already past its heyday. Several of the characteristics Ker ascribes to the romances, such as courtly love, the extensive descriptions of courtly etiquette, and their modernity, were not usually taken over by the English adapters or at least only in a very modified form. A large group of the English romances, especially those of a more religious and moral character, would not be included in Ker's definition. In others—and this applies particularly to some of the alliterative poems, such as *Sir Gawain and the Green Knight*—we find elements which Ker would probably have called epic, as for example the careful characterization and the intimate relationship between the ruler and his men. Ker's distinction between romance and epic is therefore hardly applicable to English literature and cannot help us to define the English romances, which are only mentioned in passing by Ker. Chaucer's *Knight's Tale* which he praises as a masterpiece of English romance-writing, is—apart from the fact that it forms part of the great design of the *Canterbury Tales* and should not be considered out of its context—not at all typical of the English romances and has far more in common with French and Italian courtly literature than with them.[39]

There are also some other distinctive features that have been attributed to the romances without real justification. There is, for instance, a rather bewildering variety of subject-matter. Only in some of the romances do we find the traditional 'cycles' of stories. To them were added subjects from English history, secularized legends or even long-drawn-out anecdotes, often of a very moral character. Moreover, the range seems to have widened steadily and included stories that were not primarily concerned with knighthood at all.

The metrical forms of the romances are equally varied. We find, if we exclude the prose-romances which only appear somewhat later, the alliterative long line with or without end-rhyme, various stanza-forms containing alliterative and end-rhymed lines, the tail-rhyme stanza (of which there were several quite distinctive types) and the rhyming couplet in its different forms. This variety stands in marked contrast to the comparative uniformity of the French and German romances. Finally, the length of the romances in England is not at all significant: *Robert of Sicily* contains 444 lines, *Ipomedon A* 8890 lines—that is, more than twenty times as many.

It might be asked what contemporaries meant by the term 'romance'. The valuable study by R. Hoops has shown that almost any narrative poem could be called a romance.[40] The name might refer to a French source, or it might mean any exciting adventure within a larger story, as in *Kyng Alisaunder* (ll. 668, 1916, and 6159). A complete list of works that call themselves romances would contain a large number of widely different poems which nobody would think of classing together, although, perhaps, the majority of them are romances in the modern sense of the word.[41] Rather more interesting are the lists of romance-heroes which we find occasionally in Middle English literature. They do not, of course, prove, that there were really elaborate romances about all these heroes. Rather they seem to be rhetorical devices for praising the high distinction of some particular knight by comparing him with several other famous heroes, as, for instance, in *Richard Coeur de Lion* (ll. 6723–41). This is particularly evident in the *Laud Troy Book*, which begins with a long list of famous heroes and the claim to introduce an even more famous hero:

> Many speken of men that romaunces rede
> That were sumtyme doughti in dede,
> The while that god hem lyff lente,
> That now ben dede and hennes wente:
> Off Bevis, Gy, and of Gauwayn,
> Off kyng Richard, & of Owayn,
> Off Tristram, and of Percyuale,
> Off Rouland Ris, and Aglauale,
> Off Archeroun, and of Octouian,
> Off Charles, & of Cassibaldan,
> Off Hauelok, Horne, & of Wade;—
> In Romaunces that of hem ben made
> That gestoures often dos of hem gestes
> At Mangeres and at grete ffestes.
> Here dedis ben in remembraunce
> In many fair Romaunce;
> But of the worthiest wyght in wede
> That euere by-strod any stede,
> Spekes no man, ne in romaunce redes
> Off his batayle ne of his dedis.
> Off that batayle spekes no man,
> There alle prowes of knyghtes be-gan;
> That was for-sothe of the batayle
> That at Troye was saunfayle.
> Off swyche a fyght as there was one,
> In al this world was neuere none,
> Ne neuere schal be til domysday—
> With-oute drede, I dar wel say;—
> Ne neuere better men born ware,
> Then were þan a-sembled thare;          (ll. 11–40)

This passage is particularly revealing because, although Hector plays an important part in the following poem, he is by no means the hero of the whole story. It is obvious that the poet wanted

16

above all to awaken the audience's interest in his story and to claim equal rank with other well-known romances. It would be rash indeed to conclude that he was referring to particular poems. Neither does Richard Rolle's criticism of the romances in which several heroes are mentioned by name help us much further.[42] The works he refers to were probably not the extensive romances that have survived, but shorter, ballad-like popular poems, perhaps like some of the songs of Lawrence Minot (who, incidentally, also uses the word romance). The only thing that can be concluded from these lists is that in England the word 'romance' often implied some particular hero in whose praise the romance was written. The excessive praise of particular heroes is, of course, ridiculed by Chaucer in his *Sir Thopas*, which also contains a brief list of famous knights ('romance of prys'). Such a hero, however, might be any Saint or even Christ himself, which again leaves us without a clear definition of the romances.[43] Thus, in Middle English 'romance' could mean anything we might today call 'a good story', and the lists of romance-heroes obviously referred to the actual stories rather than to particular poems. We shall see that most of the Middle English romances are devoted to the glorification of some particular hero. This is not true of the French romances to the same extent, but it partly accounts for the close connection between the English romances and Saints' legends or *exempla*; there is in this respect no real difference between the romance of *Guy of Warwick* and the Middle English legend of Pope Gregory (both in the Auchinleck Ms.). At the same time the English Saints' legends were becoming more explicitly moral and less devotional than they were in the thirteenth century and were partly influenced by the romances.[44] Thus, edifying Saints' legends and moralizing romances became more similar and are often hardly distinguishable.

This close affinity is also, as has been pointed out, revealed in the manuscripts. Many of them seem to be purely accidental and indiscriminately mixed collections of most heterogeneous products, but the grouping together of particular works in some manuscripts suggests that some system was occasionally followed. It is hardly to be expected that this will provide us with a detailed classification, but it might help us to see if a distinction is possible between secular and religious literature at least. Such a distinction is hard enough to make in French and German medieval literature, but it seems almost impossible in English. In some manuscripts, however, a rough separation of religious and secular works seems to have been attempted and the attacks of some religious authors on 'worldly' literature also seem to point in this direction.[45] Sometimes, as in the *South English Legendary*, Saints and heroes from romances are contrasted to underline the superior perfection of the Saints.[46] But such straightforward distinctions are not the rule, and only very few of the Middle English romances are so 'secular' that they would deserve to be charged with levity (unlike some of the French poems). Many of them are so pious and moral that they have been ascribed to clerical or monkish authors; even secular subjects could be adapted in a way that made them almost into Saints' legends, as is particularly the case with the Charlemagne-romances or such poems as *Sir Ysumbras* and *Emaré*. Such romances often appear in religious manuscripts that contain no really secular literature.[47] There are also some works like *Robert of Sicily* about which agreement has not yet been reached as to whether they belong to the romances or to the legends. In some of these cases even the compilers of the manuscripts seem to have been doubtful because the poems are in some collections classed as romances, in others as legends.

A look at the manuscripts reveals, too, what a small place in Middle English literature was occupied by secular works. Of the 4365 titles listed by Brown and Robbins in their *Index of Middle English Verse*, less than a third could be called secular, and many of these, it has rightly been said, were probably considered religious by contemporaries or valued primarily for their religious qualities.[48] Of course, religious works stood on the whole a better chance of survival, which may be one of the reasons why many of them are preserved in far more manuscripts than any of the romances (*The Pricke of Conscience* was the most frequently copied of all Middle English poems.) Only a few of the romances are preserved in more than three manuscripts. Many of the versions that have come down to us are badly mutilated and pages have been torn out of the manuscripts. It is significant, moreover, that those romances that have survived in the largest number of versions, like *Robert of Sicily* and *Sir Ysumbras*, are at the same time those that are most nearly related to the Saints' legends.

It may be possible, on the other hand, that many of the versions recited by minstrels were less pious and moral than the extant romances, and that it was that type of romance that may have roused the opposition of religious writers and the scorn of Chaucer. That many such versions were in circulation and are irretrievably lost, can be assumed with a fair degree of certainty.[49] The written-down versions have obviously in many cases been made more like the legends with deliberation, partly, perhaps, to make them more acceptable to moralists, partly because there was a real popular demand for such kind of instruction, or simply because it was usually the same scribe who copied romances and Saints' legends.

This close connection, however, makes it particularly difficult to establish a clear distinction between romance and legend in each case. There were many subjects which could be treated either way and many motifs make their appearance in romances as well as in legends. Thus, Sparnaay, many years ago, made an interesting study of the relationship between courtly romances and Saints' legends; the stories of Pope Gregory and of the Holy Grail served as his examples.[50] He, too, denied that a clear distinction was always possible. E. R. Curtius in studying Old French literature has come to similar conclusions,[51] while T. Wolpers, in his comprehensive survey of the English Saints' legends, tries to make a more precise distinction between the legends and all other types of narrative; but this is only possible because he confines himself rather strictly to Saints' legends in the narrowest sense and disregards all the romantic-legendary in-between types that are so numerous in Middle English.[52] When discussing the romances, however, it is not possible to narrow the field of enquiry like this; consequently we shall again and again have to come back to the close relationship between the romances and legendary literature.

Whereas in German medieval literature legends were drawn into the sphere of courtly literature, like in Hartmann von Aue's *Gregorius* and *Der arme Heinrich*, and it has been said that there was an 'incursion of the concretely religious',[53] it was rather the other way round in England. The courtly world was never as autonomous here, and the subjects borrowed from courtly literature were, from the start, treated in quite a different way. It was not a case of the religious 'breaking in' on the romances, but the romances had almost from the beginning been used as illustrations of certain moral and religious precepts. Even in Chaucer, this tendency is more frequent than is often realized.

This strongly homiletic strain in the English romances is an

important feature of the type and has to be included in any definition of it. D. Everett's attempt to draw an exact line of demarcation
by studying the narrative techniques of romances and legends,
seems to me somewhat artificial and unnecessary.[54] It is true that
most Saints' legends can be easily distinguished from the romances
by their subject and their tone, but there are still many poems
which cannot be so easily fitted into one of the two groups (e.g.
*The Siege of Jerusalem, Titus and Vespasian, The Sege off Melayne*).
The wide range of religious narrative in Middle English includes
paraphrases of the Bible (*A Stanzaic Life of Christ*), apocryphal
legends (*The Childhood of Christ*), romantically embellished Saints'
legends and, finally, exemplary romances like *Sir Ysumbras* or
*Le Bone Florence of Rome*. It is more important for an understanding of the romances to take these close links into consideration
and, where necessary, dispense with an exact classification, than to
insist on a clear-cut and rigid system.

There are, however, also some secular narrative types from
which the romances cannot be so easily distinguished. The distinction between romances and chronicles, in particular, is not as
simply made as may appear at first sight. Of course, the chronicles
are more restricted in their subject-matter and usually cover a
longer period of time; but there are some romances, too, that try
to give a survey of a certain period in national history and claim
to be read as true historical accounts, hardly less than some
chronicles proper, as for instance, some Arthur-poems, legends of
'founders', like *Havelok*, or the 'ancestral romances', like *Beues of
Hamtoun* or *Guy of Warwick*, which attempt to give a kind of
family chronicle.[55] The various descriptions of the siege and the
destruction of Troy also occupy a curious position somewhere in
between the chronicles and the romances. Some of these poems are
generally counted among the romances and have, it is true, much
in common with them; but for contemporaries they were without
doubt closely related to the chronicles. They do not have a
particularly impressive central character like most of the romances;
there are no romantic adventures and little courtly love, and the
authors seem far more concerned with portraying a certain period
in history than with telling an exciting new story. It also has to be
borne in mind that the fall of Troy was widely considered to be a
kind of prelude to the history of England (cf. the beginning of *Sir
Gawain and the Green Knight*) and would therefore be understood

more as a historical event than as some remote adventure-story. Thus, the short poem *The Seege or Batayle of Troye*, which of all the Troy-books is perhaps the most romance-like, appears in one manuscript at least (Arundel 22) as a historical work and serves as an introduction to Geoffrey of Monmouth's *History*.[56] Of course, other manuscripts include the poem together with romances, but it seems possible that it was written partly with the intention of putting this important historical subject into a form that could easily be grasped and remembered; this seems to have been the case with the *Anonymous Short Metrical Chronicle*, another poem which leaves one in doubt as to whether one should call it a romance or a chronicle.[57] Its subject is English history, of course, but it also contains several episodes and uses narrative formulas which we meet in romances as well. In this case, the manuscript tradition too, suggests a connection between the two genres; for, after the studies of Mrs. L. H. Loomis, it seems certain that the author of the *Short Metrical Chronicle* collaborated closely with the adapters of some of the 'Auchinleck romances' (*Roland and Vernagu, Richard Coeur de Lion*), if, indeed, they were not one and the same person.[58] The manner in which chronicles and romances were produced simultaneously and in collaboration for the Auchinleck Ms. again throws light on the close relationship between the literary genres in Middle English and makes it impossible to draw rigid lines of demarcation between them.

There is also a close affinity between romances and chronicles as regards their didactic intention. Again, this is particularly true of the Middle English poems. Most of the romances, like many chronicles, describe exemplary heroes and actions. La3amon's *Brut* unfolds, in a series of biographies, patterns of good and wicked government; something very similar is done, as we shall see, in *Havelok*.[59] In both cases, history serves as a lesson in political virtues and vices. It is hardly necessary to stress here that probably no one in the Middle Ages found our modern, sometimes too scrupulous, distinction between proved fact and truth embellished by fiction so very relevant.[60] This does not mean that we are unable to separate chronicles from romances in the majority of cases: the romances are usually concerned with the adventures of a particular hero or his family, whereas the chronicles are devoted to the history of larger communities or several generations. In the attitude to their subject-matter, however, the two genres have more in common than is often recognized, and again it seems more important to be aware of these similarities than to make rigid distinctions for the sake of a neat definition.

## NARRATIVE TECHNIQUE

Describing the narrative technique of the romances may be another means of arriving at a more satisfactory definition of the genre. The narrative technique of the romances has not received very much attention so far; scholars have usually been content to list a number of recurrent formulas without interpreting them within their context. The individual use made of conventional clichés, however, often illustrates the skill and originality of an author.[61] This is why the mere occurrence of such clichés does not say very much about the narrative technique of a poem; the narrator's art shows itself in the selection and adaptation of the motifs and tags he found in the rich storehouse of Middle English narrative verse. A detailed study of narrative technique can therefore only be applied to individual poems, although it is perhaps possible to make a few general observations which may help to distinguish the romances from the legends and chronicles with regard to the way they present their story-material.

It can be said of most of the Middle English romances that they are characterized by an abundant wealth of plot and incident. Some of the shorter poems, in particular, often give the impression that the author wished to tell as much as possible within the shortest space. We often find that Middle English romances are considerably shorter than their 'sources' and that this abridgement is not due to the omission of complete episodes or parts of the plot, but to a more concise mode of narration, a much sparser use of description and less reflection. Even in the very long verse novels the increase in size is not achieved by a more leisurely pace or by lengthy description, but simply by an aggregation of more episodes regardless of repetition. This predominance of plot and incident marks an important difference between the Middle English romances and their French models; for there we often find— particularly in the works of Chrétien de Troyes—that a climax in the story is accompanied by a slowing down in tempo of the narration and reflection becomes prominent. At the same time, a similar difference can be found between the romances and the legends because in the latter there is also frequently a lack of speed and a playing down of incident for its own sake.[62] I do not want to imply that the meaning of the romances is limited to the retelling of a story; in most of them indeed the story points to a deeper moral experience which is illustrated by the movements of the plot, but even where such a didactic intention is very prominent, it is conveyed by implication rather than by explicit statement. It hardly ever detracts from the interest of the plot. This is without doubt a concession to the less educated among the hearers who would at least be entertained by a lively story, even if they missed its deeper significance. Of course, this is not true of all the romances and does not quite apply, for instance, to *Sir Gawain and the Green Knight*, but even there it may be observed that description and reflection play a comparatively minor part and are strictly subordinated to the plot.[63]

A feature which is closely connected with the predominance of plot and action we noted, is the rather episodic structure of most of the romances. Similar to the legends, where we often find static scenes, like devotional paintings, many romances consist of a series of short 'vignettes' which follow each other fairly abruptly. Between these 'vignettes', the story is often summarized very sketchily.[64] This does not necessarily mean that the scenes themselves are therefore worked out in great detail. Very often they are hardly localized and consist only of short snatches of dialogue, as in *King Horn* and some of the more 'minstrel-like' romances (e.g. *Sir Tristrem*). In other romances, however, such scenes are more weighty and localities are indicated, as in *Havelok*, *Amis and Amiloun* or *Sir Perceval of Gales*, but it is not very often that we find such an extensive use of dialogue as in Chrétien's novels, in Chaucer, or in *Sir Gawain and the Green Knight*. As regards the details of the individual scenes, the romances differ among themselves considerably, but the majority of them are characterized by a sequence of short narrative units which are often quite loosely connected. This is why many romances are lacking in the kind of artistic unity and coherence that modern criticism tends to look for in evaluating poetry. In the longer poems, this lack of unity is much more striking. The way in which whole sections of plot are cut out or transposed in some versions clearly reveals their loose, episodic structure, as can be seen in the different texts of *Kyng Alisaunder* and *Richard Coeur de Lion*. In this respect, too, *Sir*

*Gawain and the Green Knight,* with its close-knit, carefully balanced structure, is a notable exception.

The narrative method of proceeding by loosely connected episodes is also evidence of the 'oral' technique of the romances. They are clearly written with the expectations and limitations of a rather mixed audience in mind. The transition between episodes often proves a useful means of freshly awakening the listeners' attention. This is probably why we find in the romances a large number of transitional formulas designed to make the sequence of the plot intelligible even for the less attentive members of the audience. Two kinds of such formulas are particularly frequent and seem to be rather typical of the English romances. Both make it very clear that a new section of the narrative is about to begin.

The first is as follows:

> Now lat we þe lady be,
> And of Sir Ywaine speke we.
>
> (*Ywain and Gawain*, ll. 869-70)

This example is rather interesting because it comes from a poem which makes less use of such clichés than many others and preserves the coherent structure of its source (Chrétien's *Yvain*) fairly well. There seems to be little reason for such an explicit change of scenery at this particular point in the narrative because no new episode begins. Nor does any similar formula occur in Chrétien's poem at the corresponding place. It seems as if the English adapter felt that the audience needed some help here. In other poems, the narrative is interrupted by such statements far more often. In many cases there is even a brief summary of the episode just concluded:

> Nou lete we William be,
> þat wente in his jorne
> Toward Arthour þe king.
>
> (*Libeaus Desconus*, ll. 457-9)

Frequently the following events are announced in a tone full of promise:

> But leue we now þat gentyl kny3t,
> And spek we of þat byrd bry3t,
> How þei gestened þat ny3t
> Carp wyll we mare.
>
> (*Sir Degrevant*, ll. 949-52)

or:

> Now of þe lyoun wyll we rest
> And ferðer telle yn owr geste,
> How þe lady rood yn þe forest,
> Hyr sones to seke,
> But sche ne herd est ne west
> Of hem no speche.
> (*Octavian*, Southern version, ll. 487–92)

It would be easy to collect hundreds of such formulas from nearly all of the romances. Often they were taken over literally from the sources, but they are just as frequent in poems which have no definite sources or whose source does not make use of such formulas. They were obviously common knowledge and were used by authors and scribes whenever some gap in the narrative had to be bridged, sometimes in a rather pedestrian and mechanical manner, but often with a shrewd sense of dramatic tension and suspense.

It is perhaps worth noting that Chaucer, too, makes use of such formulas in several of the *Canterbury Tales*. In some cases there is an unmistakable undertone of irony, as in the *Merchant's Tale*, where Damian is left by the narrator in a rather uncomfortable position, sitting on a pear-tree:

> And thus I lete hym sitte upon the pyrie,
> And Januarie and May romynge ful myrie.
> (IV, 2217–18)

Chaucer's acquaintance with the clichés of popular romance is illustrated by examples like this. At the same time, they show his brilliant skill in adapting and enlivening such worn-out formulas.

Very often in the romances, a new episode is announced by a direct appeal to the audience and a request for its special attention. In *The King of Tars*, we find within short space two such passages:

> Now ginneþ here a miri pas,
> Hou þat child y-cristned was
> Wiþ limes al hole & fere,
> & hou þe soudan of Damas
> Was cristned for þat ich cas,
> Now herken & ʒe may here. (ll. 700–705)

Only a little later we are told:

> Now herkneþ to me boþe old & ʒing,
> Hou þe soudan & þe king
> Amonges hem gun drriue,
> & hou þe Sarrazins þat day
> Opped heued-les for her pay,
> Now listen, & ʒe may liþe! (ll. 1093–8)

As the poem is so short that it could easily have been read as a whole, these explicit addresses to the audience do not mark the beginning of a new sitting, but only serve to give some prominence to the person of the narrator who wants to accentuate his story and to keep his hold on the listeners' attention. Many other formulas that have been collected also stress the situation of the narrator reading out his story and addressing his audience in order not to let their attention wander. This, it needs perhaps stressing, can in many cases be a purely literary device and does not always necessarily reflect the actual conditions under which the stories were read.[65]

Most of the romances tell the story of some hero whose glorious deeds and whose exemplary piety are praised. Two romances (*Havelok* and *Sir Gowther*) are even described as *Vita* in the manuscripts and not a few have a distinctly biographical structure. This, too, provides a close link between romances and Saints' legends, with the difference, of course, that Saints are usually extolled for different virtues from those of the romance-heroes and most legends dwell on the outward details of the plot far less than the romances do.

The tone in which the hero's biography is told as well as the attitude of the narrator towards his hero generally differ in the romances and the legends. The narrator of the former does not expect from his audience pious devotion and meditation, but rapt attention and admiration. He claims that his hero is superior in all knightly and virtuous accomplishments to all that have been celebrated before, but at the same time he wishes to establish a close bond of sympathy between his audience and the hero by expressing his own concern with the hero's fate. To this end he makes use of another set of formulas, already found in Old French poetry, like prayers for the hero's safety or denunciation of his enemies. In *Havelok*, one of the earliest and at the same time most original of the romances, this siding of the narrator with the hero against his adversaries is particularly pronounced.[66] Thus the

narrator takes leave of Goldeboru who has been imprisoned in
Dover castle by the treacherous Godrich:

> Of Goldeboru shul we nou laten,
> þat nouht ne blinneth forto graten
> þer sho liggeth in prisoun:
> Iesu Crist, that Lazarun
> To liue brouhte fro dede bondes,
> He lese hire with hise hondes;
> And leue sho mote him y-se
> Heye hangen on galwe-tre,
> þat hire haued in sorwe brouht,
> So as sho ne misdede nouht!          (ll. 328-37)

Sometimes the hero is even admonished by the narrator and reminded of his duty, as in *Sir Gawain and the Green Knight*:

> Now þenk wel, sir Gawan,
> For woþe þat þou ne wonde
> þis auenture forto frayn,
> þat þou hatȝ tan on honde.

> (ll. 487-90, end of first part)

Thus we get the impression that the narrator is deeply involved in
his story. At the same time, that story is given a greater degree of
actuality. Praying for the hero implies that his fate is still open and
can be influenced by intercession. In this way the dramatic tension
is heightened and again the plot assumes a new importance.

By his handling of perspective, too, the narrator can seem to
identify himself with the hero. In many romances we find that the
greater part of the action is told from the point of view of the hero.
The narrator often does not claim to be omniscient, instead he
describes every episode as it appears to the hero whose surprise
and astonishment we are encouraged to share.[67] The use of anticipation or direct foreshadowing of future events is comparatively
rare in the romances; on the other hand, there are usually a large
number of vague hints or warnings which arouse our expectations
without giving any reliable information as to the course of the
action. Again there are some good examples in *Sir Gawain and the
Green Knight*. When the green knight has left Arthur's hall after
his startling challenge, all we are told about him is:

> To quat kyth he be-com, knwe non þere,
> Neuermore þen þay wyste fram queþen he watȝ wonnen.

> (ll. 460-1)

27

Thus we are no wiser than the bewildered knights and a common bond of wonder and expectation is established between audience, narrator and hero, such as is rarely found in Saints' legends. In many poems this bond is strengthened by the final prayer in which the narrator includes both his hero and the audience.

All that has been said does not, perhaps, amount to a narrative technique typical of the romances, but it provides some criteria for interpreting the poems individually and for distinguishing them from other types of narrative, such as Saints' legends or chronicles.

## CONCLUSION

It seems, in conclusion, that it is practically impossible to generalize about the romances because there is so little they all have in common. The various types of narrative in Middle English are so closely related to each other that it is often pointless to bracket them together by some general definition and it is more rewarding to define the differences between the individual romances, to demonstrate what independent and varied use was made by the English adapters of the story material they found in their sources. For a start then, my subject may be defined in a negative way: I shall leave out of consideration Saints' legends in the strict sense of the word, descriptions of larger periods of English history, including the Trojan war, didactic and allegorical poems such as *Piers Plowman* or *The Parliament of the Three Ages*, and short humorous tales like *Dame Sirith*. What remains are roughly all those poems which have been traditionally described as romances and which are in particular need of critical reappraisal. Much of what these poems have in common is not confined to them alone and many of the conventional definitions do not apply to all of them.

At first sight, it seems most appropriate to define the romances in terms of their subject, but, as we have seen, neither courtly love, nor the moral code of knighthood, nor strange adventure and fighting are common to all the English poems. This is not to deny that there are some basic narrative patterns and story-outlines which keep recurring in many of the Middle English romances and that we are usually in no doubt as to whether a certain poem belongs to the 'romances' or not, however difficult it may be to give a satisfactory definition of the whole genre.[68] But more important,

28

a closer reading of the texts allows us to distinguish smaller groups of poems which clearly belong together. It is perhaps less important to decide whether these groups of poems are just different modifications of one genre, i.e. the romance, or not, than to arrive at a better understanding of the texts themselves and some of the features they have in common, which will also give us a clearer idea of the nature of romance in Middle English. This brings us to the problem of classification which will be briefly discussed in the following chapter.

# 2

# THE PROBLEM OF CLASSIFICATION

As has been shown in the previous chapter the Middle English romances have several points of similarity which to some extent justify a distinction being made between them and other genres of narrative verse. Nevertheless, it is still surprising what diversity of poems have traditionally been grouped together under this heading, from the short moral *exemplum* to the extensive novel in verse, from the humorous *novella* to the courtly epic. This bracketing together is usually not even explained or accounted for. George Kane, in his otherwise very intelligent and original survey, deals with some sixty poems in one chapter, indiscriminately comparing and evaluating them, and he expressly rejects any classification, whether according to form or subject-matter, as impracticable:

> Wherever we turn, the usefulness of classifications of the romances according to their subject, kind, form or manner is diminished for our purpose of evaluation by their refusal to run true to form.[1]

This kind of treatment, which can be said to be typical of many studies of the romances, is bound to remain unsatisfactory. The Middle English secular epic reveals the same diversity of forms as the Old French or Middle High German, and it seems quite possible, even necessary, to arrive at some classification which is not too rigid and is not just based on some external features. Certainly, the usual classifications often obscure the real literary and historical context and the individual qualities of the poems themselves.

There has, of course, been no lack of attempts to come to a more exact classification of the romances because sheer the number of extant poems makes some kind of grouping very desirable. Some of the possibilities may be briefly examined.

The most usual classification is that according to the different cycles of stories on which the romances are based. It is commonly justified by reference to the famous passage in Jean Bodel, back in the twelfth century, where he speaks of the three *matières*, 'de France, et de Bretagne, et de Rome la grant'.[2] The favour this classification has found among scholars stands in direct relation to the preoccupation of a whole generation of scholars with the history of motifs and the study of sources and analogues. It is to this same generation that we owe the most important editions of texts and the most thorough investigation of their background; and as the introductions to these older editions (apart from a study of the dialect) mainly consist of detailed examinations of all previous versions of the story, this principle of classification has become generally accepted. It has so far not been replaced and makes its appearance in most standard works of reference.[3]

The medievalist is of course inclined to discover in any passage which mentions various types of poetry a contemporary and therefore particularly authentic list of genres. Such lists, however, are not meant as a help for the systematist some centuries later, but are often quite arbitrary collections of names with no pretence to completeness or clear-cut definition. Often they are humorous or satirical.[4] Even if Bodel's list is to be taken more seriously and literally (which perhaps it is), it could still only be applied to his own period and the literature that was known to him. It is, however, hardly adequate for the situation in England one or two centuries later.[5] This is in the first place because the range of stories that went into the romances was continually widening. In England, in particular, many native subjects were added to the traditional cycles. They are usually referred to as 'matter of England', but they are often quite different from each other. Other stories, too, European or oriental, were newly discovered and adapted. To class all the romances that originated in this manner under the heading 'non-cyclic' seems rather a poor way out,[6] because these poems have not necessarily anything in common beyond the fact that they cannot be fitted into any of the *matières*. This alone makes Bodel's classification unsatisfactory.

There is, however, a more fundamental reason for this inadequacy as well. It is easy enough to demonstrate that there is in most cases no logical and unambiguous correspondence between material and form, between a certain story and a poem based on it. Even the connection between some stories and the *matières* is occasionally open to doubt and can undergo changes in the course of time. There are stories that were originally quite independent and 'non-cyclic', but which were later drawn into one of the cycles; this applies particularly to the 'matter of Britain', i.e. the stories of King Arthur and the knights of the Round Table. Thus, the story of Launfal did not at first belong to any of the cycles and was only later put into an Arthurian setting.[7] Conversely, it was quite possible for stories to loose their association with one of the 'matters'. M. van Duzee has made a very good case for *Eger and Grime* being originally an Arthurian story although the poem in its present form shows hardly any traces of this.[8]

It can, of course, generally be said that similar stories may be treated in very different ways and even the same story can appear in works that clearly belong to widely different genres. There are so many instances of this that it hardly needs arguing. A list, compiled by MacEdward Leach, of all the versions of the story of Amis and Amiloun[9] mentions the most heterogeneous works, such as legends, tales in prose and metrical romances. The story that is the ultimate source of the Middle English *Sir Ysumbras*, can also be found in Saints' legends, *exempla*, and romances, the English version being a mixture of all three.[10] The same applies to the legend of Constance (on which *Emaré* is based as well as Chaucer's *Man of Law's Tale*) and above all to the stories of King Arthur and Alexander which could be treated in a romantic and chivalrous or else in a didactic or hagiographic manner.[11] The Middle English poems on King Arthur provide a particularly good example of the uselessness of any classification based on subject-matter alone. It would be absurd to assign all these works to the same genre. Indeed, a recently published study of the rôle of King Arthur in Middle English literature reads almost like a survey of all the types of narrative we find in Middle English, from the chronicle to the ballad, from the brief metrical tale to the extensive epic.[12] There are probably not many stories that lend themselves to one particular type of narrative alone. This might be most expected of legendary material, but even here the lines of demarcation are blurred, as we have seen in the case of *Sir Ysumbras* and *Emaré*. Thus, any story can be completely transformed in the process of being told and new forms can be created which have hardly anything in common with their sources. This could easily be demonstrated by examining different versions of some stories. Take, for instance, the B-version of *Ipomedon* which, in comparison with the A-version (a rather close translation from the French), alters the story considerably, condensing it, simplifying it, and making it less courtly. Thus, the B-version, although certainly inferior to the A-version in literary merit, is rather more typical of the Middle English romances than the more elaborate and more famous *Ipomedon A*.[13]

On the other hand, it is sufficiently well known that popular heroes from all ages and continents appear in medieval literature in the shape of medieval knights and are completely adapted to a contemporary setting. The most heterogeneous stories could be made alike in tone and atmosphere by similar treatment and thus we find many poems which clearly belong to the same literary type although they would have to be grouped with quite different 'matters'. This applies, for instance, to the three novels *Kyng Alisaunder, Arthour and Merlin* and *Richard Coeur de Lion*.[14] Their dialect, transmission and narrative technique are so similar that they have often been attributed to the same author. They each centre round a hero whose biography seems the only link between the loosely connected adventures. They come from the same area (probably Kent), the same period (end of the thirteenth century) and are obviously written with the same audience in mind. The different origins of the story-material apparently did not concern the author. Similar developments could be shown by a closer study of some of the tail-rhyme romances. No doubt, by the thirteenth and fourteenth centuries the English adapters were not very conscious of a fundamental difference between the *matières*, at least they were not influenced by it in composing the romances, and this is another reason why the 'matters' are not a very useful means of classifying the romances.

Some other classifications based on the contents of the romances alone, are hardly more useful as, for instance, the term 'society romance' suggested by S. F. Barrow.[15] It can be applied to only a few of the English romances anyway, and it groups together some poems which have otherwise not very much in common. L. A. Hibbard's arrangement is rather similar, though it does not claim to be a generally applicable classification, but is only a casual grouping for the purposes of a particular book.[16] She distinguishes 'Romances of Trial and Faith', 'Romances of Legendary English Heroes' and 'Romances of Love and Adventure'. Here again, some very different works are inevitably classed together, but one advantage of her classification is that it takes into account the themes of the romances as well as their story-material. Such groupings can be useful because they point to important similarities between some otherwise very different poems, but they are not very suitable for a classification according to types.[17]

Another possible grouping of the romances is according to metrical form. In some cases we may indeed be justified in classing a number of poems together in this way. The alliterative poems of the West Midlands are examples of how a distinctive metrical form, obviously emerging from a very strong tradition, can be practically confined to a particular area; they also have many other features in common although nobody would seriously suggest that *Sir Gawain and the Green Knight, Pearl* and *Patience* belong to the same genre. They all are products of the 'alliterative revival' and as such they can be profitably compared with each other.[18] They roughly belong to the same period and they seem on the whole to be much more aristocratic and 'literary' than many of the other romances, but the differences have sometimes been exaggerated. Some of the more Northern stanzaic poems, such as *The Awntyrs off Arthure* or *The Avowynge of King Arther*, are quite close to the poems of the alliterative revival and show interesting combinations of strophic forms and the alliterative long-line.

The case of the tail-rhyme romances is similar. As A. McI. Trounce has demonstrated, they nearly all originated in the East Midlands and have so many features in common that one is almost justified in speaking of a 'school'.[19] This is, without doubt, one of the most convincing attempts at a partial classification and the identification of a distinctive type of romance. Of course, the metrical form is not the only and perhaps not even the most important element these poems have in common. Nevertheless, they are a clearly definable group of romances, following after a number of poems written in couplets, like the French models (e.g. *Floris and Blauncheflur, King Horn, Havelok*) in which the courtly atmosphere is still more clearly preserved. I would, however, count some poems among the tail-rhyme romances that are not written in tail-rhyme stanzas (e.g. *Robert of Sicily* and *Cheuelere Assigne*) and leave some out that *are*, like *Ipomedon A*, which on account of its length alone hardly belongs in the same group. There are also poems of which only some versions (and some of

34

them only in part) are written in tail-rhyme stanzas (e.g. *Guy of Warwick* and *Sir Beues of Hamtoun*), so that even here the dividing lines are far from clear. We also have to bear in mind that other kinds of poems, like Saints' legends or shorter lyrics, were composed in tail-rhyme stanzas.[20] Thus, a classification according to metrical form alone has its limitations as well, but it can be helpful in some cases, and I shall return to it from time to time.[21]

A study of the geographical distribution of the romances and their sociological background could also provide some useful data because it seems likely that the classes of people for whom the romances were written and their literary tastes varied in different parts of England. Thus, the poems from the East Midlands were obviously written for a rather bourgeois audience, less interested in courtly manners, whereas some poems from the North seem to emphasize the courtly and chivalrous aspects of their stories and show a marked preference for ceremony, polite society and the etiquette of hunting (cf. *Sir Gawain and the Green Knight*, but also a number of minor poems). The distinction between courtly and popular romances which has occasionally been suggested, has therefore also something to be said for it, but it would presuppose a rather precise interpretation of each poem, apart from the fact we noted before, that the divisions between the classes were probably much less rigid in medieval England than on the continent and courtly society less exclusive. Only a small number of the romances can with confidence be described as either courtly or popular. Few of them are courtly in the strict sense of the word, but it would be rash to conclude that all the others are necessarily 'popular' (whatever the word may mean). The problem of the audience is, as the previous chapter has tried to suggest, far from simple and it hardly provides us with a satisfactory means of classifying the romances, although it has to be carefully considered in interpreting individual poems.

Most of the classifications discussed so far seem to confine themselves to some rather accidental and superficial features of the romances and are therefore bound to be inadequate. Any grouping that hopes to say something relevant about the poems should take into account as many aspects as possible. Thus, the story can in some cases have some real importance for the definition of the literary type, not because of its origin in one of the *matières*, but for the way it has been selected, accentuated and given shape. The

35

metrical form, too, can be of value in classifying a poem, especially when it can be shown to have influenced the style and the narrative structure.

If, after all that has been said, I discuss the romances according to certain types, this does not mean a claim to a neat system into which each poem can be fitted easily. In view of the diversity of the romances such a system is hardly possible, but there are indeed certain groups of poems that have more in common than is usually appreciated, and others that are so different from them that any wholesale treatment can lead to curious misconceptions. It is surely true, as Kane writes, that most of the romances refuse to run true to type, and we probably do not know enough about them yet to make a final assessment, so that any classification can only be in the way of a compromise between various possibilities. Yet it seems desirable and possible to make some general distinctions and to point out a number of recurring types, even though not all of the extant romances will fall into one of the groups proposed. In view of the rather undecided state of scholarship on this point, even a tentative and incomplete grouping can perhaps contribute to a more precise understanding of the poems and to a more differentiated definition of Middle English romance.

First of all I propose to make a distinction between shorter and longer works. This may at first sight appear somewhat oversimplified, but even a superficial glance at some of the romances should make it obvious that a verse-novel of many thousands of lines is necessarily very different from a short tale of about a thousand and cannot be approached in the same way. In most other fields of literature this goes without saying. Only the romances have usually been treated as if their length were not an important criterion,[22] but here, too, size is by no means an external feature. It conditions the treatment of the story, the dramatic movement and the narrative structure. In the case of the Middle English romances the question of length even seems particularly relevant because they were so obviously written for recitation and with an audience in mind. Thus, it is surely significant that there is such a large number of poems of between about five and twelve-hundred lines each. If we assume (which can easily be proved by experiment) that a thousand lines can be comfortably read in about an hour (alliterative long-lines would take about twice as long), it follows that each of these poems probably would have been read in one sitting. Of course we do not know exactly in what manner these romances were actually read, but their large number suggests that they met a widespread demand. Several poems we know are about twice that standard length; they could still be read in one piece and perhaps there were longer sittings as well, but possibly they were divided in half and read in two instalments.[23] This seems to have been the case with *The Seege or Batayle of Troye*, a poem of about two thousand lines. After nearly a thousand lines, one of the manuscripts (Arundel 22) has a short passage, indicating that half the poem is over, a short blessing, and a call for drinks:

> Her ys þe haluyndell of our geste;
> God saue vs, mest and lest.
> ffyl þe cuppe & mak ous glad,
> ffor þe maker þus so bad.           (ll. 980–3)

Obviously, a short break is suggested here. Similar passages can be found in other poems as well, which seems evidence of the fact that the authors did not expect the attention of their audiences to be unlimited and that after a few hundred lines a little pause was often found appropriate.

Extensive novels in verse, which had to be read in several instalments, seem to have found less favour in England at first, at least as far as they were written in English. They were usually translations from the French or Anglo-Norman. Their number as well as their independence of the sources is appreciably smaller than that of the shorter romances although they are for the most part preserved in more manuscripts. They are also on the whole far less closely knit, and clearly divided into separate episodes, some of which could, if necessary, be omitted or read separately. This is particularly striking in the case of *Reinbrun*, which in the Auchinleck Ms. was lifted bodily out of the extensive novel *Guy of Warwick* and thus made into a separate short romance.[24]

In Anglo-Norman, on the other hand, we find a considerable number of long novels in verse which were presumably read among the ladies of aristocratic households.[25] When this kind of literature was translated into English, mainly during the second half of the thirteenth century, a number of extensive novels, such as *Guy of Warwick* or *Kyng Alisaunder*, resulted. During the fourteenth century, however, there seems to have been a marked preference for shorter tales. Very few novels we know of were

37

composed during that period. The fifteenth century again saw a rise in the popularity of longer novels, some of them now in prose.[26] This certainly reflects the rising importance of the middle classes and an increasing number of private households with literary interests and their own manuscript collections, where romances could be read more at leisure. Most of the earlier poems, however, seem to have been written for audiences who found it difficult to listen to more than a certain number of lines and who would not have appreciated extensive novels in verse, let alone in prose.

There is in Middle English also a surprisingly small number of poems of medium size, that is between three and four thousand lines, which in my opinion is another reason why the grouping of romances according to length is not just arbitrary. Most of them seem to be very condensed versions of longer novels. The adapters obviously wanted to abridge their sources, but they did not do it as radically or, perhaps, as skilfully as some authors of shorter tales (e.g. *Sir Tristrem* and *Ywain and Gawain*). In some other cases, the length of the poem is due to a more elaborate and rhetorical style and a more ambitious design, as in *Havelok* and *Sir Gawain and the Green Knight*.[27] All these poems were probably not read in one sitting, but their structure is far more closely knit and less episodic than that of the longer novels.

Thus, taking into account the approximate length of the romances can be a first step towards a more precise classification and draws our attention to some important differences which at first sight seem to have nothing to do with the size. A closer examination of some of the romances will show that this approach can indeed lead to a better recognition of some of their distinctive features.

# 3

# THE SHORTER ROMANCES (I)

As we have already noted, we find in Middle English quite a large number of short narrative poems; indeed they seem to be a typically English variety of romance. An average of about one thousand lines must have been a particularly suitable size for a tale to be read in one sitting. Apart from the shorter romances, many of the longer poems are subdivided into smaller units, as the fitts in *Sir Gawain and the Green Knight* (490, 635, 872, 533 ll., most of them alliterative long-lines).[1] The books in Chaucer's *Troilus and Criseyde* are of a similar size, and something like these fitts or books can be found in many of the longer poems. The popularity of collections of stories or 'framed' tales, like *The Seven Sages of Rome, An Alphabet of Tales*, Gower's *Confessio Amantis* and Chaucer's *Canterbury Tales*, too, is evidence of the fact that the shorter forms of narrative enjoyed particular favour with the English. Most of the shorter romances, however, are preserved in far fewer versions than the longer novels in verse;[2] many of them have only come down in one single manuscript. This can partly be explained by the fact that many of the novels are compilations of particularly famous stories, like *Guy of Warwick* or *Kyng Alisaunder*, whereas the shorter romances often treat less well known subjects and were possibly written sometimes for particular occasions.

It is very revealing that, as a rule, the shorter romances are not humorous anecdotes or *exempla* with a definite 'point', but are frequently condensed versions of novels, or if they do treat a single episode, it is at some length, more like little epics than ballads. The differences between these poems and the ballads, already noted by D. Everett, are indeed very marked, as can be seen from those romances that were later turned into ballads.[3] Of these later versions it can perhaps really be said that they were composed by wandering minstrels. Most of the shorter romances to be discussed in this chapter are, however, much more carefully constructed than any of the ballads and have to be considered in connection with some of the more literary forms of short narrative. In England, the most influential of these forms was probably the Breton lay.

## THE BRETON LAYS

It is well known that the Breton lays enjoyed particular popularity in England, a popularity that lasted for at least two centuries. It seems likely that the lays were originally a form of prose narrative, told between songs on certain heroes or local traditions, and designed to inform the hearers about the details of the story which could not be gathered from the songs alone, especially as these were probably often in the Breton language, while the prose explanation was given in French.[4] Out of these story-outlines Marie de France developed a most refined and subtle form of tale in verse. These lays usually tell a concise story in which a knight undergoes a strange adventure and which often ends with a surprising turn of plot.

The tales of Marie de France have very appropriately been called 'problem fairy-tales' and it has been noted that a very important part is played by certain symbolic objects in them.[5] The plot usually includes a discussion of problems of courtly love and is often completely subordinated to the symbolic meaning, as can be seen very clearly in the brief *Lai du Chèvrefeuil*.[6] The narrative art of Marie de France combines remarkable precision and a seemingly artless simplicity of tone with a sure command of dramatic effects and suspense. The problems of courtly love are not explicitly stated in formal debate or reflection, but become transparent through the symbolic connotations of the objects and the action. This is a new type of metrical tale which has its own distinctive features, and the more characteristic examples, at least, are quite different from other forms of short narrative.

That this new type of story was particularly popular in England can be gathered not only from a number of extant translations, but also from several later imitations which call themselves Breton lays, even some that have hardly anything in common with the original form.[7] Chaucer too uses the term 'Breton lay' and applies it to his *Franklin's Tale* which, even if it had as a source a now lost lay, is certainly a very free and sophisticated adaptation.[8]

In Middle English there are at least four poems which can with some justification be called Breton lays because they have far more in common with the lays of Marie de France than any of the later romances: they are *Sir Orfeo, Lai le Freine, Sir Landevale* and *Sire Degarre*. These poems make it seem very probable that the English shorter romances were to some extent influenced by the lays and are even, in fact, derivatives of them. Two of the English lays are direct translations from the French of Marie de France (*Lai le Freine* and *Sir Landevale*). A close comparison of these poems with their sources has established that the English versions, obviously written for a very different audience, nevertheless follow their models rather closely and more or less preserve their stylistic qualities although they introduce a large number of minor changes.[9] In the case of *Sir Orfeo* it is at least probable that there was a French source,[10] while the origin of *Sire Degarre* is, in spite of some painstaking studies, still largely conjectural,[11] although it is as likely as not that this poem, too, is the translation of a French lay. These four English poems, the only ones that can be called lays in the stricter sense of the word, were probably all composed near the beginning of the fourteenth century. Three of them are preserved in the Auchinleck Ms., a collection that is of crucial importance for the history of the romances; *Sir Landevale* was possibly once copied into a similar manuscript. All four poems, like the French lays, are quite short: *Sire Degarre*, the longest of them, only runs to just over a thousand lines.

The most marked difference between the English lays and the other short romances lies in the fairy-tale-like character of the action with its (typically Celtic) blending of reality and otherworld, particularly in those stories that deal with the union between a human being and a fairy. In contrast to most of the later romances, the lays usually place great emphasis on the disparity of the two worlds, indeed, this disparity can, as in *Sir Orfeo*, form one of the main themes of the story. Most of the later romances have completely lost this feeling of the total otherness of the supernatural; they take it very much for granted and the contrasts are often played down. The intellectual subtlety of the French lays, their suggestive use of symbols and the aristocratic refinement of tone have only partly been preserved in the English versions, but the courtly atmosphere is on the whole much more felt than in later adaptations. The more popular character of the English poems does not, as in many later romances, express itself in a kind of homely realism and a love of detail, but more in an unsophisticated simplicity of style which, however, is by no means artless and betrays a fine instinct for narrative effects and for the particular excellencies of the French models.

This is very noticeable in the handling of dramatic suspense and surprising denouement. A. Bliss, in his discussion of the best-known and most successful of the English lays, *Sir Orfeo*, has drawn attention to this point and mentions that a similar technique is used in *Lai le Freine*.[12] We find there, for instance, that the re-union of the two sisters comes as a surprising revelation, not pre-pared for by the narrator. The reader (or hearer) is not at first told the real identity of the strange lady who is introduced. Only when the marriage-contract has been concluded, are we informed that she is the sister of the hero's poor mistress (ll. 313 ff.). In *Sir Landevale*, as in the French *Lanval*, the whole story is based on suspense. Neither the hero nor the audience knows in advance how it will end and whether Landevale will be saved eventually. The tension is skilfully heightened towards the end of the poem: twice the messengers of the fairy approach and twice all the courtiers and Landevale's well-wishers begin to hope that his re-demption is near, but each time their hopes are disappointed and the trial is resumed until at last the lady herself appears and every-thing turns out well. In *Sire Degarre*, too, dramatic tension plays an important part. When, after his glorious victory in the tournament, the knight has won the fair princess, neither he nor the reader knows that she is his own mother who as a child exposed him. Only after the wedding, when he remembers the gloves (which are the token of recognition), is the dilemma discovered. Again this revelation has not been prepared for in the story up to this point (ll. 431 ff.), whereas the Middle English legend of Gregorius, which has a very similar plot, tells the story in a very different way and gives the necessary information much earlier.[13]

*Sir Orfeo* is a very good example of how the use of suspense and a less explicit narrative technique can also contribute to the exposi-tion of the theme. The apparently effortless simplicity and the per-fectly balanced structure of the poem have often been praised; they reveal a striking closeness to the lays of Marie de France. Thus the poet makes particularly subtle use of gestures which are at the same time expressive and symbolic.[14] The contrast between life and death, between this world and the other-world, which pervades the whole poem, is mirrored in the gestures of the characters, for instance in the mute exchange of looks between Orfeo and Heurodis (ll. 323 ff.), who at this point are still separated by a gulf which it seems impossible to bridge, or in the moving lament of the queen just awakened from her fatal dream (ll. 77 ff.). The suspense created by the fact that neither the King and his followers nor the readers know the cause of her distraction, effectively helps to evoke the idea of some supernatural power behind the Queen's dreams. There are also some other points in the story where dramatic suspense serves a unifying purpose. Thus the concluding episode, which might at first sight appear to be an unnecessary protraction of the final denouement, is closely linked with the rest of the poem by means of such tension. The ceremonious departure of Orfeo from his kingdom and his barons (ll. 201 ff.) leads us to expect his returning with similar solemnity.[15] His encounter with Death has not only bereft him of his wife, but also of his kingdom. His state of complete exposure in the wilderness which is described so movingly in the poem (ll. 239 ff.) is a suggestive image of an extreme spiritual isolation,[16] from which he can be saved and returned to life by nothing short of a miracle. As he has won back his queen so he has to regain his kingdom, and the testing of the steward is an appropriate sequel, corresponding to the outwitting of the fairy king. Thus the theme of the poem is clearly emphasized by its symmetrical structure. As in the lays of Marie de France, the external action is an image of a deeper truth, in this case the inseparable union between husband and wife and the temporary nature of the power of Death. At the same time there is in comparison with the later romances a complete absence of didactic and moralizing. The meaning of the poem is expressed solely through its simple, and at the same time symbolic, action. All this is clear evidence of the shaping influence of the French lays. The poem is preserved in three manuscripts which allows the inference that it was fairly popular. It is a pity that its most characteristic virtues were not imitated by later authors of romances; nevertheless, it can hardly be doubted that the form of the Breton lay served as a model for many of the short romances written during the fourteenth century; indeed, there is a close connection between the popularity of the Breton lays in England and the large number of such short romances. This may be illustrated by an examination of another English lay and its imitation.

### 'SIR LANDEVALE' AND THOMAS CHESTRE'S 'SIR LAUNFAL'

The adaptation of the English lay *Sir Landevale* by Thomas Chestre shows very clearly some of the typical resemblances and differences between the Breton lays and the shorter romances. The two versions are separated by nearly a century.

Whereas *Sir Landevale* is on the whole a rather faithful translation of Marie de France's *Lanval*, Thomas Chestre has handled the story very freely. His version has in many ways more in common with romances like *Libeaus Desconus* and *Octavian* than with the original lays. The alterations, taken singly, do not seem very remarkable, but their total effect is considerable and completely alters the character of the poem.[17] This is emphasized by the fact that Thomas Chestre did not just translate the French poem, but made free use of some other lays as well. In *Sir Launfal* the chief interest does not lie in the miraculous adventure of the knight, as in *Sir Landevale* and *Sir Orfeo*, but is firmly directed on the person of the hero. Above all, the fairy-tale world of the French poem has deliberately been rationalized and brought into closer contact with the day-to-day experience of the audience. The supernatural element which is an essential part of the story has not, of course, been eliminated, but it stands in striking contrast to the other parts of the poem and does not pervade its whole atmosphere. George Kane blames the poet for this apparent inconsistency,[18] but it seems clear that there is some artistic purpose behind it and a different type of poem from the lays was intended.

In *Sir Landevale* the story is accepted as a fairy-tale and is treated accordingly. The change from Landevale's affluence to his extreme poverty is brought about very suddenly and without any clear motivation. His election by the fairy is told with similar abruptness. His trespassing against her strict order of silence, however, is taken very seriously and he obtains the fairy's forgiveness only after abject entreaties.

In *Sir Launfal* even Arthur's court is from the start much less aristocratic and refined. This becomes apparent in the rather unfriendly description of the King's marriage (ll. 36 ff.). Unlike in

*Sir Landevale*, the Queen is introduced at a very early point in the story and from the start there is mutual dislike between her and Launfal. At the wedding-feast she gives presents to all the knights except to him (ll. 70-2) which 'greuede hym many a syde'. He, like some other knights, strongly disapproves of her because it is said that she has a great many lovers (ll. 44-8); this of course prepares us for her later behaviour when she offers her love to Launfal (ll. 673 ff.). When Launfal's companions tell her about his (pretended) wealth she is very annoyed because, we are told,

> . . sche wold wyth all her my3t
> þat he hadde be boþe day & ny3t
> Jn paynys mor & more. (ll. 178-80)

All these small details make this part of the poem a story of personal hatred and intrigue and provide a psychological motivation for the later events. When the Queen has been rejected by Launfal her disappointment and rage are far more personal and specific than in *Sir Landevale* where her reaction is only described in rather general terms:

> Tho was she ashamyd & wroth.
> She clepid her maydens bothe;
> To bede she goith alle drery—
> For doole she wold dye, and was sory. (ll. 235-9)

*Sir Launfal* gives a far more dramatic picture of her wounded pride and hatred:

> þerfore þe quene was swyþe wro3th:
> Sche takeþ hyr maydenes & forþ hy goþ
> Jnto her tour, also blyue,
> And anon sche ley doun yn her bedde;
> For wrethe, syk sche hyr bredde,
> And swore, so moste sche thryue,
> Sche wold of Launfal be so awreke
> þat all þe lond schuld of hym speke,
> Wythjnne þe dayes fyfe. (ll. 700-708)

The author of the lay was obviously not very interested in this aspect of the story or in this kind of motivation.

Another difference between the two poems is that in *Sir Launfal*

45

the story is largely told from the point of view of the hero. He is the centre of the action far more than in *Sir Landevale*. Thus his first meeting with Triamour is described as he sees it. The description of the fair lady and her tent seems to be coloured by his amazement (ll. 283 ff.; the description in *Sir Landevale*, as in the French lay, is much more formal, like a rhetorical set-piece, ll. 77 ff.). The sudden turn in Launfal's fortunes is also dramatized and given a more rational motivation by the addition of several details about his poverty and his treatment by the mayor of Caerleon. A similar purpose is served by the short episode, also added by Thomas Chestre, in which Gyfre comes into town to deliver Triamour's presents to the knight and is told the general opinion of Launfal by a bystander:

> 'Nys he but a wrecche!
> What þar any man of hym recche?
> At þe meyrys hous he takeþ soiour.'    (ll. 394–6)

Launfal himself, although he is hardly a more fully drawn character than in the source, appears more like a reckless fellow who meets with an exciting adventure than like a humble mortal encountering a completely new world which takes him entirely by surprise. The last stanza but one in which we are told that Launfal is still ready to meet any adversary who wishes to challenge him on a certain day of the year, is very typical of the rather boisterous spirit of Chestre's poem; here the fairy does not only convey happiness and riches to her lover, but she also makes him invincible, which is proved in a series of lively fights. This addition stands in strange contrast to the fairy-tale character of the original lay. Its main purpose, as Bliss has shown,[19] is to give the impression that a longer passage of time has elapsed between the first meeting and Launfal's betrayal and to make us feel that the perfect union between the two lovers has lasted a long time, whereas in *Sir Landevale* it seems to be very short. The duration and intensity of the liaison is also emphasized by Launfal's bidding farewell to his mistress before every fight.

It seems, altogether, that Chestre wants the reader to identify himself with the hero far more than can be said of *Sir Landevale*. Launfal's disappointment after the betrayal is very vividly described. After all, he has not only lost his mistress, but all his wealth, his attendant and even his bright armour. His happy state had been rather more down-to-earth and material than Landevale's. On the other hand, his breach of faith seems to be taken less seriously as a moral crime than in the lay. He hardly needs the forgiveness of the fairy because she has obviously come to save him and when she departs he follows her without another word. In *Sir Landevale* her forgiveness is by no means a matter of course and is only granted after he has expressly pleaded for it. The lady makes it very clear that he has offended against the laws of 'dern loue':

> 'Whan we ffirst togedir mete,
> With dern loue, withouten stryfe,
> J chargyd you yn all your lyff
> That ye of me neuer speke shuld;
> How dare ye now be so bolde
> With me to ride withoute leve?
> Ye ought to thyng ye shuld me greue.'       (ll. 508–14)

This is clearly the language of *amour courtois* and Landevale's failure obviously is at the core of the whole poem. In *Sir Launfal* it seems only an episode, designed to make the happy ending the more perfect. The trial-scene with the dramatic interruptions caused by the arrival of the messengers and at last the fairy herself, has been translated by Chestre rather closely because the mounting suspense towards the climax suited his purpose very well. The messengers are first noticed by the knights who are about to pass judgment on Launfal and they are described as they appear to the observers (ll. 848–52, 883–91), an interesting example of the skilful use of point of view. At the climax of the story, when Launfal himself sees Triamour approaching, his first thought is that she could save him if only she wanted to (ll. 970–2), whereas in *Sir Landevale* the knight expresses his willingness to die now he has once more cast eyes on her. This is far more in tune with the rather elaborate piece of *descriptio* that accompanies the arrival of the lady in both poems.

All these alterations contribute to a rationalizing of the fairy-tale atmosphere of the Breton lay and to a more psychological interpretation of the characters. This is also supported by the changes in narrative technique noted by Stemmler, the less varied use of tenses, the changes from indirect to direct speech, the loss of much sophisticated detail and an obvious desire to make the story more credible. All this points to the conclusion that *Sir Launfal* represents quite a different type of story and cannot really be called a lay any more. It has a distinctly epic quality as compared to the more anecdotal character of the Breton lays, and this makes it quite a typical example of the English shorter romance.[20] Its metrical form places it among the tail-rhyme romances and even apart from the metre, it has many features in common with other poems of that group. The links with *Libeaus Desconus* and *Octavian* (Southern version), already mentioned, are particularly close, so that the three poems have often been attributed to the same author. They immediately follow one another in the manuscript (Cotton Caligula A. II) and were probably all composed during the second half of the fourteenth century. The connection between the Breton lays and the shorter Middle English romances can be seen very clearly here. The original form of the lay, however, was not preserved in England after those four early adaptations, and later poems claiming to be lays, like *Emaré* or *Sir Gowther*, have only little in common with them. It seems quite likely, therefore, that the shorter romances owe their appearance at least partly to the Breton lays and are in fact a typically English development of that form.

The origin of the shorter romances cannot, however, be attributed to the Breton lays alone. The Auchinleck Ms. which contains three of the English lays, also provides us with the text of some characteristic specimens of the shorter romance. Two of them are of particular interest for our argument: *Horn Childe and Maiden Rimnild* because it is a later version of a story that had already been told in English once, and *Reinbrun* because it is an example of how a single episode from a novel (*Guy of Warwick*) could be taken out of its context and made into a short and independent romance.

### 'KING HORN' AND 'HORN CHILDE'

*King Horn* is, as far as can be ascertained, one of the earliest of the English romances and one of the few whose text goes back as far as the thirteenth century, the heyday of Anglo-Norman literature.[21] The poem seems to have enjoyed some popularity, because it has come down in three early manuscripts none of which is a direct copy of one of the others. (Cambridge University Library Gg. 4.27 (II) = C; Laud Misc. 108 = O; B. M. Harley 2253 = H.) In all three manuscripts, *King Horn* stands in some contrast to the majority of the other items, mainly Saints' legends or devotional verse. The later collections that contain a greater number of romances have not included it.

*King Horn* has some of the characteristic features of the later short romances, but it is, on the other hand, so different from them that it almost belongs to another type. Significantly, like many of the shorter romances, it is a brief version of a story that had been treated at far greater length in French. The Anglo-Norman novel about Horn runs to over five thousand lines.[22] We do not know for certain whether the English poet actually made use of that novel or a similar version of the story, but it is revealing that he tells practically the same story as Thomas, the author of the Anglo-Norman poem, in only about a quarter of the time. This remarkable abridgement is not achieved by the omission of complete episodes or a drastic simplification of the plot, but by a striking swiftness of narration, a lack of lengthy description or reflection and a very sketchy indication of localities.

*King Horn* has in some ways the same abrupt narrative technique as the ballads, with many sudden transitions,[23] short snatches of dialogue which seem to take place in an empty space, brief scenes with hardly any 'stage directions', and the bridging of long periods of time by a few words. This narrative style is on the whole very simple and lacking some of the more subtle devices we find in the lays. Nevertheless, it is not without dramatic force. The decisive moments in the story are skilfully emphasized, as, for instance, the particularly vivid scene between Horn and Rimenhild (C, ll. 381 ff.) in which she confesses her love to him and woos him in such earnest that his resistance is broken. At such points, the narrative slows down somewhat, but even here the poet does not dwell on descriptive or psychological detail, as in many of the later romances, but very quickly gets on with the business of his story. Indeed, brevity and speed seem to be his chief aims. This rapid pace and concentration on the plot are particularly suited to a poem written for recitation. As the beginning shows, the romance is put into the mouth of a minstrel:

> Alle beon he bliþe
> þat to my song lyþe:
> A sang ihc schal ʒou singe
> Of Murry þe kinge.

49

> King he was biweste
> So longe so hit laste.
> Godhild het his quen,
> Faire ne miȝte non ben.  (C, ll. 1–8)

This beginning should not, however, be taken as evidence of oral composition or transmission.[24] The skilful compression and accentuation of the story-material betrays the hand of a careful and conscious artist. The poem resembles *Havelok* in its particularly neat and coherent structure which is chiefly based on the two motifs, revenge and love. At the beginning, Horn is placed into the situation of the outcast whose actions are dictated by his desire for revenge and for the recovery of his heritage[25] (this last motif is more prominent in the Anglo-Norman poem). With the beginning of Rimenhild's love for Horn and her wooing, a new train of events is set in motion, and there is the usual introduction of a time-limit (C, ll. 555–60) until in the end the two strands of the action meet: Horn regains his kingdom, avenges his father's death, and is finally united with Rimenhild.[26]

Courtly elements are not very prominent in *King Horn*, least of all in the description of the love-story, but, as in many other English romances, there is a very clear exposition of the idea that the knight has to prove himself worthy of his lady. Curiously enough, this point is first made by Horn himself, whereas in other poems, like *Guy of Warwick* or the famous *Squire of Low Degree*, it is the lady who makes heroic deeds a condition for the granting of her love. Horn refuses to marry Rimenhild before he has done something to deserve her:

> & of vre mestere
> So is þe manere
> Wiþ sume oþere kniȝte
> Wel for his lemman fiȝte,
> Or he eni wif take:  (C, ll. 549–53)[27]

In the more homely workaday world of *Havelok* such a remark would be quite out of place. Horn's progress towards maturity does not bring him into contact with the lower classes, as is the case with Havelok. Though he is completely destitute, like Havelok, he is given a courtly education (ll. 226–44) and never has to earn his bread by menial labour.

It is also important to note that the subject of this perhaps earliest of the Middle English romances had not been chosen from one of the traditional 'matters', but treats the history of an English king. Thus, it is not just an entertaining story of love and adventure, but at the same time the biography of a famous ancestor, a vivid portrayal of the past. In its intention, the poem has, therefore, something in common with many of the native chronicles and legends though it is less definitely localized than *Havelok* and contains less specific references to the historical background.

The chief purpose of the poem lies in the praising of a hero of royal descent whose progress and whose heroic exploits are glorified. I doubt whether it is really possible to credit the poem with such a precise allegorical meaning as D. M. Hill has proposed.[28] Plot and action seem to be too prominent here to make it very likely that every detail of the story and even the minor characters have such a clearly defined function in the moral design. The conflict between love and revenge which for Hill is one of the main themes of the poem, is hardly hinted at in the text and it seems to me an overstating of the case to say that 'Aþulf and Fikenhild are aspects of Horn's character' (p. 162), but Hill is clearly right in stressing the exemplary character and intention of the poem. All the details of the action seem to be subordinated to the central theme, the glorification of the hero and the description of a perfect prince. Thus, some of the characteristics we usually associate with the romances are still absent here; for instance, the miraculous is treated in a rather detached way and only serves to put the emphasis more firmly on the hero. In contrast to the Breton lays, therefore, *King Horn* has less the character of a fairy-tale than that of a saga or chronicle, but whereas in *Havelok* we have mainly an illustration of political virtues, such as the attributes of a perfect ruler and the loyalty of subjects, it is, in *King Horn*, above all the individual prowess and determination that have a decisive bearing on the train of events. The villain and antagonist is not, as in *Havelok*, a traitor against the king, but a faithless friend, as, for instance, Wymound in *Athelston*.

*King Horn*, then, represents a type of narrative which is as different from the Breton lays as it is from the shorter romances of the fourteenth century, but there is no doubt that this form of ballad-like glorification of a king greatly influenced the development of the shorter romances.

This development can be clearly studied by a comparison between *King Horn* and *Horn Childe,* another version of the same story, probably written a few decades later. *Horn Childe* is one of the earliest of the tail-rhyme romances from the East Midlands and is preserved in the Auchinleck Ms.[29] Its length is about the same as that of *King Horn.* Though the differences between the two poems are at first sight not very great, they are sufficient to establish beyond doubt that *Horn Childe* is not an adaptation of *King Horn,* but quite an independent poem which in some details seems closer to the Anglo-Norman novel than *King Horn.* The same subject was thus adapted twice, which is perhaps another piece of evidence for the popularity of such brief versions in England.

The poem has generally not found much favour with critics and is practically ignored in many surveys of the romances. It lacks the freshness and simplicity of *King Horn* and does not attempt to give any coherent meaning to Horn's history. It is full of apparently irrelevant detail and shows more interest in the extraordinary events than in the person of the prince. There is no question that it is in many ways inferior to *King Horn,* and yet it is more typical of the English romances than the earlier poem and therefore has some claim to our attention.

The most noticeable difference is the more 'epic', less ballad-like narrative technique in *Horn Childe,* a greater emphasis on detail and a tendency to rationalize the story. Thus, at the beginning, the events leading to Horn's exile and the initial situation are far more circumstantially described, not just in a few sketchy outlines, as in *King Horn.* Horn's companions are carefully introduced and even their names are mentioned (ll. 19–34). Most of the later scenes are more clearly localized and do not just consist of brief fragments of dialogue.

A comparison between the description of the first meeting of Horn and Rimenhild in the two versions may illustrate these differences in narrative technique. In *King Horn,* the girl is introduced in a rather off-hand way and the first thing we are told about her is her love for the young prince:

> In þe curt & vte
> & elles al abute
> Luuede men horn child,
> & mest him louede Rymenhild,

> þe kynges oȝene dofter,
> He was mest in þoȝte:
> Heo louede so horn child
> þat neȝ heo gan wexe wild:                    (C, ll. 245–52)

There follows a detailed description of her passion which prepares us for her taking the initiative in the ensuing scene. The dilemma, in which Athelbrus finds himself after her request, too, is vividly portrayed although hardly any precise reason for it is given. Between such descriptions and the speeches of the characters, the progress of the action is often barely hinted at and the effect of the scenes is therefore one of abruptness and immediacy:

> Aþelbrus gan Aþulf lede
> & in to bure wiþ him ȝede.
> Anon vpon Aþulf child
> Rymenhild gan wexe wild:
> He wende þat horn hit were
> þat heo hauede þere.
> Heo sette him on bedde;
> Wiþ Aþulf child he wedde.
> On hire armes tweie
> Aþulf heo gan leie.                    (C, ll. 293–302)

Rimenhild's disappointment when her error is discovered (Athelbrus has brought Athulf instead of Horn to her) and the reaction of Athelbrus are depicted in a similarly dramatic manner and mainly by direct speech. Her first encounter with the real Horn, too, is very lively, and there is a skilful use of revealing gestures as a means of characterization.

In *Horn Childe*, however, Rimnild is introduced more deliberately and clumsily:

> Houlac king, y wene,
> Hadde no child bi þe quene,
> Bot a maid briȝt;
> Al þai seyd þat hir sene,
> Sche was a feir may & a schene,
> & maiden rimneld sche hiȝt.
> When sche herd horn speke,
> Miȝt sche him nouȝt forȝete
> Bi day no bi niȝt;                    (ll. 301–9)

Her love is described very briefly, factually and without any dramatic force. Her first interview with Arlaund (the Athelbrus of

*King Horn*), too, is rather vague, and his apprehensions, though more specific ('Lesinges schuld bi ginne;' l. 321), are somehow less disquieting than the indistinct fears of Athelbrus. Before the first meeting there is a short description of Rimnild's preparations and thus the scene of the following action is clearly set out, again in sharp contrast to the more suggestive narrative technique of *King Horn*:

> A riche cheier was vndon,
> þat seuien miȝt sit þer on,
> In swiche craft ycorn;
> A baudekin þer on was spred;
> þider þe maiden hadde hem led,
> To siten hir bi forn;
> Frout & spices sche hem bede,
> Wine to drink wite & rede,
> Boþe of coppe & horn. (ll. 328–36)

The following events give the impression that the author had not quite understood why Arlaund has brought Horn's brother with him at first instead of Horn himself. Rimnild does not notice the deception at all and on the next day the prince himself appears in her chamber without there having been a violent argument about the matter as in *King Horn*. Rimnild's wooing, too, is far less forthright and much more ceremonious than in the earlier poem. There, the girl had come to the point directly and had been so pressing that Horn was put on the defensive, whereas in *Horn Childe* she proceeds less directly. She makes him a number of noble presents until he offers to be her champion before there has been any declaration of love. The question of marriage does not arise at first and the whole affair thus starts in a far more detached and courtly manner than in *King Horn*. The betrayal of the lovers, however, is told with far more gusto and concrete detail. It is not, as in *King Horn*, prepared for by an ominous dream, but follows straight after Horn has been made a knight. Although in this version the king has rather less reason for his suspicion and does not, as in *King Horn*, surprise the two lovers in bed in the lady's chamber, his reaction is much more violent and brutal. He beats her until she bleeds and then goes to his room to let his anger cool (ll. 496–516). The narrator hastens to add, however, that

> Giltles sche was of þat dede,
> Horn hadde nouȝt hir maidenhede,
> Bot in word & þouȝt. (ll. 502–4)

When Horn visits the lady in her chamber ('Mouþe & nose al for bled', l. 521) she advises him on how to soften her enraged father. The end of the poem, too, is simpler and at the same time more circumstantial. Again Rimnild's prophetic dream is omitted; in its place there are two fairy-tale motifs: Horn's ring will change colour if the girl should betray him, and a shadow in the well will inform her of Horn's faithlessness, but in spite of these supernatural elements, the action seems more credible and consistent. On the other hand, the story is far more diffuse than in *King Horn* and less firmly controlled by a central theme. Everything is told in the same, rather pedestrian, manner which leads to a certain monotony and to an absence of any climax in the narration.

The rather loose structure of the poem is perhaps partly due to its metrical form. The tail-rhyme stanza, which is on the whole confined to more popular poetry, lends itself to a somewhat garrulous narrative style when it is used by a less skilful poet. The tail-lines (or *caudae*) often interrupt the flow of the narrative by meaningless clichés and act as a brake on the dramatic movement of the action. Since every stanza requires four rhyme-words it is easy to see why the poet was often tempted to use the same colourless tags again and again, and *Horn Childe* is particularly weak in this respect, whereas some of the later tail-rhyme romances make considerably more skilful use of that stanza-form and, in particular, of the tail-lines.[30]

Like *King Horn*, the poem begins with a promise to tell the story of a king, and it is made quite clear that we shall hear of events that took place in this country a long time ago:

> Mi leue frende dere,
> Herken & ʒe may here,
> & ʒe wil vnder stonde;
> Stories ʒe may lere
> Of our elders þat were
> Whilom in þis lond.
> Y wil ʒou telle of kinges tvo,
> Hende haþeolf was on of þo,
> þat weld al ingelond;
> Fram Humber norþ þan walt he,
> þat was in to þe wan see,
> In to his owhen hond.          (ll. 1–12)

This could almost be the beginning of a chronicle, but it soon becomes clear that the poet is neither concerned with political problems nor with the progress of an exemplary hero, but that he wants to tell a lively and adventurous story which he tries to embellish with realistic and sometimes rather trivial detail. It is difficult to see that he had any higher aim than that. The story follows the old pattern of an apparently hopeless situation being remedied and success won in the face of overwhelming odds. This simplification and rationalization of the plot is quite typical of the English shorter romances, although it must be said that *Horn Childe* is not one of the more successful and inspired specimens of that type.

### 'REINBRUN'

*Reinbrun*, another poem which is only preserved in the Auchinleck manuscript, is also an example of the clear preference for shorter tales, so noticeable in Middle English. Very often, as was perhaps the case with *Horn Childe*, such short poems are condensed versions of longer novels, whereas *Reinbrun*, as mentioned above, is just a part of the very long *Guy of Warwick* which, for the purposes of this particular collection, was separated from the novel to form a short romance on its own.[31] To achieve this, the text hardly had to be altered at all. A new introduction was added which contains the usual prayer for the audience and announces the subject of the story:

> Iesu, þat ert of miȝte most,
> Fader, & sone, & holy gost,
> Ich bidde þe a bone:
> Ase þow ert lord of our ginning,
> & madest heuene and alle þing,
> Se, and sonne, and mone,
> ȝeue hem grace wel to spede
> þat herkneþ what y schel rede,
> Iesu, god in trone.
> Of a kniȝt was to batayle boun,
> Sire Gij is sone, þat hiȝte Reynbroun,
> Of him y make my mone.          (ll. 1–12)

After that, the story of Guy of Warwick is briefly recapitulated in about twenty lines and then the adventures of Guy's son Reinbrun are told exactly as in the other versions of *Guy of Warwick* with only very slight alterations. The result is a very lively and close-knit short romance in which the fortunes of Reinbrun, who as a child is stolen by merchants, and of Heraud, who goes in search of him, are related. There are some surprising encounters and exciting fights and the whole story comes out rather more effectively than within the extensive novel of Guy of Warwick where it seems more like a long digression that has little to do with the subject of the story. The poem thus belongs to the same type as the other shorter romances which relate the wanderings and the exploits of some famous knight. It is only in this particular manuscript collection that the story of Reinbrun was thus separated from the novel itself which had been copied by a different scribe, without the parts relating to Reinbrun, in the same volume. This shows how carefully some of these collections were edited and how freely some stories could be fitted into one or more romances just as it seemed most appropriate to the redactor.[32]


## 'ROLAND AND VERNAGU' AND 'OTUEL'

Like *Reinbrun*, the two Charlemagne poems contained in the Auchinleck Ms. seem to owe their origin to the evident desire of the editor to produce short romances, whether the story was suited to that treatment or not.[33] The two poems relate episodes from the cycle of stories that centred round the legendary figures of Charlemagne and his paladins. Their sources are either similar poems in French, such as *Otinel*, or very different works, like the chronicle of Pseudo-Turpin, a compilation in Latin prose, from which the English adapter took over an episode and retold it in tail-rhyme stanzas. This is how *Roland and Vernagu* probably originated. It is a rather flat piece of work which is only interesting as another early example of the shorter romance in English. It is likely that it was composed specially for the Auchinleck collection.

*Otuel* is a rather more successful specimen of the same type. It contains some vivid scenes and the story is more skilfully adapted to the purpose of an independent little tale. In spite of the difference in metrical form (it is written in rhyming couplets), the poem stands very close to *Roland and Vernagu*, indeed it seems to be a direct continuation of it. The theory, advanced many years ago by Gaston Paris, that there was once a complete cycle of shorter Charlemagne romances, received partial confirmation when the

Fillingham Ms. with the tail-rhyme romance *Otuel and Roland* was discovered.[34] This poem makes it seem very likely that there was a now lost English romance, the hypothetical *Charlemagne and Roland*, of which *Roland and Vernagu* and *Otuel and Roland* are fragments. If this theory is correct, then the shorter poems were produced in the same way as *Reinbrun*, that is, smaller sections of an extensive tale were made into individual romances by adding brief introductions and conclusions. Another manuscript from the fifteenth century (B.M. Additional 31.042) also contains two shorter tail-rhyme romances from the same cycle of stories, *The Sege off Melayne* and *Rowlande and Ottuell*, which follow one another and relate two episodes that are more or less complete in themselves. Here, too, it is obvious that a specific type of poem was intended, a short romance with plenty of incident and a central hero.[35] This basic pattern underlies nearly all the poems dealt with in this and the following chapter.

## 'IPOMEDON' (THE A- AND B-VERSIONS)

The two English versions of the story of Ipomedon may serve as a last example in this brief survey of various short adaptations. Very likely the two poems were composed quite independently of each other, but they are both adaptations of the Anglo-Norman *Ipomedon*, a novel by Hue de Rotelande, in which courtly manners and above all *amour courtois* are portrayed with an intimate knowledge and yet with a certain degree of ironic detachment.[36] The earlier English version in tail-rhyme stanzas (A-version) is nearly as long as the Anglo-Norman poem (8890 lines). Although the tone of the source has been changed in many ways and a number of alterations are introduced which are characteristic of the differences between the two authors and their audiences,[37] the A-version follows the plot and the thematic development of the Anglo-Norman poem much more closely than the majority of English translations of French romances. Even more interesting and typical, however, is the B-version, which reduces Rotelande's novel to about a quarter of its length and makes the poem very like some of the other shorter romances in Middle English.

The A-version is something of an oddity in Middle English literature and has very little in common with any other romance, least of all with the tail-rhyme romances to which, according to its metre and provenance, it really belongs. It is only preserved in one manuscript (Chetham 8009) and has not been included in any of the major collections of romances, like Cotton Caligula A. II or Cambridge Ff. II. 38, which perhaps suggests that it was not very successful. The B-version, on the other hand, which probably was not composed before the fifteenth century, is preserved in a famous 'commonplace-book' (Harley 2252), and there are also fragments of an early printed version by Wynkyn de Worde. It is likely, therefore, that this version was more popular than the earlier one. A comparison between the two poems may cast some interesting sidelights on the peculiarities of the shorter English romances and the differences between them and their models.

*Ipomedon A* begins with a general introduction, an abridged translation of its source, in which the power of love and some of its rules are described and the story to follow is announced as an unheard-of example:

> Off love were lykynge of to lere
> And joye tille all, that wol here,
> That wote, what love may mene;
> But who so have grette haste to love
> And may not com to his above,
> That poynte dothe louers tene.
> Fayre speche brekyth never bone,
> That makythe these lovers ilkone
> Ay hope of better wene
> And put them selffe to grete travayle,
> Wheddyr it helpe or not avayle:
> Ofte sythes this hathe be sene.
>
> Be this poynte well may I prese,
> That of his love was lothe to lese
> Fro tyme that he began;
> Thereffore in þe world where euer he went,
> In justys or in turnamente,
> Euer more the pryce he wan.
> But a stravnge lover he was one:
> I hope, ye haue harde speke of non,
> That euer god made to be man,
> Ne lother knowen for to be;
> No whedure a better knyght þan he
> Was no levand than.      (ll. 1–24)

Such introductions are quite common in the French and German courtly novels, but they are very rare in the English romances of the thirteenth and fourteenth centuries.

*Ipomedon B*, however, begins with a typical minstrel-formula:

> Mekely, lordyngis gentyll and fre,
> Lystene a while and herken to me:
> I shall you telle of a kynge,
> A dowghty man, with owte lesynge;
> In his tyme he was full bolde,
> A worthy man and wele of tolde;
> Feyre he was on fote and hand
> And wele belouyd in all that lande;
> Off body he was styffe & stronge,
> And to no man he wold do wronge. (ll. 1–10)

The attention of the audience is aroused and there is the conventional description of a perfect king who, however, will play only a very minor part in the following story. The two introductions already point to a fundamental difference between the two poems. One of them is an extensive and leisurely novel on the subject of courtly love, the other is a lively tale about the adventures of a particularly valiant and daring knight. This difference is apparent throughout the two poems, particularly in the different handling of the plot and in the comments of the narrator.

In *Ipomedon A*, the several strands of the plot are skilfully interwoven, whereas in *Ipomedon B* the author firmly concentrates on those parts of the action that are concerned with the hero. Immediately after the introduction, Ipomedon's upbringing is related, whereas in *Ipomedon A*, we are first introduced to the daughter of the King of Calabria, whose beauty is described in some detail (ll. 85 ff.). The scene in which Ipomedon hears about the beautiful maiden for the first time is told more briefly in *Ipomedon A* (in spite of the greater length of that poem) than in *Ipomedon B* (cf. A, ll. 176–96, and B, ll. 109–48) where his sudden love for the girl he has never seen is better accounted for and seems more plausible because all the court appears to talk of nothing else but her perfections. In *Ipomedon A*, such an explanation is not necessary, because the suddenness of Ipomedon's love is one of the traditional features of *amour courtois* whose symptoms are described in far greater detail in this version.

In the B-version, Ipomedon's asking for leave and his departure

60

are told in a more direct manner and in the form of a short scene. Tholomew goes to the King, falls on his knees and, on Ipomedon's behalf, asks for the King's permission to leave the court. The King seems very pleased and tells him to take enough money for the journey (ll. 185–226). In *Ipomedon A*, the mother's consent has to be won too, and the whole procedure is a little more ceremonious; on the other hand, there is less use of direct speech (ll. 265–300).

The scene of Ipomedon's arrival at the court of his beloved also proves that the author of *Ipomedon B* did not abridge his source in an arbitrary fashion, but carefully selected the details he wished to retain. In *Ipomedon A*, there is a very elaborately described scene at this point (ll. 334–502); the B-version leaves out a great deal of descriptive detail and some other matter which probably seemed less relevant to the adapter (ll. 245–344), but, like the A-version, it gives a detailed account of the impression made on the girl by Ipomedon. As she looks at him she begins to suspect that he has not perhaps just come in order to be her servant, but because he loves her:

> The lady byheld Ipomydon,
> Hym semyd wele a gentilmon;
> She knew non suche in hyr londe,
> So goodly a man & wele farand;
> She saw also by his norture,
> He was a man of grete valure.
> She cast full sone in hyr thoght,
> That for no seruyce come he noght,
> But it was worship hyr vnto,
> In feyre seruyce hym to do;          (ll. 279–88)[38]

In the A-version, the reaction of the lady is more complex, and there is also a prophetic hint by the narrator, with a warning to all ladies who are too proud to show their love:

> And longe hym beheldes the fere,
> But no thynge chaunges here chere
> For carpynge of the crowde;
> Her hertte is sett so mekyll of wyte,
> Wyth love it is not dauntyd yte,
> Thowȝe she be shene in scherovde;
> But aftur sore it bande the fre,
> And so I wold, that all ye shuld be,
> That is of love so prowde!          (ll. 382–90)

There is nothing like this in the B-version, and the relationship between service and secret love is far less subtle. Ipomedon's strange behaviour is no more than an unusual adventure which is told for its own sake, not as an illustration of the etiquette of *amour courtois*.

The following events, too, are related more circumstantially in *Ipomedon A*. The young man makes a rather unfavourable impression at first because he can only hunt and seems to have no desire to engage in any other chivalrous exploits (ll. 512 ff.). Even the lady herself begins to think that he is lacking in valour:

> 'Allas', she sayd, 'so mekyll fayrenes
> Ys loste on hym wyth outen proves:
> Yt is a sory synne! . . .' (ll. 536–8)

Her disappointment is not without justification because in this version Ipomedon spends three years at her court without distinguishing himself in any way.

In the B-version, however, the development of the action is much faster. The lady falls in love with Ipomedon at first sight. She lies sleepless in her bed, thinking about him and wondering where he has come from (ll. 349 ff.). The hunting-scene, which gives her a first clue, seems to follow not very long after his arrival. It is carefully arranged by her in order that she might 'know hym by his game' (l. 364). When afterwards, during the meal, she feels that he cannot take his eyes off her, she is afraid to encourage him because she wants to avoid any gossiping which would be to her 'deshonoure' (ll. 426 ff.). This is quite natural as she has not known the knight very long, although we had been told earlier that he stayed at her court 'many a day' (l. 339). In the A-version, however, three years have already passed and the lady has another, more powerful reason for not wanting to grant him her love. She once made a solemn vow to marry only the most valiant knight that could be found (ll. 109–20), and Ipomedon has so far done nothing to deserve that distinction, as the lady herself admits ruefully:[39]

> 'For hym to love, yf I had thoughte,
> To myne avowe acordes he nought:
> That makyth myne hertte vnblythe;
> That prowde sory vowe, that I
> Made be my grette folye,
> Now makyth me wrynge & wrythe!' (ll. 705–10)

This kind of reflection is completely absent in *Ipomedon B*, and the lady's vow is only mentioned in passing. Her only reason for rejecting Ipomedon seems to be a too scrupulous regard for her reputation, whereas in the A-version she addresses a long lecture to the innocent Jason in which, for the benefit of Ipomedon, she holds forth about the proper way to win a lady's love; this, she says, is not by 'nyce lokynge', but by chivalrous deeds and prowess (ll. 840–62). The whole scene is worked out quite elaborately and there is such a meaningful exchange of loving looks that the situation becomes very tense. Jason is so struck by her reproach, which he has done nothing to deserve, that he forgets to eat. In *Ipomedon B*, the rebuff is not quite as dramatic, but when Ipomedon tells her that he wants to leave, she cuts him very short:

> 'Felaw,' she sayd, 'chese at þi wille,
> Whether þou wilt wend or abyde stille!'     (ll. 465–6)

When he has gone she is extremely sorry, but her mournful soliloquy is not so much a lover's complaint as an expression of her regret that such a perfect knight has left her 'for a word' (ll. 493 ff.). In the A-version, however, there is a formal complaint of more than one hundred and twenty lines in which she curses her pride, reflects on his beauty and goodness and bitterly reproaches herself for not taking advantage of the moment when she could have kept him had she been more reasonable (ll. 911–1036). Ipomedon, too, lies awake all night bemoaning his fate and blaming himself for his foolish behaviour (ll. 1049 ff.). The tension is much greater here than in the B-version because the lady is still in some doubt as to whether Ipomedon has really left her for good or whether she might still be able to hold him by overcoming her pride. He had parted from her the night before in somewhat ambiguous terms. When he has taken his final leave of Jason in the forest and Jason has told her about it, her grief breaks out again and she has to be comforted by her maid (ll. 1400 ff.). In no other English romance of the fourteenth century, apart from Chaucer, do we find such extensive use of reflection on the problems of courtly love and such emphasis on the thoughts and emotions of the characters. As in the Anglo-Norman poem, the action often only serves to introduce such reflections, complaints and arguments.[40] Thus, the whole episode of Ipomedon's indirect rebuff and his departure are mainly introduced as an example of the power of love which cannot be suppressed and often makes the wise look fools. This point is made very clearly by the narrator in an aside:

> Whate myghte þat be, but derne love,
> That all ways wyll be above
> To them, that shall it havnte?
> All othere thynges men davnte may,
> But, sertenly, be no waye
> Love wille not be davnte!
> Who presus ofte to serue hytte,
> Worse schall have his gurdovn quyte,
> For he be loves seruante.
> Who entrys in to loves scolys,
> The wyseste is holdyn moste foolys,
> Fro that they haue graunte.                    (ll. 797–808)

It seems that the author of the B-version either did not understand the meaning of his source or did not care to reproduce it because he omits all these more theoretical discussions and drastically reduces most of the soliloquies and complaints. This, of course, alters the character of the story considerably. It appears on the whole more superficial, although in some places it gains in speed and dramatic suspense. The two lovers who, in the A-version, part almost against their will and better judgment because they have not yet understood the real meaning of love, have become, in the B-version, a pair of rather stubborn young people who are separated because of a few rash words. In the A-version, we are pretty sure that the two lovers will meet again and will eventually be united. This is the consolation offered by her maid Imayne (ll. 1492 ff.); we are also told that Ipomedon thinks he will never love another, and she is determined that nobody shall ever wed her but he (ll. 1757 ff.). Indeed, the separation makes their love even stronger.[41] This idea is hardly present in the B-version where the suspense lies more in the external events than in the emotional experience of the main characters and the manifestations of the power of love. Kölbing rightly finds a lack of deeper motivation in the poem, but he does not seem to have realized that the adapter of the B-version was interested in a completely different aspect of the story and that his poem can therefore not be judged by the same standards. For him, Ipomedon's love is only one of his many unusual adventures. When he goes to see the lady it is partly to find out whether she is really as beautiful as he has been told (ll. 143–4). He is of course very impressed by her, but she does not, as in the A-version, govern his whole life from then on. The same applies to the lady. Her dilemma, after the knight has left her and she is asked by her nobles to take a husband, is much more distressing in *Ipomedon A* because she really loves Ipomedon and cannot bear the thought of having to marry anybody else (ll. 2148 ff.), whereas in the B-version her main concern is to marry the best knight, and as she had formed a very high opinion of Ipomedon she expects that he will come to the tournament to win her hand:

'If he be suche, as I hym holde,
Also doughty and so bolde,
For me than he wille be here
And wynne me in all manere!'          (ll. 625–8)

In the A-version, the situation is more complex. The tournament is only suggested as a last resort after long deliberation between the lady and her maid, and its purpose is clearly to attract Ipomedon and at the same time allow her to be true to the 'proude avowe' (ll. 2172 ff.). Her expectations are in substance the same as in the B-version, but very different in tone:

And yff my love be levande
And maye here tell, I vnderstond,
Thus turnament yare,
Yff he haue any þoughte on me,
Or anny provys in hym bee,
I hope, he wille be þare;
Yff he love me, I suppose,
Hee will his loue not lyghttly loose:
Yff he doo, wronge it ware;
Whedyr hit turne to wele or woo,
His loue and I shuld forgoo,
Off blis I were full bare!"          (ll. 2193–2204)

There are very similar differences in the descriptions of the three days' tournament.[42] In *Ipomedon A*, when the lady is told at the end of each day that it was Ipomedon in disguise who has won the prize, she breaks out in passionate lamentations, cursing her pride and folly, and has to be consoled by Jason and her maid (ll. 3405 ff., 3976 ff., 4706 ff.); Jason tries to detain the knight by telling him that the lady will die because of him ('My ladye dyes for love of the', l. 3959). In the B-version, the action is very similar, but the lady seems to be mainly angry with herself for being too stupid to have appreciated Ipomedon's true worth while he was still with her (ll. 871 ff.), and she consoles herself with the reflection that he cannot leave her so lightly after he has exerted himself so much for her sake (ll. 881–4, 1023–4, 1209–12), a very commonsense argument which, however, does not occur in the A-version. Another motif which the adapter of the B-version has misunderstood or altered deliberately, is the scornful amusement of the knights when Ipomedon returns from the tournament and pretends that he has only been out hunting all day. In the A-version, all the knights and ladies laugh heartily at Ipomedon's boorish behaviour, except for the Queen who rather likes him and is therefore ashamed of him because he lacks prowess (ll. 3557 ff., 4134 ff., 4898–4900). This incident is repeated three times. In the B-version, however, the Queen does not seem to think that Ipomedon has behaved dishonourably although, on the third night, the company is so much amused by his lies that some of them cannot sit upright at the table for laughing (ll. 1273–4). In both versions, Ipomedon deliberately plays the fool, but this is a far more serious matter in the courtly context of *Ipomedon A*, whereas in *Ipomedon B* it is just another entertaining episode.

It would be easy to point out similar differences throughout the two poems, for instance in the description of Ipomedon's journey with Imayne which in the B-version contains some rather burlesque elements,[43] whereas in the A-version it provides another opportunity for several reflections on the power of love because Imayne conceives a sudden passion for her companion.[44]

The endings of the two poems, too, are rather typical of their different style and theme. *Ipomedon A* gives a brief and generalized description of the final union of the two lovers as an example of complete happiness (ll. 8816 ff.) and it concludes with a message to all lovers to the effect that love's wounds cannot be healed by salves, but only by love and pity. The audience is asked to pray for all lovers:

> Ipomadon hathe sent his sonde
> To lovers, that leve in londe,
> His messyngere makythe he me;
> He commaundythe on goddis behalue,

66

To lovys wounde ye lay no salue,
But poynttis of grette pette.
Where right loue was in herte brought,
That for a littill lette ye noughte:
Sertes, no more dyd hee.
This endythe Ipomadon, iwis.
That good lorde bringe vs to his blis,
That bought vs on the rode tre!
And that ye shall for louers pray
To hym, that made bothe nyght & day.
(To brynge vs to the blysse, that lestis aye.)

(ll. 8876–8890)

There is nothing like this ending in any of the other English romances discussed in this book. The concept of love as a common human experience, let alone as a test of character and a power which has its own set of rules, is rather foreign to most English adapters of romances.[45]

Instead of this somewhat theoretical conclusion, the B-version has a detailed description of the marriage festivities with forty days of splendid dinners, minstrelsy and merry-making; there is also mention of the rich reward given to the minstrels (ll. 2269–70; see also l. 547). Even the heavenly bliss that is prayed for at the end of the poem, as in many similar conclusions, seems in the mind of the author to bear a striking resemblance to such royal entertainment and feasting:

And whan they dyed, I trow, iwis,
Bothe they yede to heuyn blysse,
There as non other thynge may bee,
But joye and blisse, game & glee:
To þat blysse god bryng vs alle,
That dyed on rode for grete & smalle! Amen. (ll. 2341–6)

Thus, even a brief comparison between the two poems has perhaps made clear that we have before us two completely different types of romance. *Ipomedon A*, which is often mentioned as a particularly successful example of the English tail-rhyme romance, is in fact very different from that group of poems in all but its metrical form and is something of an alien in Middle English literature, more akin to the Anglo-Norman courtly tradition than to the English romances. It is the history of an exemplary pair of

67

lovers (cf. ll. 8817 ff.) whose union is delayed by the folly and in-experience of the two young people, but also by the rules of courtly etiquette. Until the end, Ipomedon does not consider himself worthy enough to meet the requirements laid down in the lady's vow:

> Ipomadon thynkes aye,
> Prevely to wynd his waye,
> That no man shuld hym knawe,
> For euermore in his hert he thought:
> 'Till her vowe corde I novght,
> Therefore I will wythdrawe!'          (ll. 8156–61)

This has really been the deeper reason for his strange behaviour throughout the poem. Such conflicts are, however, not usually the subject of romances in Middle English and it is interesting to see that such a poem was actually written, but it seems more than likely that it was less popular than the shorter romances, of which *Ipomedon B* is such a characteristic example.

This poem, although evidently written by a less competent poet, tells us more about the distinctive qualities of the Middle English romances and has, in spite of its different verse-form, more in common with the tail-rhyme romances than the A-version. The adapter has obviously often misunderstood his source, but he has certainly also made many conscious alterations. The concept of courtly love which in the A-version forms the basis of the whole story, does not seem to exist for him. His hero is an accomplished knight who is deeply in love with a beautiful lady, but again and again puts off the fulfilment of his love because of an apparent delight in adventure and playful disguise. The adapter hardly ever leaves out complete scenes or episodes, but he shortens his tale considerably by a more concise mode of narration and a purposeful concentration on plot and action. Undoubtedly, the poem is an attempt to adapt the particularly attractive story of Ipomedon to the tastes of a rather mixed English audience, whereas the A-version was a very close translation of a novel written at a different time and for a different audience.

By considering several shorter romances we have seen that many of these poems can be described either as abridged versions or adaptations of more extensive works or as single episodes drawn from longer novels or compilations. There are, of course, some romances whose source we do not know and which therefore cannot be characterized in this way, such as *Sir Eglamour* and *Sir Degrevant*, but those poems too, prove that a distinct type of shorter romance developed in England of which many of the extant poems are examples.

Several kinds of such shorter romances can be distinguished according to the pattern of the action. The majority of them describe the life of a knight, often from very humble beginnings, and his first chivalrous adventures up to his marriage, sometimes with a brief glance at later fights and his death in the Holy Land. To this type belong, among others, *Horn Childe, Sir Eglamour, Torrent of Portyngale, Libeaus Desconus, Sir Perceval of Gales* and *Ipomedon B.* Closely related to these poems are tales that concentrate on one episode from the life of the hero by which his superiority is vividly illustrated, like *Sir Launfal, Sir Degrevant, Roland and Vernagu* and *Otuel.* Apart from these, there are a number of romances in which the adventures of two lovers, friends, a family, or a group of knights are related, like *Floris and Blauncheflur, The Erl of Tolous, Octavian, Amis and Amiloun, The Awntyrs off Arthure* and *The Avowynge of Kyng Arther.* These poems, too, centre round some knightly exploits, and the stories end with a wedding, a reunion or a reconciliation. The outlines of the action are often very similar in these poems, and this again is evidence of their belonging to a fairly well-defined type although the stories may derive from very different sources and there are many differences in the manner and skill of adaptation.

A definite chronology of these poems is difficult to establish. The most reliable information about the date of the poems and possible influences can be gathered from the manuscripts and at least a few general conclusions can be drawn.[46]

The most important and at the same time one of the earliest collections of romances is the Auchinleck Ms. It contains three English lays (*Sir Orfeo, Lai le Freine,* and *Sire Degarre*) as well as an appreciable number of shorter romances, like *Floris and Blauncheflur, Horn Childe, Amis and Amiloun, Reinbrun, Roland and Vernagu* and *Otuel*; it is also possible that it once included *Libeaus Desconus.*[47] It is therefore clear that shorter romances were written at least as early as the first half of the fourteenth century. Of the later collections, three are particularly important for the history of the shorter romances: Cotton Caligula A. II preserves

*Sir Eglamour, Sir Launfal, Libeaus Desconus* and *Octavian* (Southern version); the manuscript Ff.II.38 of the Cambridge University Library includes *Sir Eglamour, The Erl of Tolous, Sir Triamour, Octavian* (Northern version) and *Sire Degarre*; Lincoln Cathedral Library A. 5.2 (Thornton manuscript) contains *Sir Eglamour, The Erl of Tolous, Octavian* (Northern version), *Sir Degrevant, Sir Perceval of Gales* and *The Awntyrs off Arthure*. These manuscripts thus preserve a substantial number of shorter romances; some of the texts are contained in more than one of the collections, although none of them seems to be a direct copy of one of the others. The three later manuscripts all appear to be in some way related to the Auchinleck Ms.; the connection is particularly striking in the case of the Cambridge Ms. (like the Auchinleck Ms., it also contains texts of *Sir Beues of Hamtoun* and *Guy of Warwick*). It is also likely that some of the later tail-rhyme poems were influenced by *Amis and Amiloun* and other Auchinleck romances.[48] The majority of the poems mentioned here were copied during the fifteenth century,[49] although most of them were probably composed earlier. The few shorter romances that appear to have been written in the fifteenth century (*Torrent of Portyngale* and *Ipomedon B*) are obviously imitations of earlier poems, lacking somewhat their freshness and originality. The shorter romances are for the most part only preserved in very few manuscripts, many only in one or two, but their distribution among various collections of different dates and provenance again points to the conclusion that the type was very popular. Some of these poems will be examined more closely in the following chapter.

# 4

# THE SHORTER ROMANCES (II)

## 'LIBEAUS DESCONUS'

This Middle English romance of the Fair Unknown is a very characteristic example of the popularity of short adaptations of French novels in English and of the independent manner in which these adaptations were often produced. The poem is preserved in six manuscripts, but although all these versions are undoubtedly derived from the same original, they are so different from each other in detail that we have to assume a number of intervening versions existed which are now lost.[1] H. M. Smyser's suggestion that the romance was once contained in the important Auchinleck collection seems very plausible.[2] There are an unusual number of similarities between *Libeaus Desconus* and several poems from that manuscript which have been noticed by more than one scholar.[3] In view of the very careful editing of the Auchinleck Ms., such agreements in style and expression could be easily explained if *Libeaus Desconus* was really one of the poems that must have been lost from that collection. On the other hand, it is also quite possible that the author of *Libeaus Desconus* knew the Auchinleck Ms. or a similar collection, as seems very likely in the case of Thomas Chestre and the author of the 'Southern' *Octavian* (perhaps also Chestre), and that he was influenced by its contents. Another possible explanation is that the author or the scribe who copied *Libeaus Desconus* had access to some of the sources which were used by the authors of several Auchinleck poems. Of course this would be particularly easy if all the poems were produced or adapted in the same 'bookshop'. A particularly interesting example is the scene in which Libeaus interrupts his fight with Maugis because he is suffering from thirst, and asks his adversary for a few moments' respite until he has drunk from a little river nearby (ll. 1417 ff.). This episode is absent in the French poem *Le Bel*

*Inconnu* that may have been the author's source, but there is a very similar incident in *Guy of Warwick* (A, ll. 8132 ff.) and there are a number of verbal parallels between *Libeaus Desconus* and that novel, in particular the Auchinleck version of it.[4] It seems very likely, therefore, that the author of *Libeaus Desconus* knew either the Auchinleck redaction of *Guy of Warwick* or its source.

Whereas M. Kaluza, the first editor of *Libeaus Desconus*, believed that the poem was a direct translation of the French *Le Bel Inconnu*, most scholars now take a more cautious view and prefer to think that the source of *Libeaus Desconus* was a French adaptation, largely independent of *Le Bel Inconnu*, of some common original.[5] This is, of course, mere conjecture, but it is certain that the source-problem is more complex than earlier scholars assumed and that it will probably never be definitely solved. For our purposes, it may suffice to say that in *Libeaus Desconus*, as in several other English romances, a story that in French could run to over 6000 lines was dealt with in just over 2200 lines, which is of course more than the length of most of the shorter romances, but is still considerably briefer than the French courtly novels. This abridgement is achieved mainly by a marked increase in tempo and the leaving out of many smaller details, but also by the omission of a complete episode, Libeaus' sojourn on the 'Ile d'or' which in the French novel takes up as much space as the whole of the English poem. In *Le Bel Inconnu*, this episode evidently has a very important function, not only because the role of magic is given special prominence here, but because the author wished to lay particular stress on the dangers surrounding the hero and he wanted to describe as impressively as possible the moment in which the knight almost loses his personality and is in great peril of forfeiting his glorious destiny—a moment that also plays an important part in the structure of Chrétien's novels. Thus, the hero's triumph at the end of this episode is not just another of his exploits; it has a much more decisive and final quality.[6]

By passing over this episode in a few lines, the English adapter changed a discursive novel into a far more unified tale, a tale that does not describe a complex process of maturing and of initiation, like the French poem, but, in comparison, a rather more primitive series of adventures illustrating the prowess of the hero. Thus, not only the structure and the proportions have been radically changed, but also the exposition of the themes and the meaning. In *Le Bel*

*Inconnu,* the knight starts out from a position of complete obscurity at the court of King Arthur where his unknown origin and his namelessness relegated him to a very modest place; through a carefully graded sequence of adventures he works his way back to the court and to a new identity. As the acknowledged son of Gawain, he is now received into the company of the most respected knights. This is, though in a somewhat watered-down form, the same basic pattern we find in the novels of Chrétien.[7] In the English poem, however, there is hardly any trace of this meaningful design. *Libeaus Desconus* does not portray a significant development, but is a rather loosely constructed, though quite dramatic, story in praise of a particularly daring and at the same time virtuous knight.

The beginning of the poem is characteristic of the swaggering tone that recurs in many of these shorter romances. As in dozens of similar works, we are promised the history of a particularly valiant knight:

> Ihesu Crist, our saviour,
> And his modir, þat swete flour,
> Helpe hem at her nede,
> þat harkeneþ of a conquerour,
> Wis of witte and wiȝt werrour
> And douȝty man in dede.
> His name was called Gingelein;
> Beȝete he was of sir Gawein
> Be a forest side.
> Of stouter kniȝt and profitable
> Wiþ Arthour of þe rounde table
> Ne herde ȝe never rede. (ll. 1–12)

The illegitimate origin of the knight, his father's name, and even his own, are disclosed right at the start. In the French poem, the revealing of the hero's parentage through the voice of a fairy marks an important climax in the story. This is completely lost in the English version, where from the beginning the Fair Unknown enjoys the full confidence and favour of the King and his position at the court does not change so radically. The unity of the poem is achieved by a more concise handling of the plot; the action is practically reduced to a single extended adventure, the disenchanting of the lady in Sinadoun and the heroic exploits on the way. This simple pattern stands in striking contrast to the sophisticated structure of the French poem where several strands of narrative are intricately interwoven. Instead, *Libeaus Desconus* concentrates firmly on the person of the hero, a significant change which, as we have seen, is characteristic of several English adaptations.

When Libeaus arrives at Arthur's court, he is kindly received and made knight the same day, although he has so far done nothing to prove his valour.[8] His first opportunity comes straightaway when the messenger from Sinadoun and her dwarfish companion ask Arthur for help and beg him to send one of his knights to the rescue of their lady. This scene is even slightly elaborated in the English version. The messenger is deeply disappointed when Arthur offers to send Libeaus (because he has promised to let him have the first fight) and she thinks it will be harmful to Arthur's reputation if he puts her off with a mere child:

> 'Alas þat tide,
> þat I was hider y-sent!
> þis word schall springe wide:
> Lore, king, is þy pride,
> And þy manhod y-schent,
> Whan þou wilt sende a child,
> þat is witles and wilde,
> To dele douȝty dent,
> And hast kniȝtes of main,
> Perceval and Gawein,
> Pris in ech turnement.'          (ll. 182–92)

But Arthur refuses to send anybody else and the three depart from the court, after Libeaus has been armed by four of Arthur's best knights (Gawain, Perceval, Iwein and Agrafain), whereas in *Le Bel Inconnu* it is only Gawain who arms him. For three days, the messenger pours her anger and scorn on the knight until he has won the first fight against a powerful enemy and she gladly asks his pardon (ll. 475 ff.). In the following series of adventures, the English adapter has often tried to make his hero even more impressive than in the French poem by exaggerating his prowess, increasing the number of his enemies and the fierceness of the fights. By the drastic abridgement of the sixth adventure (the 'Ile d'or' episode) the adapter has also made sure that much less blame falls on Libeaus than in the French novel. Libeaus is not so much captivated by the fair lady's charms as overcome by her magic arts, and though he is faithless to his chief task, the rescue of

the lady in Sinadoun, we are assured that the fault lies far more
with the sorceress than with him:

> For þis fair lady
> Coupe more of sorcery,
> þen oþer swiche five.
> Sche made him melodie
> Of all maner menstralsy,
> þat any man miȝte descrive.
> Whan he siȝ her face,
> Him þouȝte, þat he was
> In paradis a live.
> Wiþ fantasme and fairie
> þus sche blered his iȝe,
> þat evell mot sche þrive!          (ll. 1513–24)

As soon as his companion, the messenger, upbraids him for his
uncourtly behaviour, however, Libeaus is deeply repentant and
sneaks out of the lady's castle through a back-door (ll. 1525 ff.).
Thus, the whole episode is only another of the dangers Libeaus
has to overcome on his way to Sinadoun, not, as in *Le Bel Inconnu*,
a real aberration and temptation.

Altogether then, *Libeaus Desconus* is a very compact adaptation
which has many features in common with other shorter romances,
such as *Sir Eglamour* or *Sir Perceval of Gales*, and is mainly concerned with the glorification of the hero. The poet deliberately
concentrates on the dramatic action which is set in motion by the
arrival of the messenger from Sinadoun at Arthur's court, and then
proceeds swiftly towards that crowning moment when they all
return to Arthur's court 'wiþ honour' (l. 2200) and the fair lady of
Sinadoun is given in marriage to Libeaus by Arthur himself. We
do not get the impression of a mere aggregation of episodes, although the number and the order of the fights on the way seem
quite arbitrary and could easily be altered without any serious
damage to the whole structure of the poem. A carefully worked-out
design in the arrangement of the episodes, such as has been claimed
for *Le Bel Inconnu*, is certainly absent here, but at least all the
episodes are directly connected with the hero's task and prove him
worthy of his father and of Arthur's patronage. Thus, the poem
could almost be described as a biographical romance, a term that
would apply to several of the English shorter romances.

In adapting his French model, the English author seems to have gone to work less drastically than other English adapters, because, in spite of deliberate abridgement, the poem is still about twice as long as *Sir Launfal* or *Sir Eglamour*. This may be due to the different sources of these poems, but we do not know enough about them to be certain. Another difference is that *Libeaus Desconus* preserves more of the courtly elements of the story than other English romances.[9] Although Libeaus is brought up in the woods 'full savage' (l. 19), like Perceval, he is not just a boor when he arrives at court and his chivalrous deeds are not only proof of his superior strength, but they show him as a knight who is ready to help all that are in need, as a champion of the unhappy and ill-treated. The description of Arthur's court, too, the reception of Libeaus and of the messenger, reveal the author's familiarity with courtly ceremony although he does not lay great stress on it. On the other hand, there is less moralizing and less religious comment in the poem although a number of the conventional didactic formulas do occur.[10] There are also some of the 'minstrel clichés', although far less than in such poems as *Horn Childe* and *Torrent of Portyngale*,[11] and there is an interesting description of minstrelsy in the enchanted palace of Sinadoun:

> Libeaus inner gan passe,
> To behelde ech place,
> þe hales in þe halle.
> Of maine more ne lasse
> Ne siȝ he body ne face,
> But menstrales cloþed in palle;
> Wiþ harpe, fiþele and rote
> And wiþ organes note
> Greet gle þey maden alle,
> Wiþ citole and sautrie;
> So moche menstralsie
> Was never wiþ inne walle.
>
> Before ech menstrale stod
> A torche fair and good,
> Brenninge faire and briȝt. (ll. 1873–87)

It is quite likely that the adapter intended his poem to be read in two instalments because after line 1296 a new episode begins which is introduced more deliberately than the others, and the poet also makes use of the convention of the *reverie* which is, of course,

chiefly a lyrical device, but can also be found in several Middle
English romances:

> Nou reste we her a while
> Of sir Otes de Lile
> And telle we oþer tales.
> Libeaus rod many a mile
> And siȝ aventurs file
> In Irland and in Wales.
> Hit fell in þe monþ of June,
> Whan þe fenell hongeþ in toun
> Grene in semely sales;
> þe someris day is long,
> Mery is þe foules song
> And notes of þe niȝtingales:      (ll. 1297-1308)

By means of this new introduction the romance is divided into two
parts of about equal length and each of the two parts contains
about the same number of lines as many of the shorter romances.

On the whole then, the poem is quite a competent adaptation,
as can also be seen from the handling of the metre. The tail-
rhyme stanza which can so easily sound flat and monotonous, is
more skilfully varied than, for instance, in *Horn Childe*, and does
not clog the dramatic movement of the story. There is also much
less frequent use of meaningless tags, especially in the tail-line; in
*Libeaus Desconus*, these lines often contain important details and
contribute to the progress of the action. On the other hand, the
poem does not come up to the mastery and the originality of *Amis
and Amiloun*.

*Libeaus Desconus* is thus another example of the English shorter
romance being a result of deliberate abridgement and adaptation. It
has very little in common with the French novel which could have
served as a model, but it represents a very distinctive type of
narrative, the brief biography of a hero whose knightly perfections
are illustrated by a series of loosely but not arbitrarily connected
adventures and his progress from obscurity to glory and honour.

### 'SIR EGLAMOUR OF ARTOIS'

The story of Sir Eglamour deserves a brief examination, if only on
account of its mediocrity and its highly eclectic character. It seems
to have been particularly popular because it is preserved in three of

the most important collections of romances (Cotton Caligula A. II, Cambridge Ff. II. 38, and Lincoln Cathedral Library A. 5.2, the Thornton Ms., and there are fragments of it in another manuscript (Egerton 2862) which presumably once contained the whole poem.[12] Five early prints and two later copies prove that its popularity lasted well into the sixteenth century; there was also a dramatic version of the story and a song about 'Sir Eglamour, the valiant knight' has survived in England to the present day.

Perhaps the first thing that strikes the reader in this romance, is the large number of commonplaces and borrowings from other stories that are here brought together. There is even less sign of original invention than in most other English romances and the skill of the author only lies in the arrangement of various motifs gleaned from other romances. The plot, which is in some ways similar to the even more famous story of Guy of Warwick, combines daring adventures for the love of a lady, fights against pagans, innocent sufferings of a lady, and the reunion of a dispersed family by means of a tournament. It would be easy to find analogues for all these motifs in earlier romance and to demonstrate that *Sir Eglamour* is rather a synthetic product.[13] There are particularly close links with *Guy of Warwick*, *Octavian* and *Sir Ysumbras*, but the adapter undoubtedly knew many more romances than can be proved by direct borrowings.

It would, however, be unjust to merely insist on the 'patchwork character' of the poem.[14] The adapter at least has to be credited with a certain degree of competence for his deft organizing of the story-material and he has succeeded in composing a fairly coherent tale which again embodies many of the characteristic features of the shorter English romances. As in several other poems, the action springs from the love of a knight for a lady who is his superior in social status, but while in *Guy of Warwick* the lady herself wants to see some proof of the knight's prowess before committing herself, he is in *Sir Eglamour* asked by her father to win her and given various tasks to perform. It soon becomes clear, however, that the father is only trying to get rid of the knight and his behaviour becomes more and more unscrupulous: for the purposes of the story, he seems at the same time to be the jealous father and to play the rôle of the 'treacherous steward'. He even exiles his own daughter when she has given birth to Eglamour's child and he falls dead from his tower when he hears of the happy reunion of the lovers after a separation of fifteen years (L, ll. 1339–44). The real reason for his hatred is never explicitly stated and we may assume that the audience was so familiar with such stories of trial and persecution that a specific motive was unnecessary. The father's villainy provides a link between the story of the knight who has to prove himself worthy of his lady's love and that of the innocently exiled woman, a story met in *Emaré* and other romances of that type. There is a certain amount of dramatic suspense because the lovers are at first not united; their child is illegitimate—not a very frequent motif in Middle English romances—and the marriage does not take place until the son himself has reached marriageable age. The last part of the poem, in which Eglamour wins his beloved, the mother of his son, in a tournament, after the son himself has already won her and nearly married her, is of course reminiscent of the Gregorius legend and the lay *Sire Degarre*.

Thus, the poem presents a curious combination of various story-types, but they are linked in such a way that they form quite a logical sequence of events. The popularity of the poem suggests that such a mixture was just what the audience expected of an effective romance. What makes it so typical of the English shorter poems, is the striking juxtaposition of chivalrous adventure and pious legend. Like the famous story of *Guy of Warwick*, *Sir Eglamour* can almost be described as an exemplum although the moral idea is less clearly formulated and obviously subordinated to the plot: the knight falls in love with the lady; he has to prove his worth; God is with him on his way (l. 633); the knight helps those who are in need and spends fifteen years fighting the heathens in the Holy Land (ll. 1012ff.). In the history of Cristabell, there is a more marked resemblance to Saints' legends. Her fate, especially her miraculous escape (l. 890) and the reunion of widely scattered members of the family, is an example of the grace of God who always stands by those who believe in him. This simple moral, also illustrated by the end of the wicked father, is briefly stated by the author:

> With God may na man stryue! (L, l. 1347)

Everything the Earl did to prevent the union of the lovers was, as it turns out, only a blasphemous attempt to run counter to the providence of God. This element of crude moralizing occurs repeatedly throughout the poem. Thus we are often told that it is

God whom Eglamour has to thank for all his amazing victories
(L, ll. 325, 406, 559, 570, 707) and his final union with Cristabell
is only the answer to his prayer near the beginning of the poem:

> To Criste his handis he lyfte vp sone:
> 'Lorde, ʒe grant me my bone,
> On þe rode als þou me boghte.
> The erlis doghetir, faire and free,
> þat scho myght myn bee-
> þat maste es in my thoughte.
> þat I myght hafe hir to my wyfe,
> And reioyse hir all my lyfe,
> To blysse þan ware I broghte.'     (L, ll. 100–108)

This prayer and the various references to the gracious guidance of
God provide the moral design of the story, although it cannot be
said that Eglamour is presented as a model of piety or that he embodies any particular Christian virtues.[15]

Nevertheless, the narrator's interest concentrates mainly on the
hero whose career is described with evident partiality. The beginning of the poem, like that of many similar romances, announces
the story of a particularly valiant knight:

> Ihesu, þat es heuens Kyng,
> Gyff vs alle his blyssyng
> And beyld vs in his boure;
> And giff þam ioye þat will here
> Of eldirs þat byfore vs were,
> þat lyued in grete honoure.
> I will ʒow telle of a knyghte
> þat was bothe hardy and wyght,
> And stythe in ilk a stoure:
> Whare dedis of armes were, fere or nere,
> þe gre he wynnes wyth iornaye clere,
> And euir in felde þe floure.     (L, ll. 1–12)

Praise of the hero is the real subject of the romance, whereas in
*Octavian* or, even more, in *Sir Ysumbras*, the course of the action
and its moral significance are more important than the hero's personal fate. Thus the poem clearly belongs to the genre of the
'romances of prys' which are ridiculed by Chaucer in *Sir Thopas*,
but it is very likely that this glorification of a central hero greatly
contributed to the poem's popularity, as it evidently did in the case
of *Guy of Warwick* and *Sir Beues of Hamtoun*.

The person of the hero, of course, gives a certain degree of unity to the poem although many verse-novels in France or Germany show that such biographical stories are often rather episodic and could sometimes be extended *ad libitum*. In *Sir Eglamour*, however, this does not happen. As we have seen, Eglamour's love is the starting-point of the action and this is never lost sight of throughout the poem, until the marriage-feast at the end brings the final fulfilment of Eglamour's desire. Each episode provides a necessary link in the story and is connected with the other parts of the action. Everything is told in a swift and purposeful manner; there are no digressions and the tempo never slacks; there is also a very limited use of description, which is strictly subordinated to the action, as can be clearly seen in the description of Degrebell's and Eglamour's arms: they are pictorial summaries of parts of the plot rather than heraldic devices. Thus, we are told of Eglamour:

> Newe armes þan beris hee:
> Herkyns! I will þam discrye.
> Of azure wyth a schippe of golde;
> A lady als scho drowne scholde;
> A child lyggand hir by—
> In þe see so grym and balde—
> Purtrayede of a nyghte alde,
> And euir in poynte to dy. (L, ll. 1199–1206)

These pictures (cf. also Degrebell's arms, ll. 1030–8) also prepare for the recognition and for the final denouement.

Brevity and a strict adherence to the concrete details of the action are the most characteristic aspects of the style of *Sir Eglamour*. In about 1370 lines, a story is told that could easily be extended to the size of a substantial novel. Although no direct source of the poem is known and the extant versions are probably very close to the original, the romance reads like a very condensed version of a much longer tale, like a brief abstract of a complicated plot. Thus, the transitions between some episodes are rather abrupt and unexpected. Sometimes, small fragments of action follow each other, as in a ballad (e.g. ll. 751 ff., 871 ff., 1039 ff.). The twelve-line tail-rhyme stanza is often used in such a way that each group of three lines forms a little narrative unit, as in the rather brief description of Cristabell's voyage:

> The lady syked with herte sare;
> The wynd rose and to a roche here bare,

And þereon gon sche lende.
Sche was full fayn, I vndurstonde:
Sche wend hyt had be byggyd londe,
And there vp gan sche wende.
Noþyng ellys syȝ sche dere
Butt see fowles þat wylde were,
That fast flew here hende.
A grype come in all hyr care:
The ȝong chyld away he bare
To a countre vnkende.                     (C, ll. 832–43)

We almost get the impression that the poem is written in three-line stanzas. Another example is the sudden appearance of the King of Sedoyne at the end of the poem who offers his daughter to Degrebell and thus makes up the two happily united couples (ll. 1321–3).

On the other hand, there is also an unnecessarily frequent use of transitional formulas. Although the whole poem is so short that the hearer (or reader) does not need such help, we are several times told that the story will now turn to somebody else (L, ll. 829–831, 877–9, 952–4). The brevity of the poem demands a rather quick pace of narration, but this does not mean that the style is very dramatic. There is not much real tension in the tale; even the surprising encounters at the end are related in a very factual manner and without any attempt to create a feeling of suspense. The audience is usually warned in advance of any surprising turns in the action, as in the meeting of Degrebell and his mother (l. 1090). Occasionally, however, the narrative is enlivened by an effective use of direct speech and brief scenes of dialogue, such as Eglamour's talks with his squire (ll. 49 ff.) and with Cristabell's father (ll. 205 ff.). Direct speech is sometimes also employed in less significant moments (ll. 896 f., 931 ff.). This, and repeated calls for the attention of the audience (ll. 15, 722, 1030, 1200), are marks of an 'oral' style.

An analysis of the style of *Sir Eglamour* might suggest that this is really a 'minstrel poem'.[16] This does not mean, however, that any of the extant versions was actually composed by a minstrel, but it is quite possible that the story was transmitted orally and that the extant versions with their considerable variants are only a few of all the versions that were once in existence. They are either copies of texts that are now lost or else they were partly written down from memory with a certain amount of improvisation.[17] In any case, it is clear that the scribes were well versed in the formulas that occur again and again in the Middle English poems and that they were more interested in the outline of the story than in the verbal details.

Sir Eglamour, then, is another very characteristic example of the Middle English shorter romance. It is the swiftly told story of an excellent knight, containing marvellous exploits, love, suffering and miraculous escapes, but all these are not related for their own sake, but are presented as examples of the power of God and the eventual triumph of goodness. The grace of God is manifested in the glorious career of the knight who puts his trust in him, but there is no suggestion of an exalted concept of knighthood or the sophisticated symbolism of the lays and the courtly novel, as we saw in the rather primitive use of Eglamour's and Degrebell's arms. Knighthood, as the poet sees it, consists mainly in defeating wicked adversaries, especially the enemies of Christianity.

In spite of the highly eclectic character of Sir Eglamour the problem of the poem's source has not yet been solved, but as no French or Anglo-Norman version of the story is known, we may safely assume that the combination of the various motifs was the work of the English adapter, and this again suggests that the poem was written to meet a particular demand for that type of shorter romance.

### 'TORRENT OF PORTYNGALE'

Torrent of Portyngale which, like Sir Eglamour of Artois, is written in tail-rhyme stanzas, may be briefly mentioned as another example of a shorter romance adapted from very similar material.[18] From the rather late and very corrupt copy in the Chetham Ms. we can conclude that the poem must have gone through several hands and perhaps through a stage of oral transmission before it was put into the form we know. Trounce thought that the original version was composed during the second half of the fourteenth century.[19] Fragments of an early print suggest that the romance enjoyed some popularity.

The outline of the poem's action is almost identical with that of Sir Eglamour, but several differences that have been listed reveal that the poet also knew some other romances and borrowed from them. Nevertheless, his chief source was probably *Sir Eglamour*, though in a better text than any that have been preserved, and his adaptation is on the whole not much more than an amplification of the earlier poem.[20] *Torrent of Portyngale* runs to 2669 lines and is thus one of the longest of the 'shorter' romances (and of the tail-rhyme romances). This extension can be explained by the more leisurely style, and, above all, by the addition of new episodes which, however, often merely repeat what has been told before. This doubling of effects largely accounts for the greater length of the poem.[21] In *Sir Eglamour*, the hero is asked to perform three tasks; in *Torrent of Portyngale*, he has to cope with five. Instead of one giant, there are now two, father and son; instead of one child, two children are born; they are both carried off, one by a griffin and one by a leopard, and are dispersed into different countries. At the end of the poem, Torrent does not only inherit his father-in-law's kingdom, as Eglamour, but he is made Emperor of Rome and his two sons become heirs to Greece and Jerusalem. All these changes seem to be due to the adapter's ambition to outdo *Sir Eglamour* and to make his hero even more perfect and exemplary. They are hardly proof that another source was used by the poet, although it seems very likely that he was at least familiar with the stories of Octavian and Sir Ysumbras.

In addition to this amplification of the hero's exploits, there is also a marked emphasis on the religious aspects of the story. None of the other poems discussed here shows such an exaggerated juxtaposition of daring adventure and simple piety.[22] Some legendary motifs are introduced, such as the voice from Heaven encouraging Torrent before his fight (ll. 1568–73), and it is made quite clear that Torrent's miraculous feats are due to the direct intervention of God. Torrent is even more reckless than Eglamour in his approach to every new adventure, but at the same time he is almost described like a Saint who is under the special protection of God and whose prayers are answered with surprising promptness. Thus, during one of his fights, God sends a shower of rain to refresh him (ll. 669 ff.) because 'Iesu wold not, he were slayne'. This combination of fantastic adventure for the sake of his love and a somewhat primitive piety seems to have been very much to the taste of the audience and was probably what was expected of a romance. It seems hardly necessary, therefore, to assume that the author was a cleric, as Adam did,[23] at least the difference in this respect between *Torrent of Portyngale* and *Sir Eglamour* is not so great as to suggest a strict distinction between minstrel romances and clerical romances, because a moral and an often rather pious tone are common to nearly all the Middle English romances.

In *Torrent of Portyngale*, the interest of the author is, however, no less attracted by the hero's love-story than by his Christian virtues. As in *Sir Eglamour*, we are told quite openly and without apparent disapproval that Torrent's children are born out of wedlock. Some other English poems are much stricter in this respect (cf. *Sir Degrevant*). In spite of all the religious embellishment, the story of Torrent is much more worldly than that of Octavian or Sir Ysumbras. Even the rather mutilated text in which the poem has come down to us reveals the hand of a competent artist who arranged his material with great skill and who seems to have had a particular liking for brief and lively scenes of dialogue, like the following exchange:

> To Torrent the kyng gan sey,
> He seyd: 'Torrent, so god me saue,
> Thow woldes fayne my dowghttyr haue
> And hast lovyd her many a day.'
> 'Ye, be trouthe,' seyd Torrent than,
> 'And yf þat I were a Ryche man,
> Ryght gladly, par ma fay!'
> 'Yf thow durst for her sake
> A poynt of armys vndyrtake,
> Thow broke her well fore ay!'
>
> 'Ye,' seyd Torrent, 'ar I ga,
> Sekyrnes ye schall me ma
> Of yowr dowghttyr hend,
> And aftyrward my ryghtys,
> Be-fore XXVII knyghtes.'          (ll. 824–38)

The story is told in a rather detached and sometimes humorous tone and with more spirit than we find in many other poems of this type. It seems likely that the original version of *Torrent of Portyngale* was one of the most lively and original of the shorter romances.[24]

## 'THE ERL OF TOLOUS'

This poem which, in spite of many differences in the plot, clearly belongs to the same type as *Sir Eglamour*, is mainly noteworthy for its concise and dramatically effective narrative technique and for its lack of that kind of sensationalism which can become rather tedious in some of the other romances. *The Erl of Tolous* has on the whole been rather neglected, and the enthusiastic praise of its editor, Gustav Lüdtke, has remained an isolated case of special pleading,[25] but it seems to me that the poem would repay closer study and that it has considerable merit. It also stands in need of a new edition.

There are a number of superficial points of contact between *The Erl of Tolous* and *Sir Eglamour*. Both poems are preserved in the two collections, Cambridge Ff. II. 38, and the Thornton Ms. (Lincoln Cathedral Library A. 5.2), and both were probably composed in the East Midlands during the second part of the fourteenth century. Neither of the two poems seems to be the adaptation of a known source although both refer to a source and claim that the story originated in Rome, which is presumably due to an erroneous etymology of the word 'romance'.[26] *The Erl of Tolous* also calls itself a 'lay of Bretayn' (l. 1220), which, however, need not be taken very literally.[27] The poem in its present form cannot really be counted among the lays unless any short narrative is to be termed lay. It is more likely that the term had become rather vague and had at the same time a certain appeal for English audiences (cf. also *Emaré* and *Sir Gowther*). To this might be added that the story on which the poem is based certainly came from France and probably had its origin in some historical events.[28] Although none of the older versions of the story can have been the source of the English poem, these versions attest to the wide distribution of many of the motifs and suggest that the English adapter must have got the story from France in some form or other. The possibility that there once was a Breton lay on the subject cannot, of course, be ruled out, but there is little doubt, that the most original and attractive features of the poem, its lively style and the effective combination of romance and legend have to go to the credit of the English adapter.

Contrary to the somewhat misleading title by which the poem is known,[29] the narrator, after the obligatory prayer at the beginning, announces the story of a lady who had to endure great distress, but was eventually made happy again:

> Jhesu Cryst, yn trynyté
> Oonly god and persons thre,

> Graunt us well to sped,
> And gyve us grace so to do,
> That we may come þy blys unto,
> On rod as thou can bled!
> Leve Lords, y schall you tell
> Of a tale, some tyme befell
> Far yn unkouthe led:
> How a lady had gret myschef,
> And how sche covyrd of hur gref.
> Y pray you, take hed! (ll. 1–12)

What in *Sir Eglamour* was only a minor theme, is here the centre of the action which is less concerned with daring fights and adventures than with treacherous intrigue and the quiet suffering of a lady. The miraculous elements have, to a considerable extent, been replaced by subtle psychology and by the tensions arising out of a clash of complex personalities. Of course there are a number of the conventional romance-motifs, such as the treacherous servant, the innocently accused woman, the tournament as vindication of her honour, and the lover disguised as a Hermit; but there is an absence of nearly everything that (even for Chaucer) often made the romances border on the ridiculous, like the giants and monsters, the miraculous union of widely dispersed families and, above all, the inhumanly perfect hero. The whole poem is told in a much quieter tone than, for instance, *Sir Eglamour*, and its scope is much narrower, but the personal conflicts are described with a much greater awareness of psychological realities.

As in many other romances, the story is based on the hero's love for a lady who is his superior; in this case, however, she is a married woman, and, in contrast to most courtly literature, her status as the Emperor's wife is an insurmountable obstacle to any honest declaration of love. The Earl, of course, wishes most earnestly that she had no husband (ll. 367 ff.), but he makes no attempt to confess his love. When he asks her for alms (ll. 378 ff.) he does it only because he hopes to get something from her that would serve as a token of remembrance:

> Myght y oght get of that free,
> Ech a day hyt for to see,
> Hyt wold covyr me of care. (ll. 382–4)

His passionate love cannot, at first, find any direct expression until he is able to appear as her champion in the trial by combat, and this he does only after he has been assured of her innocence by three different persons, the last being herself. Thus, in a sense, the action can hardly be described as a love-story, because the lady, too, does not in any way go beyond the limits of conventional politeness. When she opposes the unjust proceedings of her husband against the Earl (ll. 139–44; 151–6) and later rejects the knight who wants to deliver Barnard into her hands (ll. 253 ff.), this is only an expression of her perfect sense of justice. Her obliging behaviour when she gives Barnard an opportunity of looking at her face seems to be due mainly to her wish to enable the knight to fulfil his 'covenaunt' (ll. 289–300) because he has sworn to the Earl that he will make him see her beauty. To be sure, the gift of her ring betrays her deep affection for him and probably meant much more to the original audience of the poem than it does to us. The Empress certainly feels that she has become guilty because twice she confesses her act (ll. 1024–32 and 1071–7) though, it is added, she did it 'Yn ese of hym and for no syn' (l. 1031) and her complete innocence is never in doubt. Her spirited rejection of the two knights who want to tempt her into adultery, clearly shows how abhorrent the thought of any extra-marital relationship appears to her (ll. 565–94 and 649–61):

> 'Syr', sche seyd, 'ys þat thy wyll?
> Yf hyt were myne, þen dyd y yll.
> What woman holdst thou me?
> Yn thy kepyng y have ben:
> What hast þou herd be me or sen,
> That touchys to velané,
> That thou in herte art so bold,
> Os y were a hore or a scold?
> Nay, that schall nevyr bee!
> Had y not hyght, to hold counsayl,
> Thou schouldst be honged, wythoute fayl,
> Upon a galowtree.' (ll. 649–60)

Like her's, Barnard's love is at first without any self-interest. His longing almost seems to be satisfied when he has rescued the unhappy Empress from the unjust accusation, and the final union of the lovers after the death of the Emperor, three years later, is not the result of his own activities, but the hardly hoped-for reward for the faithfulness of the lovers and little more than an appendix to the main action of the poem.

The love-story in *The Erl of Tolous* is told with more tact and reticence than is usual in the Middle English romances and it contributes to the close-knit structure of the poem which, in contrast to *Sir Eglamour*, concentrates on one place and on two characters and does not give the impression of being a condensed version of some more extensive novel. The different parts of the story are very happily balanced and there is an effective alternation of summarizing narrative and dramatic scenes. All the more important crises in the action are told in the form of brief and lively pieces of dialogue which pointedly emphasize the particular situation, such as the short, but vivid exchange between the Empress and Barnard's treacherous companion (ll. 253–300) in which she urges him to be faithful to his oath. Perhaps the most impressive scene in the poem is the first meeting between the Earl and the Empress (ll. 322 ff.). From his hiding-place, he observes the lady as she is proceeding to church, and her beauty is described as he sees it. More and more he becomes enamoured of her as he is impressed by her perfections, while she, aware of his presence, turns her head about in order to give him a good view. The scene deserves to be quoted at some length:

> Then came that lady free;
> Two erlys hur ladd,
> Wondur rychly sche was cladd,
> In gold and rych perré.
> Whan the erl saw hur in syght,
> Hym thought, sche was as bryght,
> Os blossom on the tree;
> Of all the syghts that ever he sy,
> Raysyd nevyr none hys hert so hy:
> Sche was so bryght of blee!

> Sche stod stylle in that place
> And schewed opynly hur face
> For love of that knyght.
> He beheld ynly hur face
> And he sware be goddys grace,
> He saw nevyr none so bryght.
> Hur eyen were gray, as any glas,
> Mouth and nose schapen was
> At all maner ryght;

Fro the forhedd to the too
Bettur schapen myght none goo,
Nor none semelyer yn syght.

Twyes sche turnyd hur about
Betwen the erlys, that were stout;
For that lord schuld hur see.
When sche spake wyth mylde stevyn,
Sche semyd an aungell of hevyn:
So feyr sche was of blee!
Hur sydes long, hur myddyl small;
Schouldurs and armes therwythall
Fayrer myght none bee;
Hur hondys whyte, as whallys bone,
Wyth longe fyngurs, that fayre schone,
Hur nayles bryght of blee.

When he had behold hur well,
The lady went to hur chapell,
Masse for to her;                                              (ll. 327–63)

This is in part a conventional description of beauty, such as we find it in lyric poetry, like the *Harley Lyrics*,[30] but the traditional devices are vividly dramatized and thus do not only form a rhetorical set-piece, but are at the same time merged into the whole scene and are part of the Earl's moving experience as he becomes aware of the lady's beauty. There are not many poems outside the Chaucer canon in which we find such perfect equilibrium between stylized poetry and psychological realism. When, after Mass, the lady turns to go to her chamber, the Earl cannot bear to lose sight of her and on the spur of the moment decides to address her and ask for alms (ll. 373 ff.).

Another episode which is told in a particularly vivid and dramatic manner is the scheming of the two villainous knights against the Empress. They confess to each other that they both love her and each in turn tries his luck with her, but they are both rejected. The tone of the narrative almost reminds one of Chaucer's *Pardoner's Tale*. The dialogue does not just consist of clichés, but really characterizes the two speakers without any comment by the narrator being necessary. The first knight returns from his futile attempt:

Thus to hys felow ys he gone,
And he hym frayned soon anon:
'Syr, how hast thou spedd?'
'Ryghte noght,' seyd that othyr.
'Syth y was born, leve brothyr,
Was y nevyr so adredd;
Certys, hyt ys a botles bale,
To hur to touche soch a tale
At borde or at bedd.'
Then sayd that odur: 'Thy wytt ys thyn.
Y myselfe schall hur wyn:
Y lay my hedd to wedd!'                    (ll. 601-12)

Their pretended merriment when they proceed with their wicked design is told with similar vividness (ll. 700-32). The following episode in the lady's bedchamber is another example of the poet's skill in building up a dramatic scene. While the Empress innocently and ignorantly goes to bed and falls asleep, the poor trusting youth whom the two villains have hidden behind the curtain becomes restive and begins to think that they must have forgotten him (ll. 745-59), until they all break in on him and the Empress, and he is murdered before he can open his mouth. The realistic tone effectively brings out the wickedness of the intrigue and seems more suitable for a moral tale, like that of Chaucer's Pardoner, than for a romance. It seems certain that this realism is due to the moral intention of the author and it clearly emphasizes the exemplary character of the romance.

There are a number of other scenes which could serve as examples of the narrator's skill in presenting lively encounters, such as the trial scene in which judgment is passed and then deferred (ll. 877 ff.), the meeting between the Earl and the abbot, where Barnard learns of the lady's plight (ll. 997 ff.), and the last scene with the duel and the confession (Barnard in disguise as the Empress' confessor, ll. 1063 ff.). All these show that *The Erl of Tolous* is not the work of an artless 'hack-writer', but of a conscious and quite original artist.

The structure of the poem is not, as in *Sir Eglamour* and many similar romances, governed by emphasis on the figure of the hero, but primarily by the fate of the lady. The action is set in motion by the unjust wars of the Emperor and by the Earl's love for the wife of his enemy. The exposition of the story, which in most of the shorter romances is rather perfunctory, takes up more space here, chiefly, it seems, in order to give a portrait of the virtuous Earl who is under the special protection of God:

> Soche grace god hym send,
> That false quarrel comes to evell end
> For oght, that may betyde. (ll. 130–2)[31]

What follows is a trial of the hero's and the heroine's virtue and faith, but this trial does not, as in other romances, consist of a series of difficult tasks, but of one extended episode, and this obviously contributes to the neat structure of the poem. At the climax of the crisis, there is a sudden turn of events and the story can now end happily. This pattern is common to most of the shorter romances and also to the homiletic romances, but unlike in poems like *Sir Eglamour*, it is not the chivalrous virtues, like prowess and honour that are tested. Goodness, that is in this poem justice and chastity, prevails against all treason and intrigue without any spectacular exploits and superlative heroism. There is, in this respect, a clear resemblance to such poems as *Emaré* and *Le Bone Florence of Rome*, but in *The Erl of Tolous*, the story, though in many ways exemplary, is not told as an exemplum or as an illustration of any particular virtue. Love is the main subject of the tale, though in a much higher sense than in most of the shorter romances, and this links it with the other poems of that type rather than with the homiletic romances.

As in most romances, the narrator repeatedly interrupts the narrative with his own comments. He is not a detached chronicler, but he clearly stands on the side of his two protagonists, as is shown in expressions like 'false thef' (530) for one of the two traitors and in frequent curses like the following (the two villains have just agreed on their plan to bring about the lady's ruin):

> Now are þey both at oon assent,
> In sorow to bryng þat lady gent:
> The devell mot them sped! (ll. 694–6)

Such phrases are often found in the romances, but they seem to be particularly frequent and pointed in this poem (see also ll. 417, 600, 708, 760).[32] They help to create the impression that it is a conflict between good and evil that is presented here and that God intervenes on behalf of those who trust in him. This is also why the duel as a divine ordeal is taken so seriously, more seriously, for instance, than in *Amis and Amiloun*. The transmission of the romance (it is preserved in four manuscripts that seem to be independent of each other) suggests that *The Erl of Tolous*, with its effective combination of love-interest and moral didacticism, was one of the most popular of the shorter romances. That this popularity did not last, may be partly due to the absence of a memorable hero who impresses himself on the imagination of the hearers, but the poem is nevertheless one of the most successful of the Middle English romances and deserves more attention than it has received so far.

### 'SIR DEGREVANT'

*Sir Degrevant* represents a somewhat different type of shorter romance from those discussed so far. The poem was probably not composed before the end of the fourteenth century and is preserved in two fifteenth-century manuscripts, Lincoln Cathedral Library A. 5.2 (Thornton Ms.) and Cambridge University Library Ff. I. 6, both rather mixed collections which, apart from romances, contain mainly didactic and devotional literature.[33] Neither of the two versions is a copy of the other. The editor of the poem, L. F. Casson, believes the text was influenced by oral transmission although, as he himself can demonstrate, the two extant versions are both copies of some written originals. Most of the discrepancies he lists, such as the transposition of certain parts of the poem to different places, can be explained in other ways. A free redaction by a scribe could have produced very similar results and it does not, therefore, seem necessary to assume that the poem was once written down from memory, but it would be unwise to be dogmatic on this point.

The romance is clearly distinguished from the tail-rhyme romances that were written in the East Midlands by its metrical form, the sixteen-line tail-rhyme stanza. However we may try to explain that stanza-form, its most striking feature is certainly the peculiar combination of rhyming stanza and alliterative long-line. The lines of the stanza correspond partly to the alternating verse of the twelve-line stanza, and partly to the alliterative half-lines.

The great number of alliterative formulas which, according to Casson, can be found in about a third of the lines of the poem,[34] clearly show that the poet was familiar with the alliterative poetry of the West Midlands. There are, in particular, a fair number of parallels with the *Morte Arthure*. On the other hand, there is a skilful use of rhyme, especially in the technique of stanza-linking, which proves the poet to have been experienced in the art of rhyming as well.[35] About three-quarters of the stanzas are linked to each other. This device is characteristic of several romances that were composed in the North of England. There, a number of poems were written which seem to be particularly independent of their sources (as far as these can be made out) and reveal a far more highly developed metrical art than the majority of the East-Midland poems. There is also a closer familiarity with courtly manners and ideas, a more marked attempt to provide a psychological motivation for the action and less emphasis on the moral and religious elements of the story. All this is particularly noticeable in *Sir Degrevant*.

The story of *Sir Degrevant* probably originated in England; a French source has not been found, nor is it very likely that one ever existed. Nevertheless, the originality of the poet does not lie in the invention of a completely new story, but in the effective combination of various motifs gleaned from other romances, such as the love of a knight for the daughter of his enemy who is also socially his superior, the treacherous steward, and the three days' tournament in which the hero defeats all the lady's suitors. At first sight, there is a striking similarity with *The Erl of Tolous*, but the author has given a completely different turn to the plot. The motif of the innocently accused lady is absent here and the action is rather more simple and straightforward. There is no doubt that the knight, who in this poem is particularly daring and impulsive, is the centre of the action. There are no moral problems here of the sort that play such an important part in *The Erl of Tolous*, because the lady is not the wife but the daughter of the enemy. On the other hand, there are a number of realistic scenes in the poem which seem to owe their existence more to a close observation of reality than to literary borrowing, such as the lively scene in Melidor's chamber with the popular custom of 'bundling', not found in any other Middle English romance.[36] In contrast to poems like *Sir Eglamour*, *Torrent of Portyngale* and *Amis and Amiloun*, the girl refuses to grant the last favour to the knight. Her reply to his pleading suggests a common-sense morality rather than *amour courtois:*

> Righte a-bowte midnyght
> Sayd Sir Degreuant þe knyghte:
> 'When will ȝe, swete wyghte,
> Lystyn me till?
> For lufe myn hert will brist;
> When þou gase to thi ryste
> Lady, wysse me the beste,
> Giff it be thi will.'
> The birde answerde ful ȝare:
> 'Neuen þou it any mare,
> þou sall rewe it full sare,
> And lyke it full ill.
> Certis, sir, ef þou were a kyng,
> þou solde do me no swylke thing
> Or þou wede me with a rynge,
> And maryage full-fill.           (L, ll. 1521–36)
>
> .    .    .    .    .    .    .
>
> For-thi, sir, halde the styll
> Till ȝe gete my fadirs wyll.'
> þe knyght grauntid þer-till,
> And þare þay trouthes plyghte.   (L, ll. 1549–52)

It can be said of *Sir Degrevant*, even more than of some of the other shorter romances, that the whole poem centres round the hero and tries to present an idealized portrait of him. Everything else seems to be subordinated to this aim. The figure of Degrevant was obviously not invented by the author; he is probably to be identified with the Sir Agravayn mentioned in *Sir Perceval of Gales, Libeaus Desconus* and *Sir Gawain and the Green Knight,* who, like Degrevant, is described as King Arthur's nephew. A hitherto very vague character was thus made the hero of a new poem and given an exciting history; this is probably not a very unique example of how new romance-heroes could be produced. Some other knights of the Round Table were 'promoted' in a similar way.[37] The connection with the Arthurian material is, of course, not very important for the poem, but it may have given the story some weight, because for the audience Degrevant was not a completely new character and this may have made them more willing to hear more about him.

Among the many heroes of Middle English romance, Degrevant is certainly one of the most individualized and at the same time likeable. He is not only a most daring fighter who is always victorious, but he has also some more personal traits. At the beginning of the poem, more space is used for the description of him than is usual in the romances. Not only his exemplary prowess and piety are praised, but also his efficiency as a landowner, his skill in hunting, playing and singing, his generosity towards minstrels and even his chastity and lack of interest in women:

> Certis, wyfe wolde he nane,
> Wenche ne no lemman,
> Bot als an ankyre in a stane
> He lyued here trewe. (L, ll. 61–4)

All this seems more personal and closer to reality than many similar portraits in the romances.

Perhaps Degrevant's most striking trait is his reckless daring and his undaunted spirit in the face of any danger, particularly where his right or his love are at stake. Thus he makes the most of his victories over the Earl and over Melidor's suitors and teases the defeated by challenging them to fight him again (cf. ll. 385 ff. and 1217 ff.). The first time, the Earl grudgingly has to admit that he is unable to fight any more; the second time a personal combat ensues. Degrevant's love-suit, too, is more adventurous and daring than that of most other romance-heroes. There is a particularly lively description of how he creeps past the sleeping porter, watches the lady as she goes to Mass, and then practically waylays her (ll. 609 ff.). When she threatens to hand him over to her father, he just laughs, and when she tells him that she would be glad of his death, he cheerfully replies that she would regret it afterwards and renews his suit. He disregards the warnings of her maid just as he has disregarded the fears of his squire before. When, some time later, he is surprised by sixty knights on his way to Melidor, he kills most of them and afterwards appears in her chamber as if nothing had happened and gives some harmless explanation for his torn clothes (ll. 1685 ff.). He is equally impulsive when he knights his squire on the spot and promises him as a husband to Melidor's maid (ll. 881 ff.).

The girl, too, seems to be more spirited than many ladies in other romances. The awakening of her love is at first only hinted at and the knight gets nothing but reproaches from her, but she betrays herself by her scorn after her maid has led Sir Degrevant whom Melidor had rejected, into her own chamber and has set a meal before him. By her derisive inquiry Melidor tries to find out what really happened in the maid's chamber, and her relief when she hears that Degrevant has only given his squire to the maid, but has sent a ring for herself, is the first clear sign of her love for him:

> 'Had þou Syr Degriuaunt had,
> þen had þou wel i-gon.'  (C, ll. 979–80)

Later, she cruelly scorns the defeated suitor (ll. 1313 ff.) and with proud decision confesses her love for Degrevant to her father (ll. 1745 ff.).

There is a striking and perhaps typically English mixture of courtly and moral elements. The author thinks it necessary to state emphatically that the lovers did not sin before their wedding-day although they were very fond of each other (ll. 1559–60). Every night Degrevant visits Melidor's chamber, is lavishly entertained, and the two enjoy their mutual affection. At the same time, Degrevant is a particularly religious knight; he asks for God's assistance before each fight, gives thanks to God for his victories and fights in the Holy Land before his courtship (ll. 117 ff.) and after Melidor's death. Finally he is slain during one of the crusades and thus dies a martyr.[38] For the author he is obviously the ideal of a Christian knight.

Side by side with the more realistic features of the poem there are also a number of courtly elements, such as are less frequent in the English romances. Hunting, festivities, beautiful clothes, good food, and social entertainment are usually described with great relish and provide an atmosphere of aristocratic living. There is a very interesting and particularly circumstantial description of Melidor's chamber (ll. 1397 ff.) which is even called 'chaumbur of loue' (C, ll. 1439 and 1442). The room is most splendidly adorned with paintings, statues and embroidery, but it is rather unusual that the various pictures and portraits do not represent romance-heroes, as in similar descriptions in French romance, but Apostles, Saints and Fathers of the Church:

> þer men myght, who so wolde,
> Se archangells of golde,
> Fefty made on þe molde,

97

Gleterand full bright;
With þe Pokalypps of John,
Paulis Pistils ylkone,
The Parabylls of Salomone
Paynted full righte.

And þe foure Gospellers
Standand on þe pelers;
Hend, herkyns and heris,
Giff it be ȝoure will.
Austyn and Gregorius,
Jerome and Ambrosius:
Thir are þe foure doctours;
Lystyn þam till.                                    (L, ll. 1449–64)

Only on the hangings of the bed is there an embroidery of the story
of Amadas and Idoine (ll. 1493 ff.). Even this remarkable detail is
typical of the peculiar juxtaposition of courtly and religious
elements in this poem. The whole scene is obviously indebted to
the French courtly novel and any reader would, after the elaborate
description of the chamber, expect a courtly love scene; on the
other hand, the moral element is never absent and thus we are
hardly surprised to see the lady reject the advances of the knight.
The description of the pictures emphasizes this contrast. It puts
the whole scene in the centre of the story and it also delays the
beginning of the conversation between Melidor and the knight, in
which they come to an understanding. The 'chamber of love'
seems to be, in a way, spiritualized and points to a deeper aspect
of love, but its original function as the setting of a love-scene is also
still present. It would probably be difficult to find a similar combination of contrasting elements in the French romances.[39]

The denouement is unusually simple in this poem. The enraged father is quickly reconciled by the entreaties of his wife and
his daughter and gives his assent to the marriage, more it seems,
because he is unable to resist his daughter than out of any real
affection for his future son-in-law. The end is told very swiftly.
Indeed, the whole poem seems particularly unified and compact.
This is due partly to the rather simple and uncomplicated action
which, without any noticeable digression, leads straight to the
union of the lovers, and partly to the particularly vivid and outspoken style. The author seems to have had a rather shrewd sense
of dramatic irony. An example is the scene in which Melidor's

father warns her suitor about Degrevant. After describing his prowess, he adds:

> Couþe he loue par amoure,
> I knew neuer hys mak. (C, ll. 1063–4)

He little suspects that Degrevant has already given convincing proof of his abilities in this respect. The author often shows a humorous detachment from his story and not content with simply retelling it, he seems anxious to establish some connexion between the world of the poem and the world of the audience, as in the description of the quarrel between the Earl and Degrevant at the beginning of the poem which is told with evident interest and knowledge (ll. 97 ff.).

The frequent mention of minstrels, who are richly rewarded whenever there is an occasion for it (ll. 86–92, 1173–6, 1346, 1877–80), and the ironic assurance that a minstrel would never commit treason (ll. 1585–8) might suggest that the poem was written for a minstrel; perhaps the author wished to provide a more dignified form of entertainment than that normally offered by minstrels. Degrevant's liberality, however, is primarily related as evidence of his own nobility of character and does not necessarily say anything about the person of the author.

*Sir Degrevant*, then, is a particularly successful example of the typically English form of the shorter romance with its original blending of courtly, popular and religious elements. The way in which these elements are combined is, however, noticeably different from that in the East Midlands tail-rhyme romances. Courtly ceremony is given more prominence here, miraculous and incredible incidents play a much smaller part. The tone of the poem is rather down-to-earth and there is a refreshing absence of meaningless clichés. It is probably right to account for the courtly setting and the realistic manner of the poem by reference to the rather more isolated North of England where a strictly feudal form of society survived longer than in the South and certain courtly and popular traditions were kept alive. This conclusion is also supported by the fact that most of the later Arthur-poems originated in that part of the country, as well as by the style of those poems that in provenance and form stand particularly close to *Sir Degrevant*, such as *Sir Perceval of Gales* and *The Avowynge of King Arther*.

## 'SIR PERCEVAL OF GALES'

This poem, which is also preserved in the Thornton Ms., has much in common with *Sir Degrevant*. This applies less to the subject-matter of the two romances (the reason why they have not usually been grouped together), but to their form and style. Like *Sir Degrevant* and *The Avowynge of King Arther*, *Sir Perceval* is composed in a sixteen-line tail-rhyme stanza which is rather rare in Middle English, but is used with astonishing skill and competence in this poem. The author has, in particular, employed the technique of stanza-linking much more consistently than the author of *Sir Degrevant* so that practically every stanza is linked to the last and to the following stanzas in some way or other.[40] This device is common not only in Latin and Old French, but also in the more sophisticated Middle English lyrics[41] and thus, in *Sir Perceval*, it is not a sign of popular and oral origin, but a highly literary and rhetorical ornament which shows the author to have been a very conscious artist, familiar with stylistic traditions. On the whole, the stanzas are linked less by rhyme (as in the stanzas 81–2 and 110–11) or by the repetition of single words (as in stanzas 74–5, 121–2, 126–7) than by the doubling of complete lines, either in a slightly modified form (see stanzas 5–6, 36–7, 101–2, 114–15) or in exactly the same words (as in stanzas 3-4, 9–10, 80–1). The latter is particularly frequent in direct speech where the technique of verbal repetition often helps to bring out the importance of a certain point although it can sometimes sound rather mechanical (see for instance stanzas 67–8, 105–6, 116–17, 118–19, 130–1). The various kinds of stanza-linking in this poem have been exactly classified by M. P. Medary and others and there is little doubt that certain rules were observed in employing this device, but it is even more interesting to study the different examples in their context and to see whether, apart from merely formal virtuosity, they serve a purpose in the narrative. It would be possible, for instance, to demonstrate that stanza-linking is not only used occasionally, but with deliberate consistency throughout the poem and that in the few cases where stanzas do not seem to be linked at first sight, there is always a definite reason for it. This technique may be due to the fact that the individual stanzas form rather close and self-contained metrical units which could lead to a somewhat halting progress in the narration. This danger, however, is not completely avoided by the excessive use of stanza-linking because the gaps between the stanzas are often even more emphasized in this way.

The two poems, *Sir Degrevant* and *Sir Perceval of Gales*, are of about the same length and they both describe the adventures of a hero up to his happy marriage, with a short preview of his death in the Holy Land. Both poems belong to the Arthurian cycle, although, as we have seen, this connection is rather loose in the case of *Sir Degrevant* and was perhaps only an afterthought, and in both we find an interesting combination of a courtly setting and the glorification of a particularly reckless and easy-going knight. The two stories are so different that the two romances inevitably disagree in many details of plot and action, but their similarities are more remarkable and it is particularly interesting to see to what extent the story of Perceval has been adapted to the style and manner of the English shorter romance. A detailed comparison of the English poem with Chrétien's *Perceval*, as has several times been attempted, [42] does not, in fact, contribute much to an understanding of it, because *Sir Perceval* is certainly not an adaptation of Chrétien's novel and is related to it only through some earlier versions of the story. [43] The main outline of the action is, of course, the same in both poems, and there are even some episodes which are quite similar, but apart from that the two works are so completely different from each other in their treatment of the story-material and in their concept of chivalry that some superficial resemblances do not count for much. That part of Chrétien's novel which roughly corresponds to the English poem is more than twice as long and it only forms a small part of the whole work. In *Sir Perceval of Gales*, not only the whole of the Gawain plot is lacking, but there is also no mention of the Holy Grail and many other episodes without which the French poem would become quite meaningless. The few episodes that are common to both poems, thus have a completely different function in *Sir Perceval*. In the English poem, Perceval's childhood in the woods and his strange behaviour when he first meets some of King Arthur's knights are not a significant part of the hero's education and the lowest point in a meaningful development towards chivalrous perfection, but hardly more than a curious adventure which already throws light on the hero's undaunted spirit. His naive recklessness is only seen as the natural consequence of his peculiar upbringing, not as the first step in a complex process of maturing and initiation. The tone of the poem rather implies that for the author, Perceval's boorish daring is just as admirable as the sophisticated etiquette at the court of Arthur. Perceval's early exploits are particularly worthy of praise because they only spring from his personal prowess and strength and reveal his superiority without any of the paraphernalia of courtly knighthood. The killing of the Red Knight, which in Chrétien's novel is due to a lucky stroke by the ignorant and inexperienced youth and is on the whole rather deplorable, appears in the English poem as his first deed of honour, and when the English poet crudely exaggerates Perceval's clumsiness in handling weapons, he does it mainly for the sake of a comic effect, not because he wants us to despise the young hero. Furthermore, the poem does not tell us how Perceval acquires a courtly education and there are no scenes, like those in the French novel, where the hero is systematically instructed in all the knightly virtues. In Chrétien's poem, of course, this aspect is of vital importance, whereas *Sir Perceval of Gales* could appropriately be described as the 'History of the Boorish Knight', because it was evidently this part of the action which interested the English adapter, whereas the later parts of the story left him rather cold. He seems to have felt a certain pleasure in confronting the higher claims of a courtly code with the crude forthrightness of the young savage. Similar confrontations appear and seem to have been relished in several other romances, mainly from the North of England, such as *Sir Gawain and the Green Knight*, *Morte Arthure*, *The Taill of Rauf Coilƺear* and *The Carl of Carlisle*. In all these works, there is deliberate emphasis on courtly ceremony, but also an implied criticism of its artificial character because it is not always justified by a higher moral standard.

The drastic abridgement and simplification of the story give greater unity to the poem and firmly put the hero in its centre. The various adventures are not arbitrarily selected, but they form part of a larger episode: the ignorant child from the woods avenges his father and by his inborn prowess alone earns himself an honourable place among Arthur's knights. He also brings his mother back to the court from which she had been driven by the death of the old Perceval. All the exploits of the hero contribute in some way to this development of the plot and they are also related to each other by other incidents, such as the story of the ring that he takes from the sleeping lady (ll. 433 ff. and 1820 ff.) and the various family relationships by which nearly all the characters in the story are connected. The unity of the poem is also supported by such minor motifs as the 'water of þe welle' (l. 7) which is said to have been Perceval's drink at the outset of the story. Later, when he is married, he suddenly remembers his mother and the 'Drynkes of welles, þer þay spryng' (l. 1777) and he goes out to find her until he comes to the well again (ll. 2205–9). What at first seems perhaps a meaningless tag, has thus an important function in linking the beginning and the end of the story.

Like many of the other shorter romances, then, *Sir Perceval* is a 'romance of prys'. Its chief subject is the glorification of a hero who, in spite of his uncourtly upbringing and his lack of proper instruction, becomes a model of prowess and of piety.

The narrative technique of the poem is characterized by particular liveliness. As in *Sir Degrevant*, the action is not related in sketchy outlines (as it is in some of the East Midlands tail-rhyme romances), but in a series of dramatic and sometimes quite elaborate scenes. There is also a particularly effective use of varying points of view. Events are often described as they appear to one of the characters, not from the point of view of the omniscient narrator, and this can contribute to a more sympathetic picture of the characters, as in the rather pathetic scene when Perceval's mother sees him return from the woods with a steed:

> Scho saw hym horse hame brynge;
> Scho wiste wele by þat thynge,
> þat þe kynde wolde oute sprynge
> For thynge, þat be moughte.
> þan als sone saide þe lady:
> 'þat ever solde I sorowe dry
> 'For love of þi body,
> 'þat I hafe dere boghte!          (ll. 353–60)

The scene is given a rather emotional quality in this way and its importance for the action of the poem is emphasized. A similar technique is used when Perceval first appears at Arthur's court. The King looks at him and is put in mind of Perceval's father:

> The kyng by-holdez hym on hy;
> Than wexe he sone sory,
> When he sawe þat syghte.

> The teres oute of his eghne glade,
> Never one anoþer habade:
> 'Allas', he sayde, 'þat I was made
> 'Be day or by nyghte!
> 'One lyve I scholde after hym bee,
> 'þat me thynke was lyke the;
> 'þou arte so semely to see,
> 'And þou were wele dighte.'      (ll. 534–44)

and a little later:

> The kyng bi-holdez þe vesage free,
> And ever more trowed hee,
> þat þe childe scholde bee
> Sir Percyvell son.
> It ran in the kynges mode
> His syster Acheflour þe gude,
> How scho went into þe wodde,
> With hym for to wonn.      (ll. 585–92)

The visual impression produces a particular train of thought and this not only gives the scene a certain spatial quality, but it also heightens our interest in the characters concerned. This technique can be seen as an early example of dramatic use of point of view which is not so very different from similar devices employed in the modern novel.[44] There are several scenes in this poem where the narrator seems to retreat and describe events through the eyes of one of the characters. Sometimes the point of view alternates between several characters, as in the scene where Arthur appears before Lufamour's castle (ll. 1381 ff.). He is first seen by Perceval who prepares to meet the newcomers. At the same time Perceval is watched by the lady who begins to fear for his life. Again, there is an effective portrayal of her feelings as she observes the scene in front of her:

> Then was the lady full wo,
> When scho sawe hym go
> A-gaynes foure knyghtys tho
> With schafte and with schelde.
> They were so mekyl and unryde,
> þat wele wende scho þat tyde,
> With bale þay solde gare hym byde,
> þat was hir beste belde.      (ll. 1405–12)

104

After that, we are told of the reaction of Arthur and his knights when they see Perceval galloping towards them. Only very few of the popular romances treat their story with such detachment and with such an acute awareness of the personal drama involved. There are also some instances of a wry humour, as after the killing of the Red Knight, when Perceval addresses the dead and the narrator remarks drily:

> The knyghte lay still in þe stede:
> What sulde he say, when he was dede?  (ll. 737–8)

It is, above all, this unconventional liveliness and originality of the narrative technique that make *Sir Perceval of Gales* one of the most readable of the Middle English romances.

### 'AMIS AND AMILOUN'

Like *Sir Perceval of Gales*, the romance of Amis and Amiloun relates a story which was popular not only in England, but seems to have been known all over Europe, although in widely differing versions. The extensive investigations of MacEdward Leach have shown that the story was usually interpreted in one of two ways, either as a romance or as a hagiographic tale.[45] The adventures of the two friends could be told as an example of true friendship and loyalty or as a trial sent by God to test his Saints. The romantic versions end with the happy union of the friends, the hagiographic with their martyrdom. The English version clearly belongs to the first group, but it is also markedly didactic and less courtly than the Anglo-Norman poem *Amis e Amilun* which may have been its source, although in a different version from those extant. *Amis and Amiloun* seems to have been one of the most popular of the Middle English romances. It is preserved in four manuscripts, which for a poem of this kind is quite a high number, and its influence can be traced in several later poems, although the romance itself was not included in any of the larger collections of the fifteenth century. As it is preserved in the Auchinleck Ms., it must have been composed early in the fourteenth century and was probably known to most later authors of romances. The other three versions are in B.M. Egerton 2862 (S), B.M. Harley 2386 (H) and Douce 326 (D).

It is rather striking that the English poem is more than twice as long as its probable source so that this is perhaps one of the few cases where an English adapter has expanded and enlarged on his source although it is possible that he had before him a more extensive French version which is now lost. Since, however, the Anglo-Norman poem is preserved in three texts, none of them substantially different from the others, this possibility can probably be ruled out. *Amis e Amilun* is a particularly brief and concise tale which in style and narrative technique shows many resemblances with the Breton lays, whereas *Amis and Amiloun* is a typical and particularly successful example of the English shorter romance and is quite different from the lays.[46]

This can be seen in the way the story is embellished and dramatized. The poet's particular gift seems to have been his ability to compose vivid scenes which are often exactly localized and show an astonishing mastery in handling dialogue. In many cases the English adapter adds considerably to his source. An example is the lively scene in the orchard with the first meeting of the lovers, Amis and Belisaunt (ll. 493 ff.). The traditional motifs of springtime and the song of the birds are skilfully woven into the story. The encounter is seen first from Belisaunt's point of view, then from Amis', so that there is a change of perspective which gives the scene a more dramatic quality. The dialogue, with the impulsive wooing of the lady, his hesitation and his attempt to put her off, and her scorn which soon turns into threats, is considerably more effective than in the Anglo-Norman poem and has quite a realistic flavour. Amis' dilemma which is briefly and precisely described in his short monologue (ll. 637–51), comes out much clearer through the technique of changing point of view. The discovery of the love-affair, too, is described in a short scene (ll. 685 ff.). The steward observes how Belisaunt casts loving looks on the knight and from then on he spies on them until he can clearly incriminate them. It is interesting to see the way in which looks alone indicate the situation:

> þe steward ful of felonie,
> Wel fast he gan hem aspie,
> Til he wist of her fare,
> & bi her siȝt he parceiued þo
> þat gret loue was bi-tvix hem to,
> & was agreued ful sare,          (ll. 700–5)

Very similarly, love is betrayed by looks alone in the two versions of *Ipomedon*.

This trend towards a more scenic technique where the source-poem often only gives a brief summary, could be demonstrated throughout the English poem, for instance in Belisaunt's visit to Amis' bedroom (ll. 721 ff.), the parting of the two friends (ll. 277 ff.), the trial by combat (ll. 1285 ff.) and, above all, in the healing of Amiloun by the blood of Amis' children. The description of this episode is one of the finest passages in all the Middle English romances. It has a moving simplicity and directness which are quite rare in these poems and show the poet at his best (ll. 2251 ff.). It is Christmas, the feast of love and reconciliation; Amis alone stays at home from church and he goes to his children's bedroom to take a last look at them. Again, the interrelation between the scene and his emotions is very effectively dramatized:

> Alon him self, wiþ-outen mo,
> Into þe chaumber he gan to go,
> þer þat his childer were,
> & biheld hem boþe to,
> Hou fair þai lay to-gider þo
> & slepe boþe yfere.
> þan seyd him-selue, 'Bi Seyn Jon,
> It were gret reweþe ʒou to slon,
> þat god haþ bouʒt so dere!'
> His kniif he had drawen þat tide,
> For sorwe he sleynt oway biside
> & wepe wiþ reweful chere.          (ll. 2281–92)

The scene impressively illustrates Amis' loyalty towards his friend; his deep grief is a sign of the greatness of the sacrifice he is making for the sake of his sworn brother.

The English adapter has in fact subordinated the whole poem to what seemed to him its real theme, that is the faith and loyalty of the two friends, which overrule any other relationship or commitment. In spite of its more leisurely and scenic style, the English poem appears more unified and purposeful than the Anglo-Norman version and several changes that were introduced in it can be explained by this emphasis on the theme of friendship which also provides a better motivation for some parts of the plot.

Thus, in *Amis and Amiloun* the description of the pledging of friendship is more elaborate and it is clear that it forms the basis of the whole story. The episode of the two beakers, too, which is only briefly mentioned in the Anglo-Norman poem, is told in greater detail and is introduced much earlier. At parting Amiloun presents one of the beakers to his friend (ll. 313 ff.) and his excitement when later he sees the same beaker in the hands of the leper (ll. 2053 ff.), is therefore much more convincing. Obviously the beakers are the symbol of their loyalty. A minor change which, however, also serves to underline the theme of friendship, is that in the English poem Amis is expressly forbidden by the King to accompany his friend home (ll. 265 ff.), whereas in the Anglo-Norman poem he himself refuses to go out of loyalty towards his sovereign.

Throughout the story, the English adapter has altered episodes in order to make them illustrate and deepen the theme of the poem. For instance, after the departure of Amiloun, the wicked steward offers his friendship to Amis (ll. 349 ff.). In *Amis e Amilun*, this is told in rather general terms and the steward's rejection seems to spring mainly from a personal dislike, a dislike that is perfectly justified in view of the steward's behaviour earlier in the poem. In *Amis and Amiloun*, however, the point of the episode is that the steward in fact offers to replace Amiloun by swearing brotherhood with Amis. Amis has to reject the offer if he wants to remain faithful to his friend, and his decided refusal shows that for him the bond of sworn brotherhood is not affected by time or by the absence of the friend:

> For ones y pliȝt him treuþe, þat hende,
> Where so he in warld wende,
> Y schal be to him trewe;
> & ȝif y were now forsworn
> & breke mi treuþe, ye were forlorn,
> Wel sore it schuld me rewe.
> Gete me frendes whare y may,
> Y no schal neuer bi niȝt no day
> Chaunge him for no newe.'                    (ll. 376–84)

Another test of the friendship is implied in the duel which Amiloun undertakes in order to save his friend, and here, too, the English poet has made some significant changes. In the Anglo-Norman version, Amilun marries Florie (Belisaunt) after the duel. On his way to church he is warned by a voice from heaven and his punishment by the infliction of leprosy is announced. The illness is thus God's judgement for his second marriage. In the English poem, however, the warning comes before the fight, and the sin

Amiloun commits is not bigamy (because he departs without marrying Belisaunt), but the acceptance of the duel itself on behalf of his friend although he knows that Amis is in the wrong. By Amiloun's decision to fight, the divine judgement by ordeal is falsified and the steward is killed although his accusation was true, as the two lovers of course, realize (ll. 908, 940–1). Thus, by the voice from heaven Amiloun was faced with the choice whether to undertake the fight and draw upon himself the judgement of God or whether to abandon his friend to his fate and thus break his faith:

> þat kniȝt gan houe stille so ston
> & herd þo wordes euerichon,
> þat were so gret & grille.
> He nist what him was best to don,
> To flen, oþer to fiȝting gon;
> In hert him liked ille.
> He þouȝt, 'ȝif y beknowe mi name,
> þan schal mi broþer go to schame,
> Wiþ sorwe þai schul him spille.
> Certes,' he seyd, 'for drede of care
> To hold mi treuþe schal y nouȝt spare,
> Lete god don alle his wille.' (ll. 1273–84)

This conflict is absent in the French poem.

In the English one, Amiloun decides to be true to his friend and is soon afterwards stricken with leprosy. Thus his loyalty is tested in a far more agonizing way than in the Anglo-Norman version.

The scene between Amiloun and his wife, again dramatized in the English poem, shows that in the meantime Amis was equally true to his friend (ll. 1459 ff.). The second parting of the friends is a repetition of the first, and this time it is Amis who asks his friend to come to him should he ever be in need (ll. 1441 ff.).

The theme of friendship is further illustrated by the figure of the young boy who stays with Amiloun when everybody else has forsaken him. He does for Amiloun what his friend is, for the moment, unable to do because he does not know about his plight. When Amis hears about the loyalty of the boy who refuses an advantageous offer to remain at court with him because he does not want to forsake Amiloun, he is full of admiration for it, while the knight who has told him about it thinks it a good joke (ll. 1954 ff.). By his emphatic approval Amis shows how much he values true friendship and this reflects on his own loyalty. His explanation of the boy's behaviour is also a comment on the theme of friendship:

> Oþer þe child is of his blod yborn,
> Oþer he haþ him oþes sworn
> His liif wiþ him to lede.
> Weþer he be fremd or of his blod,
> þe child,' he seyd, 'is trewe & gode,
> Also god me spede. (ll. 1996–2001)

He is obviously put in mind of his own vow of friendship to Amiloun whom he has not yet recognized in the leper.[47]

After Amiloun has given such convincing and painful proof of his loyalty, Amis is soon faced with a similar decision, whether to leave his friend with his dreadful disease or to save him by committing another sin. Thus the scene in the children's bedroom, quoted above, corresponds exactly to the scene before the duel, and again the loyalty of the friend is stressed by the difficulty of the dilemma.

A further comment on the theme of the poem is provided by the different behaviour of the two wives. Amiloun's wife bitterly reproaches him for standing by his friend and endangering his own life and she turns him away when he is disfigured by his leprosy, whereas Belisaunt praises Amis for his loyalty and comforts him for the loss of their children (ll. 2389 ff.). This again throws light on the conflict between loyalty and selfishness which runs through the poem. Nearly every episode is in some way related to this problem, especially those that have been expanded in the adaptation. Only the wooing of Belisaunt at the beginning of the story seems to come from a more romantic version and almost detracts from the main concern of the poem. It is quite similar to the parallel incident in *King Horn*. *Amis and Amiloun* thus does not belong among the hagiographic versions of the story although it is not just a courtly romance either, because the adventures of the two friends are, as we have seen, told as an example of true friendship and loyalty. No sin is as great as the breaking of faith sworn to a friend. The sanctity of friendship is upheld in a very similar way in the short poem *Athelston* which is dealt with in the following chapter.

It seems likely that the compilers of the Auchinleck manuscript considered the poem not a romance, but a didactic tale, because they put it among homiletic works, not next to the romances. It stands in the first, largely devotional and didactic half of the manuscript, between *Speculum Guidonis* and *Marie Maudelayne*, whereas in the manuscript Egerton 2862 it is put among romances.[48] The transmission thus supports the conclusion that the poem combines elements from the romances and from legendary tales, and the obvious success of the poem shows that it was just this combination that appealed to English audiences.

In spite of the legendary elements, it seems preferable to group the poem with the shorter romances rather than with the homiletic romances. Although it is evidently written to praise a particular virtue, i.e. loyalty, it is also considerably indebted to the more romantic versions of the story and to other romances and is clearly different from the hagiographic versions, but it is certainly one of those shorter romances which are particularly close to homiletic tales like *Athelston* or *Sir Gowther* and little would be gained by an exaggeration of the differences between the two groups.

### 'OCTAVIAN'

The Middle English poem about the Emperor Octavian is another characteristic example of the shorter romances described in this chapter. The poem is preserved in two different versions which are included in three of the most important collections of romances: the Southern version is preserved in the manuscript Cotton Caligula A. II, together with *Libeaus Desconus* and *Sir Launfal*, the Northern version in Cambridge Ff. II. 38 and in the Thornton Ms. (Lincoln A. 5.2.). The English versions are probably free adaptations of an Anglo-Norman poem of some 5300 lines, which in turn was based on the French novel *Florent* (about 18500 lines).[49] It thus appears that the English adapters reduced their source to about a third of its size although that source was already a drastic abridgement of an extensive novel. A comparison between the two English versions reveals that they both treated the Anglo-Norman poem in a very independent way although the Northern version is somewhat closer to it than the Southern one. Both are typical of the freedom with which such stories were adapted and shortened in English. The two poems are of about the same length; the Southern version runs to 1962 lines, the Northern version to about

1700, which means they are among the more extensive of the shorter romances. This is probably due to the story itself for it would indeed be difficult to tell it in even fewer words.

While most of the lays and the romances that were influenced by them (like *Sir Launfal*) consist of only one or two episodes and tell a comparatively simple story, we find in *Octavian* a rather complicated and diffuse plot ranging over a variety of countries and involving many characters none of whom can really be described as the hero of the poem. Such a plot seems to be particularly unsuitable for treatment in a brief and condensed version and it is therefore interesting to see how two different adapters tried to cope with this problem and to compress the story into a work that could be read at one sitting.

It seems, as we have already noticed in the case of other English romances, that the adapters were above all attracted by the colourful mixture of romantic, legendary and even comic elements in the story. This mixture is already evident in the French and Anglo-Norman versions, but the English adapters have, both, each in his own way emphasized the contrasts. A brief analysis of the plot may illustrate this variety and also draw attention to the resemblances between *Octavian* and several other English romances, particularly *The Erl of Tolous*, *Sir Eglamour* and *Sir Ysumbras*.

The first part of the poem, relating the childless state of the Emperor and his wife, the hatred of the mother-in-law and the exiling of the innocent Empress, might equally well be the introduction to a legend as to a romance and the situation is reminiscent of *The Erl of Tolous* as well as of *Emaré* and *Le Bone Florence of Rome*. In the course of the story, particular prominence is often given to the legendary features, such as the decision of the Empress to join a group of pilgrims sailing off to the Holy Land and the fierce wars against the pagans which occupy nearly all the second half of the poem and create a crusading atmosphere. The innocently persecuted Empress is portrayed almost like a Saint, particularly in the Northern version. On the other hand, the style and tone of the poems suggest that the adapters were less interested in the didactic side of the story and in moral edification than in the colourful series of events and the complications of the plot. Thus the Emperor is not criticized for his unjust wrath and the cruel treatment of his wife because the poet is in an evident hurry to pass on to the consequences of his action, the wanderings of the lady and the dispersal of the family with the eventual happy reunion.

The humorous scenes, too, give the impression that the adapters were more concerned with momentary effects than with a larger design; they are told with more gusto and emphasis than in the sources. For instance, the contrast between the courtly youth (the Empress' son) and his boorish foster-father is presented in such a way that the sympathy of the hearer is rather more on the side of the cunning old citizen who by a crude trick makes the knights pay for the entertainment he has provided for them and who often has occasion to be disappointed with his foster-son, whose noble birth has made him completely incapable of the more practical arts of bartering and trading.

All these heterogeneous elements are, in spite of the brevity of the English poems, linked together with such competence that we do not get the impression of a mere hotch-potch of story-motifs, but of a pleasant variety which is unified by the narrator's evident enjoyment of his craft. This applies, in a greater or lesser degree, to both English versions, although there are considerable differences in the arrangement of the material and in the manner of presentation.

As mentioned above, the adapter of the Northern version follows the order of events in the French poem more closely than the Southern one and it is probable that he had a copy of the French text in front of him when composing his romance. The verse-form, too, the twelve-line tail-rhyme stanza, is handled with more skill and artistry and the whole poem is clearly more 'literary' than the rather ballad-like Southern version. Sarrazin thought the Northern version to be one of the most successful Middle English poems before Chaucer.[50]

The author of this version brings out the legendary as well as the humorous elements in the story with particular force. The Empress' earnest wish for a child is miraculously granted when she and her husband vow to found an abbey (ll. 37 ff.); by the grace of God she gives birth to twin-boys. Like a Saint she endures all the hardships that the jealousy of her mother-in-law has brought upon her, as is shown by her meek prayer in the woods after she has lost her two sons (ll. 385–402):

> Lorde, the sorowe, that y am ynne,
> Welle y wot, hyt ys for my synne:

Welcome be thy sonde!
To the worlde y wylle me neuer yeue,
But serue the, lorde, whylle y leue,
Into the holy londe.'                    (C, ll. 397–402)

There is no suggestion in the poem that the lady has deserved her
hard fate and her sense of guilt does not spring from any particular
act she has committed, but from a deeply Christian insight into her
own sinfulness. After this scene, the hearer would probably expect
quite a different continuation of the story from that which actually
follows.

The humorous scenes, too, are drawn with particular vividness,
although not as coarsely as in the Southern version. Typical of the
way in which courtly elements are burlesqued here, is the episode
in which Clement (Florent's foster-father) and his wife provide
their foster-son with arms which rust and age have made completely useless (C, ll. 877 ff.; L, ll. 792 ff.). The narrator is particularly
amused by their combined efforts to pull the old sword out of its
scabbard:

Clement the swyrde drawe owt wolde,
Gladwyn, hys wyfe, schoulde þe scabard holde,
And bothe faste they drowe;
When the swyrde owt glente,
Bothe to the erthe they wente:
There was game y-nowe!
Clement felle to a benche so faste,
That mowth and nose alle to-braste,
And Florent stode and loghe.
Hyt ys gode bowrde to telle,
How they to the erthe felle,
And Clement lay in swoghe!        (C, ll. 889–900)

It is a far cry from the elaborate descriptions of the arming of the
hero in French courtly novels, or in *Sir Gawain and the Green
Knight*, to the broadly comic scene which is reminiscent of such
burlesque romances as *The Tournament of Tottenham* and shows
that even such an emphatically religious poem as *Octavian* was
designed to provide pure entertainment as well as instruction.
There are several other passages which betray the author's lively
sense of the grotesque, such as the reaction of the Princess when
Florent brings her the giant's head which he has cut off,[51] or the
loud laughter of the knights when the Emperor's mother cuts her

throat (C, ll. 1720–1). On the other hand, we are told that Florent is ashamed of his foster-father's boorish behaviour (C, l. 1140) and it is clear that the adapter was not unaware of the courtly background of the story. When the Empress comes to Jerusalem, she is royally entertained by the king and treated with all respect due to her high state (C, l. 505), whereas in the Southern version she earns her living by sewing fine robes (ll. 619 ff.). In Florent's love-suit and his knightly exploits, too, the courtly tone of the French poem can still be felt.

The narrative technique of the poem does not give the impression that it was composed by or for a minstrel.[52] At the beginning, and once or twice in the course of the action, there is the usual call for attention (cf. C, ll. 204 and 207), but otherwise such formulas are comparatively rare in this poem. The transitions, too, are not announced explicitly by the narrator, as in many more minstrel-like romances, but are usually made in a quite unobtrusive way and woven into the story. By putting together parts of the action which in the Southern version are separated by other episodes, the adapter evidently tried to avoid the danger of the poem becoming disconnected because of a continual shifting of scene. At the same time, as a comparison with the Southern version shows, the adapter has tried to focus the action in a number of more elaborate scenes and to present the story less by summarizing narrative than by a concentration on some particularly important moments, a technique similar to that used in *Amis and Amiloun*, *Sir Degrevant* and *Sir Perceval of Gales*.

Thus, right at the beginning of the poem, the conversation between the Emperor and his wife is reproduced in the form of a clearly localized scene with some very expressive gestures (C, ll. 37 ff.), not as an isolated piece of dialogue, as many scenes in the Southern version. Similarly, the Emperor's first meeting with his mother after the birth of the children (ll. 97 ff.) is placed in a definite setting and is made into a brief and dramatic scene. Even the transitions between different episodes are sometimes disguised by such a clear indication of localities; the characters proceed from one locality to the next without the narrator explicitly announcing the change, as when the Emperor hears the news of his children's birth and then goes to chapel to give thanks and there meets his mother (C, ll. 91–102), or in the transition from Florent's exploits to the story of his mother and brother (C, ll. 1561–72): the rumour of the fighting in France spreads fast and is heard in Jerusalem. The author of the Northern version has also tried to avoid frequent changes of scene by telling the story of each child as a whole (contrary to the Anglo-Norman poem), whereas in the Southern version there is far more shifting from one scene of action to another. It is evident that the author of the Northern version was not content to give a brief summary of the story, but he tried to reorganize it for the purposes of a shorter poem and also to bring out the more emotional qualities of the action by his concentration on individual scenes and encounters between characters.[53]

As we have seen, the author of the Northern version also puts particular emphasis on the religious aspects of the story and stresses the piety of the main characters. Sarrazin thought, that even for medieval times there was a rather unusual amount of praying in the poem and he concluded that the author must have been a cleric.[54] Another feature that might be used as an argument against minstrel-origin is the scene in which Clement beats all the minstrels away from his feast (L, ll. 1059–64). The French version inserts an emphatic defence of minstrels at this point whereas the English author does not seem to find Clement's behaviour particularly reprehensible, although the whole episode serves to illustrate Clement's boorishness. I doubt whether from details like this any definite conclusions can be drawn as to the calling of the author. The artistic unity of the poem and the skilful organization of the plot suggest an educated scribe rather than an improvising minstrel, but whether he was a cleric or not is probably impossible to decide, because the religious tone of the poem is quite in keeping with the style of many other East Midlands tail-rhyme romances and there is no reason why this poem should have been written by a cleric, unless we assume the same of *The Erl of Tolous*, *Libeaus Desconus* and *Sir Eglamour*.

The Southern version of *Octavian*, on the other hand, shows a far greater number of those stylistic traits which we usually associate with minstrel-poetry, although it should be noted that this says less about the person of the author than about the transmission of the poem and the audience it was written for.[55] The narrative technique seems far more adapted for the situation in which the poem would be read aloud; there are many direct addresses to the audience and calls for attention. New episodes are

often announced in a tone suggestive of the street-crier (cf.
ll. 113-14, 299-300, 471-2, 903-4, 1163-4, 1277-8, 1373-4,
1811-12) even when there is nothing sensational about them or
they are only very brief. An example of this rather popular and
salesmanlike style is the following announcement:

> He, þat wyll harkene dystresse,
> Now he may here! (ll. 437-8)

This introduces an account of the sufferings of the Empress. Many
changes of scenery and transitions between episodes are announced
in a similar manner (cf. ll. 425 ff., 661 ff., 1323 ff., 1459 ff., 1549 ff.,
1777 ff.), as for instance:

> Now reste we her a lytyll wyȝt,
> And forþer telle, as hyt ys ryȝt,
> How þat oðer chyld was dyȝt,
> That dwellede yn Fraunce. (ll. 661-4)

Thus the flow of the narrative is time and again interrupted and we
get the impression of a rather loose sequence of separate episodes.
There is a very extensive use of direct speech, even for minor
incidents, but the short snatches of dialogue are often hardly
localized and there are no elaborate scenes as in the Northern
version. This ballad-like technique and the unsystematic arrangement of the plot, which can be seen in the description of the
children's fates or of the fights near the end of the poem, show that
the author of this poem was a far less careful artist than that of the
Northern version and was mainly thinking in terms of oral
recitation.

He, too, stresses the religious aspects of the story, but he does it
in a more openly didactic manner and intrudes with his own
comments, as when he states at the end:

> þus god kan turne wrong to ryȝt
> þoruȝ hys poste. (ll. 1949-50)

or when he announces:

> Now mowe ye here greet merueyle,
> How god man helpys: (ll. 471-2)

The beginning of the poem, more verbose than many similar
introductions, stresses the homiletic value of such a tale and
speaks very disapprovingly of those who do not want to hear

edifying stories. This little sermon is interesting because it shows again that many of the romances want to provide popular entertainment and moral instruction at the same time. They cannot thus be described as either minstrel or clerical poetry because they obviously try to bridge the gap between mere amusement and didacticism. The introduction to the Southern *Octavian* shows that this was not always easy:

> But fele men be of swyche manere,
> Goodnesse when hy scholden here,
> Hy nylleð naght lesste with her ere,
> To lerny wyt,
> But as a swyn with lowryng cher
> All gronne he sytte,
>
> And fele of hem casteð a cry
> Of thyng, þat fallyð to rybaudy,
> That noon of hem, that sytte hym by,
> May haue no lest.
> God schylde all thys company
> Fram swych a gest,
>
> And ʒeue vs grace goodnesse to lere
> Of ham, that before vs were,
> Crystendom how they gonne arere,
> Tho hyt began!                    (ll. 7–22)

Thus the romance is announced as an instructive tale about the beginnings of Christianity—on the whole not a very accurate description, but as in the Charlemagne romances, nearly every fight in this poem is part of a crusade and a manifestation of the superiority of God. The Sultan, when he hears of his daughter's marriage to a Christian, rushes to his temple and knocks all his Gods to pieces (ll. 1303–14); his daughter has been converted by Clement (ll. 1263–6). On the other hand, Clement's uncourtly pranks are described even more crudely than in the Northern version and little remains of the courtly atmosphere of the French novel. In spite of its claims, the poem is a simple retelling of the story of Octavian, written for a rather undiscriminating audience, and its didacticism is only very superficial.

Nevertheless, the two English versions belong to the same type of shorter romance which is both adventurous and edifying and condenses a long story into a brief poem, but they also show how very differently the English adapters often went to work. The Northern version, as we have seen, is a fairly close-knit and artistically balanced tale which successfully tries to give a certain unity to a rather rambling story. Its lively style reminds one of *Amis and Amiloun* and of *Sir Ysumbras*,[56] two poems which were particularly popular. The Southern version, on the other hand, is a rather artless product, which was possibly written down from memory and is much less original, with its use of meaningless clichés and the careless stringing together of episodes. Both versions, however, throw light on the close connection between such romantic tales and popular legend. Even though very secular adventures are described in them, their religious tone and their obvious moral intention bring them particularly near to the 'homiletic' romances which will be discussed in the following chapter.

# 5

# HOMILETIC ROMANCES

In discussing the shorter romances, it has several times been necessary to stress their affinity with religious literature, especially with the Saints' legends. This affinity shows itself in the moral and often didactic tone of these tales and in many story-motifs which are common to the romances and the legends. Most of the shorter romances centre round a hero who is not only an exemplary knight and warrior, but such a faithful servant of God that he becomes almost a Saint. Some of these heroes, like Degrevant and Perceval, even suffer martyrdom in the Holy Land. Nearly all the shorter romances, however, are basically love-stories; by his extraordinary deeds, the knight proves himself worthy of marrying the lady he has loved for so long. The poet does not only want to instruct, he wants to entertain as well.

Apart from these romances, there is, however, another group of poems which are even closer to the legends and which could be described as homiletic romances.[1] These works are, as a rule, indiscriminately classed with the romances and it cannot be denied that they have much in common with them, particularly in their style and in the manner of transmission. On the other hand, they can be clearly distinguished from most of the shorter romances. Their story-material does not usually come from one of the traditional cycles, but often from legends. Although the homiletic romances do not portray any canonized Saints, they are sometimes related to such Saints, as *Athelston*, or they describe biographies which are very like those of Saints (cf. *The King of Tars*, *Emaré*, *Le Bone Florence of Rome*). Apart from that, there are many story-motifs which we also find in the shorter romances although here they are usually treated in a more pointedly religious manner, such as the sufferings of an innocent lady (*The Erl of Tolous*, *Octavian*, *Emaré*, *Le Bone Florence of Rome*), the impoverished knight (often by his own liberality), such as Sir Launfal, Sir Cleges, Sir Amadace and Sir Ysumbras, or a longer stay in the Holy Land or in Rome (*Sir Eglamour, Torrent of Portyngale, Octavian, Emaré*). In all the homiletic poems, the plot is completely subordinated to the moral and religious theme, even though this is occasionally lost sight of, as in the first part of *Le Bone Florence of Rome*, and all the adventures of the hero or heroine contribute to it, either by illustrating some particular Christian virtue in the hero or by commenting on the exemplary pattern of the action. One could describe these works, therefore, as either secularized Saints' legends or legendary romances because they occupy a position exactly in the middle between these two genres.

Two story-patterns are particularly typical of the homiletic romances. Several of them describe the history of men in whose lives God intervenes very directly, usually by a miracle, in order to chastize them and eventually to save them, as in *Robert of Sicily, Sir Ysumbras, Sir Gowther* and to some extent in *Sir Amadace*. The miraculous element often plays an important part in these poems, but this is not for the sake of sensational effects, but to point the moral. Even *Sir Cleges*, which is a particularly attractive combination of pious legend and popular *fabliau*,[2] may be counted among this group. The pretty little miracle by which the impoverished knight is suddenly enabled to mend his fortunes and to get his revenge on the avaricious court officials, is very characteristic of the simple, almost calculating piety of some of these tales and of the hearer's expectations. The poet could evidently depend on a certain animosity towards overbearing courtiers and porters in his audience. Sir Cleges is by no means a Saint and the poem has not many devotional qualities, but it is clear that the knight is rewarded for his liberality and Christian charity which have made him destitute. The moral is simple enough and we may assume that such humorous praise of generosity was not composed without some ulterior motive on the part of the author and that it held a pointed message to the patron or the lord of the manor who might listen to the tale.

The second group of homiletic romances is even nearer to the Saints' legends. They describe the fate of women who, though innocent, have to endure great hardships and persecution, but at last withstand all sufferings and dangers by their exemplary constancy and piety. The difference between these poems and the

Saints' legends proper can be seen in the sometimes rather colourful adventures of the lady and above all in the conclusion of the story. There is no martyrdom, and the heroine returns to a life of happiness and earthly wealth.

It might be useful to glance briefly at one or two characteristic examples before discussing some of the poems in more detail.

## 'THE KING OF TARS'

Like the lays and the shorter romances, the homiletic romances are represented in the early Auchinleck Ms. The tale of the King of Tars which is preserved there, is a typical example; it occurs in the first part of the collection, between the legend of Gregory and *Adam and Eve*, quite apart from the romances. It is also preserved in the Vernon Ms., an almost entirely religious and devotional collection. Thus the transmission makes it seem very likely that the compilers of the two manuscripts considered the poem a legend or a devotional tale rather than a romance.

The poem tells the story of the miraculous conversion of a pagan Sultan by the faith and the persuasive constancy of his wife.[3] Its militantly Christian tone is reminiscent of the Charlemagne romances. Here, too, God is always on the side of the believers and intervenes on their behalf in a very spectacular manner. Deception and cruelty are perfectly justified when they are employed in the cause of the Christian faith. At the end of the poem, all the Saracens are told that they either have to be baptized or killed (A, ll. 1027–50).

The poet obviously tried to make a legend out of a somewhat romantic tale and there is often a curious mixture of a pious and crusading atmosphere and crudely humorous elements. Thus the Sultan is described first as a choleric villain who begins to rave madly when the messengers return with the refusal of the King's daughter to marry him (A, ll. 97–111). When she has changed her mind and given her consent he remains stubborn and refuses to marry her until she has forsworn her Christian faith (A, ll. 400 ff.). His wrath is equally violent when he has to admit the superiority of the Christian God; in his rage he smashes all the statues of his gods (A, ll. 646–57).

The main character of the poem is, however, the daughter of the King of Tars. Her inner conflict is described with particular vividness. On the one hand, she does not want to marry a heathen and proudly confesses her faith to the Sultan, on the other hand, she cannot bear to see all the best of her father's knights being slaughtered because of her. Thus she decides to sacrifice herself and to accept the proposal of the Sultan. Contrary to the source of the poem, she does not, at first, have the approval of her parents, but it takes some persuading before they consent to let her go (A, ll. 217 ff.). Another deviation from the source is that the maiden does not go in the hope of converting the Sultan, but out of pity for the Christians who suffer for her sake (A, ll. 229–37, 265–78, 328–32). When she realizes that she can save her parents only by accepting the Sultan's faith, she makes even that sacrifice and at least pretends to submit to his wishes, but whenever she is alone she prays to Christ who in a dream has promised to save her. When at last God has demonstrated his superiority before all eyes she addresses a long sermon to the Sultan, teaching him the fundamentals of the Christian faith (A, ll. 823–70). Although his real conversion is brought about by a miracle, a kind of competition of gods, such as we find in the Old Testament and in several medieval legends,[4] there is no doubt that it was primarily the meek submission and sacrifice of the lady which made the miracle possible and thus brought about the conversion of all the heathens. Thus in many ways she assumes the attributes of a Saint.

It should be obvious that such a story is very different from the love-affairs of Sir Launfal and Sir Degrevant and that it has more in common with the Charlemagne romances which have usually been assigned to clerical authors.[5] The homiletic tendency of the poem is very marked, for instance in the catechizing of the Sultan by his wife or in the circumstantial description of his baptism, with the additional miracle that he changes colour and becomes 'Al white' (A, ll. 922 ff.). This in turn convinces his wife that his conversion is now complete:

> þe leuedi þonked god þat day,
> For ioie sche wepe wiþ eyʒen gray,
> Vnneþe hir lord sche knewe.
> þan wist sche wele in hir þouʒt,
> þat on Mahoun leued he nouʒt,
> For chaunged was his hewe.          (A, ll. 934–9)

In the more romantic versions of the story, the birth of the lady's misshapen child arouses the suspicion that it might be illegitimate, whereas in *The King of Tars* it is seen by all present as proof of the fact that either the mother or the father does not believe in the true God (ll. 574 ff.). Such changes show how much the adapter of the English version tried to bring out the religious element in the story.

On the other hand, there is in form and style an undeniable resemblance to the shorter romances. The poem is composed in twelve-line tail-rhyme stanzas and has much in common with many other tail-rhyme romances; in particular it makes free use of formulas which we associate with minstrel-poetry, like calls for attention (ll. 700-5, 1078-80, 1093-8), transitional formulas (ll. 370-2), or the mention of gifts to the minstrels (ll. 550-61). The miraculous christening of the child is announced in this promising way:

> Now ginneþ here a miri pas,
> Hou þat child y-cristned was        (A, ll. 700-1)[6]

The Christian miracle is presented like a sensational adventure, another example of the close connection between entertainment and edification in these poems. There is little doubt that this tale was intended for recitation to the same kind of audience that enjoyed romances, but, as we have seen, it has as least as much in common with Saints' legends as with romances. The fact that it is always classed with romances again reveals how inadequate some of our definitions of medieval genres are.

### 'ROBERT OF SICILY'

This poem represents a slightly different type of homiletic romance. Its legendary character has often been noticed.[7] The poem was included by Horstmann in his collection of legends, and in the manuscripts, too, it is usually grouped with legends or devotional tales, but it has also been discussed in connection with the romances.[8]

The outline of the plot at once makes it clear that this is a moral and didactic tale. The action is set in motion not by an intrigue or by some knightly adventure, but alone by the King's pride and God's decision to punish him for it. It is only to this end that the angel assumes Robert's shape and his humiliation is made perfect. At the end of the poem this moral is clearly formulated. All the embellishment, possibly due to the influence of the romances, helps to underline the central theme of the little poem. The contrast between the angel who, in the guise of Robert, introduces a perfectly just government, and the humiliated King, is very vividly portrayed. The gift of beautiful cloth to the messengers (ll. 233 ff.) is a sign of the heavenly origin of the new King. On the other hand, Robert's grief and repentance occupy much space and are particularly important for the homiletic intention of the poem. He thinks of the sinful careers of Nebuchadnezzar and Holofernes (whose story is briefly described) and he breaks out in a devoutly humble prayer which, with its almost liturgical form (cf. the refrain), reminds one of some of the Middle English penitential lyrics and seems to be the moral centre of the poem. After the deep inner transformation of the King, God's forgiveness and the complete reversal of his fortunes with a return of his former power and wealth seem to be almost a matter of course.

This very brief poem, to judge from its transmission, seems to have been more popular than most of the romances, because it is preserved in eight manuscripts, that is in more than any of the shorter romances. It is a particularly interesting example of the brief exemplary tale because again the story is not reduced to a bare outline, but told with evident gusto, for instance in the almost comic porter episode, and presented in a series of quite dramatic scenes. Robert's prayer, too, shows that brevity was not the poet's first concern. On the other hand, there are hardly any of the meaningless clichés we find so often in the shorter romances. Although the poem has much in common with the tail-rhyme poems, it seems, on the whole, slightly more literary and it is possible that it has suffered less than many of the romances from the accidents of transmission.

### 'SIR GOWTHER'

The homiletic romance of Sir Gowther is in many ways similar to *Robert of Sicily* and the two poems have several motifs in common. Here, too, the central figure is a knight who by God's direct intervention, is brought to a consciousness of his guilt and sinfulness, and who by intensive penitence achieves his return to a righteous and happy life.[9] Like *The King of Tars*, the poem belongs to the tail-rhyme romances and contains some of the traditional formulas, although less direct addresses to the audience. Its editor, Karl Breul, thought that it was composed by a minstrel. The two manuscripts in which the poem is preserved seem to count it among the legends. One of them (Advocates 19.3.1) is a mainly religious and devotional collection, the other (Royal 17 B XLIII) even calls the poem *Vita Sancti*.

The story of the poem was known all over Europe and has survived in many different versions; the majority of them have given a religious twist to the original fairy-tale.[10] The English version for which a definite source has not yet been found, claims to be a Breton lay (ll. 751–3). We do not know whether this is more than a vague and conventional formula, but even if there was a lay on the subject, the English adapter has changed and moralized it. However, it is more likely, he just wanted to write something like a religious counterpart to the traditional lays. Thus the scene in the orchard where Gowther's mother is visited by the devil (ll. 67–78) is clearly a Christian version of similar episodes in the lays[11] and the devil takes the place of the fairy or another visitor from the other-world. The motif of the three days' tournament comes from more secular tales and is treated very similarly as in *Ipomedon*; the knight's disguise as a beggar also has many parallels in the romances (*Amis and Amiloun, The Erl of Tolous, Guy of Warwick*).[12] There is no doubt that the author was famliar with a great number of romances, as is also suggested by the style of the poem, and that he tried to combine romantic and legendary elements in his treatment of the story. The wicked deeds of the knight which are, of course, only the visible expression of his infernal origin, and his sudden conversion are related in a very moral tone and there is no attempt to create an atmosphere of dramatic suspense; surprising turns of plot are either explicitly announced or told in a very factual manner as, for instance, the miracle by which the Emperor's daughter regains the power of speech (ll. 657–60). The poet seems to have been equally attracted by the romantic and by the religious aspects of the story and he does not bring out his homiletic theme with the same conciseness and clarity as the author of *Robert of Sicily*. He neither makes the most of Gowther's sudden conversion nor of his penitence and his hero does not undergo a convincing process of moral regeneration as do Robert of Sicily and Sir Ysumbras. It is not quite clear how he has really deserved to be forgiven all his sins unless his knightly exploits and his spectacular victories in the tournament are counted as part of his penance. Thus the combination of legend and romance is not very successful here and we may ask whether the poet really knew what he was doing or whether he just retold the story without any clear idea of its religious meaning.

The hero of the poem is a particularly valiant knight and also an exemplary Christian, but the two conceptions of his character do not add up to a convincing whole and it comes somewhat as a surprise to hear at the end of the poem that we are meant to think of him almost as of a Saint:

> And when he dyed, þo sothe to sey,
> Was beryd at þo same abbey,
> þat hym selfe gart make;
> And he is a varre corsent parfytt
> And with cryston pepull wele belovyd.
> God hase done for his sake
> Myrrakull, for he was hym hold,
> þer he lyse in schryne of gold,
> þat suffurd for goddus sake.
>
> Who so sechys hym with hart fre,
> Of hor bale bote mey bee,
> For so god hase hym hyȝt.
> þes wordus of hym þar no mon wast,
> For he is inspyryd with þo holy gost,
> þat was þo cursod knyȝt.      (ll. 724–38)

The identification of Sir Gowther with 'Seynt Gotlake' which is made in one version of the poem[13] is probably a later addition, but, like the word 'corsent' (l. 727), it shows that for the compilers of the two manuscripts at least, the hero was a kind of Saint and they tried to incorporate the poem in the traditional canon of Saints' legends. One is inclined to suspect that they partly misunderstood this homiletic romance, but there is no doubt that *Sir Gowther* holds a particularly interesting position between the romances and the legends.

The poems I have briefly tried to characterize in this way show that in Middle English there was a considerable number of works which are neither romances in the strict sense of the word nor

Saints' legends, but are closely related to both genres and draw on both for their story-motifs and stylistic devices. Some are more like romantically embellished legends, like *Sir Gowther*, others are adventure-stories which have been given a particularly religious interpretation, like *The King of Tars*. Such poems, as we have seen, appear as early as the Auchinleck Ms. and they can be found in religious collections, such as the Vernon Ms., as well as in those manuscripts that contain many romances, like Cotton Caligula A. II (*Emaré, Sir Ysumbras, Cheuelere Assigne*), Cambridge Ff. II. 38 (*Robert of Sicily, Le Bone Florence of Rome*) and the Thornton Ms. (*Sir Ysumbras*). As I have tried to demonstrate, these poems are sufficiently different from the shorter romances to be treated as a separate group. Most of them are not love-stories; they have a definite moral theme and romantic motifs are usually given a distinctly moral or religious interpretation. These differences are perhaps not always as clear-cut as that, but with most of the homiletic romances there is little doubt that they belong to a different literary type than, for instance, *Sir Eglamour* and *Sir Perceval of Gales*. A discussion of some of these poems will, it is hoped, give a clearer idea of this type.

### 'SIR YSUMBRAS'

Few Middle English poems can illustrate so well the close connection between religious and secular, edifying and entertaining tales as the story of Sir Ysumbras. Judging by the transmission, it was one of the most popular of all tales, because it is preserved in more manuscripts and early prints than any other of the romances.[14] This can probably be interpreted as evidence of the fact that the poem was considered to be more than just an entertaining romance. In most of the manuscripts, too, it is grouped with legends or devotional literature, as in Gonville & Caius 175 and Advocates 19.3.1, where it stands next to the legend of St. Catherine, and in Cotton Caligula A. II where it comes between *Cheuelere Assigne* and two devotional poems (*Quinque Vulnera* and *Quinque Gaudia*). Only in the Thornton Ms. it is placed between two 'romantic' tales (*The Erl of Tolous* and *Octavian*), but the order of items in this collection seems on the whole unsystematic and unrelated to the contents of the individual works.

The transmission of *Sir Ysumbras* thus reflects the mixed

character of the poem. From its subject-matter it could be described as a romantically embellished legend, but the moral and religious character of the story has been preserved more clearly than in the case of *Sir Gowther*. We do not know the immediate source of the poem, but it is clearly one of the many derivatives of the legend of Saint Eustace of which countless versions existed all over Europe.[15] It is interesting to see that many of these versions are extensive novels, whereas the English adapter has compressed the whole, rather complicated story into a short poem of less than a thousand lines. By this drastic abridgement he has not only altered the character of the plot, but he has also succeeded in stressing its moral pattern. As in most versions of the Eustace legend, two very common motifs are combined in the story: the trial and salvation of the hero by suffering, and the eventful dispersal and reunion of a family. The first motif was known to the Middle Ages chiefly through the Book of Job and reappears in many different forms.[16] The second motif, which ultimately derives from the Greek novel, also occurs in many romances (cf. *Octavian*); it obviously demands a certain breadth of epic treatment and cannot be unfolded very effectively in the space of a few lines. This is why in *Sir Ysumbras*, where the many wanderings of the hero and his family are passed over rather briefly, the adventurous elements play a less prominent part. The poem does not attempt to give a colourful description of romantic incidents, but concentrates on the exemplary story of a knight whose happiness is suddenly turned into misery and who in all his sufferings proves himself a humble and patient Christian until everything that he has lost is returned to him.

From the beginning it is clear that the poem portrays a deliberate process of education which is controlled by God and from which the knight emerges purified and humbled. The series of misfortunes that befall him are God's punishment for his pride, as the poem states with almost programmatic directness at the outset of the story:

> In his hert a pride was broghte:
> Of goddis werkes gafe he righte noghte
> His mercy for to neuen.
> So longe he reyngned in þat pride,
> That god wolde no lenger habyde:
> To hym he sent a steuen.          (ll. 31-6)

Ysumbras admits at once the justice of his fate and realizes that he has amply deserved all his sufferings. Thus he can even comfort his wife with pious reflections:

> God, þat sent me alle this woo,
> Hase sent me joye and blys also,
> And ȝitt may send ynoghe'. (ll. 94–6)

and:

> For alle þe bale, þat we aryn in,
> It es for oure wyked syn:
> We are worthi wele mare! (ll. 112–14)

The knight accepts God's punishment with such perfect humility that any further testing of his Christian virtue seems unnecessary (see also ll. 130–2 and XVI b, 10–2); however, not only his patience in adversity, but also his loyalty to the Christian faith are put to the test, as when the Sultan offers food, clothes and a home to him, if he forsakes God (ll. 253 ff.). At his indignant refusal, he is beaten up and cast out again, and the second and more extensive part of his sufferings begins. First he works as a simple blacksmith for seven years until he has earned a suit of armour for himself. His spectacular victory over the heathens seems to mark the end of his trial, but he flees from all the honours due to him and goes as a pilgrim to the Holy Land where he stays for another seven years. For the poet, this is obviously an even more extreme stage in the penitential career of the hero:

> Goddes werkkes for to wyrke
> Of penance was he neuer irke
> For his are-mysdede. (ll. 526–8)

At this very lowest point in his fortunes, he is told that now at last his sins are forgiven:

> All þe cete he hase thurgh gone,
> Mete ne drynke ne gat he none
> Ne house to herbere in.
> Besyde þe burghe of Jerusalem
> He sette hym by a welle streme
> Sore wepande for pyne.
> And, als he satt, abowte mydnyghte
> þare come an angelle faire and bryghte

130

And broghte hym brede and wyne.
'Palmere', he saide, 'welcome þou bee!
The kynge of heuen wele gretis the:
Forgyffen erre synnes thyn.

Rest þe wele, sir Ysumbras:
Forgeffen es alle thi tryspase, . . .          (ll. 529–42)

From this moment the course of his fortunes is reversed and not only his peace of conscience, but also all his former wealth and his family are restored to him.

The English poet, although concentrating on his moral theme, tells the story with an evident sense of dramatic effect and he tries to give us some insight into the feelings of his characters. When Ysumbras comes to the castle of the beautiful queen to ask for alms, we are not at once told that she is his wife, but only after she herself has realized who he is (ll. 661ff.). This particularly moving episode is also told in greater detail than other parts of the story and there is a very effective scene, when Ysumbras sits at the Queen's table and is reminded of all his former wealth. His grief is observed by the lady who then wants to hear his story:

Mete and drynke was forthe broghte:
þe palmere satt and ete righte noghte,
Bot luked abowte the haulle.
So mekill he sawe of gamen and glee
And thoghte, what he was wonnt to be:
Terys he lete downe falle.

So lange he satt and ete righte noghte:
The qwene byhelde, and wondir thoughte,
And till a knyghte gan saye:          (ll. 583–91)

Then he is at least relieved of his bodily wants. The memory of his family, too, is reawakened in him by an outward sign: he finds his cloak and the money which the heathens had forced on him in payment for his wife (ll. 637 ff.). These objects put him in mind of his heavy loss and his grief returns with renewed force. At the same time, this discovery leads to the reunion with his wife.

Thus the poem is rich in surprising and entertaining adventures and scenes that are charged with emotion; but they are not told for their own sake, because the whole tale centres round the hero and every episode throws some light on his career. For this reason, the fate of Ysumbras' wife and children is practically passed over;

131

they vanish completely from the scene and suddenly make their appearance again when the time of the hero's trials is over, whereas in *Octavian* and similar tales the author follows the fortunes of all the dispersed members of the family one after the other because this variety of adventures is one of the chief attractions of that kind of work. *Sir Ysumbras* is much more unified and its structure is far simpler than that of many other versions of the Eustace legend; with its firm concentration on the person of the hero, it is related to the 'romances of prys' as well as to the Saints' legends.

The introduction to the poem, praising the deeds of ancestors and announcing the history of a knight who is far superior to all those around him, could belong to one of the shorter romances as well as to a legend, although it soon becomes clear that an edifying story is being told which has nothing to do with chivalrous exploits or love-affairs. The romance-motifs pointedly emphasize the difference between many conventional heroic tales and the history of Sir Ysumbras:

> Hende in haule, and ჳe will here
> Of eldirs, þat byfore vs were,
> þat lyffede in arethede
> (Jesu Crist, heuen kynge,
> Graunte vs alle his blyssynge
> And heuen to oure mede):
> I will ჳow telle of a knyghte,
> þat was bothe hardy and wyghte
> And doghty man of dede.
> His name was called sir Ysumbras:
> Swilke a knyghte, als he was,
> Now lyffes nane in lede.
>
> He was mekill man and lange,
> With schuldirs brode and armes strange,
> þat semly was to see.
> He was large man and heghe:
> Alle hym loffede, þat hym seghe:
> Se hende a man was hee.
> Glewmen he luffede wele in haulle
> And gafe þam riche robis of palle,
> Bothe golde and also fee.
> Of curtasye he was kynge,
> Of mete and drynke no nythynge:
> In worlde was none so fre.     (ll. 1–24)

All these perfections of body and mind, which add up to a conventional portrait of an ideal knight, are, however, deceptive because they have made him proud and forgetful of God's grace. His fall appears all the greater, coming after such excessive praise. There is no doubt that the poet consciously stressed this contrast in order to interest his audience in the hero and at the same time to criticize traditional ideals of knighthood.[17] The conventions of romance are thus given a new meaning. The sufferings of the knight are a consequence of his pride and thoughtlessness and the happy end is the reward for his humility and penitence. It is clear that Ysumbras is portrayed as a model for all Christians. His superiority in all the traditional chivalric virtues is a visible sign of God's grace and of the hero's uniqueness. Like Gregory, he is singled out by God and is at the same time a perfect knight and a perfect penitent. Like many other romance-heroes, he distinguishes himself in fighting the heathens (ll. 433 ff.), but even this incident is chiefly used as an illustration of his humility: when the Christian King asks for his name, Ysumbras only calls himself a 'smethyman' (l. 479) and retires again into obscurity. The miracles that happen to him, too, set him apart and almost make a Saint of him, as when an angel brings him bread and wine (ll. 535 ff.) or when his two sons are returned to him by an angel just at the right moment (ll. 751 ff.).

There is, of course, a certain inconsistency here. As we have seen, Ysumbras acknowledges his guilt as soon as the first tribulation has fallen on him, and thus we cannot say that the long series of sufferings is necessary to bring him to a consciousness of his sinful state. He is not, like Robert of Sicily, led through an extreme situation of spiritual isolation, even madness, to undergo a complete change of heart; at least we get the impression that Ysumbras casts off his pride and his sinful thoughtlessness very soon and that all his further trials only serve to make him a model of Christian humility and repentance. The poem seems to combine two quite different patterns: the punishment and purification of a sinner and the prolonged demonstration of patience and constancy in adversity.[18] The latter is typical of most of the less romantic versions of the Eustace-legend, whereas the former is more appropriate to moral exempla and is didactic rather than devotional. *Sir Ysumbras* is a very successful attempt to bring these two story-patterns together, but it cannot be denied that this detracts somewhat from the interest we take in the character of the hero because the carefully graded sequence of his trials does not correspond to a significant development in him and he remains rather static in his perfect submission.

Of course, Ysumbras is no Saint and, contrary to Saint Eustace or Gregory, he is neither martyred nor does he attain to high religious honours, but like Job, he regains everything he has lost and his earthly happiness and prosperity at the end are greater than at the beginning, as the poet explicitly mentions (cf. ll. 709–10 and 793–4). It is also easy to see that the poem has several features in common with some rather more secular works. On account of its metrical form, it belongs to the tail-rhyme romances and as in many other of these poems, the author often dwells on homely and vividly observed detail more than the meaning of the story would demand, as in the description of the smithy (ll. 397–420) or the events at the court of the Queen (ll. 613–36). There is also a touching little scene when Ysumbras wants to carry his two sons across the river. As he leaves the eldest to go back and fetch his brother, he admonishes him tenderly:

> 'Luke, sone, þat þou be styll,
> To I feche thi breþer the till,
> And playe the with a blome'. (ll. 172–4)

All this does not make *Sir Ysumbras* a romance,[19] but again illustrates how impossible it is to make clear-cut distinctions between secular and religious poems and attests to the popularity of tales which combine elements from legends and romances.

It is also difficult to arrive at a positive decision as to the authorship of these poems. Various formulas and the mention of the hero's generosity towards minstrels might suggest that the poem was written for a minstrel, and it also appears from several details, like the description of the smithy, that the author was acquainted with the life of the lower classes, but all this does not justify the assumption of a 'humble minstrel author'.[20] The adaptation of a legend for the purposes of an edifying moral tale reveals considerable artistic skill and a certain amount of careful planning and could easily be the work of a cleric, but at any rate we can assume that the author must have been at home in both worlds, because the poem combines such different elements. If he was a cleric, he had an extensive, but by no means surprising knowledge of popular romances and their stylistic devices; if he was a minstrel, whatever our interpretation of that term, he was familiar with Saints' legends and was more concerned with presenting an exemplary story than with 'game & glee'.

## 'EMARÉ'

The tale of the sufferings of the innocent and beautiful Emaré is preserved in the important collection Cotton Caligula A. II, but it is not placed there among the shorter romances, like *Sir Launfal*, *Libeaus Desconus* and *Octavian*, but among religious works, and this suggests, as we found in the case of other homiletic romances, that the poem was, for the compilers of the collection, a legend or a devotional tale.[21] The plot, too, supports this conclusion because it clearly derives from the exemplary story of Constance and from the legend of Crescentia. We do not know the immediate source of the poem, but it seems likely that it is based on a French version of the story, as Edith Rickert suggested. The poem itself claims to be a Breton lay (ll. 1030–2), but as we have seen, such statements have to be treated with caution, and the poem in its present shape has not much in common with the original form of the lays. It is also probable that the source of the poem was much longer than *Emaré* because there are evident signs of abridgement[22] and the story is so eventful and moves between so many different places that it would be particularly suitable for an extensive novel. Thus the English adapter has reduced the size of the source in order to write a poem that could be read at one sitting.

*Emaré* is usually classed with the romances because of its romantic embellishment of the legendary material and because of its style which proves a close relationship between this poem and the tail-rhyme romances. In contrast to romances on similar subjects, however, the colourful and pathetic adventures of the heroine are not related for the sake of entertainment, but are clearly subordinated to the central theme of the poem, the demonstration of patient suffering and the survival of true virtue through all afflictions. The initial situation, too, is different from that of comparable shorter romances, like *The Erl of Tolous* and *Octavian*. Emaré is not exiled in consequence of any unjust accusation, but because she refuses to trespass against God's laws by committing incest. Her situation is that of a Christian martyr who suffers for her obedience to the laws of God (ll. 241 ff.). Her second voyage on the wild seas is, of course, due to an intrigue, but it is still a consequence of her first refusal and its chief cause is the old Queen's suspicion of Emaré's celestial beauty. The end of the poem, too, has a distinctly legendary quality. The two men who have injured Emaré both come to Rome in order to do penance for their sin and there they meet Emaré as a visible sign of the grace and forgiveness of God. It is not only the usual happy end of many romances, with the miraculous reunion of a dispersed family, but a triumphant vindication of Emaré's innocence and the end of the penance for the two men. The whole poem is a glorification of the heroine who, wherever she goes, awakens love and admiration. Not only her deeds and her practical skills (cf. ll. 373–84, 424–9, 730–1), but especially her perfect beauty are outward expressions of her goodness. Even the wicked old Queen has to admit that she never saw such a beautiful woman (ll. 443–4), but it is a sign of her vicious character that she cannot recognize this beauty for what it is, but thinks it must be a mark of the devil. Several times we are told that Emaré's beauty makes her appear like a being from another world:

> She semed non erþely wommon,
> That marked was of molde. (ll. 245–6)

Very similar expressions are used on two other occasions (ll. 394–6, 700–2). It is quite clear that her beauty is more than mere prettiness, and is an inseparable attribute of her moral perfection and it is also the cause of all her sufferings. Her patience in adversity is as exemplary as her beauty. She submits to the injustice of her treatment without trying to defend herself (ll. 625 ff.) and when adrift on the sea she puts all her grief before God whose providence never forsakes her, as the poet repeatedly reminds us.[23] The exemplary nature of Emaré's fate is also emphasized by repetition. Twice she suffers exactly the same misfortune and the author makes very little attempt at variation or at a dramatic climax. Thus several scenes and episodes recur in a nearly identical form, as the scenes where her father and her husband are suddenly struck by her appearance at dinner (ll. 220–31 and 397–408), the despair and repentance of the two men when she has left (ll. 280–300 and 769–83), and her double exile and miraculous salvation. These repetitions, far from being a sign of the author's incompetence and lack of imagination, bring home the exemplary character of the whole action and make it clear that we are not just listening to a tale of individual sorrow.[24]

In other ways, too, the narrative technique contributes to the pious tone of the poem. The prayer at the beginning is longer and more devotional than in most of the romances, and it is followed by the famous passage about the duty of the minstrels to begin their tales with a prayer:

> Menstrelles þat walken fer and wyde,
> Her and þer in euery a syde,
> In mony a dyuerse londe,
> Sholde, at her bygynnyng,
> Speke of þat ryghtwes kyng
> That made both see and sonde.
> Who-so wylle a stounde dwelle,
> Of mykylle myrght y may ȝou telle,
> And mornyng þer a-monge;
> Of a lady fayr and fre,
> Her name was called Emare,
> As I here synge in songe. (ll. 13–24)

This is more than the usual introductory formula; it seems like the pious admonition of an author who is trying to employ the popular form of a romantic tale to a more edifying purpose and who takes this opportunity of demanding more seriousness than was usual from the minstrel or whoever might recite the poem. This does by no means imply that the author was 'doubtless a wandering minstrel, who sang in the market-place,'[25] but it is probable that he had such people in mind and knew that they might make use of his poem. In its present form, however, *Emaré* shows a considerable degree of conscious artistry and could have been written by a cleric or by a professional scribe. At any rate, like the author of *Sir Ysumbras*, he tried to combine legendary material with romantic elements, but although the moral significance of the tale might be less precisely formulated than in *Sir Ysumbras*, the mode of narration is more like that of the legends and has an almost devotional quality.[26]

The story of Emaré is told in an unembellished and not very varied style, a style that is marked by the use of stereotyped formulas and repetition and by a lack of dramatic tension. Apart from the elaborate description of the beautiful cloth (ll. 88–168) to which I shall presently return, there are no extended descriptive passages in the poem, nor is there any appreciable use of swift and pointed summary, quite in contrast to the highly sophisticated and varied narrative technique of Chaucer's *Man of Law's Tale* which tells a very similar story.[27] The conventional formulas of transition (ll. 70-2, 310-12, 742-4, 946-8) which in such a brief tale seem somewhat unnecessary, also make for a certain monotony and absence of tension. In spite of the brevity of the poem, the narrator proceeds without any hurry and there are often short scenes with dialogue which create a rather leisurely atmosphere. Hardly ever do we feel that we are reading a very condensed version of an extensive tale. This impression of an unhurried sequence of events is also strengthened by the repetition of several situations which are then related in nearly the same words, such as the swooning of various characters which is nearly always accompanied by the formula: 'they took him up hastily' (cf. ll. 283-8, 550-5, 607-12, 780-3), or the journey of the messenger with his two stays at the house of the old Queen (ll. 514 ff.). In the same leisurely manner we are told how the King discovers the deception by comparing the letters and by asking the messenger about his journey (ll. 757 ff.). The ordering of events also is typical of the unreflecting, merely additive mode of narration. After Emaré's second exile, her fortunes are told up to the point when her son is seven years of age and wins general admiration (ll. 733-41). Then we return to the King, her husband, who learns what has happened in his absence and, after grieving for seven years, decides to go to Rome. All this shows that the author was not interested in a sophisticated and dramatically effective presentation of his story. On the other hand, the poem has a lucid simplicity of structure and style which clearly brings out the exemplary meaning of the story. It falls into three parts, of which the first describes the lady's constancy and her first exile (ll. 1-309), the second her further trials and sufferings (ll. 310-741), and the last her vindication and her return from Rome (ll. 742-1035). This simple ordering of episodes and the plainness of the narration clearly relate the poem to the Saints' legends and their techniques. We are presented less with a swiftly moving action than with a series of images which are particularly designed to arouse our sympathy with the lady and her unmerited fate,[28] and this again serves to focus our attention on the exemplary character of the story. Thus it would be quite wrong to account for the rather unimaginative and often monotonous style of the poem merely by charging the author with triteness and incompetence, because he obviously did not want to write a romance like *Sir Eglamour*, but a tale that moves us to contemplation and devotion.

The moral significance of the poem does not lie in any educational process to which the heroine is submitted, nor can her sufferings in any way be understood as a punishment for any sins she has committed. As we have seen, Emaré is portrayed as an absolutely blameless woman whose moral integrity is expressed in her almost unearthly beauty and the significance of her pitiable fate depends on its being completely unmerited. Just because she has done nothing to deserve her sufferings, she becomes such a model of patience in adversity and at the same time an example of the unfailing justice of God's providence. The moral and spiritual perfections of the lady are also effectively mirrored in the extensive description of the beautiful cloth that is given to her father by the King of Sicily (ll. 88–168). This elaborate piece of descriptive writing, rather reminiscent of the description of Melidor's chamber in *Sir Degrevant*, seems at first sight rather out of keeping with the rest of the poem and its important function long went unrecognized, but has now been convincingly explained by Hanspeter Schelp.[29] The cloth, that is the beautiful robe made out of it for Emaré, clearly serves to set off her beauty to even better effect, because her robe is always mentioned whenever her beauty impresses the beholders (cf. ll. 244–6, 394–6, 697–702, 932–3); in fact, the robe is an inseparable attribute, like her outward beauty, and a closer examination of the description reveals that it is in many ways symbolic of her inner perfections. The portraits of famous lovers can be seen as an allegorical representation of faith, just as the unicorn (ll. 163–5) embodies chastity; the precious stones, in particular, illustrate the virtues of the lady, and as Schelp has demonstrated by reference to medieval lapidaries, the magic powers traditionally attributed to most of them are connected with the preservation of chastity and an unwavering faith in God's providence. The precious robe thus has a vital function and its description is completely integrated into the poem. By its symbolic implications, the exceptional character of the heroine is even more stressed and she comes very near to being a kind of secularized Saint, the incorporation of chastity and constant faith, and her

story shows the glorious survival of Christian virtue in all afflic-
tion. Like the beautiful robe, Emaré's exemplary character has
remained to the end 'bryght and shene' (l. 933).

### 'LE BONE FLORENCE OF ROME'

This poem, too, the longest of the homiletic romances (2187 lines),
represents an interesting combination of romantic and religious
elements. It is only preserved in one manuscript (Cambridge Ff.
II. 38) where it is placed among a group of partly adventurous and
partly edifying stories, between *Guy of Warwick* and *Robert of
Sicily*. The work was probably composed towards the end of the
fourteenth century and, like *Emaré*, it belongs to the East Mid-
land tail-rhyme romances.[30]

*Le Bone Florence of Rome* derives, like *Sir Ysumbras*, from a
legend which was known all over Europe and of which many
different versions existed, the Crescentia-legend. The source of the
English poem was probably a French version, closely related to the
extant novel *Florence de Rome*;[31] the English adapter seems to have
abridged it considerably and he has produced a version that shows
a remarkable degree of independence. A comparison with the
extant French versions reveals that the poet has eliminated or re-
interpreted quite a number of rather phantastic and miraculous
incidents and stressed the legendary and morally edifying aspects
of the story.

It seems, however, that he was not very clear in his mind as to
what kind of tale he really wanted to write. In reading the poem we
get the impression that he set out to compose a rather burlesque
and humorous adventure-story and that it was only in the course
of his work that he realized the homiletic possibilities inherent in
his material. This can be illustrated by a brief glance at the different
treatment of the same story in *The King of Tars*.[32] In the latter
poem, there is no doubt that it is a war between Christians and
heathens that is described, and the refusal of the King's daughter
to marry the Sultan is not based on any personal dislike, but on his
different faith. When she realizes how much sorrow is brought on
her country because of her steadfastness, she decides to accept the
proposal, even against the wishes of her parents. In *Le Bone
Florence of Rome*, however, this opportunity of giving a Christian
interpretation to the story has not been exploited. We are not even

told in so many words whether the old Garcy is a Christian or not and there is certainly no crusading spirit. Instead, it seems at first as if we are about to hear a *fabliau*, like that of January and May.[33] Garcy's old age and his rather decrepit state are described with merciless realism (ll. 94 ff.) and his wooing of Florence has a very comic aspect. He needs a wife to warm his cold limbs, and the poet comments sarcastically that he would have been better served with a bright fire, a good bath and a warm bed (ll. 97 ff.) than with a young maiden, nor do the messengers, when delivering his proposal, make any attempt to conceal what it is she is wanted for:

> He byddyth wyth owte avysement
> That þy doghtur be to hym sent
> For to lygg hym by
> Hys body ys bresyd hys bones are olde
> That sche may kepe hym fro þe colde
> Haue done now hastelye (ll. 205–10)

Her answer to his proposal is not an expression of Christian constancy, as in *The King of Tars*, but of a young girl's understandable abhorrence of such an unequal union. Again, her words reveal quite a humorous sense of reality:

> And sche seyde Jhesu for bede
> Sche seyde be god þat boght me dere
> Me had leuyr þe warste bachylere
> Jn all my Fadurs thede
> Then for to lye be hys bresyd boones
> When he coghyth and oldely grones
> J can not on hys lede (ll. 243–9)

The tone of this beginning stands in marked contrast to the following parts of the story. When Garcy moves towards Rome with an enormous army, the girl begins to realize the disastrous consequences of her refusal and she offers to go out and marry old Garcy:

> Allas seyde that maydyn clere
> Whedur all þe ȝonde folke and þere
> Schoulde dye for my sake
> And y but a sympull woman
> The terys on hur chekys ranne
> Hur ble be ganne to blake
> Put me owt to olde Garcy
> Yf all þes men schulde for me dye
> Hyt were a dolefull wrake (ll. 574–82)

141

Her father, however, refuses to let her go, and a murderous battle ensues. After the defeat of Garcy, the more legendary part of the romance begins, with the extended trials of Florence, until at the end of the poem she returns to Rome in triumph and is finally reunited with Emere. Thus the poem clearly falls into two parts. The first part describes the wars with Garcy up to his being taken prisoner by Emere (ll. 1–1265), whereas the second part is entirely devoted to the sufferings of Florence and her miraculous preservation in the midst of all temptation and persecution. Near the beginning of the second part, there is a brief summary of part of the story (ll. 1330 ff.) which perhaps suggests that the poem could be read in two instalments.

The beginning of the poem shows that Florence does not bring all her sufferings on herself by a positive Christian decision, like Emaré or the daughter of the King of Tars, but that she is presented as a victim of outward circumstances and, in particular, of her beauty. What makes her an exemplary figure, and indeed almost a Saint, is her patience and her trust in God, but especially her firmness in the face of all threats to her chastity. Whereas her first refusal to marry Garcy cannot be explained by any very exalted motives, all her later trials are seen as a consequence of her faithfulness towards Emere, her husband:

> Sche had leuyr to haue be dedd
> Then þere to haue loste hur maydyn hedd    (ll. 1867–8)

This applies to the whole of her story. Wherever Florence goes, she awakens the sinful appetite of wicked men which turns into violent hate when she resists them. The deeper her sufferings, the clearer her chastity and constancy assert themselves and the more manifest the divine protection of her virtue becomes, until indeed at the end of the story, she resembles more a Saint than an earthly Empress. Her beauty, like that of Emaré, has something celestial about it. Thus the knight whom she has rebuffed in a very forceful manner, says as part of his wicked accusation that her unearthly beauty alone was a sign that she must be 'some false fende of helle' (l. 1669). When she rides through the forest it begins to shine (ll. 1708–9) and on board the ship all the men fall in love with her immediately (ll. 1828–33; see also ll. 1568–72). The state of true sanctity seems to be reached, however, when after the shipwreck she comes to a lonely monastery; at her approach, all the bells begin to ring 'þorow godys grace / Wyth owten helpe of hande' (ll. 1892–3) and miracles begin to happen through her presence so that her fame spreads far and wide. After that, it seems rather an anti-climax and a return into the less saintly world of romance when the 'holy nonne' (l. 1981) goes back to Rome to be united with Emere and to begin a life of secular wealth and happiness.

The legendary character of the story is also underlined by frequent forebodings which bring out the uniqueness of the heroine. From her birth she is destined to suffer great unhappiness and to be the innocent cause of sufferings to many others (ll. 67–9), and in the course of the action the narrator repeatedly gives warning of more woe and mischief (cf. ll. 367–9, 715–17, 1280–1, 1596, 1622–3, 1629, 1743). Such prophetic hints are much rarer in the majority of similar tales. The author does not, however, imply that Florence's sufferings are intended as a divine trial, but he lays particular emphasis on the idea of God's justice which punishes the wicked and preserves the faithful. This is, of course, particularly evident in the miracles by means of which God directly intervenes in the action of the poem to preserve and glorify the heroine. As the poet says in one place referring to his source:

> The boke seyþ god þat vs boght
> Many myrakyls for hur he wroght
> Many a con and thyck folde           (ll. 871–3)

Most important for her are the three miracles by which her chastity is preserved. Twice her prayer saves her from the advances of Milon. By the grace of God his wicked desire suddenly disappears and he lets go of her (ll. 1438–44 and 1496–1500). More elaborate is the description of her miraculous escape from the brutality of the captain of the boat who has bought her. Again it is her faith in God and her earnest prayer that save her:

> Sche seyde lady mary free
> Now thou haue mercy on me
> Thou faylyst me neuyr at nede
> Here my errande as þou well may
> That y take no schame to day
> Nor lose my maydyn hede           (ll. 1852–7)

At once a violent storm breaks out and the ship sinks, only Florence and the captain surviving. The story reaches a climax when all the four men who have injured her are stricken with repellent diseases and come to the monastery to be healed by her. Their public confession of all their attempts to inflict harm on Florence is a further demonstration of the justice of God, and the realistic description of their pains and their symptoms serves as a warning example (ll. 2020 ff.) and stresses the contrast between divine reward and punishment. This aspect of the story is also singled out in the last stanza of the poem where it appears as a rather simple moral:

> For þy schulde men and women als
> Them be thynke or þey be false
> Hyt makyth so fowle an ende
> Be hyt neuyr so slylylye caste
> 3yt hyt schamyþ þe maystyr at þe laste
> Jn what londe þat euyr þey lende
> J meene be thes IIIJ fekyll
> That harmed feyre florence so mykyll
> The trewest that men kende
> And þus endyth þys Romance gode
> Jhesu that boght vs on the rode
> Vn to hys blysse vs sende (ll. 2176–87)

By several minor changes and additions the English adapter has underlined the religious character of his tale which he claims was composed by the Pope Simon (l. 2173). The Pope is mentioned several times and he takes an active part in the story by absolving Egravayne from the oath he has sworn to the traitors (ll. 1111 ff., 1360 ff.). At the end of the story Florence is welcomed back to Rome by a solemn procession of the Pope and his Cardinals who praise God for her preservation (ll. 2143–51). Other additions of the English poet are the brief description of the painting in the Emperor's palace representing the Seven Deadly Sins (ll. 329–33), the references to the doctrine of transubstantiation (ll. 1004–5, 1099–1101), and the mention of St. Hilary's day (ll. 1894–6).

As in the French poem, the history of Florence is closely bound up with the fate of Rome. At her Christening, there are sinister portents which foreshadow the tribulations that will come over the town because of her (ll. 40–54). Her beauty nearly leads to the destruction of Rome, but God intervenes and sends the two sons of the Hungarian King. Florence at once realizes that this is a sign of divine providence (ll. 481–9). When at the end the poem is described as part of the 'Cronykyls of Rome' (l. 2174), this might originally be due to a simple misunderstanding or refer to an early version of the *Gesta Romanorum*, but the connection between Florence and the history of Rome is very appropriate in the English poem and was probably understood very literally by the English adapter. Thus at the beginning of the story, there is a brief description of Troy and of the founding of Rome (a kind of second Troy), which was to become the 'chefe Cyte of Crystendome' (l. 17). This also explains the detailed account of Garcy's messenger who is deeply impressed by the greatness of Rome (ll. 310–45); it is important as an eloquent eulogy of the town from the mouth of an enemy and as a description of the power Garcy wants to fight against. When he has been defeated in battle, his own knights reproach him for starting such an adventure to satisfy his pride (ll. 1210–21). It is a humorous reference to the same theme of Rome's greatness when Emere tells Garcy whom he has taken prisoner that now he will have an opportunity of seeing the town from within (ll. 1238–41). On the whole, however, the exemplary fate of the heroine is more important for the author than the history of Rome, and the historical background is mainly used by him to give more weight to the moral and religious aspects of the story.

Although by the end of the poem it has become very clear that the fate of Florence is related mainly for a homiletic purpose, the author sometimes seems to have lost sight of his aim, or at least have felt that he had to embellish the story with entertaining incidents. Thus *Le Bone Florence of Rome* offers a much greater variety of incident and of mood than, for instance, *Emaré* and the influence of more romantic tales is more noticeable. The realism of the poet which often stresses the exemplary character of the tale, as in the description of Florence's persecutors, is also used to less edifying purposes, particularly during the first part of the poem, the wooing of Garcy, which, as we have seen, has more in common with a *fabliau* than with a legend. The author clearly enjoys a good fight; he tells us that in the heat of the battle heads fell down to the ground ('hopped vndur hors fete') like hailstones in the streets (ll. 640–1) and a little later he comments excitedly, 'Gode olde fyghtyng was there' (l. 681). There is also the traditional reference to the rewards given to minstrels (ll. 2155–7), and the noble rank of Florence is proved by her generous gifts to the messenger who told her about the defeat of Garcy (ll. 1265-9). The death of the Emperor is lamented by his barons chiefly because of his liberality (ll. 838-43).[34] All this shows that the author was very familiar with the secular poetry of his time and that he tried to make his tale more interesting by such borrowings from the romances. This is, of course, not surprising if we bear in mind that *Le Bone Florence of Rome*, like *Emaré*, comes out of the school of the East Midlands tail-rhyme romances and could indeed have been written by the same author as some of the less homiletic tales. Our poem illustrates the juxtaposition of romance and legend particularly clearly because neither genre is completely subordinated to the other. The romantic elements, irrelevant to the moral purpose, heighten our interest in the story, but there is no doubt that the chief meaning, the 'message' of the poem, is expressed in the delight of all those who have seen the final reunion of Florence and Emere:

> They loouyd god wyth my3t and mayne
> That þe lady was comyn a gayne
> And kept hur chaste and clene (ll. 2161-3)

## 'ATHELSTON'

This short poem (it has only 812 lines) is an interesting example of how a certain theme, like that of sworn brotherhood, could not only be treated in the form of a romance but also more in the manner of a legend. In *Amis and Amiloun*, as we have seen, a particularly happy combination of the two genres was achieved, but on the whole, the poem had to be classed with the more romantic versions of the story. In *Athelston*, however, a poem that was probably very indebted to *Amis and Amiloun*,[35] the legendary elements are much more prominent and clearly relate the poem to the homiletic romances. The transmission, too, makes it probable that *Athelston* was considered to be a moral or religious tale by the scribe or collector of the manuscript (Gonville & Caius 175). It comes after a devotional poem (*Matutinas de cruce*), and the whole collection is rather more religious than secular, the only romances in it being *Richard Coeur de Lion* and *Beues of Hamtoun*. Another possible connection between the items is perhaps their Englishness.

Nearly all of them are based on native subjects. This combination of the religious and the traditional can be clearly seen in *Athelston* and is manifested, above all, in the reference to St. Edmund, the Saint of East-Anglia, and in the powerful figure of the Archbishop of Canterbury.

There are few poems in which localities are described in such detail, as is, for instance, the way from London to Canterbury (ll. 321–56), and in which native customs or historical features play such an important part (cf. the trial at the end or the interdict and its consequences, ll. 465 ff.). At the same time, the narrative technique of the poem is distinguished by a particular forcefulness and dramatic realism. As in *Amis and Amiloun*, there is a striking preference for vivid scenes and lively dialogue and very little summary. This is especially noticeable in the manner in which important messages are exchanged in this poem. The figure of the messenger has an important function in linking various episodes and localities. His ride to Canterbury is circumstantially described as well as his arrival there and his return to London. The argument about his dead horse (see ll. 384 ff. and 729 ff.) adds an entertaining detail to his journey and also gives greater prominence to his rôle in the poem.

The most important events are nearly always related in the form of dialogue, as can be seen in the meeting between the King and the traitor (ll. 91–180). Although the scene is not very long, it gives a vivid picture of the human situation. The indirect approach of the calumniator who presents his accusation, but at the same time tries to clear himself of all suspicion by claiming to be the friend of the accused and by pretending to give his treacherous information most unwillingly, and the violent reaction of the King whose blood rises so quickly that he is unable to think clearly, are brilliantly portrayed in the space of a few lines. The author's sense of the dramatic also comes out in his use of significant and often very emotional gestures: the King kicks his wife when she tries to plead for the accused Egeland (ll. 282–4); the Bishop breaks out in tears when he reads the letter from the Queen (ll. 366–8) and Egeland's children laugh in the fire (ll. 609–10).[36] Such gestures, though often only briefly indicated, heighten the narrative tempo and effectively accentuate the story. The poem is also enlivened by a simple but purposefully employed point-of-view technique which often helps to avoid clumsy transitions and prepares for new encounters. Thus the dramatic meeting between Athelston and the Archbishop is introduced quite naturally:

> And whene he hadde maad his prayer,
> He lokyd vp into þe qweer;
> þe erchebysschop sawȝ he stande.
> He was forwondryd off þat caas,
> And to hym he wente apas,
> And took hym be þe hande. (ll. 429–34)

The transitions made by the journeys of the messenger are also part of this technique (ll. 199 ff., 333 ff., 381 ff., 711 ff.).

In spite of the brevity of the poem then, the style is completely different from that of the ballads, it is truly epic, like that of most of the more successful shorter romances. Conciseness is not achieved at the expense of fully-drawn characters and a clearly defined setting, but by the tempo of the narrative and by the lack of descriptive detail. The shorter romances and the homiletic romances developed their own distinctive epic technique which can be seen at its best in *Athelston*.

The poem is also quite original in its use of the tail-rhyme stanza which often helps to bring out particular narrative effects. The author knew how to avoid monotony by skilful variation of the metre and of the sentence structure, especially in dialogue. The tail-line, which in many poems of this group tends to be a meaningless annex to the stanza, is more successfully integrated here and often contains an important piece of information or a surprising point. The flow of the narrative is thus much smoother and at the same time more varied than in many of the less interesting tail-rhyme poems.[37]

The dramatic art of the English poet is also revealed very impressively in his drawing of memorable and individualized characters. The portrayal of the King himself is perhaps least original. He seems completely unreasonable and has the simple credulity of some fairy-tale character. When his wrath has once been aroused he is inaccessible to any sensible argument, as the Queen and the Archbishop experience. He is, however, faithful to his promise when he refuses to reveal the name of the traitor and has to be forced by the spiritual authority of the Archbishop (ll. 663–98).

The Archbishop is even more violent, but he is above all moved by a desire for absolute justice. He imposes the highest ecclesiastical penalties on the King when he refuses to grant the accused Egeland a just trial (ll. 465 ff.) and he compels the King to name the traitor by most terrible threats. As soon as Athelston has revealed the name 'Be schryffte off mouþe' (l. 688), no regard for the confidential nature of such a confession hinders the Archbishop from arresting and convicting the traitor at once. There are not many romances in which such a powerful and unconventional character occurs. It seems quite likely that, as Trounce suggests, he was modelled on a contemporary Bishop (William Bateman), though this does not, of course, in any way detract from the originality of the poet.[38]

The traitor, too, is something more than the traditional villain of romance. He has a convincing motive for his hatred, the King's particular love for Egeland (ll. 73–84). The poet seems to have felt the importance of this motive, because after Wimound has been convicted, he is earnestly entreated to reveal the reason for his treachery. His simple answer, 'He louyd hym to mekyl and me to lyte' (l. 799), perhaps an allusion to the sin of Cain, makes him a much more convincing figure than many of the wicked stewards and mothers-in-law who cause so much innocent sorrow in the romances. This also gives more coherence to the whole action. There are few Middle English tales which are governed by human passions to this extent and are so full of dramatic tension from beginning to end.

Thus the action and the narrative technique contribute to the particularly close-knit structure which, above all, arises from the theme of the poem: sworn brotherhood and its absolutely binding power. In contrast to *Amis and Amiloun*, this theme is treated in a predominantly negative way. Whereas in *Amis and Amiloun*, friendship manifests itself in convincing deeds of love and sacrifice, we are told in *Athelston* of the disastrous consequences of any breach of loyalty and of the judgement which the traitor brings upon himself. On the other hand, the theme is widened by the inclusion of a whole group of friends. The poem demonstrates that sworn brotherhood between four men is just as binding as between two. The first consequence of the mutual agreement is that the King puts his brothers in high offices which all stand in some relation to each other. Two of them are given Earldoms on the way to Canterbury where the third brother reigns as Archbishop.

All the action takes place in this small and well-defined area and there is hardly any romantic embellishment, no love-story and no knightly exploits. Instead of some unidentifiable fairy-tale court, there is the Royal Court in Westminster. All this helps to bring out the exemplary character of the tale. Its chief subject, as the poet states it, is falsehood:

> Lord, þat is off myʒtys most,
> Fadyr and sone and holy gost,
> Bryng vs out off synne,
> And lene vs grace so for to wyrke,
> And loue boþe God and holy kyrke,
> þat we may heuene wynne.
> Lystnes, lordyngys þat ben hende,
> Off falsnesse, hou it wil ende
> A man þat ledes hym þerin.
> Off foure weddyd breþeryn I wole ʒow tel,
> þat wolden yn Yngelond go dwel,
> þat sybbe were nouʒt off kyn.                (ll. 1–12)

The story shows the endangering of this friendship by envy and lack of trust. Wimound breaks the friendship because he thinks himself unjustly treated. The narrator leaves us in no doubt as to who is the real villain of the piece (see ll. 131–2, 156, 180). He curses the traitor and he points the moral by explicit comment (ll. 294–6, 807–12). In this passionate indictment of all treason, the poem is clearly related to *Havelok*.[39]

However, the King too betrays a lack of understanding of the deeper significance of the bond by his ready belief in the brother's guilt and his quick decision to remove the Archbishop, who pleads for the brother and for justice, from office. There is thus a certain irony in the fact that the King's love which arouses the envy of the traitor, proves to be so inconstant.[40] The Archbishop, as the militant spokesman for justice and friendship, realizes that the unreasonable behaviour of the King violates the bond of brotherhood just as much as the calumny of Wimound and he stakes all his authority to help the unjustly accused. The fourth brother remains a more shadowy figure; his main function is to be the victim of falsehood and envy. Thus, all the episodes of the poem are strongly linked by the theme of friendship and the dramatic style helps to give greater force and concreteness to the moral.

The subject of sworn brotherhood is, in this poem, also related to the larger problem of the rival authorities of Church and State. In the quarrel between Athelston and Alryke it is not only the two estranged brothers who are confronted, but at the same time the highest representatives of earthly and spiritual power, and it seems likely that the author was reminded of similar clashes in English history, for instance that between Henry II and Thomas à Becket.[41] But the problem is not further pursued by the author, and the political conflict is seen mainly as a consequence of Wimound's falsehood which is the chief subject of the poem and which appears particularly sinful because it has such far-reaching repercussions. As in *Havelok*, the conclusion brings a return of order and just government. This happy ending has an exemplary force which is stressed by the important event of Egeland's wife giving birth to the later Saint Edmund in the same hour in which God proves her innocence (ll. 636–62). Athelston at once makes the child his heir, and the narrator praises the happy significance of that moment: 'Now iblessyd be þat stounde!' (l. 662). The symbolic implication of the end is supported by the fact that Athelston in his unjust wrath had killed his own heir, yet unborn, by kicking the Queen (ll. 282–93). This, too, was a consequence of Wimound's treachery:

> Ladyys and maydenys þat þere were,
> þe qwene to here chaumbyr bere,
> And þere was dool inowȝ.
> Soone withinne a lytyl spase
> A knaue-chyld iborn þer wase,
> As bryȝt as blosme on bowȝ.
> He was boþe whyt and red;
> Off þat dynt was he ded—
> Hys owne fadyr hym slowȝ.
> þus may a traytour baret rayse,
> And make manye men ful euele at ayse,
> Hymselff nouȝt afftyr it lowȝ.          (ll. 285–96)

With the birth of Saint Edmund this sin of Athelston is forgiven and the evil consequences of the treason are turned into blessings, but the poem ends with the evil fate of the traitor and a prayer for stern justice:

> Now Iesu, þat is heuene-kyng,
> Leue neuere traytour haue betere endyng,
> But swych dome for to dye.          (ll. 810–12)

On the whole then, this is hardly a political poem, but a didactic legend whose lively style and dramatic unity make it one of the most impressive of the homiletic romances.[42]

## 'THE SEGE OFF MELAYNE'

It has often been noticed that only a very limited selection of the stories about Charlemagne were ever translated into English. Many of the original *chansons de geste* were stamped by a very nationalistic tendency and were for this reason perhaps less attractive to the English adapters who often tried to glorify their own history. Thus, apart from a short fragment of the *Chanson de Roland* in English translation (Ms. Lansdowne 388), practically all the English Charlemagne romances centre round the figures of Otuel and Firumbras in whose story the strange fascination of the pagan world and the superiority of the Christian faith found a particularly memorable expression. It was, in fact, chiefly the militant and completely intolerant Christianity of the Charlemagne stories that interested the English adapters, and it seems very likely that most of the English versions are to attributed to clerical authors.[43] This may partly account for the considerable length of some. The romance *Sir Ferumbras*, which is preserved in the manuscript Ashmole 33, is evidently a bookish compilation, not a brief tale to be recited in one sitting, and the same applies to the poem *Firumbras* in the Fillingham Ms., a rather faithful translation,[44] whereas several of the Charlemagne romances are free adaptations which in size and style follow the shorter or the homiletic romances very closely.

Such brief versions of individual tales from the Charlemagne cycle are, as we have seen, as old as the Auchinleck Ms.[45] The close parallels between *The King of Tars* and *Otuel and Roland* show how much the English Charlemagne poems are adapted to the style of the homiletic romances. This applies particularly to the two poems *The Sege off Melayne* and *The Romance of Duke Rowlande and of Sir Ottuell of Spayne* preserved in the manuscript Additional 31.042 of the British Museum. They, too, belong to the tail-rhyme romances, and their editor, S. Herrtage, suggested that they might have been written by the same author as *Sir Perceval of Gales*.[46] None of the parallels he lists are, however, convincing as evidence of common authorship; on the other hand, there are undoubtedly some very near resemblances and it cannot be denied that these two poems have more in common with the homiletic tail-rhyme romances than with the English versions of the Firumbras story.

Of the two works, *The Sege off Melayne* is by far the more interesting, because it tells a story which does not occur in any of the French poems on Charlemagne and evidently originated in England. As in the tales about Otuel, the chief point of the episode described here seems to be the drastic demonstration of the superiority of the Christian faith. In spite of some initial setbacks, the Christian warriors are always victorious in the end, although not always due to their own greater strength and prowess, but to the direct intervention of God, who does not tolerate any blasphemy. This story-pattern gives a rather legendary character to the poem which is also stressed by several miracles, proving that the fight against the heathens is a holy war. The beginning of the poem puts the emphasis on Charles' fame as a killer of heathens:

> All werthy men that luffes to here
> Off cheuallry þat by fore vs were
> þat doughty weren of dede,
> Off charlles of Fraunce, þe heghe kinge of alle,
> þat ofte sythes made hethyn men for to falle,
> þat styffely satte one stede. (ll. 1–6)

The siege of Milan is an example of such a war: Alantyne refuses to save the town by abandoning his faith. God hears his earnest prayer (ll. 67–84) and sends a vision in a dream to Charles, ordering him to come to the rescue of Milan (ll. 109 ff.). Later in the story, when Roland and his companions have been taken prisoner, they are freed by a very picturesque miracle: the crucifix that the heathens want to burn fails to be consumed by the fire and blinds all the Saracens instead (ll. 421 ff.). The return of the knights is announced by the sudden ringing of all bells, a frequent miracle in the legends (ll. 514–19). Another miracle happens during the celebration of Holy Mass (bread and wine are sent from heaven, ll. 889–912) which confirms the sanctity of this war. That the slaughter of Saracens is pleasing to God also becomes clear in the vision of Richard of Normandy before his death (ll. 313 ff.) where he sees all the slain French knights being led to heaven by a host of angels. Turpin's indignant reproach of the squire who wants to spoil the dead body of one of the heathens (ll. 973 ff.) is obviously intended to show that the French fight only to the glory of God, not for any personal advantage. *The Sege off Melayne* is thus a true crusading poem, very much like *The King of Tars*, but also related to *Sir Eglamour* and *Torrent of Portyngale*.

Particularly striking is the unquestioned supremacy of the Church as represented in this poem. Bishop Turpin's priests are ready and armed for the march against Milan long before the King's barons (ll. 613–48), and the army of clerics leads the van in the first battle against the Saracens (ll. 925 ff.). The Bishop is Charlemagne's chief adviser (see ll. 601 ff. and 1167 ff.); he exhorts the Emperor to think of the Holy Virgin when he is threatened and tempted by a Saracen (ll. 1042 ff.); it is obviously he who is the driving force behind the whole expedition. The portrait of Turpin is perhaps the most remarkable contribution of the English adapter. There is hardly anything in the other English romances to compare with the passionate and domineering character of the Bishop. Not for him the meek and passive humility of many a romance-hero. When Roland returns defeated from his first encounter with the heathens, the Bishop's disappointment breaks out in a rather reproachful prayer to Mary, blaming her for the disaster:

> A! Mary mylde, whare was thi myght,
> þat þou lete thi men thus to dede be dighte,
> þat wighte & worthy were?
> Art þou noghte halden of myghtis moste,
> Full Conceyuede of þe holy goste?
> Me ferlys of thy fare.
>
> Had þou noghte, Marye, ȝitt bene borne
> Ne had noghte oure gud men thus bene lorne?
> þe wyte is all in the.
> Thay faughte holly in thy ryghte,
> þat þus with dole to dede es dyghte,
> A! Marie, how may this bee?'          (ll. 547–58)

This rather truculent attitude towards God whose duty is considered to be not to forsake his knights, is quite typical of the English Charlemagne romances, but nowhere is it expressed in such a dramatic manner as in this poem. The Bishop is so annoyed about the first success of the Saracens that he refuses to say 'Good morning' to the King (ll. 568–73) and later, during the battle, he makes a vow neither to eat nor drink before the taking of Milan (ll. 1189 ff.) although he nearly dies with exhaustion because of it (ll. 1339–56, 1579–93). His irascible nature reveals itself with particular force in his conflict with Charles at whom, in an impassioned speech, he throws the most violent accusations because he hesitates to march against the Saracens. He calls the King a heretic, worse than any Saracen, and solemnly excommunicates him (ll. 679–708). The Bishop even proceeds to assemble his clerics and march against Paris until the King yields and asks his forgiveness.

The King is on the whole a rather weak representative of earthly power and reminds one of some similarly unflattering and critical portraits of King Arthur found in Middle English. How limited his authority over his barons and knights is, comes out clearly in the scene in which he needs a messenger to go to France and tries to persuade several of his knights who all refuse him until Barnard at last agrees to go, on condition that he is first knighted (ll. 1366 ff.). Charlemagne's lack of firmness and real authority are also exposed by his unsuspicious acceptance of the wicked advice of the traitor Ganelon (ll. 169 ff. and 649 ff.) and by his impotent raging against Turpin (ll. 709 ff.) which only makes his humiliation more complete. The scene in which the King humbles himself before the Bishop is strongly reminiscent of *Athelston* and, like the whole episode, illustrates impressively the superiority of spiritual over earthly power in this war.[47] The dramatic argument about the question whether the King should act upon his divine vision and go to the rescue of Milan also brings home the fact that the war between Christians and heathens is the real subject of the poem. Ganelon turns traitor because he puts his personal interest before the common cause.

The quick movement of the action is supported by a very forceful and robust narrative style, by the short and vivid scenes and by the dramatic dialogue as well as by the genuine involvement of the narrator who passionately sides with the Christians (cf. ll. 289, 348, 945) and proudly calls their army 'oure Cristen men'.[48] The following passage is typical of the militant and committed tone of the narration:

> We may thanke gode þat is in heuen
> þat lent vs myghte & mayne.

Thay sloughe þam downn with swerdis bright
þe Cristynnes faughte in goddis righte,
þe Bischoppe loughe for fayne.     (ll. 1100-1104)

By several prophetic hints, too, the narrator betrays his personal
interest in the story (ll. 178–80, 196–8, 223–5, 490–2). On the
whole though, the poem contains less formulas by which the
narrator draws attention to his own person than many other tail-
rhyme romances, but the beginning of *Rowlande and Ottuell* shows
that both these tales were written to be recited before a group of
listeners and that the author tried to create an atmosphere of
minstrelsy and romance:

Lordynges, þat bene hende and Free,
Herkyns alle hedir-wardes to mee,
Gif þat it be ȝour will.
Now lates alle ȝour noyse be,
And herkyns nowe of gamen & glee,
þat I schall tell ȝow till.
Of doghety men I schall ȝow telle,
þat were full fayre of flesche & fell,
And Semely appon Sille.
And with þaire wapyns wele couthe melle,
And boldly durste in batell duelle,
And doghety proued one hill.     (ll. 1–12)

Both poems are less concerned with the glorification of a particular
hero or Saint than with an exemplary story; although Turpin in
*The Sege off Melayne* and Roland in some other poems are presented as models of Christian warriors, it is not their biography
that is the prime interest in the Charlemagne-romances,[49] but the
irreconcilable conflict between Christianity and all other religions,
and the indisputable superiority of God. Thus the romantic story-
material is, as far as this had not already been done in the French
sources, given a strictly religious interpretation and is often embellished in the manner of Saints' legends. This is why the shorter
English Charlemagne romances are of the same type as the other
homiletic romances discussed in this chapter.[50]

### 'CHEUELERE ASSIGNE'

The tale of the swan-knight is another characteristic example of the
English adapters' tendency to extract single episodes from longer

novels and make them into independent romances. It is a résumé of the first eleven hundred lines of a French novel, about six times as long.[51] The episode is quite self-contained and dramatically coherent. The English adapter has tied up a few loose ends, but apart from that he has left the story more or less unchanged. Nevertheless, its character is completely altered by its amputation from the novel. The French poem is mainly concerned with the family-history of Godfrey of Bouillon, and the episode of the swan-knight is only one of several remarkable adventures of his ancestors. The English poem practically disregards this genealogical framework. It describes the birth of the children and the rescue of the mother, who was innocently sentenced to death, only as an example of the grace of God who upholds justice and protects the helpless. Thus the poem belongs to the homiletic romances, like *Emaré* with which it is preserved together in the collection Cotton Caligula A. II. Its position between *Sir Ysumbras* and *The Siege of Jerusalem* allows the conclusion that the compilers considered it a legendary and edifying poem rather than a romance. The motif of the wicked mother who without any apparent reason, persecutes the wife of her son, is reminiscent of tales of the Constance-type (like *Emaré*), but it is even more obviously interpreted in terms of a religious legend. God intervenes directly on behalf of the innocent by sending an angel to the foster-father of her supposedly dead son (ll. 191 ff.).

The knight himself is only portrayed as the instrument of God's grace, not as the hero of the whole story, which thus cannot be described as a 'romance of prys'. He grows up, like young Perceval, far from all courtly arts and manners, but again the treatment of this motif illustrates the completely different intention of the author of *Cheuelere Assigne*. In *Sir Perceval of Gales*, the ignorance of the knight contrasts effectively with his natural prowess that enables him to perform wonders even without the benefits of a courtly education. Here, however, a religious miracle happens: the ignorant youth who has never in his life before watched a fight, is instructed by an experienced knight in all the rudiments of armed combat within the space of a few moments (ll. 287 ff.) and after this brief prompting he is at once ready to meet the sinister Malkedras in single fight. That the twelve-year-old defeats the practised warrior after a short encounter is not so much due to his superior valour and strength, but to the justice of his cause and the intervention of God by another miracle: during the fight a snake darts out from the cross on Enyas' shield and blinds Malkedras who has spoken blasphemously of the crucifix (1. 329). The scene is very much like some similarly unequal encounters in the Charlemagne romances where victory is always granted to the faithful. The religious, almost ritual character of the duel is also underlined by the miraculous ringing of all bells (ll. 272–4), as in *The Sege off Melayne*.

In spite of the different metre (the poem is written in alliterative long-lines), *Cheuelere Assigne* belongs with the homiletic tales from the East Midlands with which in language and style it has far more in common than with the alliterative poems from the West and the North. Whether the original version of the poem was a product of the 'alliterative revival', cannot, however, be definitely ascertained.[52] Since the tail-rhyme poems frequently contain alliterative formulas, the connection between the various 'schools' was probably closer than is often suspected and it is not advisable to overemphasize the differences between alliterative and rhyming romances. In its present form, at any rate, *Cheuelere Assigne* is one of the homiletic romances, although it has undergone a slightly different development than, say, *Emaré* and does not present such a popular and minstrel-like appearance as most of the tail-rhyme romances.[53]

# 6

# THE LONGER ROMANCES

Between the shorter romances and the extensive novels in verse there are a number of poems of a medium size which, perhaps, have not so much in common with each other that they can be treated as a distinctive group, but which all attempt (each in its own way) to present a more extensive yet strictly unified kind of romantic tale, not a brief episode, nor a comprehensive compilation. It is worth noting that only a comparatively small number of such romances from the thirteenth and fourteenth centuries are extant and this confirms the assumption that the shorter tale which could be read in one sitting and the additive, less unified compilation were more or less clearly defined types which had proved useful and generally served as models for most adapters. Neither does any of the works discussed in this chapter seem to have enjoyed particular popularity because none has survived in more than one manuscript.[1]

Most of these romances—*Sir Gawain and the Green Knight* is an exception in this as in many other respects—are condensed versions of long and complex stories, but these have not, as in the shorter romances, been simplified and subordinated to a definite theme, but are retold in some detail and without substantial omissions. This applies not only to the English version of the Tristan-saga, the rather badly preserved *Sir Tristrem*, but also to the far more carefully constructed poems *Ywain and Gawain* and *Le Morte Arthur*. All these poems are characterized by a wealth of incident and detail that is usually found only in much more extensive works.

Another feature these longer romances have in common is that they try to keep alive the memory of heroic deeds from the English past and to hold up former ages to the present as models of prowess and loyalty, as can be seen from the introductions of *Havelok*, *Ywain and Gawain, Le Morte Arthur* and *Sir Gawain and the Green Knight.* Thus, most of these poems take their story-material from the *matière de Bretagne*, that is from Arthurian literature, and they usually emphasize native elements and the bearing of the events on the present. With the exception of *Havelok*, all the longer romances come from the North of England where oral traditions were kept alive longer and were preserved more carefully than in the South. The didactic and religious tendency is also far less obtrusive in these poems than in the shorter or the homiletic romances. The story is often told in a detached manner which could at first sight be interpreted as moral indifference, but only reveals the authors' intention of presenting their material as faithfully as possible and to leave the moral application to the hearer. None of the longer romances—except, perhaps, *Sir Gawain and the Green Knight*—could be described as courtly in the strict sense of the word, but the aristocratic and courtly elements in the stories are usually much better preserved in them than in the more popular and edifying shorter poems. They were probably written for listeners who had more than a passing acquaintance with aristocratic ways of life and who were particularly interested in their own past. It is reasonable to assume that such an audience could be found especially on the large aristocratic estates in the North of England.

The transmission is, unfortunately, of little help in this matter, because all the longer romances must have passed through several hands before they found their way into the manuscripts we know. This is particularly striking in the case of *Sir Tristrem* because the Auchinleck Ms. in which the poem is preserved, was probably written in London and catered for quite a different audience from that of the original poem. The extant text of *Ywain and Gawain* is somewhat closer to the original, but here, too, there are remarkable differences between the dialect of the manuscript (Cotton Galba E. IX) and that in which the poem was presumably first composed.[2] The carefully written manuscript contains for the most part religious and political poems (e.g. *The Pricke of Conscience, The Seven Sages of Rome* and poems of Lawrence Minot) and it seems clear that *Ywain and Gawain* was included more for its historical and moral content than for its merits as a romance. The 'commonplace book' which preserves *Le Morte Arthur* (Harley 2252) and was jotted down during the sixteenth century in London, admits of even less definite conclusions as to the provenance and purpose of the original poem.[3] Only the *Gawain* manuscript (Cotton Nero A. X) reproduces the original dialect of the poem quite faithfully and was probably written not long after the composition of *Sir Gawain and the Green Knight*.[4] For all we know, it might even be an autograph, though this is not very likely. Here again it is tempting to surmise that the poem was included in the collection mainly on the strength of its religious and ethical meaning, not as a romance. The unity of tone and dialect distinguishes this manuscript strikingly from the majority of Middle English romance-collections. The theory, held by several scholars, that it was written down by some cleric for one of the aristocratic households in the North-West of England would account for the individual character of the manuscript, but there is no conclusive proof. It can be said, however, that with the exception of *Sir Tristrem*, the transmission of the longer romances puts them somewhat apart from the main-stream of the more popular shorter poems and from the novels in verse.

On the whole, then, the longer romances have at least some superficial features in common. They are perhaps nearest to some of the more Northern tail-rhyme romances, like *Sir Perceval of Gales, Sir Degrevant* and *The Avowynge of King Arther*, but as a group they are distinguished from the shorter romances by more than just their size and can with some justification be classed together, although, I should like to repeat, I do not claim that they form a very distinctive and clearly definable literary type. A closer examination of the individual poems will perhaps clarify these introductory remarks and throw some light on the similarities as well as the considerable differences between the longer romances.

### 'HAVELOK THE DANE'

It seems at first sight as if *Havelok the Dane* and *King Horn* are only slightly different variations of the same type of tale and they are therefore often grouped together in literary histories. They are both among the earliest Middle English romances, are preserved side by side in the same manuscript (Laud Misc. 108), and have several story-motifs in common. On closer inspection, however, it appears that in structure, theme and narrative technique the two poems are very different from each other and this is why they are discussed in different chapters here. *King Horn* is obviously the condensed version of a story which, as the Anglo-Norman version shows, could be treated equally well in the form of a long novel, whereas *Havelok* seems to be by far the longest of all the early versions of the saga; the two French versions are both much shorter.[5] For once it was the English adapter who deliberately embellished his story-material and made something like a brief novel out of it.

The author's tendency to expand the story and to slow down the narrative tempo can be seen in the description of individual episodes as well as in the structure of the whole poem. One of the first things that strike the reader of this poem is the extensive use of direct speech even where the action does not demand dialogue, and brief summary might be thought to fulfil the same purpose. The author's preference for direct speech is apparent in his use of dramatic dialogue, like the vivid scene between Godard and Grim (ll. 663–90) in which Grim is told that his services will not be rewarded, in several revealing soliloquies, like that of Godard (ll. 507–22) in which he reasons with himself as to whether he should let Havelok live (see also Godrich's similar monologue, ll. 291–311), and, particularly, in formal orations, addressing some larger assembly, as the dying speeches of Athelwold and Birkabeyn (ll. 166–75 and 384–96) and Ubbe's long address to the Danes (ll. 2204–51; see also Godrich's speech to his knights, ll. 2576–2605). Ubbe's account is also an example of the frequent use of recapitulation in this poem. Some important parts of the plot are thus deliberately impressed on the memory of the hearers. Other instances are Havelok's prayer (ll. 1359–84) and his address to Grim's children (ll. 1400–44). It is possible that such recapitulations were inserted with particular regard to the situation in which the poem would be read and that they were meant as a help to newcomers or less attentive listeners, but this is only a fanciful surmise. At any rate, the technique clearly contributes to an accentuation of the story and to the epic quality of the poem. The use of recapitulation is also related to the device of parallelism in the structure of the plot to which I shall return and it clearly shows that the poem, despite its apparently simple structure, was carefully planned and designed.

Apart from his preference for long speeches, the author of

*Havelok* devoted particular artistry to the description of often brief, but vivid scenes. Not only the more important stages of the story, the two death-scenes at the beginning, Havelok's marriage and the raid on Barnard's house are depicted in some detail, but also less decisive events are presented in the form of colourful scenes, like Havelok's successful attempt to earn his keep as a porter (ll. 863 ff.). Some scenes are given a particularly dramatic and at the same time spatial quality by the immediate reaction of one of the characters, as when Havelok has to watch the slaughter of his two sisters:

> þer was sorwe, hwo so it sawe,
> Hwan þe children bi þe wawe
> Leyen and sprauleden in þe blod:
> Hauelok it saw, and þer-bi stod.
> Ful sori was þat seli knaue,
> Mikel dred he mouhte haue;
> For at hise herte he saw a knif,
> For to reuen him hise lyf.                    (ll. 473–80)

Havelok's horror and fear are effectively portrayed and the scene gives a vivid picture of the injury done to the young prince. Twice in the course of the action Havelok recalls the scene in very similar words (ll. 1364–8 and ll. 1411–16) as a concrete image of his sufferings.

The three miraculous lights by which Havelok's royal birth is disclosed, are also described in the way they appear to the beholders. The effect of the miracles on those around the prince helps to focus our attention on the hero and his exceptional fate and at the same time contributes to the development of the action. The first miracle saves Havelok's life and provides him with an invaluable ally (ll. 586 ff.); the second reveals to Goldeboru that her husband, like herself, is of royal blood and thus the two strands of the action are finally united (ll. 1247 ff.); the third convinces Ubbe, and he and his men do homage to Havelok who can now regain his inheritance (ll. 2092 ff.). This is not a case of simple repetition, as in some other romances, but an obvious attempt to give more shape to the story and to bring out the central theme of the poem. The three scenes also show that the author was not at all concerned with condensing his story, but aimed at a certain breadth in the narrative and made use of the time-honoured devices of the epic poet, parallelism and repetition. Thus the events

163

do not pass swiftly before the reader's eyes, as, for instance, in *King Horn*, but there is a carefully designed dramatic development and a deliberately graded sequence of episodes building up the tension towards the final climax.

Another way of embellishing the story, frequently found in *Havelok*, is the elaborate description of situations and events, enriching the action with apparently superfluous detail. This is another point of difference between this poem and *King Horn* where the rapid flow of the narrative allows of no pauses. It is interesting to see that all the more extensive descriptions in *Havelok* refer to rather homely and uncourtly subjects. In one place where there would have been an opportunity of enlarging on a more courtly entertainment, the poet passes it over with a revealing *occupatio*:

> Of þe mete forto telle,
> Ne of þe win bidde i nouht dwelle;
> þat is þe storie for to lenge,
> It wolde anuye þis fayre genge.     (ll. 1732–5)

This does not at all mean, however, that the style of the poem is simple and artless. Though the subjects described are often ordinary enough, the method of description clearly betrays the poet's familiarity with the art of rhetoric. Impressive instances are the picture of an ideal commonwealth under Athelwold (ll. 27–105), the feast of Havelok's knighting (ll. 2266–353), or the elaborate catalogue of Grim's prey:

> Grim was fishere swiþe god,
> And mikel couþe on the flod;
> Mani god fish þer-inne he tok,
> Boþe with net, and ek with hok.
> He tok þe sturgiun, and þe qual,
> And þe turbut, and lax with-al,
> He tok þe sele, and ek þe el;
> He spedde ofte swiþe wel:
> Keling he tok, and tumberel,
> Hering, and þe makerel,
> þe butte, þe schulle, þe þornbake:     (ll. 749–59)

The modern reader is inclined to notice here above all the 'realistic' detail which is indeed remarkable, but such descriptions are at the same time rhetorical devices and products of a very conscious art. Their homely content does in no way detract from their literary character. Indeed, it is this remarkable mixture of an ornamented style and very plain subject-matter that makes *Havelok* such an intriguing poem. Notwithstanding many statements to the contrary, the style of the poem is anything but 'popular'; it reveals an astonishing degree of sophistication, although the poet is clearly anxious to achieve popular appeal. The descriptions are not arbitrary digressions or signs of garrulousness, but are indispensable to the unassuming and yet ceremonious tone of the poem and have an important function in the whole design. Thus the rhymed tirade on Athelwold's government, which at first sight seems only an elaborate but slightly irrelevant rhetorical set-piece, is, as we shall see, a vital part of the exposition of the theme (ll. 87–105).

The poet's thorough acquaintance with rhetorical devices can be seen not only in his use of description, but throughout the poem. There is abundant use of alliteration, anaphora, formulaic patterns, and other comparatively simple ornaments of style, belonging with the *ornatus facilis*.[6] Often such repetitions sound like the primitive mannerisms of an oral style, and this may in some cases be true, but they also belong to a rhetorical tradition and show a degree of conscious artistry which accords very little with the picture, often drawn, of a popular minstrel entertaining a group of illiterate peasants in a market-place or a tavern.

A particularly elaborate passage, illustrating various stylistic devices, is the speech in which Grim's children express their homage to Havelok:

> 'Welkome, louerd dere!
> And welkome be þi fayre fere!
> Blessed be þat ilke þrawe
> þat þou hire toke in Godes lawe!
> Wel is us we sen þe on lyue,
> þou maght us boþe selle and yeue;
> þou maght us hoþe yeue and selle,
> With-þat þou wilt here dwelle.
> We hauen, louerd, alle gode,
> Hors, and net, and ship on flode,
> Gold, and siluer, and michel auhte,
> þat Grim ure fader us bitawhte.
> Gold, and siluer, and oþer fe
> Bad he us bi-taken þe.
> We hauen shep, we hauen swin,
> Bi-leue her, louerd, and al be þin!

> þou shalt ben louerd, þou shalt ben syre,
> And we sholen seruen þe and hire;
> And ure sistres sholen do
> Al that euere biddes sho;
> He sholen hire cloþes washen and wringen,
> And to hondes water bringen;
> He sholen bedden hire and þe,
> For leuedi wile we þat she be.'  (ll. 1213–36)

Only ignorance of medieval rhetorical traditions could lead one to mistake this highly stylized rhetoric for the primitive product of an unlearned minstrel. Undoubtedly, the poet knew that such simple patterns would be particularly effective in recitation, but this applies, with varying degrees of sophistication, to all medieval rhetoric. The fact that he mainly uses rather uncomplicated *colores* does not necessarily mean that he was unfamiliar with more sophisticated language or that he did not know what he was doing. He evidently aimed at suiting his style to the story and to his audience. This can also be seen from his particularly vivid comparisons which often give picturesque glimpses of everyday experience and never take their material from the world of courtly refinement. Thus, the thieves that invade Bernard's house are soundly beaten:

> He maden here backes al-so bloute
> Als here wombes, and made hem rowte
> Als he weren kradelbarnes:
> So dos þe child þat moder þarnes.  (ll. 1910–13)

Of the bright cross that appears miraculously on Havelok's back during the night, we are told:

> It sparkede, and ful brihte shon
> So doth þe gode charbucle-ston,
> þat men se mouhte, by þe liht,
> A peni chesen, so it was briht.  (ll. 2144–7)[7]

There is no doubt that the poem is addressed not to a courtly, but to a middle-class audience, with the intention of appealing to a great variety of tastes. There is no indication in the text, however, that illiterate peasants or labourers were the chief listeners, and from the little we know about the living-conditions of those people, this appears very unlikely. It can safely be assumed that 'a cuppe of ful god ale' which the narrator asks for at the beginning (l. 14) was available not only in a market-place or a tavern, but in any bourgeois household throughout the country. We cannot tell, of course, whether the author had a more extensive knowledge of courtly manners or not, but it is clear that he did not want to give detailed descriptions of things his audience would not be interested in and that he made a very conscious effort to popularize his material. This is why we get circumstantial accounts of Grim's fishing, Havelok's endeavours to find a job for himself, his extra-ordinary feats at the country games and his heroic thrashing of the thieves. The poem is rich in descriptions of native or even local customs, like the popular games (ll. 980 ff., 1007 ff., 2320 ff.), the table-manners (ll. 1722 ff.), the wedding-ceremony (ll. 1169 ff.) and the gruesome details of the traitor's execution (ll. 2488 ff.). Another mark of this deliberately popular style is the great number of proverbial expressions and generalizing aphorisms (see, for instance, ll. 307, 600, 1338, 1352, 1693, 1712–3, 2461, 2813, 2983). By such expressions of popular wisdom rather than by direct moralizing, the author draws attention to the general applicability of his story. There is no doubt that he was familiar with the life and the customs of his audience.

Another device to heighten the effect of the poem in recitation is the emphasis on the rôle of the narrator as an intermediary be-tween the story and the audience. In *Havelok*, this is more con-sistently employed than in most other English romances. Thus, the prologue is particularly extensive, and it has been suggested that it was interpolated,[8] but there is no need for this assumption, because the first 26 lines of the poem successfully evoke an atmos-phere of conviviality and establish a certain personal contact be-tween the narrator and the audience. Often in the course of the story, the narrator intrudes in order to show his personal involve-ment in it. In most cases he makes use of traditional formulas, such as can be found in many romances and in Old French epic liter-ature, but they are here employed with particular gusto and with an assured sense of dramatic effect. Very striking are the repeated curses on the two traitors, Godard and Godrich (e.g. ll. 422–36, 446, 542–4, 1100–2, 1157–8, 2447, 2511), which also emphasize the partiality of the narrator. In one passage, the brief curse is ex-tended into a rhetorical incantation:

þanne Godard was sikerlike
Vnder God þe moste swike,

> þat eure in erþe shaped was,
> With-uten on, þe wike Iudas.
> Haue he þe malisun to-day
> Of alle þat eure speken may!
> Of patriarke, and of pope,
> And of prest with loken kope,
> Of monekes and hermites boþe! . . .
> And of þe leue holi rode
> (þar) God him-selue ran on blode!
> Crist him warie with his mouth!
> Waried wurthe he of norþ and suþ!
> Of alle men, þat speken kunne,
> Of Crist, þat made mone and sunne!　　　(ll. 422–36)

Sometimes such malediction is combined with a prayer for one of the main characters, as in the passage quoted in Chapter 1 above (p. 27, ll. 331–7), or in the short prayer:

> Iesu Crist, þat makede go
> þe halte, and þe doumbe speke,
> Hauelok, þe of Godard wreke!　　　(ll. 542–4)

There are a number of similar blessings in the poem (e.g. ll. 403–7) and also several transitional or explanatory formulas which remind us of the narrator's presence (ll. 328–30, 338, 731–2, 2369).

Thus the poet enlivens the story and heightens the dramatic tension. In spite of the stylistic embellishment, there is no lack of narrative tempo and suspense. The author's craftsmanship is not, however, confined to rhetorical devices and vivid scenes, but the whole structure of the poem reveals careful planning and conscious artistry. As the use of recapitulation shows, the poet was anxious to present the action of the poem as a coherent and meaningful whole and to point to inner correspondences between the episodes. The simplest correspondence is that between treason and punishment, between innocent suffering and final happiness. The repeated references to the scene in which Godard threatened Havelok's life (cf. ll. 1364–8, 1411–16, 2222–9) not only keep this episode in our minds, but also bring home the justice of Godard's terrible fate. Havelok's kingship, impressively confirmed by the three miraculous light-appearances, can only be usurped temporarily by Godard's treason, but triumphantly asserts itself in the end. Goldeboru's very similar fate serves as a commentary on the story of Havelok and points to its exemplary character. Like

Havelok, she is the legitimate heir to a kingdom, bereft of her rightful inheritance until, by the grace of God, she is fully reinstated in all she has lost. In contrast to the French versions, where Havelok's story is presented on its own, and Goldeboru's similar fate is only briefly summarized later, the English poet emphasizes the resemblances by devoting practically the same amount of space to both strands of the narrative. This contributes to the symmetrical structure of the poem: first we are told about Athelwold's death and Godrich's treason, then, in very similar words, about Birkabeyn's death and Godard's crime. The central section of the poem tells of the union of the two disinherited children, their journey together to Denmark, and, as a preparation for the last part, Havelok's glorious defeat of the robbers. The two victories over Godard and Godrich and the execution of the two traitors correspond exactly to the first parts of the poem and herald a return to the blissful state of law and order described at the beginning. Poetic justice even extends to a minor figure like Bertram the cook, who is royally rewarded for his kindness towards Havelok in his misery (ll. 2896 ff.).

This doubling of plots is a means of intensifying the drama and underlining its significance. It was a particularly successful stroke of the author to begin the poem with Goldeboru's youth and Godrich's treason. Only after her story has been told so far is Havelok himself introduced. His fate appears even harder, and Godard's treachery more abhorrent than Godrich's. A comparison of these parallel episodes shows that the author stresses the common features, but at the same time avoids monotony by skilful variation in detail (Birkabeyn's death is described more briefly than Athelwold's, but Godard's villainy is related more circumstantially than Godrich's). The two strands meet when Havelok is forced to marry Goldeboru. This seems to be the lowest point in their fortunes and is meant as the crowning humiliation of Goldeboru. Both the royal children feel that it is the end of their hopes, but the reader can already detect the working of God's providence in Godrich's wicked plan. The subtle irony of the episode lies in the fact that Godrich means to be true to his oath and yet to avoid the consequences of Athelwold's last will by this literal fulfilling of his promise to marry Goldeboru to the strongest and best man that can be found (ll. 198–200, 1077 ff.), but by his very treachery he unintentionally acts according to Athelston's dying wish and helps to bring about the happy turn of events. Thus the prosperous end is foreshadowed at a very early point in the story. The almost pyramidal structure of the poem is also underlined by the three miraculous lights which, as we have seen, introduce three new phases of the action and clearly accentuate the story of Havelok's recovery of his inheritance.

Even a brief outline of the action reveals that the unity of the poem lies just as much in its theme as in its plot. Behind the exciting story of treason, exile, trial and return there is the concept of an ideal government which upholds peace and prosperity for all, whereas the usurper can rule only by force and injustice. The raid on Bernard's house, which is described at such length, stands in pointed contrast to the vivid picture of a well-governed commonwealth at the beginning of the poem (ll. 51 ff.) where we are told that nobody had to be in fear of robbers. Both passages could at first sight appear to be unnecessary digressions, but they are essential to the intention of the poem. The fighting in Bernard's house illustrates the lawlessness that has spread under Godard's rule and presents Havelok as the champion of law and order, whereas the long introductory description of Athelwold's just government sets the standard by which all the following events are to be judged. This remarkable passage is quite unique in Middle English romance; in no other poem do we find such an extensive and concrete exposition of a well-ordered state, not an idealized Utopia, but a very realistic expression of any citizen's longings and, at the same time, of the poem's 'message'. After this introduction, the treason of Godrich and Godard is bound to appear the more revolting, a contrast which is heightened by the narrator's curses on the traitor. Both are repeatedly compared with the arch-traitor Judas and with the devil himself (see ll. 319, 425, 482, 1100-1, 1133-4, 1411, 2512); this illustrates that in the context of this poem, disloyalty and perjury are the greatest sins imaginable. The traitors' oaths of loyalty are repeatedly referred to (ll. 313-5, 419, 2216-19, 2708-15), and it is probably significant that Havelok cuts the traitor's hand off in the fight (ll. 2751-3). Surely we are meant to remember the false oath Godrich has sworn to Athelwold (ll. 184-203) at this point.[9] Only the legitimate King and heir can bring back peace and order. Thus *Havelok* presents the picture of an ideal government by a strong and rightful King and a severe warning against disloyalty and lawlessness. It also contains the portrait of a perfect ruler who combines royal birth and divine sanction with personal integrity and strength. Havelok's progress from Grim's cottage to the thrones of Denmark and England illustrates the maturing of an ideal King, not in any systematic educational process, but in an effective dramatic as well as thematic climax. It is characteristic of the particular appeal of the poem that Havelok does not prove his superiority by any marvellous feats of knighthood or in courtly surroundings, but by rather down-to-earth exploits, fighting for a job, carrying tremendous loads, and winning the prize in the unsophisticated country games. His triumph at 'putting the stone' is the uncourtly equivalent of the glorious victories in tournaments won by other heroes of romance. Without any help from others, Havelok earns respect by his strength, but also by his kindness and purity (ll. 991–8). When Godrich tells him to marry Goldeboru, he wants to refuse because he is unable to support a wife (ll. 1136–46), whereas the girl's reason is much more aristocratic and shows that she is well aware of what is due to her (ll. 1111–16). When the two arrive in Denmark, Havelok again tries to earn his bread by a rather lowly occupation, until his victory over the robbers proves him worthy of knighthood. Then his rise to power begins; its visible climax is his defeat of Godrich. His regard for order and justice is illustrated by his honourable treatment of the traitor who has to be lawfully tried by his knights, not simply slain in battle (ll. 2754–65).

Havelok is thus a truly popular King who is not just surrounded by a group of select noblemen, but is intimately acquainted with the lower classes, their struggle for food and drink and their simple loyalty. Havelok's generosity towards Bertram the cook shows that class-distinctions are of no importance to him. Though the poet clearly enjoys telling a good story and embellishing it with picturesque detail, we should not overlook the exemplary if not didactic quality of the poem. *Havelok* is not a 'mirror for magistrates', but it obviously wants to glorify the blessings of a well-ordered commonwealth and of loyalty towards the legitimate ruler. Every character is judged by these standards. Grim and Ubbe are faithful to the legitimate King although they endanger themselves seriously by their loyalty, and Grim's children do homage to Havelok without any hope of reward. *Havelok* therefore belongs to a type of romance quite different from poems like *King Horn*. It does not relate miraculous adventures in the service of love or personal trials, passions and virtues, but above all tries to portray historical incidents as a model and a warning for the present. The person of the hero is less important than the political virtues he embodies and the ideas of law and order that are illustrated by his fate. The historical claim of the poem is enforced by its reference to the founding of Grimsby:

> And for þat Grim þat place auhte,
> þe stede of Grim þe name lauhte;
> So þat Grimesbi it calle
> He þat þer-of speken alle;
> And so shulen men it callen ay,
> Bituene þis and domesday.
>
> (ll. 743–8; see also 2528–9)

In its subject-matter the poem shows a marked resemblance to *Athelston*, where the authority of historical events and authentic scenery also help to bring home the moral, and loyalty, though in a different form, is extolled. Another interesting link is suggested by Raouf de Boun's chronicle *Petit Brut d'Angleterre* (c. 1310) where Guy of Warwick is connected with Havelok's son.[10]

Havelok does not seem to have enjoyed the same popularity as Horn, Guy or Beves of Hamtoun. It may be that the rather more sober tone of the poem did not appeal to later audiences as much as the romantic and often phantastic biographies of other romance-heroes. It is worth noting that in the manuscript *Havelok* is called a *vita*, not a very common term for the romances, but the poem certainly resembles the *vitae* of some Saints in that it presents models of human behaviour and provides instruction as well as entertainment, in a more specific sense than can be said of the shorter romances. There is no 'escapism' in this poem, unless we consider as escapism the genuine craving for a just and peaceful order of society which is so movingly expressed in this poem.[11]

## 'SIR TRISTREM'

This poem which is only preserved in the Auchinleck Ms., probably belongs to the earliest of the Middle English romances. Its size places it between the shorter romances and the novels in verse; the whole poem presumably ran to just over three thousand five hundred lines. In some ways its position among the Middle

English romances is quite unique, because more than most other poems discussed here it shows traces of oral transmission. We cannot prove, of course, that this is the romance of Sir Tristrem referred to by Robert Manning in the famous prologue to his chronicle where he complains of some texts, especially those in complicated stanza-forms, being disfigured to the point of unintelligibility by oral transmission,[12] but his remarks would fit *Sir Tristrem* very well, and as long as no other English version of the story is known, we have no reason to doubt that the two works are identical. The poem has obviously suffered badly from careless transmission and it seems quite believable that even contemporary listeners found some parts of it hard to understand. The reason given by Robert Manning, too, is very plausible: the stanza-form chosen by the poet is so complicated that only a particularly competent artist could have handled it without the use of many meaningless tags, but the author of *Sir Tristrem* was no such skilful craftsman and he often had to sacrifice clarity of expression and sense to the exacting metre. It is quite possible that even the original poem was sometimes flawed by obscure passages, and this would make it particularly liable to negligent copying or oral transmission. The scribe who copied the Auchinleck version must certainly have had in front of him a text that was already much the worse for wear. The clumsiness of the style can thus partly be explained by the stanza-form, and a comparison with other poems written in the same form shows how much more competently even such intricate metres could be handled by other, more gifted poets.[13]

The stanza-form of *Sir Tristrem* is quite different from the tail-rhyme stanzas in that it has a tripartite structure, like most of the Romanic lyrics and many Middle English poems. Its rhyme-scheme (*ababababcbc*) is the same as that of one of the *Harley Lyrics* ('Middelerd for mon wes mad,') though that poem lacks the most characteristic feature of the *Tristrem*-stanza, the *bob*, which is a line of two or three syllables (line nine in the stanza), linked by its rhyme to the last line of the stanza, but in most cases connected to the first half of the stanza by the syntax. Kölbing stated that in about 105 out of 304 stanzas the bob is linked to the preceding line by alliteration. The last two lines are usually separated from the rest of the stanza by the syntax and by their content: sometimes they give a brief summary of the stanza or add a general observation (as in ll. 439–40 and 626–7). Very often a completely new idea

is expressed in the last two lines, as in ll. 1000–1 or in 1737–8,
where we are all of a sudden told that Ysonde wants to kill Breng-
wain, or a new episode is introduced, as in the following stanza
which is a very characteristic example of the way the poet handles
his chosen form; Tristrem and Ysonde return from the woods:

> To court were comen þo to,
> þat in þe forest were;
> Mark kist Ysonde þo
> And Tristrem, trewe fere.
> Forȝeuen hem was her wo,
> No were þai neuer so dere.
> Tristrem þe bailie gan to
> Swiftly for to stere
> A stounde.
> Of loue who wil lere,
> Listen now þe grounde!            (ll. 2564–74)

This provides a link with the following stanza (see also ll. 1429–30).

Apart from connecting stanzas by their content, the poet has
also made use of some more formal devices of stanza-linking, such
as verbal repetition or use of the same rhyme. Altogether about a
hundred stanzas are linked in some way or other; often more than
one device is used. In general, the poet is not as consistent in this
respect as the author of *Sir Perceval of Gales*, and there are long
sections of the poem in which hardly any trace of stanza-linking
can be detected; on the other hand, it is interesting to see that often
a whole group of stanzas are linked, and this is usually the case when
part of the plot is briefly summarized, whereas in those episodes
which are related in some detail, the poet usually felt that he could
dispense with this device.[14] The use of stanza-linking, as well as
variations in the handling of the individual stanza, show that the
poet made some attempt to relieve the monotony of his metre, but
it is sometimes difficult to decide whether he was acting from a
conscious artistic impulse or, which often seems more likely, from
mere carelessness. It can hardly be denied that the stanzas of *Sir
Tristrem* frequently sound like the 'rym dogerel' of Sir Thopas.
This is mainly due to the extreme triteness and poverty of the
rhymes and the unusually high number of meaningless tags which
often make even quite dramatic scenes sound rather irrelevant.
The obvious explanation seems to be that such formulas are the

result of improvisation or that they were inserted as an aid to the minstrel's memory. The poem was evidently composed to be recited, and it is quite possible that it was written down from memory, as Kölbing though,[15] though I prefer to think that it was originally quite a literary product. This is suggested by the comparatively sophisticated metre and by the close resemblance of episodes in the English poem to some other versions of the story, especially the Norse saga. Undoubtedly the original poet had in front of him some literary version of the story. Some obscurities in the English poem can also be accounted for by the fact that the scribe of the Auchinleck Ms. was unused to the dialect of the poem (in all probability it was originally Northern) and that he tried, with varying consistency, to adapt it to his own idiom.

Not only the style of the poem, but also the management of the plot, suggest the possibility of oral transmission. In contrast to the technique of many tail-rhyme romances, the action does not proceed by a logical sequence of events, but often in fits and starts. Sometimes a whole episode is briefly summarized only to be told later in great detail. In most cases this cannot be explained as deliberate anticipation, but only as thoughtless bungling on the part of the author (or scribe). Thus Rouland is introduced three times, as if the author had forgotten that he had already mentioned him earlier (ll. 23, 43-4, 89-94); the dwarf is brought into the story with similar abruptness (l. 2062), as Kölbing noted, and, most surprising of all, Tristrem's assumed name is mentioned immediately after his birth (ll. 252-3), even before he has been given his real name,[16] a completely irrelevant anticipation. In other places, the poet forgets to mention important facts and thus makes some episodes rather puzzling, as in the passage beginning at line 1013, where we are not at first told that the fight between Tristrem and Moraunt is to take place on an island. Tristrem's behaviour (he lets one of the two boats go because, he says, only one of the two adversaries will return), therefore seems at first rather pointless and is only explained in the following stanza. Also there are often sudden transitions from one episode to the next, a very fragmentary use of dialogue, and abrupt changes of subject from one sentence to the next (e.g. ll. 1629-39). All this is not what we expect from a competent and consciously planning artist, but from a scribe who found the complications of the story rather too much for him and who only seemed to remember details when he came to them or felt that he had to put them down before he forgot them again, without any regard for logic or for a larger design.

The unusual style of the poem is also partly due to the author's striving for the utmost brevity. The versions of the Tristan-saga that are nearest to *Sir Tristrem* are all much longer than the English poem. The French poem of Thomas which, if not the source of *Sir Tristrem*, is at least very closely related to its source, runs to about 3000 lines, but it only contains a fragment of the story so that the complete work must have been much longer,[17] whereas it is unlikely that more than about sixteen stanzas, that is 176 lines, are missing from the English poem. The Norse saga, which probably goes back to an English source, too, is about twice as long as *Sir Tristrem*. Gottfried von Strassburg's novel is of course full of digressions and rhetorical embellishment, but it is interesting to note that it takes about 19,500 lines, as against 2673 lines of *Sir Tristrem*, to reach the same point in the plot, and this again illustrates how concise the English poem is in comparison. It contains roughly the same number of episodes, and no substantial part of the plot has been omitted, so that the abridgement is mainly due to the swift and often almost too laconic mode of narration. As in many of the shorter romances, the author evidently tried to condense his complicated and rambling plot as much as possible without making any drastic changes in the sequence of events. This explains the compressed and sometimes enigmatic style and the size of the poem which could be described as the abridged version of a novel, but is considerably longer than the shorter romances because the poet evidently did not try to write a poem that could be read at one sitting. A comparison with *Ywain and Gawain* would show how much more skilfully that poem has been adapted, although the underlying story is admittedly more lucid and easy to grasp.

It would be rather pointless to make a detailed comparison of *Sir Tristrem* and Gottfried von Strassburg's astonishing novel.[18] Such a comparison could only list a great number of fundamental differences which would contribute little to our understanding of either poem. Few Middle English poems come off so badly when compared with other versions, as *Sir Tristrem* does, if we fail to take into account the completely different character and purpose of the English adaptation. For the English adapter, as even a brief glance at the different versions shows, the story of Tristrem was not predominantly a love-story. Several of the episodes which in

Gottfried's novel are embellished and sophisticated to such an extent that they form the core of the whole poem, are passed over with particular brevity in *Sir Tristrem*, such as the episode of the love-potion, which takes up about 1200 lines in Gottfried's novel and about 80 in *Sir Tristrem*. Other instances are the sojourn of the lovers in the wood, and the divine ordeal. On the other hand, the first part of the story, before the first meeting of Tristrem and Ysonde, takes up comparatively more space than in Gottfried's poem and, what is more important, there the prologue and the various reflections on the theme of courtly love make even the first part of the story appear as a preparation for the love-story, whereas in *Sir Tristrem*, Ysonde is not mentioned at all until about a third of the poem is over. The meeting of the lovers is not told with any more sympathy or emphasis than Tristrem's fights against giants and dragons. By confining himself to the mere outline of the plot and to a simple retelling of the events, the poet completely alters the character of the story. It becomes the history of a fatal error, by which a noble and promising knight is brought to misery. Only in a few places do we get the impression that the two lovers are attracted to each other by more than simple magic, and there are only occasional glimpses of something like a deeper bond between the two, as in Tristrem's reflections after his marriage to Ysonde with the white hand:

> Tristrem biheld þat ring,
> þo was his hert ful wo:
> 'Oӡain me swiche a þing
> Dede neuer Ysonde so;
> Mark, her lord, þe king,
> Wiþ tresoun may hir to.
> Mine hert may no man bring
> For no þing hir fro,
> þat fre.
> Ich haue tvinned ous to,
> þe wrong is al in me!' (ll. 2685-95)

The magic of the ring evidently puts him under an obligation to be faithful to her, although it has struck them both through no fault of theirs and forces them into a sinful passion. The English adapter obviously did not quite know what to do with this motif. Neither the problems of such fatal love nor the question of adultery are raised in so many words, and thus Marke only appears as the rather ludicrous figure of the deceived husband who is continually outwitted by the cunning of the lovers. The deeper implications of this passion do not seem to concern the author. We hardly ever see the two lovers alone together and all the author has to tell us about them is that they 'pleyen' as often as opportunity offers itself. The rather burlesque character of some episodes—in Gottfried's novel often skilfully disguised by a sophisticated narrative technique—comes out very clearly in *Sir Tristrem*. Wit is employed against wit, and the narrator does not hide his conviction that Meriadok who warns the deceived king and spies after the lovers, is a traitor. The situation is not unlike that in *Le Morte Arthur*. There, too, adultery is accepted as a fact which the author does not find it worth his while to deplore.

The unsubtle and heavy-handed narrative technique makes the whole poem appear as an adventure-story, which cannot, of course, end with the victory and the happy marriage of the hero, as so many shorter romances do. Tristrem has, however, much in common with other heroes of romance. The story of his childhood reminds one of that of Horn; like Ipomedon he proves himself a knight by his expertness in courtly etiquette, and the situation into which he is put by his love is in many ways similar to that of Lancelot. Tristrem is the centre of the plot much more than this can be said of Gottfried's poem. His love for Ysonde constitutes the most important episode of the poem, of course, but it is only told from his point of view, not as a mutual experience. His prowess and his exploits are given particular prominence; his superiority in battle (against Moraunt, ll. 1013 ff., a dragon, ll. 1431 ff., Beliagog, ll. 2751 ff., and others) is just as exceptional as his courtly education and his skill at playing the harp, at chess or at hunting. The ideal of knighthood implied here is different from that of many later romances. The poet probably had a rather courtly version of the story in front of him from which he took its more aristocratic elements. Later adapters usually departed from their sources more noticeably in this respect (cf., for instance, *Ipomedon B*). On the other hand, *Sir Tristrem* lacks the religious trend of most later romances and we are not told that exceptional piety is one of the hero's virtues. Even the almost obligatory prayer at the beginning of the poem is missing.

Thus the poem is not in all respects typical of the Middle

English romances. This can partly be explained by its early date. There is hardly any trace of the bourgeois tone yet, which is so characteristic of some of the later tail-rhyme romances. The action takes place in a distinctly aristocratic society, whose customs the author seems to know well enough. Singing, harp-playing and romance-reading are mentioned several times, and there are few romances in which minstrels play such an important part. Tristrem disguises himself as a minstrel, and it is a minstrel who by a clever trick abducts Ysonde. Several times there is mention of the rich rewards given to minstrels, messengers or other court-officials, and once we are told that

> He was ful wise, y say,
> þat first ȝaue ȝift in land. (ll. 626–7)

The occasion on which this remark is made, the porter-episode (ll. 619 ff.), rather reminiscent of *Sir Cleges*, shows that the author was quite familiar with the particular troubles of wandering professions, and would be quite appropriate in a poem written for recital by a minstrel. The same also applies to those passages where the audience is addressed, as in the announcements of new episodes (ll. 199–200, 1429–30, 2573–4) or in the references to the author's source (ll. 1–22, 397–407). These, together with the rather monotonous metre and the high number of clichés, give the poem that ballad-like tone which we also find in some of the other early romances, like *King Horn* and *Floris and Blauncheflur*.

On the other hand, *Sir Tristrem* has neither the structural coherence nor the religious seriousness of *King Horn* or *Havelok*. The poem provides quite a revealing illustration of the fact that even towards the end of the thirteenth century, some very different types of romance were already in existence. It is reasonable to suppose that the more 'oral' of these poems were the least likely to survive, and perhaps these were also the less edifying romances. The exemplary and religious elements were usually the result of a more literary redaction in some *scriptorium*. It does not seem as if the type represented by *Sir Tristrem* was revived by later adapters, nor was the stanza-form used in this poem ever taken up again by a romance-writer, at least not in any poem that has come down to us.

## 'YWAIN AND GAWAIN'

*Ywain and Gawain* is another interesting example of the longer English romances and like *Sir Tristrem*, though in a different way, it seems to stand somewhat apart from the other romances. This is partly on account of its source; *Ywain and Gawain* is the only English translation of one of Chrétien's novels. Unlike many other adapters, the poet does not present the mere outline of the story, but he obviously worked from a text of the French poem and followed his source with astonishing closeness down to many smaller details.[19] At the same time he reduced the poem to little more than half its size so that the events follow each other much more closely and the tempo is considerably increased. This kind of adaptation is, as we noted several times, typical of many English romances, but in *Ywain and Gawain* it was achieved in a rather more literary way than is usual. The particularly careful text makes it very unlikely that oral transmission was involved, and the manuscript, obviously a very faithful copy, gives the impression of having been composed by a professional and at some expense (Cotton Galba E. IX).[20] The poem is divided into more or less coherent paragraphs, and after line 2428 there is a red rubric 'here es þe myddes of þis boke' which also proves that the scribe paid some attention to the structure of the poem and wanted to offer some help to anybody who might want to read the poem from the manuscript. Perhaps he thought that this could be done in two instalments. The metre, too, is very skilfully handled. In contrast to *Sir Tristrem* and *Le Morte Arthur*, the poem is written in rhyming couplets, with a liberal use of alliteration, run-on lines, and some simple rhetorical devices. There is much less use of clichés and meaningless formulas, and the style of the poem reveals far more competence than that of *Sir Tristrem*, though perhaps not a great deal of imagination and originality.[21]

The English poem has been compared with Chrétien's *Yvain* several times, so that it seems unnecessary to compile another detailed list of differences and parallels between the two romances. As we might expect, the English adapter had not much use for extensive descriptions of courtly ceremony, the rhetorical embellishment of many episodes, or, least of all, for the theoretical discussion of problems of courtly love, and he abridged such passages drastically.[22] The whole intellectual design of the French poem, the subtle and meaningful interrelation of the various episodes, and the deliberately graded progress of the hero towards courtly perfection seem to have been beyond his comprehension. The differentiated and carefully worked-out process of spiritual maturing found in Chrétien's poem,[23] becomes a more or less arbitrary sequence of exciting adventures, connected often more by a sense of drama and tension than by a deeper meaning. The characters have for the most part been simplified; the hero, in particular, is a much less complex personality than in the French poem and resembles some of the more primitive warriors in English romance, so that his madness from excessive grief appears far less convincingly motivated. All these changes show that the English adapter wrote for a completely different audience from that of Chrétien, an audience not very interested in ideals of knighthood and *amour courtois*, but expecting to hear of strange exploits, surprising adventures and manly trials.

Less striking than the alterations made by the English adapter, but just as significant, is his comparatively close adherence to his model. Although he obviously tried to adapt the story to the tastes of his audience, he nevertheless preserved the structure and the proportions of the French poem. *Ywain and Gawain* exhibits the same neatness of design and the same balanced symmetry of the episodes as Chrétien's *Yvain*, and this is partly what makes it so different from many other Middle English romances. The logical coherence of the plot and the tight structure are even brought out to better effect by the omission of many rhetorical flourishes and digressions, and there are a number of impressive scenes, such as are rare in the shorter romances. In all these respects, *Ywain and Gawain* is much nearer to its source than, for instance, *Libeaus Desconus* or similar versions of French novels. Thus, to mention one example, the extensive scene at the beginning of the poem has only been slightly abridged and the long tale of Colgrevance (ll. 135–456) appears almost like a little independent romance told in the first person. The dialogue between the Queen and the knights is also reproduced at some length by means of direct speech, and thus from the beginning there is a certain ceremonious quality in the narration which continues throughout the poem and is quite different from the swift pace of many of the shorter romances. Although the adapter has missed many sophisticated effects and psychological subtleties, he seems to have grasped the artistic design and the effective interplay of Chrétien's characters. He usually managed to reproduce quite faithfully many of the most successful scenes of dialogue in *Yvain* though he often coarsened them, as can be illustrated by a comparison of the scenes in which Alundyne is persuaded by Lunet to receive Ywain back into her favour.[24] Here, as in many other places, long and formal speeches are replaced by brief and pointed repartees, and stylized dialogue by swift and dramatic exchanges. Another example is Colgrevance's account of his duel with Alundyne's husband. In Chrétien's poem, the knight introduces himself by a lengthy speech and explains to Colgrevance his fault; the English version only gives a brief summary of his speech, and the short, but all the more threatening sentence 'þou sal aby' (l. 413) is the only piece of directly quoted dialogue. The scene in which Ywain comes to Alundyne's castle and is protected by Lunet from the revenge of the lady's knights, is also stripped of much of its sophistication and reduced to its dramatic essentials by the English adapter; this seems to give some additional vividness to Lunet's character.[25] However, some other important passages, like Ywain's decision to leave Arthur's court and his parting from Alundyne (ll. 1499 ff.), are hardly abridged at all.

*Ywain and Gawain* is thus an unusually close-knit and effective novel of adventure, lacking the wit and subtlety of Chrétien, but superior to most of the more pedestrian adaptations of French novels. It is undoubtedly the product of conscious and careful reshaping, not an artless retelling of the plot. The poem shows how much the authors of English romances could have learnt from Chrétien, even though they did not share his courtly ideology, and how a completely new genre could have developed under his influence. Like the majority of the shorter romances, *Ywain and Gawain* presents the story of a knight's trial and success, not in a single episode or a hasty series of adventures, but in a skilfully linked chain of events. In contrast to most shorter romances, the narrative does not follow the fortunes of the hero only, but devotes much space to the adventures of other persons as well, such as the fate of Lunet and the quarrel of the two sisters; but all these episodes, though they give more scope and breadth to the novel, are eventually linked with Ywain's story and there is no doubt that he is the real centre of the poem.

For the English adapter, though not for Chrétien, the story of

Ywain was part of his own country's early history and Arthur a predecessor to the English Kings, as is illustrated by the reference he inserted to native laws of inheritance (ll. 3767–72). The poet evidently wanted to confront his own contemporaries with an account of a past far superior to the present in true virtue and nobility (cf. ll. 7–46). Whereas Chrétien deplores the decline of courtly refinement and tries to depict the ideal of a courtly society, the English adapter is concerned with simpler virtues. He regrets the lack of truth and loyalty among his contemporaries and he sees in Arthur's court the perfect realization of his ideals. Arthur and his knights represent the model of a society united by loyalty and a desire for fame, and as in Chrétien's poem, colour is added to this picture by the fact that there is also an uncourtly boor in the midst of the knights (Kay) who, by his offensive talk, arouses the indignation of his fellows, but is tolerated by them because he belongs to them. In the friendship between Ywain and Gawain this spirit of brotherhood finds particularly clear expression. That this friendship was felt to be an important part of the story is suggested by the title of the English poem (see also ll. 2299 ff. and ll. 2785 ff.). The poet realized the symbolic significance of the duel between Ywain and Gawain although he reduced Chrétien's highly rhetorical and sophisticated reflections on the theme of love and enmity to a few lines (3509 ff.). Although they do not recognize each other, neither of the friends can hurt the other because they are so equally matched:

> Al þat ever saw þat batayl,
> Of þaire might had grete mervayl;
> þai saw never under þe hevyn
> Twa knightes þat war copled so evyn.
> Of all þe folk was none so wise,
> þat wist wheþer sold have þe prise;  (ll. 3593–8)

The English adapter evidently saw the inner unity of the poem in its portrayal of a loyal knight. In contrast to Chrétien's hero, Ywain sins against Alundyne not so much by his lack of love and his failure to understand the nature of true communion with the beloved as by his breach of faith. This central episode is much simpler and at the same time has a more moral flavour in the English poem than in the French, although the English adapter has only condensed it a little and his alterations seem at first sight not very great. The lady dismisses Ywain with the earnest entreaty not to forget the date fixed for his return:

> Hir lord, Sir Ywayne, sho bisekes
> With teris trikland on hir chekes,
> On al wise þat he noght let
> To halde þe day þat he had set.     (ll. 1557–60)

After that, it is not Gawain who persuades Ywain to delay his return (as in Chrétien's poem), but their chivalrous deeds make them forget everything else (ll. 1561 ff.). Because of the omission of nearly all passages describing the love between Ywain and Alundyne, Ywain's promise of return appears more in the nature of a contract between the two, and the considerably abridged speech of Alundyne's messenger, too, emphasizes Ywain's lack of loyalty rather than the grief of the lady which is described at some length in *Yvain* (cf. *Yvain*, ll. 2695 ff., *Ywain and Gawain*, ll. 1583 ff.). Thus the words of the messenger form a parallel to the prologue of the poem where faith and loyalty are extolled and the lack of these virtues in the present is deplored:

> þai tald of more trewth þam bitwene
> þan now omang men here es sene,
> For trowth and luf es al bylaft;
> Men uses now anoþer craft.
> With worde men makes it trew and stabil,
> Bot in þaire faith es noght bot fabil;
> With þe mowth men makes it hale,
> Bot trew trowth es nane in þe tale.     (ll. 33–40)

Ywain's complaint at the well, too, is mainly concerned with his breach of faith (ll. 2087–102), whereas the corresponding passage in Chrétien's poem is rather more general. It is appropriate that Ywain has to go through a series of adventures in which his loyalty is put to the test before he can regain the favour of his wife. Thus he demonstrates his faithfulness to Alundyne by refusing the love of a lady whom he has helped (ll. 1959 ff.), his loyalty to Gawain, by undertaking a dangerous fight on his behalf (ll. 2299 ff.), and his loyalty to Lunet by coming to her rescue (ll. 2151 ff.), even though he finds it very difficult to keep his promise (ll. 2499 ff.): he has to leave the castle where he has been received very kindly, only to be in time for his appointment. None of the adventures that follow is a merely arbitrary addition, but they all bear some

184

relation to the theme of loyalty. When Ywain agrees to be the champion of the younger of the two sisters (ll. 2923 ff.), this prepares for the battle between Ywain and his friend, as the reader realizes. The night spent in the enchanted castle (ll. 2931 ff.) only delays the fight, heightens the dramatic tension and again puts Ywain's loyalty to Alundyne to the test. Once more he refuses the love that is offered to him and moves on in order to fulfil his obligation.

The reconciliation which at last takes place between Ywain and Alundyne is the reward for his heroic adventures on behalf of those who were in desperate need of help. His fame has spread so far that Alundyne herself wants the Knight with the Lion (of whose identity she is ignorant) as her champion against Ywain because he has already done her a service by saving Lunet, and Lunet herself pays back a debt when she succeeds in her endeavours to bring about the reunion of the lovers. On the whole, the logic of events is certainly simpler in this poem than in *Yvain*, but it is nevertheless apparent. The persistent emphasis on the virtue of loyalty is an interesting point *Ywain and Gawain* has in common with *Sir Gawain and the Green Knight*, another poem in which true knighthood is portrayed as consisting above all in faithful keeping of contracts and a regard for loyalty and truth.

The English adapter evidently realized that Chrétien's novel, quite apart from its courtly and sophisticated content, is also a story of simple faithfulness and readiness to help those who are in need. Ywain's loyalty to his friend, to Lunet and, above all, to his wife, is the centre of the action, and it is paralleled by Lunet's inventive and efficient services to Ywain which, as she knows, are absolutely compatible with her loyalty to Alundyne, even when she outwits her mistress and draws upon herself the significant reproach, 'I wend þou sold be to me lele' (l. 3986), because both Ywain's and Alundyne's interests are served by a speedy reconciliation. Thus, the joyful end of the poem includes the well-earned reward for 'trew Lunet' as well (ll. 4014-19). In these simple human relationships the English poet saw the chief appeal of Chrétien's story and he thus gave it a new kind of unity, intelligible to a less courtly audience. We do not know whether the poem met with particular success, but it certainly achieves, like *Le Morte Arthur* and *Sir Gawain and the Green Knight*, a very felicitous combination of French courtly and native traditions.

### 'LE MORTE ARTHUR'

This poem which, like *Ipomedon B*, is preserved in a sixteenth-century commonplace-book (Harley 2252) is one of the best-known Middle English romances. It has been edited several times and has been a favourite with most critics who have praised its alleged simplicity and naïveté, but rarely troubled to give a more detailed description of these qualities.[26] Most studies are confined to questions of dialect, provenance and analogues of the story. In contrast to D. Bruce and others who thought the poem a plain and unsophisticated reproduction of an earlier version (which, however, is lost, if ever it existed), I feel we should credit the author with a considerable degree of independence and artistic refinement.

The by no means simple, but skilfully handled metrical form alone suggests that the poet aimed at conciseness and unity of style. The rhyme-scheme which makes some demands on the author's ingenuity (*abab_abab*), the frequent alliterative formulas, and the effective use of stanza-linking, especially in the more important episodes, show clearly that this is no naïve story-telling, but that the author was a conscious stylist who tried to give some shape to his poem. There is also a rare balance in the structure of the plot, a strict subordination of details to the theme of the poem, and a notable lack of any digressions which could slow down the tempo of the narration. The unity of the whole poem is also strengthened by the well-weighed alternation of summarizing narrative and extended scenes; both techniques are used with equal competence, and there is not the slightest suggestion of monotony in the poem. As we do not know the poet's source, we cannot, of course, determine exactly his share in the successful composition of the poem, but there is no reason to think that it was inconsiderable.

The subject of *Le Morte Arthur* is the fall of Arthur and his Round Table. This tragic event is not, as in the alliterative *Morte Arthure*, presented as a just punishment for Arthur's pride, but as an inescapable destiny which is deplored by all and for which Lancelot and Gaynor are ultimately responsible although they are overtaken by the terrible force of events like all the others. From the rather elegiac, but not in any way accusatory tone of the poem we can gather that the author does not, of course, approve of the adulterous *liaison* between the two, but that he accepts it as a fact whose origins he has no reason to inquire into and which it is futile to condemn. A dissolution of the fatal union is never considered, nor could it, under the circumstances, stop the disastrous course of events, because the conflict of loyalties, once broken out, cannot be allayed any more by simple reconciliation. The author understood that this was not a story of knightly adventure depending on surprising turns of plot, but above all a clash of personalities and conflicting claims, all inherent in the traditional concept of knighthood and developing with the irresistible power of true tragedy. This is why he lays particular emphasis on all those episodes in which psychological processes and struggles are described. An interesting example is the scene in which the Queen, after she has been unjustly accused of a crime she never committed, implores Arthur's knights, one after the other, to stand by her and be her champion (ll. 1318 ff.). All the knights know that Lancelot has left the court because of her and they are angry with her for it; since, furthermore, appearances are against her in the case under dispute, they have a certain justification for refusing to help her although they do not really want her to come to grief. Thus their refusal is really dictated by their annoyance at Lancelot's departure, although they use quite different arguments, and their protest when at last Sir Bors promises to help her, clearly reveals the deeper reason for their behaviour:

> The knyghtis answerd with wo and wrake,
> And sayd they wyste wetterlye
> That 'she hathe launcelot du lake
> Browght oute of ouere companye.
> Nys non that nolde thys bataile take,
> Er she hade any vylanye,
> But we nylle not so glad hyr make
> By-fore we ne suffre hyr to be sorye.'      (ll. 1451–8)

In other words, they are all really prepared to help her, but not before she has been severely punished. Thus, the Queen, though completely innocent of the crime she is reproached with, as the reader knows, still deserves to suffer. By the dramatic description of this scene, the author prepares us for the subsequent turn of events and effectively shows what strong emotions are aroused in all those concerned by the love affair between Lancelot and the Queen. For the first time, there is a hint of the conflicting loyalties which will eventually bring about the disaster. The scene also indicates that Arthur's knights (and presumably the author, too), do not take exception to the *liaison* because of any moral scruples, but they strongly resent anyone who, like the Queen in this case, makes this love affair a liability for the whole community by unreasonable behaviour. It is clear that such an affair, if kept secret by the partners and by all who know about it, would not in any way endanger the peace and harmony of the Round Table; obviously the story belongs to a world in which such secret unions were celebrated and were not at all to the discredit of the two lovers.

In the course of the story, the author never passes a moral judgement on the Queen's adultery. The debate between Agrawayn and the other knights, again described in some detail (ll. 1672 ff.), once more indicates where the real problem lies. Agrawayn's conviction that Lancelot is a traitor and that it is their duty to warn the King, is not questioned by the knights or by the narrator, but, as Gawayn's reply (ll. 1688 ff.) points out, it is mainly the consequences of Agrawayn's proposal they have to consider. Gawayn's friendship for Lancelot makes it impossible for him to denounce Lancelot behind his back, but his chief reason for not doing so is *realpolitik*. He knows that Lancelot is the most powerful member of the Round Table and that a conflict between him and Arthur is bound to have far-reaching repercussions. This more pragmatic view leads him to dissuade Agrawayn from doing anything rash, and it is evident that the author is on Gawayn's side in this matter. It is only after Gawayn's brothers have been killed—again without any personal fault of Lancelot's—that Gawayn becomes Lancelot's fiercest enemy because his duty to avenge his brothers overrides all claims of friendship. From then on, all attempts at a reconciliation are made impossible by Gawayn's implacable desire for revenge. Thus, the story is not based on an ethical conflict or Christian morality, but on a clash of loyalties which can only end in tragedy and which, with its sinister and unavoidable logic, rather suggests a Germanic and pre-Christian mentality. Nor is Lancelot's crime condemned as an immoral act, but as treason against the King (cf. l. 1683).[27]

The rather legendary ending slightly disguises the heroic and unchristian quality of the story and is not consistent with the earlier parts of the poem. Looking back, the Queen realizes that her sinful passion for Lancelot was the real reason for the catastrophe. Her long and elaborate conversation with Lancelot (ll. 3638 ff.)

shows that the poet was very concerned to emphasize her penitence and that he took her guilt very seriously. This does not necessarily mean that he was unaware of the contrast between the two halves of the poem or that he was morally indifferent.[28] The Queen's repentance gives her a deeper insight than the first part of the poem leads us to expect. We are never told about the origins of their love but only about the situation in which they and the Court find themselves after it has gone too far for separation to be possible. The moving episode of the maid of Ascalot illustrates very impressively the intensity of their love and already gives us a glimpse of later conflicts. After Agrawayn's 'treason' (although he proves his loyalty to the King by warning him about Lancelot, he is, in the context of the poem, a traitor, causing enormous mischief) Lancelot is left no choice but to resist the King, but, as the conclusion of the poem proves, the author is not ignorant of the fact that Lancelot has in the last resort only himself to blame. It is only a sign of the poet's assured sense of dramatic tension and climax, even where the moral interpretation of the story is concerned, that Gaynor's recognition of the deeper cause of the disaster does not come before events have taken their sad course. A strictly moral presentation of the whole story from the beginning would certainly have detracted from its tragic force and from the pathetic effect of human powerlessness in the face of destiny. Thus, Lancelot and Gaynor are guilty, but they are so much enmeshed in the logic of the events that they still gain the reader's sympathy.

The ending of the poem does not only add a new moral dimension to the story; it also contributes to the unrealistic and almost fairy-tale character of the poem which has even less 'realistic' qualities than most other English Arthur-poems and seems to speak to us at several removes. The introductory assurance of the author, often no more than a conventional formula, is very much in keeping with the spirit of the whole romance:

> Lordingis that ar leff And dere,
> lystenyth and I shall you tell
> By olde dayes what aunturs were
> Amonge oure eldris þat by-felle:
> In Arthur dayes, that noble kinge,
> By-felle Aunturs ferly fele,
> And I shall telle of there endinge
> That mykell wiste of wo and wele. (ll. 1–8)

The narrative style of the poem is distinguished above all by the subtle and unobtrusive way in which mental processes are portrayed and made visible by slight gestures without the help of explicit commentary. Outward actions are often described in such a way that we can feel the seething passions behind them although nothing is said about the emotions of the characters.

The story of the maid of Ascalot is a particularly impressive example of the poet's art (ll. 177 ff.). As the reader knows without having been told in so many words, Lancelot has rejected her touching confession of love mainly because of his loyalty to the Queen. Gawayn's report from Ascalot which he gives in good faith and without any intention of wronging Lancelot, is the cause of the Queen's unfounded jealousy and Lancelot's new departure, as Gawayn and the other knights know very well (ll. 796 ff.). All this gives particular poignancy to the scene in which Arthur and Gawayn meet the boat from Ascalot with the dead body of the maid and her letter, containing a true account of the affair (ll. 956 ff.), especially of Lancelot's refusal to be her lover. Although the poet seems to do nothing but give a plain statement of events, we recognize at once the complex emotions of the two characters: Arthur reproaches the absent Lancelot because of his uncourtly behaviour (ll. 1098 ff.) and thus clearly betrays his ignorance of Gaynor's adultery. Gawayn, however, tries to excuse Lancelot and at the same time keep the King ignorant of the real situation. At the same time Gawayn realizes with dismay what mischief he has done by his false report from Ascalot. This we can gather from the fact that he immediately leaves the King and goes to the Queen to confess his fatal error (ll. 1128 ff.). This effective technique, working by delicate hint and implication rather than by direct statement, is characteristic of the whole poem and distinguishes it from many other romances. Only in a few cases, as in the passage following line 720 (a description of Lancelot's feelings on returning to the court), are emotions portrayed more directly; but even then the detached tone stands in contrast to the strong emotions which the reader senses behind it.

It is part of the author's rather detached narrative technique that he makes particularly frequent use of direct speech and reproduces long passages of dialogue. By these means he does not only create vivid scenes or emphasize particular highlights of the plot, as we observed in other romances, but the action itself often seems to be

implied in the dialogue so that there is no need for any explanatory
narrative since we can gather all we are meant to know from the
speeches of the characters only, as in Lancelot's refusal of the maid
of Ascalot's love (ll. 185 ff.) or Agrawayn's warning of the King
(ll. 1728 ff.). The speeches often seem to be pregnant with suppressed passions and inner conflicts although these are disguised
by a facade of courtly ceremony and good breeding.[29] This translation of action into dialogue is to be found to some extent in many
Middle English romances and also in the French *Mort Artu*, but
it is used with especial consistency and purpose here. Between
crucial scenes the action is often summarized in a rather perfunctory
manner and the author seems to seize every opportunity that offers
itself to introduce some dialogue (see, for instance, ll. 544 ff.). This
is why the formula, 'Than it by-felle' (cf. ll. 624, 728, 880, 888,
1672, and others), introducing an important scene, is quite typical
of the narrative style of the poem.

Another technique that is employed several times, is the portrayal of events as witnessed by one of the characters. Thus the
arrival of a knight or a messenger is sometimes watched from a
tower, and thus immediately related to those characters who are to
be involved with the newcomer (see ll. 105 ff., 704 ff.). For example
the arrival of the boat containing the dead body of the maid of
Ascalot (ll. 958 ff.) is described as it appears to Arthur and Gawayn
who watch it approaching. This technique adds considerable
vividness and tension to the whole scene and it is used with similar
effect in various other places in the poem, sometimes with a
deliberate change of perspective (see ll. 289 ff., 440 ff., 664 ff.,
1459 ff., 2620 ff.). Another example is the trial by combat (ll. 1520
ff.), where the dramatic suspense is heightened by a brief description of Arthur's emotions. E.g.:

> The kyng lokyde one All hys knyghtis,
> Was he neuere yet so woo,
> Sawhe neuyr on hym dyght
> A-yenste Sir mador for to goo;    (ll. 1520–3)

Gawayn's change of heart which has such fatal consequences,
appears much more convincing, too, because it is described by
means of a moving scene (ll. 1994 ff.). The formula, 'he saw', so
common in the Middle English romances, is here employed with
more skill and originality than usual.[30] It often helps to add a new

dimension to the events described and gives a more objective quality to the narration because the narrator seems to step back and leave all comment and evaluation to the characters themselves. The author of the alliterative *Morte Arthure* is, in comparison, far more outspoken and makes no secret of his moral convictions and of his own attitude to the events he describes. One of the few passages in which our poet makes a direct accusation, is expressed in such vague terms that it seems to refer less to some particular person than to the course of events in general:

> he that by-ganne thys wrechyd playe,
> What wondyr thoughe he had grete synne!
>
> (ll. 2212–13)[31]

The reactions of the characters to the tragedy also emphasize its inescapability; this applies, above all, to Arthur himself. A typical example is the little scene during the battle between the King and Lancelot. The King is unhorsed in the fight, but Lancelot helps him back onto his steed:

> Whan the kynge was horsyd there,
> Launcelot lokys he vppon,
> How corteise was in hym more
> Then euyr was in Any man;
> He thought on thyngis that had bene ore,
> The teres from hys yȝen Ranne;
> He Sayde 'Allas!' with syghynge sore,
> 'That euyr yit thys werre be-gan!'        (ll. 2198–2205)

Arthur does not accuse Lancelot in any way, but only deplores the sad turn of fate. He, who has been wronged more than anybody else, most eagerly longs for a reconciliation with Lancelot; Lancelot's own attitude is very similar (cf. ll. 2082 ff, and 2116–17); he is completely free from any personal hatred, and it is only with great reluctance that he lifts up his sword against his former friends. We are also told that the people are involved in Arthur's quarrels and suffer because of them.[32] The objective tone of the narrative brings home the fact that it is no longer within the power of the individual actors to avert the general catastrophe. This impotence is brought home with particular force in the episode of the snake (ll. 3336 ff.) in which the precarious truce between Arthur and Mordred is broken, but the whole poem is pervaded by a feeling of resignation and mute acceptance, already present in Lancelot's words when he returns from his interrupted meeting with the Queen:

> We haue be-gonne thys ilke nyght
> That shall brynge many A man full colde.'
>
> (ll. 1886–7)

and in Bors' answer:

> 'sithe it is so,
> We shalle be of hertis good
> Aftyr the wele to take the wo.'      (ll. 1889–91)

The detailed description of the peace talks with Lancelot and afterwards with Mordred shows how strong the general longing for peace has become (e.g. ll. 2636 ff.). On the other hand, the prolonged fight between Lancelot and Gawain illustrates the tragic futility of events, the undiminished nobility of Lancelot and the implacable pride of Gawayn.

The author seems to have been aware of a certain distance between himself and the story because he made no attempt to 'modernize' it, as so many other English adapters did, and he generally let the events speak for themselves. It is this conscious simplicity and detachment that distinguish *Le Morte Arthur* from most other romances and make it so particularly attractive and appealing to modern taste.

## 'SIR GAWAIN AND THE GREEN KNIGHT'

As far as size is concerned, this poem, too, comes between the shorter romances and the novels in verse. It is too long to be read in one sitting, but it is clear that the poet was anxious to achieve that degree of unity and coherence which we usually only find in much shorter works. Whereas *Sir Tristrem* and *Le Morte Arthur* can be described as condensed novels, *Sir Gawain and the Green Knight* might more appropriately be considered as an extended *novella* whose plot could have been told much more briefly.

It is hardly necessary to point out that the poem is in many essentials very different from the other romances discussed in this chapter. What it has in common with them is the explicit reference to the English past—emphasized by the short historical sketch from the siege of Troy to the founding of Britain—the close-knit structure and the careful handling of the metre. Apart from this,

*Sir Gawain and the Green Knight* can only with some reservations be grouped among the 'longer romances' and it does not quite belong to the same literary type as *Havelok* or *Sir Tristrem*. The problem of classification seems particularly intractable in this case.

*Sir Gawain and the Green Knight* has always, with justice, been regarded as the most significant English contribution to the genre of romance and it has provoked countless and often conflicting interpretations.[33] It is, however, important to remember that the poem is in many ways quite unique in Middle English literature and can be compared with very few of the other romances. In its intellectual and moral scope it is clearly distinguished from other English works on similar subjects and is more nearly related to the other poems of the *Gawain*-poet. Nevertheless, it cannot be denied that the poet used the story-material and many conventions of chivalrous romance, that is, he obviously wanted to write a romance. This is why it might be useful to discuss the literary form of the poem and, in particular, its position within the canon of Middle English romances.

What, perhaps impresses the reader most on first perusing *Sir Gawain and the Green Knight*, is the exceptionally neat and coherent structure, the organic interrelation of the individual parts and the skilful subordination of every detail to the astonishing design of the whole poem. This even applies to the metrical form.[34] The *Gawain*-stanza is a very close and at the same time flexible narrative unit, quite unlike most other stanza-forms in Middle English. While the variable main part of the stanza in alliterative long lines can easily be adapted to the tempo and the particular style demanded by each episode, the rhyming conclusion provides a clear-cut caesura between the stanzas and at the same time acts as a metrical refrain, establishing an important link between them. D. Everett has shown in how many different ways the 'wheel' (the last four lines of each stanza) can be used. Sometimes it briefly summarizes the preceding narrative (see ll. 362–5 and 512–15) or adds some explanatory comment (as in ll. 1788–91); sometimes it concludes a descriptive passage and returns to the story (e.g. ll. 532–5) or it leads directly into the next stanza (as in ll. 319–22); and sometimes it contains a surprising piece of information (ll. 147–50) or gives additional force to a pointed reply (e.g. ll. 1788–91 and 1813–16).[35] This imaginative and often brilliant use of a metrical device which seems at first sight rather inflexible, is clear evidence of the poet's consummate art. The alliterative long lines, too, show an astonishing degree of variation; they are extended or shortened, slowed down or speeded up just as the context makes it desirable. The number of long lines in each stanza varies from twelve (I, 2) to thirty-seven (II, 18) so that the poet is completely free to put as much information or plot into each stanza as he thinks fit and there is no danger of a monotonous repetition of identical narrative units, a danger which becomes apparent in many tail-rhyme romances. The *Gawain*-stanzas are just as effective in long and elaborate description (cf. the description of the 'pentangel', ll. 640 ff., or of the deer-hunt, ll. 1150 ff.) as in quick and pointed dialogue (cf. ll. 1208 ff.). Sometimes the scene shifts in the middle of a stanza, which is another means of avoiding any undue prominence of the stanzaic pattern (cf. ll. 1731 ff.). Thus the metrical variety in *Sir Gawain* is perhaps even more remarkable than in Chaucer's poetry; the poet manages to combine to an exceptional degree the solemn gravity of the old alliterative epic with the elegance and polish of courtly novels.

This flexibility in detail within a larger design that is never lost sight of, is also characteristic of the poem's plot-structure. This is marked by a strict symmetry and consistency, quite different from what we find in many other Middle English romances. At the beginning of the poem, as at its conclusion, there is a scene that takes place in Arthur's court.[36] Even the destruction of Troy, mentioned in the first lines, is taken up again near the end (ll. 2524–5).[37] Gawain sets out from Arthur's court, and returns to it a completely different person. The return-motif, which is rather more typical of the French courtly novel than of the English romances, is paralleled by the change of seasons in whose periodic cycle the action is closely involved. The season of Christmas is the date for Gawain's perilous adventure and it links the ending of the poem to its beginning, just as the axe-stroke in the first fitt is returned in the last. Inserted between these two scenes is Gawain's adventure in Bertilak's castle; thus the two central fitts are framed by the story of the 'beheading game' to which they repeatedly refer. The three temptations and the hunting-scenes appear like an extended digression, an obstacle in Gawain's way to the Green Chapel. All the time, during the seemingly light-hearted encounter with the lady of the castle, Gawain is oppressed by his disquieting apprehensions and the poet takes care that we do not forget it (cf., for instance, ll. 1836–8). Gawain's 'fault', too, is directly connected with the threatening encounter, because Gawain's dread of the unknown danger is the only point in which he is vulnerable and susceptible to the lady's offers.[38] In this way the temptation scenes are very closely related to the last part of the poem.

The symmetrical structure of the poem is above all, as has often been remarked, the result of the brilliant fusion of the two stories, the 'beheading game' and the temptation, on which the poem is based. However we try to solve the source-problem—few scholars would still subscribe to G. L. Kittredge's elaborate reconstruction —it seems very likely that the *Gawain* poet's share in the interrelation of the various motifs was considerable.[39] In the centre of both episodes stands the trial of Gawain and of his 'trawþe'; for even in the temptation scenes, it is Gawain's loyalty to his host and to the contract that is at stake, rather than his chastity (see especially ll. 1773–5).[40] A contract lies at the heart of both stories, and this leads to a number of parallel details which strengthen the connection between the two chief adventures. The parallels between the first and the second fitts are particularly noticeable. Both culminate in a contract that seems to be nothing but the expression of the general gaiety at the Christmas-festivities; these contracts are outwardly just a 'crystemas gomen' (l. 283) and they both put Gawain under an obligation. The second appears to Gawain (and to the reader) as by far the less serious, but it turns out to be the more dangerous in the end. Compared with this subtle and skilful motivation, the late and not particularly convincing introduction of Morgan le Fay as the real cause of all the mischief seems rather unimportant. For the contemporary reader, this mysterious figure might have added to the authenticity of the story, but it would be wrong to ascribe to her a major rôle in the design of the poem.[41]

The inner connections between the various parts of the poem are repeatedly underlined by parallels and contrasts in style and narrative technique. The gaiety at Bertilak's castle obviously corresponds to the merry atmosphere at Arthur's court, and both stand in pointed contrast to the lonely winter landscape Gawain has to pass through. The skilful interrelation between the hunting-scenes and Gawain's temptation has been noticed by several scholars.[42] Apart from possible allegorical suggestions, which, however, are at best intriguing hints and certainly do not make up the central meaning of the episode, the whole of the third fitt is a masterpiece of dramatic suspense and effective climax. By subtle variation, each of the three days has its own distinctive character. Whereas each of the hunts is even merrier than the one that went before, and at the same time the trophies become less valuable, the 'winnings' of the knight increase in value, the lady's intentions become more and more unmistakeable, and the tone of the conversation accordingly more suggestive and dangerous.

The poet knows how to create tension and richness of effect even within a single scene. The first scene of the poem is carefully built up and has the unity of a dramatic performance, in which the actors come to life by their gestures as well as by their speeches. The scene is 'framed' by Arthur's custom of not touching any food before something extraordinary has happened. The suspense created by his announcement is at first fully satisfied by the appearance of the Green Knight, but it is newly aroused first by the awkward silence and fear of the knights and then by Gawain's readiness to undertake the adventure. The contract between the two knights again heightens the suspense, and the tension never slackens until the end of the poem. The first scene, however, is pointedly concluded by Arthur's observation that now he can indeed begin his meal because he has really witnessed an astonishing adventure (ll. 474–5).

The importance of each detail for the whole plan of the poem can also be seen in those passages where the tempo of the narrative slows down and the action comes to a temporary standstill because of elaborate digressions. We find such rhetorical insertions at one or two crucial points in the story which are made more conspicuous by this means and assume particular importance. Most noticeable is the extensive description of Gawain's armour and the interpretation of the 'pentangel' on his shield (ll. 566 ff.). This is certainly no mere rhetorical flourish, but an important exposition of the theme of the poem. Another passage which considerably adds to the effect and the meaning of the poem is the description of the seasons at the beginning of the second part.[43] It is a most dramatic and impressive image of the passing of time and the approach of the appointed date. The icy winter landscape movingly reflects Gawain's loneliness and isolation and stands in significant contrast to the physical, social and also spiritual comforts of courtly society. It also serves as a background to the Green Chapel, which is associated with the Devil by Gawain (ll. 2187–8).

It is a particularly successful and surprising effect that these two worlds, the wintry wasteland and the heartwarming cheerfulness of the convivial company, are both embodied in the impressive figure of Bertilak. This effect would be considerably diminished, however, if we were meant to regard Bertilak from his first appearance as the sinister and deceptive representative of evil powers and the Green Knight as the uncourtly opposite of Arthur's knights or as the 'wild man' of popular custom.[44] All these interpretations are of course vaguely suggested by the poet in one or two places, but the Green Knight as well as Bertilak (for the reader and for Gawain they are at first two completely separate characters) are presented in a quite positive way when we first meet them, and it would be a simplification to explain this fact merely as the difference between appearance and reality, in fact the narrator intentionally refrains from any explicit comment or evaluation which would detract from the intriguing ambivalence and openness of the action.

Another digression which slows down the narrative tempo and might at first sight appear to be an irrelevant side-track, is the extensive description of the three hunts with a circumstantial account of the etiquette belonging to the courtly art of venery. The leisurely dwelling on so many details of an aristocratic way of life provides an effective background for the swiftly moving dialogue between Gawain and the lady in which the more negative and indeed dangerous side of the courtly world becomes apparent. At the same time, the epic breadth and ceremonious character of these descriptions heighten the tension between the temptations and emphasize their importance. Although the scenes in Gawain's bedchamber are comparatively short, they stretch over a considerable part of the whole poem and thus appear to take up more space than they actually do, which is largely due to the elaborate hunting-scenes.

The alternation of broad and stylized description which at first sight seems to digress from the subject of the poem, and swiftly-told, brief scenes in which the really important events take place, points to another feature of the poem, illustrating the astonishing virtuosity of the poet's narrative art: the hiding of crucial statements behind seemingly irrelevant detail, superficial etiquette and courtly love of game and entertainment. The deepest and most serious questions raised by the poet are often not explicitly stated, but implied between the lines. Thus, for instance, the whole poem itself is much more than is claimed at the beginning, where we are only led to expect another of Arthur's unusual adventures (ll. 27–29). The author's announcement does not get beyond many similar promises introducing conventional romances. The exchange of blows is at first sight nothing but a chivalric game, quite in keeping with the general mood of boisterous merriment. The knight himself calls it a 'crystemas gomen' (l. 283), and a similarly harmless explanation is given by Arthur in his attempt to calm the Queen (ll. 470 ff.), although his behaviour clearly gives the lie to his outward gaiety:

> þaʒ Arþer þe hende kyng at hert hade wonder,
> He let no semblaunt be sene, bot sayde ful hyʒe
> To þe comlych quene, wyth cortays speche . . .
>
> (ll. 467–9)

There is a very similar effect of suggestive understatement when the knights have relapsed into terrified silence after the Green Knight's challenge, and the narrator innocently remarks:

> I deme hit not al for doute,
> Bot sum for cortaysye;
> Bot let hym þat al schulde loute,
> Cast vnto þat wyʒe.          (ll. 246–9)

The second contract, too, in which the exchange of 'winnings' is agreed upon, is introduced like a harmless courtly entertainment, and it is only towards the end that we realize what a serious trial it involves.[45]

The poet's art of conveying a deep and complex meaning in apparently light and even flippant language, reaches a particularly impressive climax in the temptation scenes. They too begin like a courtly game. As soon as Gawain has arrived at Bertilak's castle, the lords and ladies begin to hope for a demonstration of true courtesy and 'þe teccheles termes of talkyng noble' (l. 917), because 'þat fyne fader of nurture' is among them (l. 919).[46] What they would particularly welcome, however, are examples of 'luf-talkyng' (l. 927); significantly, this is the last word in the stanza. It is this art of refined talk that the lady wants to practise with him on her visit to his bed-chamber. At first sight it seems as if all she expects is to converse with him in a courtly way, especially on the subject of love, a point to which she frequently returns (see, for instance, ll. 1508 ff.). The tone of the first temptation has frequently been misunderstood because of a mistaken reading of the line '3e ar welcum to my cors,' (l. 1237).[47] It is more harmless and at the same time more dangerous than a superficial interpretation would suggest. The whole conversation remains on the surface of courtly polish, but beneath the playful repartees the real argument takes place without ever being mentioned in so many words. The courtly refinement acts as a kind of shield, disguising the serious issue. Although Gawain's whole reputation, and indeed his life, are at stake, the three temptations pass without an unkind or violent word being spoken, and the two part in complete amity.

The temptation-scenes are at first presented by the poet almost without any comment, only by means of direct speech, and it is left to the reader to discover beneath the gay dialogue the deeper intentions of the lady and the brilliant fencing of Gawain. It is only in the course of the third temptation that the poet gives us a direct glimpse of the technique employed in this dialogue:

> With luf-la3yng a lyt he layd hym by-syde
> Alle þe speche3 of specialte þat sprange of her mouthe.
>
> (ll. 1777–8)

This is exactly what happens in all the three temptations, and, moreover, it is a fairly accurate description of the poet's own narrative technique.

During the third exchange of winnings, it is still Gawain who delights all the court by his cheerful gaiety although, as we know, he is no longer guiltless and the decisive encounter with the Green Knight is close upon him (ll. 1926 ff.). Here again, it is the description of playful merriment that points to a deeper and much more serious meaning; this is the same technique as that we noted in the first part of the poem.

All this expresses an artistic variety and subtlety hardly found anywhere else in Middle English literature apart from Chaucer. *Sir Gawain* is quite unique in its effortless combination of courtly, Arthurian knighthood, a tolerant and realistic sense of humour and uncompromising religious seriousness. By using diverse narrative techniques, the *Gawain* poet achieves at the same time the stylized artistry of a courtly novel and the down-to-earth, unidealistic directness of a Christian homily.[48]

The poem is obviously addressed to an audience familiar with the aristocratic manners described. It is probable that for listeners completely unacquainted with courtly ideals, Gawain's inner conflict between disloyalty and discourtesy (ll. 1770–5) would seem rather strange and far-fetched. The detailed descriptions of refined etiquette, evidently written by an expert, the composition of the manuscript, and the ideal of knighthood embodied in Gawain, very different from that of most other romances, lead to the same conclusion. By proving himself true and loyal in every sense of the words, Gawain demonstrates his perfection in all chivalric virtues. This is also the meaning of the elaborately described 'pentangel', as an all-inclusive symbol of perfection.[49] It only adds to Gawain's stature and to the success of his trial that in the end he alone is oppressed by a strong sense of failure. This does not mean, however, as has recently been suggested, that his ideal of knighthood has from the start been unrealistic and 'superhuman' and that Arthur's knights justly make fun of him in the end.[50] On the contrary, Gawain's disappointment reveals the poet's mature Christian realism and his recognition of the biblical concept that nobody is perfect who has lost the sense of his own fallibility or who has ceased to strive for an even higher degree of perfection. The laughter of the knights (l. 2514), as that of the Green Knight earlier on (ll. 2389 ff.), does not express derision of an idealist, but sympathy and comfort. Even after his adventure and his partial failure, indeed, because of it, Gawain remains the most perfect knight of the Round Table.

*Sir Gawain and the Green Knight* is related to many other romances in that it describes an excellent knight who in the course of the action gives convincing proof of his superiority. On the other hand, the poem is different from many similar works in that the knight's greatness is not illustrated in a loose sequence of brilliant exploits or exercises in penitence, but by a number of skilfully interrelated and subtly graded tests. Moreover, the virtues that the knight is meant to embody do not, as usual, consist merely in prowess or faithfulness and mercy, but in 'trawþe', which, like the 'pentangel', comprises all other virtues as well. Such 'trawþe' even binds the knight when neither his fame nor his reputation of loyalty are at stake, but only his own conscience is witness. This is the meaning of the last temptation, that by Bertilak's guide (ll. 2118 ff.). Again Gawain is tempted to avoid fulfilling his contract, but, as his answer shows (ll. 2126–39), it is not his reputation which concerns him. Even the secrecy of his guide could not prevent Gawain from feeling a 'kny3t kowarde' (l. 2131), an expression that clearly implies much more than the idea of simple cowardice in the face of danger.

It is rather striking that two essential ingredients of chivalric literature, love and fighting, are only touched on in passing. Apart from the exchange of blows between Gawain and the Green Knight, the hero is involved in no serious fight, whereas in nearly every other romance he has to prove his superiority by an impressive single combat. That Gawain has to fight with countless monsters on his journey to the Green Chapel (ll. 715 ff.), is only mentioned by the way, perhaps as an indispensable requisite of romance, perhaps as an ironic comment on the traditional clichés which had become quite meaningless. In any case, it is quite obvious that the poet does not attach very much importance to this aspect of Gawain's knighthood. The exaggeration of the incredible and the piling up of unusual effects, so typical of many English romances, are completely absent here. In the few places, however, where the poet does want to achieve startling effects, he succeeds with unparalleled brilliance, as at the first appearance of the Green Knight where it is above all the description of the knights, frozen with terror, and the also rather startled King that creates the atmosphere of a truly unheard-of adventure. This is the more impressive as the tone of the narrative so far has not at all prepared us for such a sudden intrusion of the miraculous.

Neither does courtly love play a significant part in this poem. In a Middle English romance, this is perhaps less surprising than the absence of spectacular battles, but in a poem which seems to put so much emphasis on the details of courtly behaviour as *Sir Gawain*, we would certainly expect a sophisticated love-story. In this point, however, the poem is nearer to the more popular literature of England than to the courtly poetry of France or even to the world of Chaucer. Courtly love makes its appearance in the speeches of the lady only, who tries to seduce Gawain into disloyalty. Her eloquent praise of love as portrayed in conventional romance, is above all employed as a weapon against his higher ideal of knighthood. As in Spenser's *Faerie Queene*, two centuries later, the word 'bliss' (1519) has a distinctly negative flavour:

> & of alle cheualry to chose, þe chef þyng a-losed
> Is þe lel layk of luf, þe lettrure of armes;

For to telle of þis teuelyng of þis trwe knyʒteʒ,
Hit is þe tytelet token & tyxt of her werkkeʒ,
How ledes for her lele luf hor lyueʒ han auntered,
Endured for her drury dulful stoundeʒ,
& after wenged with her walour & voyded her care
& broʒt blysse in-to boure with bountees hor awen.

(ll. 1512–19)

The picture of a knight's occupation evoked here by the lady, exactly agrees with the spirit and the conventions of many French and English romances, but the lady's speech reveals only a very limited idea of what true knighthood means for the *Gawain* poet and stands in significant contrast to the moral depth of the whole poem. What the lady, in her almost mechanical list of clichés, understands by 'lele luf' (l. 1516) is practically the opposite of Gawain's 'trawþe'. Thus, the whole edifice of *amour courtois* (as far as it is interpreted in such a superficial way) is shown to be deceptive and unworthy of a true knight, and this in a poem which, more than most other English romances, conforms to the pattern and style of a courtly novel. It is perhaps the most intelligent and serious comment on the world of courtly romance in Middle English literature.[51]

The rejection of extra-marital love (Gawain pointedly refers the lady to her husband, l. 1276) is, however, combined with an extraordinary regard for the lady herself. Gawain never becomes guilty of the slightest discourtesy towards his temptress; indeed, the seriousness of his dilemma lies in his duty to decline her advances without any personal rebuff ('Oþer lach þer hir luf oþer lodly refuse;', l. 1772). This is why he can spend the day with her in friendly conversation as if nothing had ever happened. The conflict between extra-marital love and the laws of Christianity is clearly resolved here as in many popular romances,[52] but not at the expense of womanhood in general or by simple moralizing. It seems quite clear that Gawain's violent harangue against women (ll. 2414–28) is an expression of his disappointment with himself and a collection of medieval commonplaces, not a statement of the author's own views.[53]

It appears from what has been said before, that the ideal of knighthood celebrated in this poem is not so much based on the courtly romances of France and England, but, as has been noted by many recent critics, has a very marked religious aspect.[54] Without attributing a consistently religious, let alone allegorical meaning to the whole poem,[55] it can be said that Gawain is seen above all as a Christian knight and that the ideal he embodies has very little in common with his traditional reputation as a great lover of women.[56] It may even be that the poet consciously emphasized this contrast. For the 'traditional' Gawain, as he appears in many other romances and as he is seen, incidentally, by the knights and ladies in Bertilak's castle (ll. 908 ff.), it would not have been a mortal sin to return the lady's favours in kind.

The extremely intelligent and careful art of the poet which makes *Sir Gawain and the Green Knight* so different from most other English romances, can also be illustrated by his effective narrative technique. The beautiful balance between extended scenes of dialogue, rhetorical description and swift summary has already been mentioned. Whereas in many other romances, time is treated in a rather negligent way, the *Gawain* poet accentuates the story by his skilful handling of time and place. The main action takes place in a few elaborately described scenes which are connected by concise summary. (This is one of the few things *Sir Gawain* has in common with Chaucer's *Troilus and Criseyde*). By subtle variations in the narrative point of view, the author also achieves scenic effects such as are quite rare in Middle English literature. Thus, when describing a particular object or person, the poet often sees it in relation to its surroundings from which it is by degrees singled out so that a more spatial impression is created (see, for instance, ll. 995–1019).[57] Even more effective is his handling of point of view in the description of whole scenes and episodes. The arrival of the Green Knight, for example, is told from the point of view of the knights, gathered in Arthur's hall. The whole description of his strange appearance seems to be informed with their mute bewilderment and anxiety (ll. 134 ff.). The omniscient narrator has almost completely disappeared from the scene, even at the end, when the frightening guest leaves the hall and nobody knows where he is going. This method of description strongly influences the reader's impression of the whole scene. The Green Knight remains a strange and remote figure because we, too, see only his outside and look forward to the coming events with the same uncertainty and suspense as Gawain and his companions.[58]

From the second part (fitt) of the poem on, events and objects are for the most part described as they appear to Gawain, so that the reader can, to some extent, identify himself with the hero. Gawain is the only character in the poem whose thoughts and emotions we are enabled to share. The description of Bertilak's castle, appearing before his eyes (ll. 763 ff.) has often been praised,[59] and indeed it contributes considerably to the portrayal of Gawain's relief at the approaching end of his winter journey and to the significant contrast between the desolate landscape and the hospitality of the cheerful court.

In the following part, too, there are a number of scenes which gain remarkably in effect from the narrative technique employed. Again it is the three temptation scenes that come to mind. In them, the narrative point of view changes repeatedly. On the first morning, it is Gawain who experiences the approach of the lady (ll. 1178 ff.). His almost comic reactions, his pretended sleep, his peeping through half-closed lids, and at last his arrival at the conclusion that he will have to face the encounter after all, help to make us realize the unusual nature of this temptation and the extent of Gawain's predicament. The silent little scene also sets the tone for the following conversation in which long sections of the dialogue are reproduced almost without comment so that we largely share Gawain's viewpoint. The motives and feelings of the lady are only hinted at in one or two places, but we are never given any real insight into her thoughts.[60] Up to the end, we are left in doubt about her real intentions, and this in turn helps us to sympathize with Gawain's difficult situation.

A similar technique is used in the description of the last morning: Gawain in his bed is kept awake by the wild winter storms outside, and the crowing of the cock reminds him of his contract.[61] The journey to the Green Chapel and his encounter with the Green Knight are again described from his point of view. Particularly impressive is the moment when he first hears strange sounds from the direction of the 'Chapel':

> þene herde he of þat hyȝe hil, in a harde roche,
> Biȝonde þe broke, in a bonk, a wonder breme noyse.
> Quat! hit clatered in þe clyff as hit cleue schulde,
> As one vpon a gryndelston hade grounden a syþe;
> What! hit wharred & whette as water at a mulle.
> What! hit rusched & ronge, rawþe to here. (ll. 2199–204)

The vivid description gives such an immediate and impressive picture of Gawain's surprise and shock that it resembles the technique of reported speech used in the modern novel. The same applies to the three blows (see, for instance, Gawain's sideways glance at the swiftly descending axe, ll. 2265 ff.). It is perhaps in consequence of the reader's identification with Gawain, achieved by such technical devices, that Gawain's penitence and disappointment at the end have a more lasting effect on us than the merriment of the knights who try to console him, but whose judgement is evidently based on a more superficial knowledge of Gawain's story than ours. The main function of the effective narrative technique, then, seems to lie in the depth of the characterization of the hero who is the focal point of the whole poem. On the other hand, the narrator also succeeds in making us see Gawain more objectively, especially towards the end of the poem, so that eventually we arrive at a somewhat different view of his experience from his own and judge him less harshly than he judges himself.

*Sir Gawain and the Green Knight* is, by its own claims, no more than a chivalric story of adventure, and the poet modestly puts it in the same category as many another 'aunter' (ll. 27 ff.). In its moral seriousness, however, and in the astonishing scope of its artistry, it is markedly distinguished from any other romance in Middle English. Other poets, too, attempted in their own manner to use Arthurian material for the exposition of a Christian ideal of knighthood, such as the author of the alliterative *Morte Arthure*, but only the *Gawain* poet achieved such a perfect combination of formal unity, as we find it in some lays and a few shorter romances, and epic dimensions, created by elaborate description and extensive scenes of dialogue. The poem seems to be an ideal compromise between the short tale so popular in England, with its rather limited possibilities, and the ambitious novel in verse which does not appear to have found favour before the fifteenth century. The traditional romance was a point of departure for the *Gawain* poet in his endeavour to transcend its moral code, and thus he composed a poem which cannot be described by any of the conventional terms. Unfortunately, it stands as a quite unique achievement in Middle English literature; it seems to have had no influence on the subsequent development of English romance, just as it appeared, as far as we can see, without warning and cannot be explained by anything that went before.

# 7

# NOVELS IN VERSE

Apart from short tales in verse and the longer romances, the thirteenth and fourteenth centuries also produced a number of extensive verse-novels of between five and twelve thousand lines. There are considerably fewer of them than of the shorter poems, but most of them have been preserved in more versions. This does not necessarily mean that the type was generally more popular than the smaller epic forms which naturally could more easily get lost and which certainly often existed in many more versions than those that are still extant. Many of the verse-novels are also compilations of widely known legends, whereas the shorter poems often only contain single episodes from these story-cycles or deal with other, less famous heroes and their adventures. With the exception of a few, not very characteristic examples, the novels usually contain the life-history of some particularly famous hero of history or legend, from his birth until his death. They are compilations covering a long period of time and a multitude of adventures without any great regard for unity of structure and theme. This alone makes it rather pointless to put them on the same level as *Amis and Amiloun* or even *Sir Perceval of Gales*, poems in which a decisive phase in the life of the hero or a series of significant adventures united by a common theme, are singled out.

It is worth noting that the length of the verse-novels is achieved mainly by an aggregation of adventures and single episodes, not by a more circumstantial or ceremonious epic style and a particularly slow narrative tempo. Only in a few cases—most clearly, perhaps in *Ipomedon A*—do the style and the narrative technique differ radically from that in the shorter romances. The difference lies rather in the more economical choice of material and the concentration on a particular theme in the shorter romances; they confine themselves to a few important episodes, whereas often in the novels very similar events are told more than once and, as the different versions of some novels show, large sections could simply be inserted or left out *ad libitum*.[1] The descriptions of battles are, perhaps, an exception because they are often more extensive and detailed in the novels than in the shorter tales. They are usually fairly close translations from the French or Anglo-Norman. In this as in some other respects, the novels are much less original and reveal less individuality in the manner of adaptation than the shorter romances. They are often surprisingly faithful to their sources and make no attempt at creating a new literary type, whereas the less extensive romances, as I have tried to show, handle their material with astonishing independence and seem to have aimed at something very different from many of their sources.

A glance at the transmission of the novels shows that a fair number of them, at least those about particularly renowned heroes, were translated into English at an early date. Among these are two works based on Anglo-Norman novels, *Sir Beues of Hamtoun* and *Guy of Warwick*, both of which are adaptations of indigenous stories and clearly represent an attempt to glorify native popular heroes who could claim equal status with the heroes of the older story-cycles and often have to go through very similar trials and adventures as these.[2] Though originally written for the Anglo-Norman nobility, perhaps even on behalf of particular families, these novels soon achieved remarkable popularity and the number of English versions shows that before long a much wider audience was appealed to than that originally addressed.

Also dating back to a comparatively early period are three novels from the London area which are often attributed to the same author and for the most part likewise derive from Anglo-Norman models: *Kyng Alisaunder*, *Arthour and Merlin* and *Richard Coeur de Lion*. Each has as its subject the biography of a famous king, and they are on the whole even less unified than *Beues of Hamtoun* and *Guy of Warwick*. They largely consist of a series of battles and often rather fantastic adventures. In these novels, it is generally less the hero himself than his whole army and the cause it represents that claim our chief attention, particularly in the militantly Christian novel about Richard Coeur de Lion. As far as their style is concerned, these novels are, however, more dependent on courtly literature and the art of rhetoric than the more popular and didactic stories about the founders of famous English families, as is particularly noticeable in the case of *Kyng Alisaunder*.

Apart from these novels, which are, by the way, all preserved in the Auchinleck Ms. and probably date back to the thirteenth century, there are a few other attempts to create poems of some length in English after French models, but none of them seems to have been particularly successful.

*William of Palerne* is a fairly close translation of the French novel *Guillaume de Palerne*, written at the request of some noble, in which the most remarkable thing is the chosen verse-form (alliterative long lines) that makes this novel quite unique in fourteenth century literature of England. The tail-rhyme version of the story of Ipomedon (*Ipomedon A*), an artistically very successful translation of Hue de Rotelande's *Ipomedon*, which captures the courtly and graceful tone of its model very well, is also a rather special case and seems to have had no influence on the development of English romance.[3] It is an extremely interesting, but quite isolated attempt to transpose a highly sophisticated and psychologically subtle story into the traditional and homely form of the tail-rhyme romance without substantial alteration. If we exclude the alliterative *Morte Arthure*, which belongs to a completely different tradition, and the extensive compilations of the story of Troy, such as the *Laud Troy Book*, which can hardly be termed romances in any precise sense of the word, it is not until the fifteenth century that we find again more lengthy and comprehensive works, especially the long and rather bookish compilations of Lydgate and the novels about Partenope and Generides, two quite successful translations from the French, which, however, lie already outside the period dealt with here and illustrate a new trend in literary taste.[4]

Thus, most of the surviving verse-novels are translations in a much stricter sense than, for instance, *King Horn, Libeaus Desconus* or even *Ywain and Gawain*. They all were probably written out of a desire to make famous subjects, with a long literary or historical tradition, available to an audience no longer familiar with French. The prologues of *Arthour and Merlin* and *Richard Coeur de Lion* make this very clear, and the information provided by *William of Palerne* points in the same direction (see ll. 163 ff. and ll. 5529 ff.). We certainly cannot speak of minstrel-poetry here, whatever we may mean by the term, because these novels are highly literary products, written either at the instigation of some patron, as *William of Palerne*, or to satisfy the translator's own wish to appeal to a wider pubic. Undoubtedly they were intended to be read before an audience and the frequent occurrence of clichés which we tend to associate with minstrel-poetry is therefore quite appropriate. The brief allusion to the widespread ignorance of French round about 1300 in *Arthour and Merlin* (ll. 25–6) indicates that we are not only to think of the lower classes in this connection, but that the nobility were also included in the circles of those for whom these poems were translated.[5] The extent and emphasis of the remarks referring to the purpose of the translations, so interesting for the historian of the language, are also clear signs of the deliberation with which the adapters went to work. Such information is lacking in the majority of the shorter works because they never claim to be translations in the same ambitious sense, but even where they refer to their sources, they only want to retell the same story, not to produce an exact equivalent.

All this is partly the reason why the verse-novels are for the most part not the most successful of the Middle English romances. Comparing them with their French models, one cannot help noticing that the form of the artistically unified and close-knit novel that is not just an aggregation of separate episodes, but a well-planned structural and thematic whole, is lacking in English, if we leave out of consideration the alliterative *Morte Arthure*. The courtly novels of Chrétien de Troyes and his successors did not act as a stimulus to the writing of similar works in England, and the only translation of a novel by Chrétien, the English *Ywain and Gawain*, characteristically avoids the extensive novel-form as far as possible and, by drastic abridgement, attempts to present the story in a more concise and lucid way, whereby, it must be admitted, much of the actual meaning of the original is lost.[6] Only *Ipomedon A* has some claim to be considered a unified and thematically coherent novel in verse, but it stands very much on its own in Middle English and it follows a source which in itself does not represent the highest form of the courtly novel.

Thus, it is not possible, even in the case of the verse-novels, to arrive at a completely satisfactory classification of the individual works, but we can at least describe a few characteristic types whose similarities and differences lie not so much in their subject-matter as in the way in which this is treated and in the style. This will be illustrated by a closer examination of a few poems.

## 'SIR BEUES OF HAMTOUN'

*Sir Beues of Hamtoun* was probably one of the best known of the Middle English romances; in popularity it was probably second only to *Guy of Warwick* with which it has several features in common. Its wide appeal is attested by the transmission alone: the poem is preserved in six manuscripts and a number of early prints; there are also some versions that were current on the continent.[7] The English versions are mainly to be found in larger collections, like the Auchinleck Ms. (A) and Cambridge Ff. II. 38 (C), where they are put among other secular works, or Gonville & Caius 175 (E), Chetham 8009 (M) and Egerton 2862 (S), where they are copied together with some more historical and legendary works. (The sixth manuscript, Royal Library of Naples, XIII, B 29 (N), is of particularly mixed content.) It may be coincidence that *Sir Beues of Hamtoun* stands next to poems like *Arthour and Merlin* (in A), *Athelston* (in E) and *Richard Coeur de Lion* (in S) in some of the manuscripts, but it could also indicate that the novel was felt to be a kind of family chronicle or at least a tale from England's past which had some important bearing on the present.

In the poem's source, the Anglo-Norman *Boeve de Haumtone*, this is even more obvious; it belongs to the type, suitably described as 'ancestral romance' by M. D. Legge.[8] Its most characteristic motifs are the founding of a family, exile, and the achievement of extraordinary exploits abroad. The English version has taken over and dramatized just these 'native' qualities of the ancestral romances so that the term could also be applied to *Sir Beues of Hamtoun*, though perhaps in a wider and less specific sense.

The form of the work presents some problems. Unlike its source, it begins in tail-rhyme stanzas, which, however, break off after some four hundred lines; after that, the poem continues in rhyming couplets. As the Auchinleck version of *Guy of Warwick* has a similar change in metre, it is possible that the scribes of the manuscript or of its immediate source were responsible for the introduction of the tail-rhyme stanzas and, in the case of *Sir Beues*, simply continued in the metre of the preceding item

(*Reinbrun*). *Horn Childe* and *Amis and Amiloun* show that this manuscript is particularly important for the history of the tail-rhyme romances.[9]

On the other hand, some other manuscripts, not immediately dependent on A, also have the strophic beginning. In two of them (S and N) there is an attempt to carry on the metre by adding a *cauda* (tail-line) after every couplet, though only for about a hundred lines, while in another version (M) the beginning is completely altered and consists of rhyming couplets only. Thus it is hardly possible to say anything definite about the reasons which may have led the scribe to abandon the tail-rhyme stanzas in favour of couplets. All the same, the close relationship between the two metrical forms becomes apparent here. Kölbing maintained that the beginning of the romance could not originally have been written in couplets because he felt that many of the tail-lines were quite indispensable for the meaning;[10] this may be so, yet it is noticeable that the form of the tail-rhyme stanzas used here is quite different from that found in most of the tail-rhyme romances. Thus, only very few of the couplets are linked to each other by rhyme (see, for instance, ll. 301–5) and the tail-lines usually only rhyme in pairs; in other words, we have here six-line stanzas, not the usual twelve-line stanzas. The *caudae* are for the most part quite unimportant for the development of the plot; often they are only very loosely integrated in the syntax, just as in the passage of lines 409–509[21] of the manuscripts S and N, where it is obvious that the *caudae* are an afterthought. Essential parts of a sentence or of the plot are hardly ever contained in the tail-lines, as, for instance in *Reinbrun*.[11] Thus, it seems to me quite possible that the first part of the poem was also originally written in rhyming couplets which by slight alterations, in many cases merely by the insertion of *caudae*, were turned into tail-rhyme stanzas. The lines 409–509[21] in S and N prove that such a procedure was occasionally followed. The M-version, on the other hand, which is in rhyming couplets throughout, obviously belongs to a slightly different line of transmission. It is sometimes rather more formal than the other versions and occasionally tries to be more precise (cf. the indirect speech in M, ll. 708 ff., as compared with direct speech in A, ll. 917 ff., or the more exact details in M, ll. 241 ff. and the vaguer ones in A, ll. 301 ff.). Kölbing's 'stemma' describes very accurately the textual relationship between the individual manuscripts, but it is more than doubtful whether it gives an adequate explanation of the actual origins of the different versions.[12]

The plot of the poem has several points in common with *King Horn*. Both romances apparently go back to a *chanson de geste* and have some uncourtly, or rather pre-courtly characteristics, such as the resolute wooing by the lady, by which the knight is almost forced into loving her.[13] As in *King Horn*, the story combines the motifs of love, revenge and the progress of a knight from an inexperienced youth to a victorious fighter and king. In both poems the boy is deprived of his inheritance, and a long series of fights is necessary before he can win it back. The similarities between the two poems are hardly sufficient to prove that they have a common source, but they do show that this is a type of plot which was obviously a particular favourite in England.

An important difference between the two poems lies of course in their length. *King Horn* is a short tale, summarizing an extensive plot within a brief space, so that it could easily be read in one sitting, whereas *Sir Beues of Hamtoun* is a verse-novel of three times the length, with clear divisions and pauses, obviously aiming at a series of effective episodes rather than a unified whole. The work is not expressly divided into 'fitts' or '*partes*' (nor are any of the other verse-novels dealt with in this chapter), and so in reciting the poem, breaks could be introduced at various undetermined points, according to circumstances. However, the story itself suggests several clearly marked caesuras, dividing the novel into five almost equal sections of about nine hundred lines each.

The first part briefly describes the hero's youth, his escape and his first heroic deeds at the court of King Ermin. His boyish displays of strength already give a foretaste of his later glorious exploits, and his rescue by Josiane hints at the love relationship between the two. The injustice done to Beves and his vow of revenge (ll. 301 ff.), foreshadowing later events, create enough suspense to hold the attention of the listeners and make them eager to hear the continuation of the story (see also the anticipation in ll. 328-30 and the repetition of his vow, l. 552). Thus, although complete in itself, this first part of the poem contains several motifs that prepare for the further development of the story. The opposition between Christians and heathens, too, which runs through the whole novel, is introduced at an early point. In the first description of Josiane we are expressly told that she is a pagan ('Boute of cristene lawe ȝhe kouþe nauȝt', l. 526), and Beves soon has an opportunity of proving his loyalty to the Christian faith when Ermin offers to make him his heir and give him Josiane for a wife if he renounces his faith (ll. 555–68). Beves' determined refusal, which only increases Ermin's regard for him (ll. 569–70), is the more remarkable as he obviously only has a very vague idea of the Christian creed and has to have the meaning of Christmas explained to him by a heathen (ll. 585–606). That he can only remember the jolly tournaments and feasting in honour of Christmas from his early childhood, but nothing about the deeper meaning of the festival, is quite characteristic of the unconcerned and at the same time realistic tone of the poem.

At line 909 a new section of the novel begins, outwardly marked by the passing over of three years and by the appearance of Brademond as Josiane's suitor. What makes the break between the two parts particularly clear, is the detailed recapitulation of an episode told only a few lines earlier (ll. 934–59). This recapitulation is included in most of the English versions, but is lacking in M, which, as we noted before, is a more bookish redaction, less adapted to oral recitation. The repeated reference to Beves' heroic deeds at this point seems completely unnecessary and probably has no other function than that of giving the second part a certain amount of unity by providing a few helpful clues for all those who would not recall every detail of the first part (or had not listened to it). The second section of the poem describes Josiane's wooing of Beves, his seven-years' imprisonment by Brademond and his miraculous rescue. On his way to Brademond, as well as after his escape from prison, he gives further examples of his prowess and gains victories against overwhelming odds, particularly, of course, against heathens. Beves is called 'þe cristene kniȝt' (l. 1011), and there is a real crusading spirit in this part of the story, as in the English Charlemagne-romances and, by the way, in nearly all the verse-novels discussed in this chapter. The meeting with Terri recalls the first part of the poem with the story of Terri and Saber; both characters are to play an important part in the later course of the plot. Josiane's own fate, her despair at Beves' supposed infidelity and her marriage, are also described in this section. Thus, the second part, too, is in a way self-contained; it includes several complete episodes and all the most important characters of the story make their appearance.

Again at line 1959 a new section begins, which is also introduced by some glances at the previous parts of the story, reminding us of the most important elements in the plot that has already become somewhat complicated. Beves gives an account of his life-story up to this point and vows that he will only marry a virgin, a motif that may have something to do with the family-chronicle character of the poem and points forward to later events in the poem. The French version does not mention Beves' promise to marry a virgin at this point. The A-version of the poem has in addition some more recapitulations and backward glances (ll. 1991–2004, 2013–36). More recapitulations follow, usually extended by the English adapter, some in the form of dialogue. They recall Beves' own adventures (even the wicked part played by his step-father is briefly mentioned) and those of Josiane. The narrator also seems very interested in the fate of Beves' horse Arundel (ll. 2139–46), presumably because of its association with the founding of Arundel castle.

Beves arrives at the conclusion that he is not yet in a position to reconquer his inheritance, and so first of all he sets out to find his lady again. The section which now follows gives an account of their flight together and their arrival in Cologne where Josiane is baptized. Another clear caesura in the plot can be discovered after line 2596, but the subsequent episode, which is only to be found in the English versions of the story (ll. 2597–2910), probably has to be counted as part of the previous section. Beves' glorious feat of killing a most dangerous dragon gives added importance to his sojourn in Cologne. The regaining of Beves' inheritance is again delayed by this interlude, as well as by Josiane's short marriage to Miles which is told in the following section (ll. 3117–3304). Thus, the third section of the poem (ll. 1959–2910) is just as long as the first two, whereas the fourth part, ending with Beves' re-establishment in his inheritance, and his marriage to Josiane, is somewhat shorter, though particularly rich in exciting incidents.

Between this and the following (fifth) section of the poem the division is less clearly marked;[14] indeed all the divisions suggested here are not meant as a strict scheme, but rather as reflecting the basic structure of the poem and the principle of its composition, with a view to oral recitation. These divisions are, however, by no means clearly marked in all the manuscripts. Just at this point (between the fourth and the fifth section) there is a very clear break in the plot, though not in the text of the poem. Beves has achieved his end, and the poem could quite conceivably stop here, but with the introduction of the English King new complications begin to arise, involving Beves' own sons and a number of his former enemies. They start with a quarrel about Arundel, the faithful horse, and a new separation from Josiane, lasting for seven years. At the end of the novel, Beves has won a kingdom for each of his sons, for Terri and for himself. After twenty years of happiness he and Josiane die, almost at the same moment, and Arundel, too, falls down dead.

This last part of the poem is of course linked to the preceeding sections by most of the characters taking part, but it still gives the impression of a later addition which is not absolutely necessary for the continuity of the story. On the other hand, we are at the end of the fourth part still in ignorance about the fate of Josiane's father and her first husband. Thus the poem is indeed a unified whole in so far that all the threads of the story are not tied up until the end; nevertheless there are several places where we can see that the plot is spun out in a purely episodic manner, suggesting that there was no very definite masterplan for the whole novel, such as we can discover in Chrétien's poems. The three extensive additions made by the English adapter can be quoted in support of this observation. They each consist of an episode, complete in itself (see ll. 585–738, 2597–2910, 4287–4538) and by no means clumsily inserted, but heightening the suspense; however, they seem to prove that the adapter was more interested in the individual episode than in the structure of the whole poem. Thus, the fight with the dragon is obviously added with the intention of putting Beves on an equal footing with Guy of Warwick and Lancelot, as the express reference to these two famous heroes shows. Beves has to be given a similar adventure as Guy. The fight is told almost in terms of a Saint's legend. It is prepared for by a dream, such as we would expect in a legend (ll. 2681 ff.), and Beves' victory is celebrated by bell-ringing and by a solemn procession (ll. 2893–2910).

The London street fight, too, has the effect of an independent insertion which was bound to appeal particularly to an English audience of less refined tastes and must have been especially successful when read somewhere in the London area. The scene does not only prove that the poet had a pretty exact knowledge of the topography of London,[15] but also that he was capable of describing this battle against citizens of flesh and blood with more precision and artistic energy than the conventional encounters with blood-less monsters. It is less likely, however, that he wanted to allude to definite historical events. In this case, the wholesale slaughtering of London citizens would not have been an exploit apt to endear Beves and his sons to a London audience of the lower classes.

There are also some other aspects of the poem which give the impression that the author was mainly concerned with satisfying the audience's desire for simple amusement. Thus, we find quite a number of rather burlesque scenes, suggesting that the poet had no very subtle sense of humour, such as Ascopard's attempted bap-tism and his very unchivalrous way of fighting (ll. 3420 ff.), the messenger scene, obviously only included to raise a laugh (ll. 3061 ff.), and the description of Josiane's and Miles' wedding night (ll. 3117-3304). This whole episode is clearly not taken very seriously by the author; otherwise it would give rather an un-favourable picture of Beves' future spouse. There are also some other instances of the poet's grim and not very delicate humour.[16]

In spite of the episodic structure of the poem, there is no lack of coherence and tension, although we cannot detect a systematic plan or any sophisticated principles of composition. The dramatic unity of the poem is above all achieved by the character of the hero, who gets his revenge on his step-father, regains his inheritance, and founds a family which rules over several kingdoms. At the same time, the novel describes the career of a knight who by his natural valour alone overcomes all obstacles and all resistance. There is a certain climax in the series of his exploits. His first trials of strength (except his fight against Brademond) have something of the swaggering youth about them; his battles against his pur-suers after his escape from prison are mainly fought in self-defence, but his great fight with the dragon shows him as a Christian cham-pion who with God's help frees the country from a satanic plague and is honoured by the Bishop with a ceremonial procession. All the time Beves has to rely entirely on himself; indeed, he insists on being left to himself in all his fights and he twice rejects Josiane's offer of help (ll. 2413-20 and 2474-8), the second time with a brutal threat. Truly heroic courage and obstinate ambition seem to be closely related here, which fits in with the portrait of a popu-lar hero rather than one of a courtly knight. The dramatic prin-ciple of increasing tension is applied time and again, but the repetition of similar episodes and the prominence of the external mechanism of the plot make it impossible for us to feel that this is a novel about the maturing and the chivalric education of a king, as is the case with *King Horn*, *Havelok*, and, to some extent, *Guy of Warwick*.

Beves is not only a valiant knight, but also a warrior of God who succeeds in decimating the heathens, freeing the Christians from wicked enemies and converting Josiane to the Christian faith. All this, however, does not amount to a consistent spiritual design, but is presented as part of the swiftly moving plot. The theory that the author of the original poem was a cleric could account for the pious tone of several episodes, but the style of the English versions is not so obviously religious that we are forced to assume the English adapter, too, must have been a cleric. The poem only shows once more to what extent love of God and hatred of the Saracens are part of the make-up of the perfect knight in many of the English popular romances and these qualities are just as important as physical superiority and courage. It is hardly surprising that these characteristics are particularly emphasized in a work describing the origins of a powerful English family and praising its famous ancestor. The term 'romance of prys' would be especially fitting in the case of this poem.

Apart from prowess and exemplary piety,[17] it is above all liberality by which the true knight is distinguished, and this is also a virtue which, in a somewhat watered-down form greatly appealed to the adapters of the English romances. Thus, Josiane's chamberlain who comes to Beves in order to reconcile him with his mistress, receives a princely reward from the knight, although his request is refused (ll. 1153 ff.), and it is just this reward that convinces Josiane that Beves cannot possibly be of low degree because

> . . . hit nas neuer a cherles dede,
> To ȝeue a maseger swiche a wede!     (ll. 1173–4)

Indeed, it is this proof of his noble character that finally causes her to abandon her faith in order to win his love.

The on the whole very pointed and well-balanced structure of the poem shows that, within his modest limits, the English adapter had a conscious artistic design which, in spite of all episodic rambling and embellishment, he never quite lost sight of and tried to impress on his audience. Thus, even the Anglo-Norman version contains various prophetic hints, designed to create a feeling of suspense and to give some unity to the whole story. The English adapter took over some of these anticipations more or less literally (as, for instance, ll. 1063–8), extended them (as in ll. 205–10), or added new ones (ll. 832–6, 3637–8). They usually, however, refer to events that follow fairly soon, at least in the same section of the poem, whereas the recapitulations, as we have seen, mainly serve to connect the various sections and help the audience to keep up with the somewhat intricate plot.

The frequent premonitions also have another function which is characteristic of the style of the poem. They give some prominence to the figure of the narrator by revealing his deep involvement in the events he has to relate. Thus, some of the premonitions are in the form of powerless complaints about the unavoidable disaster that is to befall one of the characters, as the distressed warning when Beves' father rides into the forest where he will meet his death (ll. 205–10).[18] The prayers for individual characters, particularly frequent in this poem, and the cursing of villains have a similar effect.[19] Such formulas are not infrequent in the source of the poem, but they can also be found in those passages that were added by the English adapter. The frequently inserted proverbs and general aphorisms are also characteristic of the style of the poem; they mostly seem to be added by the English adapter and are reminiscent of *Havelok*, particularly such homely truths as the following:

> For, whan a man is in pouerte falle,
> He haþ fewe frendes wiþ alle.    (ll. 3593–4)[20]

These proverbial sayings also allow the narrator to come to the fore and to establish closer contact with his audience. In addition, there are the numerous conventional formulas, pointing out transitions and changes of scene or announcing some particularly exciting events, like 'Herkneþ now a wonder-cas!' (l. 1792) and similar clichés.[21] As in *Havelok*, the narrator in one place asks for a drink before he can continue his story:

> Ac er þan we be-ginne fiȝte,
> Ful vs þe koppe anon riȝte!    (ll. 4107–8)

Here, too, we are not to think of an ale-house, but of some larger social gathering or a domestic circle. The passage, like several other

219

formulas, creates a feeling of a community between the narrator and his audience, whether the invitation was really meant to be followed or, as is more likely, it is to be understood as a literary convention.

The narrative style of the poem has much in common with that of the Anglo-Norman poem which, as M. D. Legge says, 'has no nonsense about it'.[22] In spite of its length, the poem never seems monotonous or long-winded. The action develops rapidly throughout, and the narrator hardly ever troubles to give us a more detailed description of things and persons. Even the descriptions of feasts, so common in many other romances, are sometimes passed over by an *occupatio*, like the following:

> þou3 ich discriue nou3t þe bredale,
> 3e mai wel wite, hit was riale,
> þat þer was in alle wise
> Mete and drinke & riche seruise.  (ll. 3479–82)[23]

Only certain climaxes, like the fight with the dragon and the London street-fight, are related in more detail, but the long and elaborate speeches, so frequent in *Havelok*, are almost entirely absent here, although many events are portrayed in the form of brief scenes of dialogue in direct speech. Thus, in A (ll. 70–174), the sending of the messenger as well as the delivery of his message and his report on his return are presented in direct speech. In many ways, the style of the poem is much more like that of the shorter romances than that of *Havelok* or *Ywain and Gawain*.

*Beues of Hamtoun*, then, is an extremely lively and entertaining, though on the whole rather artless verse-novel, which is mainly concerned with presenting an exciting plot and with engaging the listeners' interest by a swift narrative and a wealth of colourful episodes. If the number of manuscripts is anything to go by, it was certainly very successful in this limited aim.

### 'GUY OF WARWICK'

The equally popular and well-known verse-novel of Guy of Warwick can be dealt with more briefly because the English versions follow their Anglo-Norman source for the most part rather closely and do not change the character of the poem to any significant degree. Extensive alterations, abridgements or expansions are rare; most editorial changes are to be found in the second half of the poem which even in the sources was rather diffuse and even more episodic than the rest.[24] The version contained in the manuscript Ff. II. 38 of the Cambridge University Library keeps most closely to the original. The version in Gonville & Caius 107 (C) also follows it very exactly, but it breaks off with Guy's death.[25] In contrast, the redaction of the story in the Auchinleck Ms. is particularly illuminating because it divides the novel into three completely separate poems of which the first is composed in rhyming couplets and takes the story as far as Guy's return to Warwick. The following part is not included in the contemporary numbering of the manuscript items and was probably counted as part of the first section. It begins in the same column where the first poem leaves off, but it has its own introduction, not to be found in any other version of the story, and it is clear that a new beginning is being made:

> God graunt hem heuen blis to mede
> þat herken to mi romaunce rede
> Al of a gentil kniȝt:
> þe best bodi he was at nede
> þat euer miȝt bistriden stede,
> & freest founde in fiȝt.
> þe word of him ful wide it ran,
> Ouer al þis warld þe priis he wan
> As man most of miȝt.
> Balder bern was non in bi:
> His name was hoten sir Gij
> Of Warwike, wise & wiȝt. (ll. 1–12)

The explicit introduction of the hero and the change in the metre (the poem continues in tail-rhyme stanzas) show that this is more than the beginning of a new section and that the poem is quite independent of the first part. It contains the story of Guy from his marriage until his death. The poem also keeps closely to the French source, but it carefully leaves out the first part of Reinbrun's story which in the other versions is related before Guy's death (cf. C, ll. 8654–9029 and the Cambridge version, ll. 8397–8744). The transition from A 141.12 (= C, l. 8653) to A 142.1 (corresponding to C, l. 9030) reveals no trace of a break and is obviously the result of some careful editing. The story of Guy is thus much more unified and the omission makes the structure more coherent and close-knit. At the same time the adapter was then enabled to combine the various parts of Reinbrun's story which in the source, as in the Cambridge version, were separated by the account of Guy's death.

In A, the second *Guy* poem ends with the death of the hero and a conventional conclusion with a brief summary and a prayer. After that, a completely new poem begins (it has a number of its own in the contemporary numbering of items) with its own prologue, briefly summarizing the preceding events, and a complete version of Reinbrun's history on its own. The first part contains the section which was left out between stanzas 141 and 142 of the second *Guy* poem, and then there follows—without any break at all—an account of all those events which in the Anglo-Norman poem and in the Cambridge version are only related after Guy's death (see stanza 32). This rather skilful redaction suggests, as L. H. Loomis has shown, that some deliberate editing, possibly under supervision, went on in the 'bookshop' in which the manuscript was produced.[26] Above all, this division of the Anglo-Norman novel into three separate works makes it very likely that the English adapters recognized the episodic and composite character of the whole story and did not therefore consider it a unified work of art, but a series of effective adventures which could be rearranged without any harm to the consistency of the whole work. The fact that such novels were usually read in instalments, probably to variable audiences, appears to have had an important influence on the forms of the individual poems in England.

On reading *Guy of Warwick*, it soon becomes clear that this is a particularly mixed patchwork composition, in which the most diversified romance-motifs follow each other in a rather loose sequence. Of course the various episodes are linked by the figure of the hero and some continuous threads in the plot, but they do not, as, for instance, in Chrétien's poems or in *Havelok*, logically arise one from the other or add up to an organic whole. Many of them remain superfluous, interchangeable, and could easily be taken out of their context without any loss to the story. The C-version in particular shows that often large sections could be left out or be summarized in a few words without seriously affecting the structure of the poem. Such works as Lydgate's poem about Guy of Warwick can serve as examples of the fact that single episodes from the bulk of the stories about Guy, in particular his fight with Colbrond, began to have a life of their own and were very popular even out of their original context.[27]

Though the English versions do not indicate any clear-cut division into separate sections, and it was probably left to the reciter to decide at which point he wanted to break off, at least the Auchinleck version shows a tendency to announce clearly new episodes and to bring out the caesuras in the plot. Thus the first section (ll. 1–1266) relates the beginning of Guy's love for Felice and his knighting, the second section contains his first heroic deeds and the inception of his fight against the Emperor (ll. 1267–2448), the third gives an account of the reconciliation and Guy's killing of the heathen Sultan (ll. 2449–3996). After that the individual episodes are less easily disentangled and the divisions between separate sections cannot be so clearly established, but in this part of the story too, we find frequent caesuras where new episodes are announced and the plot seems to come to a standstill, at least in the versions A and C. Formulas by which transitions are explicitly made and new events are introduced, usually combined with a request for the audience's attention, are spread throughout the whole work in considerable number. It is perhaps worth noting that these formulas are used particularly frequently in such extensive verse-novels. It seems certain that the adapters had an audience in mind whose attention had to be awakened from time to time by such reminders and which was mainly used to shorter works. In the Cambridge version the transitions are as a rule less clearly marked. It appears to be a rather more bookish version, less deliberately adapted for oral recitation, but even here there are a few places where the audience is addressed, and some requests to fill the glasses, which are absent in the Anglo-Norman poem (ll. 5859–5860, 6687–8, 7117–18).

The rather patchwork character of the novel which in places reads like a collection of romance-clichés, certainly contributed to its popularity. Even more than *Sir Beues of Hamtoun*, *Guy of Warwick* is a combination of a Saint's legend and a courtly romance. It contains even more bloody fights than *Sir Beues*, but at the same time it is much clearer that the hero does not take on all these adventures out of mere desire for glory, but because of a genuine pity for the oppressed. This becomes particularly important in the second part of the poem when Guy prays to God, apologizing for his many fights and explaining that he is not concerned about any worldly gains. Thus he assures God when his attempt to help his friend Tirri has brought him into a rather desperate situation:

> Whi is me fallen þus strong cumbring?
> & y no fiȝt for to win no þing,
> Noiþer gold no fe,
> For no cite no no castel,
> Bot for mi felawe y loued so wel,
> þat was of gret bounte.
> For he was sumtyim so douhti,
> & now he is so pouer a bodi,
> Certes, it reweþ me.' (A, 197, ll. 4–12)[28]

Thus the author can revel in endless descriptions of fights and adventures without seeming to offer only worldly entertainment because Guy always fights for a good cause.

Guy's mission as a champion of God becomes most apparent in his great fight against Colbrond (A, 242, ll. 1 ff.; C, ll. 10,432 ff.; Cambridge version ll. 10,065 ff.). The whole episode is told like a devotional tale. All night King Athelstan prays for help until an angel appears to him and announces that Guy will fight on his behalf. Guy only seems to be the instrument by which God saves England from the Danes. The function of this episode in the context of the poem is quite similar to that of Beves' fight against the dragon. Guy's death, again announced by an angel, is described like the edifying end of a Saint. It is rather significant and shows the markedly homiletic character of the novel, that Guy's story does not end with the happy union of the lovers, as most romances do, but in the solitude of a hermitage in the woods. Miracles take place near his dead body: a sweet perfume arises from the corpse, and even a hundred men cannot move Guy's body to take it away from the hermitage (A 294.1; C, ll. 10,949 ff.). All this shows that the poem turns into a legend towards the end and it is quite possible that it was originally written by a cleric who wished to glorify the family of the Earl of Warwick by presenting such a saintly portrait of their ancestor and at the same time to appeal to a wider audience by the description of an exemplary hero who combines the virtues of a knight with those of a Saint.

In contrast to the legendary character of the second part, the first, rather more extensive section of the poem is a courtly romance on the well-known theme of the Squire of Low Degree.

224

The knight loves a lady who is socially far above him. She rejects him until he has proved himself worthy of knighthood, as he soon succeeds in doing. After a series of increasingly difficult fights against more and more overpowering odds, he finally reaches the goal of his ambition and is united to her. Guy is the traditional lover who exhibits all the typical symptoms of courtly love, and Felice the rather forbidding lady who only wants to belong to the very bravest knight—quite different from the resolute and spirited girl-characters in *King Horn*, *Amis and Amiloun* and *Sir Beues of Hamtoun* who press their love upon the hero. Felice's reply, when Guy, after being knighted and after having won a triumphant victory in a tournament, comes to her and renews his suit, is typical of many courtly romances, though perhaps more of the French ones than of the English adaptations. She tells him that he is not yet so famous that she could not find many equally distinguished knights. Above all, she suspects that he would become lazy and inactive if she were to grant him her love so that she would actually wrong him by her too ready consent:

> & ʒif ich þe hadde mi loue y-ʒeue,
> To welden it while þat y liue,
> Sleuþe þe schuld ouercome:
> Namore wostow of armes loue,
> No comen in turnament no in fiʒt.
> So amerous þou were anon riʒt.
> Y schuld misdo, so þenkeþ me,
> & miche agilt oʒaines te,
> & ich þi manschip schuld schone,
> Wit me euer more to wone.          (A, ll. 1137–46)

This answer which is very close to the central problem in Chrétien's *Erec*, betrays a more courtly attitude of mind than we find in most English romances. In what follows, the poem shows that Felice behaved quite rightly, although, as Guy later complains, many a good knight lost his life because of Guy's love of Felice (A, ll. 1555–66).

The story of Guy's love and his endeavours to prove himself worthy of her, keep the first part of the poem together. After each new heroic feat he remembers that he wants to go back to her, but again and again he is diverted from his path by a cry for help from someone in distress and he rushes to their assistance (see, for example, ll. 4197 ff., 4931 ff., 7035 ff.). This first part is a typical example of that kind of chivalric novel (on the whole not very common in England) which consists of a series of adventures, illustrating the knight's pity and desire to help the oppressed. Thus, a whole series of episodes is introduced by Guy's meeting with someone who is in great distress and persuades him to interrupt his journey.[29] This is each time the beginning of a new episode which regularly ends with Guy's solemn parting from the grateful object of his kindness. Guy's readiness to help all who need his protection is emphasized time and again. Only his very first exploits, such as his victory in the tournament, are mere demonstrations of strength and valour. After that, all his adventures are services, first against the unjust Emperor of the West, then on behalf of the Emperor of the East, greatly oppressed by the heathens, and finally in support of Tirri whom he wins as a true friend and comrade in battle by his generous help. Thus, the two parts of the poem are not sharply divided from each other, but there is a clear thematic connection. The happy union of the lovers is only described very briefly in most versions (C even has an *occupatio* at this point). A has the most extensive description of the feast, but this feast here only serves as an introduction to the story of Guy's pilgrimage. It is rather interesting that this redaction does not make Guy's wedding part of the first section, but uses it as a preliminary to Guy's sudden conversion, thus emphasizing the inner connection between the two parts of the poem. For the English adapter there was no inconsistency in the juxtaposition of courtly romance and Saint's legend; the legendary second part of the poem arises out of Guy's sudden realization that all he has done so far has been for his own glory, not for the honour of God. This crucial scene is one of the finest passages in *Guy of Warwick*, though it consists largely of conventional motifs:

> To a turet sir Gij is went,
> & biheld þat firmament,
> þat thicke wiþ steres stode.
> On Iesu omnipotent,
> þat alle his honour hadde him lent,
> He þouȝt wiþ dreri mode;
> Hou he hadde euer ben strong werrour,
> For Iesu loue, our saueour,
> Neuer no dede he gode.

Mani man he hadde slayn wiþ wrong.
'Allas, allas!' it was his song:
For sorwe he ȝede ner wode.           (A, 21, ll. 1-12)

Guy now gives up everything he has won and dedicates himself to
God. In a way, his second series of adventures can be seen as a re-
enactment of his former career, only in a very different spirit. The
structure of the second part parallels that of the first part in many
ways, but it puts a very different interpretation on Guy's heroic
exploits, as we have seen. Thus, *Guy of Warwick* is a particularly
characteristic example of the close connection between romances
and legends. It is a truly exemplary and homiletic romance. Guy is
not only a successful lover and a brave fighter, but he is above all
a model of Christian piety and penitence. Though the poem has
neither the freshness and vitality of *Sir Beues of Hamtoun*, nor the
rhetorical elegance and pretentiousness of *Kyng Alisaunder*, it combines in a particularly obvious manner many of the features that
characterize the Middle English romances, and it was probably
because of this that it enjoyed such wide and lasting popularity.[30]

## 'KYNG ALISAUNDER'

*Kyng Alisaunder*, a fairly extensive novel in rhyming couplets, is
perhaps by the same author as *Arthour and Merlin, Richard Coeur
de Lion* and, possibly, *The Seven Sages of Rome*, but even though
the identity of the author cannot be proved conclusively, it is
certain that the four poems were written about the same time (end
of thirteenth century) in or around London and are addressed to
the same audience.[31] *Kyng Alisaunder* reveals the individuality of
this group most clearly and can be considered by far the most
successful of the four works. It is the translation of the Anglo-
Norman *Roman de Toute Cheualerie* by Thomas of Kent; M. D.
Legge particularly emphasizes the moral tone of this work[32]
which is of some importance within the medieval Alexander-
tradition, though it keeps fairly closely to its sources, especially the
*Zacher Epitome* of Pseudo-Callisthenes.[33] In view of the fact that
the affiliation of manuscripts of the Anglo-Norman poem have
not been fully investigated yet, it is hardly possible to make an
exact comparison between the English version and its source.
Some passages in the English poem which appear to have no direct
model in any of the versions known to us, may have been available

to the adapter in some other, not yet discovered, version. Nevertheless, it is true to say that, in spite of the closeness of the translation, a completely new and in several ways original work was created by the English adapter in which his individuality as an artist is unmistakeably expressed.

Undoubtedly the novel enjoyed a certain popularity in England because it has come down in at least three manuscripts, and a printed fragment is also preserved in the 'Bagford Ballads'. Of the three manuscripts, the Auchinleck collection is particularly interesting although it contains only a small section of the novel, because it preserves the oldest text and thus gives some clue as to the date of the poem. What is more, this is the only manuscript which contains all four of the poems usually ascribed to the same author. Since many pages have been lost from the volume, it is no longer possible to say exactly at which point in the collection the poem was originally placed; it seems to have been inserted next to the two Charlemagne poems *Roland and Vernagu* and *Otuel*.

The most complete and reliable text is found in Laud Misc. 622 (end of fourteenth century). The manuscript contains almost only religious and didactic poetry; *Kyng Alisaunder* is the only item that could be called secular. It is reasonable to suppose that the poem was included mainly because of its instructive character, not as an entertaining romance; this is partly confirmed by the fact that the poem is followed in the manuscript by a brief description, in a later hand, of memorable things and places seen in the Holy Land. It can also be taken as proof of the instructive and homiletic character of the collection that the scribe took over a whole section from the *South English Legendary*.[34] The evenness of the tone is to some extent explained by the fact that the manuscript, apart from the *mirabilia*, was written continuously by one scribe. Each item begins immediately after the preceding one, usually on the same page or column. It seems that *Kyng Alisaunder* was originally the last entry and that the order of items was later altered by misbinding.

The third manuscript, Lincoln's Inn 150 (L), is of a completely different character. Because of its narrow, oblong shape it has been suggested that it was intended for the pocket of a wandering minstrel, but this can only be a fanciful surmise.[35] Most of the works included in it are, however, of a more entertaining character (e.g. *Libeaus Desconus*, *Arthour and Merlin*, and *The Seege or*

*Batayle of Troye*) so that it is possible that it was written as a portable anthology for reading aloud to convivial gatherings. The text is not nearly as good as that in Laud Misc. 622 (B), and G. V. Smithers has shown that many of the mistakes in it could be 'auditory rather than palaeographical errors' (p. 12). It is unfortunate that we still know too little about the actual production of these manuscripts to say with confidence how such auditory errors came about. They may just as easily have arisen in copying, possibly after dictation, as by oral transmission which seems unlikely in the case of such a literary and extensive work.[36] It is particularly important to note that a complete section of about 1200 lines has been left out in this manuscript (between B 4762 and 5979) which is evidence of some deliberate editing because there is no gap in the L-version at this point and the omitted part is so complete in itself that no reader or listener would notice its absence.[37] As the passage consisted almost only of descriptions of exotic countries and their inhabitants, one is inclined to think that the adapter made this abridgement for the benefit of an audience that wanted more entertainment than instruction.

There can be no doubt that the original adapter of the novel, especially if he was also the author of *Arthour and Merlin* and *Richard Coeur de Lion*, aimed first of all at making available to a wider public an entertaining and at the same time instructive work which already enjoyed a certain popularity in Anglo-Norman and was a compilation of well-known material. The unusually elaborate introduction, with its curious combination of didactic seriousness and a popular minstrel-tone, is obviously addressed to a public used to light-weight entertainment and needing constant encouragement, but considered capable of higher interests by the adapter. It may be because of this that he reveals a particular preference for the formula 'lewed and lered' (ll. 2, 213, 598, 1713, 2969, 8017), usually employed as a fairly general description of the diversity of people inhabiting the Earth; its formulaic character is emphasized by the stereotyped rhyme 'myddelerde'. Nevertheless, the adapter certainly wanted to create a work that would appeal to the more educated as well as to the 'lewed', i.e. those without clerical learning.

The juxtaposition of a popular, salesman-like tone, rhetorical embellishment and solid learning is characteristic of the whole novel. A comparison of *Kyng Alisaunder* with the shorter poems in the Auchinleck Ms. or even with *Sir Beues of Hamtoun* and *Guy of Warwick*, would show how much more artistic and elaborate the style of this poem is. There can be no doubt that the author had a thorough literary education, that he was well-read and, as Smithers has impressively demonstrated, that he was familiar with rhetorical traditions, especially with the wealth of epic formulas derived via Old French poetry from classical and medieval Latin literature.[38] Such close adherence to literary tradition is very rare in Middle English narrative literature of the early fourteenth century. For instance, the use of the word 'coloure', meaning rhetorical embellishment, half a century or more before Chaucer and Gower, is indeed remarkable. The whole passage shows with what artistic awareness the author went to work:

> þis bataile distincted is
> Jn þe Freinsshe, wel jwys.
> þerefore J habbe hit to coloure
> Borowed of Latyn a nature,
> Hou hiȝtten þe gentyl kniȝttes,
> Hou hij contened hem in fiȝttes,
> On Alisaunders half and Darries also.
> ȝif ȝee willeþ listnen to,
> ȝee shullen yhere geste of mounde—
> Ne may non better ben yfounde.     (ll. 2195–2204)

The way in which the theoretical description of the rhetorical method is followed by the more popular invitation to listen, promising a great battle and trying to make the whole episode sound very sensational, is characteristic of the poem's stylistic range. The desire to educate and instruct by an artistic presentation of the material is one of the most interesting features of this novel. It can also be seen in the adapter's treatment of his source.

*Kyng Alisaunder* is not a romance in the same sense as poems like *Beues of Hamtoun* and *Guy of Warwick*. It is in the first place a biography in which the suspense cannot be sustained in the same way as, for instance, by the 'exile-return motif' or by the hero's love-story. The unity of the plot seems to be achieved only by the person of the hero, but his character does not undergo any visible development and his feelings and impressions appear to be of little interest to the author. No spiritual conflicts are described, but only external events and political intrigues. The briefly related love-story (see ll. 6648 ff. and, particularly, ll. 7616 ff.) is told with remarkable frankness, but takes up only little space in the course of the poem and puts the emphasis more on the calculating artfulness of Candace and on the exotic quality of the whole episode than on the personal experience of Alexander.[39] The adapter follows his source in that he does not present Alexander as the courtly lover, but rather as the victim of female seductive charms.[40] Apart from this episode, however, most space is taken up in this poem by the accounts of military and exploratory expeditions and the dealing with recalcitrant adversaries.

*Kyng Alisaunder* is, in a way, chiefly a collection of *mirabilia*, of geographical, zoological, and anthropological curiosities which are described with evident relish and were obviously just as important to the author as the actual plot. Alexander, thirsty for knowledge and novel adventures, enjoys all these strange sights, but his personal fate often recedes completely into the background, and large sections of the novel have almost the character of a scientific treatise. The author's claim that 'þis is nouȝth romaunce of skof,/ Ac storye ymade of maistres wyse' (ll. 668–9), is thus confirmed by the tone and contents of the narrative: when the poet tells us about the siege of Thebes, he inserts a circumstantial account of the history and the distinctive character of the town (ll. 2639 ff.). The description of Egypt relates one miracle after the other (ll. 6160 ff.), and the passage omitted in the L-version (ll. 4763–5979) consists mainly in a list of curiosities. It is typical of this poem that the translator did not abridge any of these passages (except in L), but occasionally even added some details himself.

In other parts, too, the poem is rich in detailed and rhetorically stylized descriptions. Thus, at the beginning, the scene in which Queen Olympias shows herself to the people, is carefully elaborated (ll. 167–214) and the astrological reflections which follow soon afterwards, are also reproduced in full. There are several lengthy descriptions of battles (as in ll. 2159 ff.), where the formal character of the passage is emphasized by the repetition of the same rhyme (ll. 2159–72).[41] It is hardly necessary to point out that no realistic portrayal of actual events is intended here. The formulaic nature of these and many other passages only confirms the impression that they serve mainly as rhetorical decoration and are quite in line with time-honoured epic traditions. The battle-scenes, in particular, with their almost identical sequence of events, the regular alternation of individual combats and mass slaughter, the rhetorical catalogues and the almost ritual listing of proper names, are clearly in the tradition of the Latin and Old French epic. The author's preference for long catalogues and enumerations is rather striking and also illustrates his rhetorical education, witness his list of names (ll. 1691–8), of authorities (ll. 4763–84), of countries (ll. 2581–6), or of *exempla* (ll. 7703–9), the description of a feast (ll. 1039–46) or the particularly elaborate and stylized account of Alexander's host (ll. 3200–14). Candace's letter to Alexander (ll. 6674–717) is largely a catalogue of promises. It is quite obvious that here we have to do with a writer who is not interested in the mere reporting of sensational events, nor in moral instruction only, but above all in the passing on of culture and learning and in the art of stylistic embellishment.

The broad epic style of the poem is also reflected in the reproduction of dialogue and long speeches. Consultations or exchanges of messages and embassies are often described very elaborately and formally, as for instance in the debate of the Athenians (ll. 2915 ff.) or of Darius and his counsellors (ll. 3295 ff.) and several similar scenes. Even such a dramatic episode as that of Alexander's incognito appearance at the court of Darius (ll. 4137 ff.) is mainly told in the form of lengthy speeches. The locality and the feelings of the characters involved are only very briefly outlined. The same applies, for example, to the scene in which the treacherous Persian knight is tried by Alexander and his noblemen (ll. 3962 ff.). Thus the reader (or listener) seldom receives the impression that the plot is only moving slowly, because the long speeches, although they often seem to retard the progress of the action, do at the same time give a feeling of lively movement and dramatic activity. This combination of vivacious narrative style and rhetorical elaboration almost reminds one of *Havelok*, a poem that has otherwise not much in common with *Kyng Alisaunder*.

For all his learning and his stylistic virtuosity, the author was anxious, as has already been pointed out, to make his work appeal to a large and mixed audience and to make the most of the situation in which the poem would be read aloud. The poem is very rich in formulas by which the audience is directly addressed. Important climaxes in the plot are announced by the narrator who also adds his own observations on the action and hints at the moral implications of the story. At the same time, these authorial comments help to give the otherwise rather sprawling novel a certain structure and break it up into smaller narrative units which could be read at one sitting or not, just as circumstances might require. The same kind of device was noticed in *Sir Beues of Hamtoun* and *Guy of Warwick*, above. In the case of *Kyng Alisaunder*, however, this division into smaller episodes is facilitated by the lack of unity in the action and thus determines the character of the poem more noticeably. The author makes particularly frequent use of the conventional call for attention. It often introduces only rather short passages without any new development in the action. Thus, concluding a short description of Alexander's childhood, the author tells us:

> þe childe waxeþ a wiȝth ȝongelyng.
> Now hereþ geste and ȝiueþ listnyng.　　(ll. 655–6)

What follows is really only a continuation of the preceding events. Often such formulas are only to draw the audience's attention to some particularly interesting incident or detail which is to follow; this occurs frequently before battles or descriptions of marvellous events. Thus, the description of Egypt is introduced by these promising remarks:

> Sitteþ stille and ȝiueþ listnynge,
> And ȝe shullen here wonder þinge!　　(ll. 6502–3)

or a little later, even more specificly:

> NOw listneþ (and sitteþ stille!)
> What beest is þe cokedrylle.　　(ll. 6586–7)

Such formulas strike us as being a simple attempt to relieve the monotony of some descriptive passages and to retain the attention of the audience which might otherwise get bored. Similar invitations can be found in many other places in the poem.[42] Occasionally they are combined with a brief summary of the preceding events:

> Now resteþ Alisaunder jn þis siggyng—
> Yhereþ now al oþer þing.
> HErd ȝee habbeþ, Ich wil reherce,
> Hou þe messagers comen from Perce
> For trowage and Philippe ennoyed—
> Hou Alisaunder it hem wiþseide.
> 　　(ll. 1661–6; see also ll. 6008–15 and ll. 6496–6503)

Such passages show clearly how consciously the author tried to organize his material and how anxious he was to make it interesting as well as comprehensible to an audience that was probably used to very different stories.

A similar kind of accentuation is provided by the inserted prayers, such as we often meet at the end of romances or legends. Often they are only short blessings (e.g. ll. 992, 2046, 2566, 3438), but sometimes they are more extensive and seem to mark clear pauses in the narrative; it is reasonable to suppose that they served to indicate where the reciter might conveniently break off. A typical example comes after the siege and destruction of Thebes:

> þus ended Tebes cite.
> God on vs haue pyte,
> And lene vs so to þryue
> We moten come to his lyue,
> Whan we shullen hennes wende,
> And lyuen wiþ hym wiþouten ende.     (ll. 2891–6)

After that, a new introduction follows and a new section of the plot begins. Most of these passages are conventional clichés and can be found in many other romances. Here, however, they are not only used more frequently, but also often more to the point and fit in more naturally with the loose and episodic structure of the plot.[43]

Another distinctive feature of the author's style is the frequent insertion of moralizing commentaries and reflections. Often they only consist of a line or two (see ll. 166, 284, 751–2), but occasionally they are more weighty, as in the description of Olympias:

> OLympyas stant tofore Neptanabus
> Of her nywe loue wel desirous.
> So dooþ womman after mysdoyng,
> Ne can no shame ne no repentyng,
> Er she be lauȝtte in her folye
> So in þe lyme is þe fleiȝe.     (ll. 415–20)

Sometimes an episode is given a moral interpretation afterwards (see ll. 4597–4600, 4719–24, and, particularly, 6978–87) and sometimes such moral reflections seem to be inserted in the action at random. Thus, after the description of Darius' desperate appeal to his knights, the poet comments rather abruptly:

> Lorde Crist, what þis wordeles iȝth
> Js leef to duk and to kniȝth!

þere nys non so slowe wiȝth jnne,
And he wene mychel wynne,
þat he ne wolde for grete tresure
Done hym-self in auenture.                    (ll. 3880–5)

However, we later realize that this is the anticipated moral of the
following episode, containing the story of the Persian knight who
hazards his life in order to kill Alexander and earn the promised
reward. Similarly, at another point, a general moral precedes an
illustration of its truth (ll. 4038–41). In this way, as by many
shorter prophetic hints, an element of suspense is created, undoubtedly intended by the author, and the action is given a moral
interpretation. These moralizing commentaries do not, however,
amount to a definite framework of ethical standards, and the story
of Alexander is not here presented as an *exemplum*, as in some other
versions of his life. The whole method of presentation rather reveals
that the author was mainly interested in enlivening and breaking
up his extensive material in order to make it more acceptable to
his audience. The moral commentaries have the same effect; they
are meant to draw attention to the relevance of the story and at the
same time provide breathing spaces in the otherwise somewhat
monotonous narrative.

This applies particularly to the so-called 'head-pieces', which
are a very striking and attractive feature of this novel and deserve
a closer examination. Unlike most of the conventional minstrel-
formulas, they are highly original, and none the less so because
they can be traced back, as Smithers has shown, to similar
formulas in Latin and Old French poetry. Their large number—
there are about twenty-nine in *Kyng Alisaunder*—and their varied
usage have no parallel in English, not even in *Arthour and Merlin*,
the only work in which an appreciable number of similar devices
can be found.[44]

The 'head-pieces' in *Kyng Alisaunder* appear at first sight to be
isolated lyrical insertions in the text, separating the various
episodes from each other. It has even been supposed that they
were sung which, however, is very unlikely, if only because of
their close metrical connection with their context. Undoubtedly,
they make an important contribution to the structure of the poem
and mark clear caesuras between several episodes. It is significant
that they are almost evenly spread throughout the whole novel.
Only in one place are two such head-pieces separated by a space of

as many as about a thousand lines (between ll. 5981 and 6988); otherwise they are never more than about four to five hundred lines apart, usually the size of a self-contained episode that can easily be read in one sitting.[45] The caesura is especially marked after line 4738, that is after about half the poem is over. Darius is finally defeated, and the first part of the campaign is over. After a moralizing and religious head-piece (ll. 4739-46), the poet announces that the second part of the poem is about to begin (ll. 4747-8). There can be no doubt that here a pause in the reading was intended.

Smithers and others have already drawn attention to the variety of themes introduced by the head-pieces.[46] It is certain that they did not follow any particular model, although there are obvious points of contact with the Middle English lyric, especially the *reverie*, a very common device taken over from the Latin and French lyric, but freely adapted by the English poets. The head-pieces in *Kyng Alisaunder* usually describe the seasons of the year or times of the day (mostly the morning) with characteristic human activities; sometimes, however, they only consist of a few general aphorisms (e.g. ll. 4313-18). They are not always clearly separated from the rest of the poem, but in most cases they are distinguished by the repeated use of the same rhyme.

The head-pieces are almost always inserted at the beginning of a new episode. This is often emphasized because they are preceded by a blessing or a prayer indicating the conclusion of a certain section so that the head-pieces mark a new start (see ll. 2566-72, 2891-902, 3438-41). Often the head-pieces are also introduced by a call for attention or a similar formula (e.g. ll. 455-64, 1572-6, 2046-56, 3287-94, 4099-104, 5742-50, 7351-61); sometimes the head-piece is in turn followed by such a formula (see ll. 4739-48, 5201-6), and in one place we have a combination of both, which makes the caesura particularly noticeable (ll. 3577-86). Occasionally the action is interrupted and retarded by a head-piece and a heightening of the dramatic tension is achieved (ll. 1163-4, 5201-4, 5741-50).

The majority of head-pieces consist of between four and eight lines, usually connected by one common rhyme. A typical example is found at lines 4056-64:

> MEry it is in þe day graukynge,
> Whan þe foules gynneþ synge,

And jolyf herte so gynneþ sprynge.
To sone it þencheþ þe slow gadelynge!
Jn mychel loue is grete mournynge;
Jn mychel nede is grete þankynge.
A ferly þouȝth is wiþ þe kyng—
Erly he riseþ, and makeþ boost,
And hoteþ quyk armen al þe ost.

What appears particularly interesting here (as in many other places), is not only the decidedly lyrical and aphoristic character of this inserted set-piece, but also its clear connection with the context by the rhyme as well as by the indication of the time. The head-pieces are not, therefore, arbitrary additions which could be changed about or omitted altogether, but they are part of the rhetorical embellishment of the story and often have a definite function at certain points in the plot. This becomes clearer still in another part of the novel where day-break is indicated in a similar manner and at the same time the passing of the night, as part of the story, is suggested:

Niȝth it is—hij takeþ rest.
Amorowe ariseþ newe gest.
DAy-spryngynge is jolif tyde.
He þat can his tyme abide,
Often hym shal his wille bitide.
Looþ is gentil-man to chide.
Alisaunder dooþ cryen wyde
His loges setten on þe water-syde.          (ll. 4281–8)

It may even be that the little piece of popular wisdom about the man who can bide his time is directed at Alexander and partly accounts for his success. Similar indications of time can be found in other head-pieces and are directly connected with the plot (see ll. 139–46, 3289–96). Often such a connection is established by the content of the head-pieces. Thus, the general remarks about 'gamen' (ll. 235–41) are followed by the description of Queen Olympias' escapade, which is also termed 'game' (l. 243). In the head-piece between lines 457 and 464 it is briefly suggested that wicked deeds cannot escape discovery, which is confirmed by the following episode. The attentive and thoughtful listener would not only recognize the general truth of such statements, but he might also try to apply them to the story he is about to hear and thus discover a deeper meaning in the events. The brief meditation about

joy and sorrow before the decisive battle of Mantona certainly also
has to be understood in this way (ll. 1239–44), and other head-
pieces are connected with the plot of the poem by suggestive hints
in a similar manner (see ll. 1843–8, 7352–61).

One theme which is touched on particularly frequently in the
head-pieces, is that of inconstancy and transitoriness, of which the
novel offers of course a whole series of examples. Several head-
pieces provide an explicit commentary on this theme, the following
with especial urgency:

> MErcy, Jesu! þou vs socoure!
> Jt fareþ wiþ man so dooþ wiþ floure—
> Bot a stirte ne may it dure;
> He glyt away so dooþ þessure.
> Fair is lefdy in boure,
> And also kniȝth in armoure. (ll. 4313–8)

This is very much like some of the early Middle English religious
lyrics, bewailing the transitoriness of human existence. Another
head-piece eloquently points out the fickleness of all earthly joy:

> þoo þou miȝttest on many wise
> Yseen solace and game aryse,
> Leighȝen, syngen, and daunces make,
> Dysoures talen and resouns crake.
> Swiche chaunce þe werlde kepeþ—
> Now man leigȝeþ, now man wepeþ!
> Now man is hool, now man is seek;
> Nys no day oþer ylyk.
> Noman þat lyues haþ borowe
> From euene libbe forto amorowe. (ll. 6978–87)

This is immediately followed by another head-piece about April
(ll. 6988–94) with some general reflections on the same subject.
In another place the theme is illustrated by a series of *exempla*
(ll. 7820–32), but most of the head-pieces about the seasons or
times of the day imply this changeableness, the timeless correspondence between the outward signs of the ever-changing nature
and the fate of man. Within this framework, Alexander's rise and
fall acquires the force and meaning of a parable, underlined by
suggestive hints throughout the whole novel, but never obtruded
on the reader by glib didacticism. Thus the head-pieces are not

only connected to the various episodes they introduce, but by their regular occurrence and their insistence on the theme of mutability they create a system of values by which Alexander's fate can be assessed. This fact does not seem to have been sufficiently recognized so far.

By the addition of the head-pieces the adapter has therefore considerably changed the character of his source and has added a new dimension. He certainly did not see Alexander's story primarily as an *exemplum*. The whole plot and the *mirabilia* he describes with such gusto, show that his interests were more varied than that and that he was more than a moralist. This is also suggested by his faithful rendering of his source, especially the more scientific and factual parts. Nevertheless, he does indicate that in the rise and fall of Alexander, as in that of some of his enemies, the same everlasting law is manifested that at all times has subjected nature and mankind to the periodic changes of days and seasons.

## 'ARTHOUR AND MERLIN'

This novel which, though incomplete, runs to 9938 lines, can be dealt with more briefly here because it does not differ in essentials from *Kyng Alisaunder* and does not add anything new to the history of the English novel in verse. It belongs to the same type and is also a compilation of well-known material taken over rather uncritically from the source.[47] The poem is probably based on some prose-novels written in the wake of Robert of Boron or similar compilations. Whereas the first part is at least held together by a certain tension and unity of plot, the second, more extensive part consists almost entirely of an aimless sequence of military campaigns and mass-battles which are described in great detail and with evident relish, but whose monotony is perhaps one of the reasons why the novel was never finished.[48] The later version, which confines itself to the first part of the story, makes it seem likely that the later adapter, aware of the confusion of the second part, decided to dispense with it altogether. This later version, though in some ways more pedestrian than *Arthour and Merlin*, is at least far more unified, concluding with Pendragon's death and burial and with a short conventional prayer (ll. 2488–92). The end of the poem corresponds roughly to line 2160 of *Arthour and Merlin*.

Without going into detail about the supposed common authorship of *Arthour and Merlin* and *Kyng Alisaunder*, it is perhaps
possible to throw light on their connection with each other by a
brief comparison. Apart from the fact that they were written at the
same time and probably in the same district, the story-material
alone reveals a number of similarities which do not really bear on
the question of authorship. It is particularly in the first part, where
we are told about the miraculous story of the hero's birth, that the
close relationship of the two poems as regards their subject-matter
is apparent. This is mainly explained by the obvious influence of
the legends of Alexander on the Arthur-stories.[49] As the poems go
on, however, the differences between the sources become clearly
apparent. The author of *Kyng Alisaunder* already had a complete
novel in front of him and was therefore enabled to concentrate on
the stylistic refinement of his version. This can hardly have been
the case in *Arthour and Merlin*. In the first part, the adapter at least
had to deal with a fairly unified story and so here we find some
skilfully told episodes although the dramatic flow of the action is
often hampered by a certain awkwardness and lack of precision, as
in the descriptions of Vortiger's attempt to build a castle (ll. 494 ff.),
of the five-year-old Merlin and his astonishing gifts (ll. 1195 ff.),
or also of Uterpendragon's love for Ygerne (ll. 2239 ff.). The
diffuse and purely episodic character of *Arthour and Merlin* is therefore partly due to the nature of the source, but the endless monotony
of the battles in the second part reveals a lack of imagination and a
degree of artistic clumsiness which we hardly ever find in *Kyng
Alisaunder*.

On the other hand, the novel does show that the adapter made
an occasional modest attempt to introduce rhetorical ornament and
that he was acquainted with many of the literary formulas typical
of the Old French epic. One can agree with Göller who feels that
the poem was in the first place written for a rather simple audience,
but it would be quite mistaken to conclude that the author must
therefore have been a popular story-teller, using only the language
of unlearned people. The comparisons taken from the sphere of
ordinary craftsmen which Göller quotes in this connection, are not
so much examples of a realistic style, as epic formulas, however
adapted to the experience of a middle-class audience.[50] In the
descriptions of battles, too, there is, in spite of repetitive monotony, an obvious striving for rhetorical effects and stylization,

mainly expressed in the stereotyped repetition of particular heroic deeds, the unvaried sequences of single fights and mass-encounters and the interminable lists of combatants (e.g. ll. 9329–48). One may, as Göller does,[51] regret that the author failed to see the unintentional humour in all these ferocious battles, but a description like the following was surely not written without deliberate, if grim irony:

> Alder next him was Galathin,
> þat him halp wiþ miȝt fin;
> What Sarrazin so he mett,
> Wel soriliche he hem grett,
> þat, wom euer þat he hitt,
> þe heued to þe chinne he slitt,
> Oþer þe scholder oþer þe heued
> Fro þe bodi was bireued,
> Oþer legge oþer fest
> Oþer what he miȝt take best;
> Who so euer he atrauȝt,
> Tombel of hors he him tauȝt.          (ll. 4807–18)

It would be doing the writer an unnecessary injustice to read this as a piece of absurd and clumsy realism. It is precisely the use of formulas and the frequent repetition of identical scenes which indicate that the author made an attempt, though not very imaginative, to write in the traditional epic style which would be unthinkable without Old French models. There is unmistakable irony in the use of the words 'grett' and 'tauȝt', and it is exactly the sort of irony that is characteristic of the epic style.[52]

Certain other artistic devices, listed by Kölbing, such as the recurring rhymes, the large number of stereotyped clichés, and particularly the 'head-pieces' reveal that the author had some skill in the practical details of his craft and they suggest that he had enjoyed a very similar literary education as the adapter of *Kyng Alisaunder*, though the latter did indeed handle such rhetorical conventions with much more freedom and originality.[53]

As in *Kyng Alisaunder*, an attempt is made to organize the extensive work into a form suitable for oral delivery. To this end, many of the traditional calls for attention and transitional formulas of the type 'Now lete we . . .' (e.g. ll. 623–30) are employed, often with some hint as to coming events, designed to rouse expectation and to create a minimum of dramatic suspense. All these devices are, however, used far more mechanically than in *Kyng Alisaunder*. The same applies to the 'head-pieces' (about ten in number); they are only very loosely connected with the plot and seem to have been inserted in a rather arbitrary way. They are usually shorter and more formulaic in character; most of them consist merely of two or three rhyming couplets. Only one of them shows the same repetition of the same rhyme as the head-pieces in *Kyng Alisaunder*, and in this case there is also a certain connection between the time mentioned in the lyrical introduction and that of the action described in the poem:

> Mirie is June, þat scheweþ flour;
> þe meden ben of swete odour,
> Lilye & rose of fair colour,
> þe riuer cler wiþ outen sour;
> Boþe kniȝtes & vauasour
> þis damisels loue paramour.
> On Mononday in þe pentecost
> Leodegan & alle his ost
> Armed hem. . . .                    (ll. 8657–65)

Even this passage does not, however, have the freshness of many head-pieces in *Kyng Alisaunder*, so that I would rather attribute it to some inferior imitator than to the same author. Thus, there is on the whole not the same lively relationship between narrator and audience as in *Kyng Alisaunder* and the individual narrative units in the poem are both more extensive and less clearly defined and coherent.

The whole novel, therefore, gives the impression of a compilation intended for the greatest possible variety of listeners, in which a great and shapeless mass of material is collected without any overall thematic design. It is true that the adapter did abbreviate and simplify the story in places and by the use of inherited formulas tried to provide some modest rhetorical embellishment, but it is obvious that the sheer extent and variety of his material left him on the whole rather helpless, and I find it difficult to accept the idea that this pedestrian work was composed by the same author as the far more unified and sophisticated *Kyng Alisaunder*.

## 'RICHARD COEUR DE LION'

Much of what has been said about *Arthour and Merlin* applies equally to the romance on the life of Richard Coeur de Lion. It is also a biographical compilation, describing the life of a famous ruler and consisting chiefly of descriptions of military campaigns and battles. The episodic structure of the novel is particularly noticeable here because, as the manuscripts show, the later versions are the result of repeated redaction by which the novel was extended several times.[54] Since the French source of the poem is not known (though it is likely that such a source existed), it is impossible to assess the achievement of the first adapter. Later additions and expansions increased the size of the work by more than two thousand lines, however, and some longer sections were inserted which emphasize above all the sensational character of the narrative and contain episodes that are no less fantastic than the adventures of Alexander or Merlin. Thus, the extended version at least, written less than two hundred years after Richard's death, is no more 'historical' than *Kyng Alisaunder* and *Arthour and Merlin*, and it is hardly apparent any more that the work was originally, it seems, based on a chronicle. For the author, Richard is a romance-hero just like all the others whose names he lists at the beginning of the poem, indeed the whole point of his elaborate introduction is to prove that Richard is equal to all the other heroes glorified in the romances. The passage is also interesting because of the clue it gives as to the audience the poet wants to appeal to:

> Ffele romaunses men maken newe,
> Off goode kny3tes, stronge and trewe;
> Off here dedys men rede romaunce,
> Boþe in Engeland and in Ffraunce:
> Off Rowelond, and off Olyuer,
> And off euery Doseper;
> Off Alisaundre, and Charlemayn;
> Off kyng Arthour, and off Gawayn,
> How þey were knyghtes goode and curteys;
> Off Turpyn, and of Oger Daneys;
> Off Troye men rede in ryme,
> What werre þer was in olde tyme;
> Off Ector, and off Achylles,
> What folk þey slowe in þat pres.
> In Frenssche bookys þis rym is wrou3t,
> Lewede men ne knowe it nou3t—
> Lewede men cune Ffrensch non,
> Among an hondryd vnneþis on—;

Neuerþeles, wiþ glad chere,
Ffele off hem þat wolde here
Noble iestes, j vndyrstonde,
Off douȝty knyȝtes off Yngelonde.
þerfore now j wole ȝow rede
Off a kyng, douȝty in dede:
Kyng Rychard, þe werryour beste
þat men fynde in ony ieste.
Now alle þat here þis talkyng,
God geue hem alle good endyng!                    (ll. 7–34)

There could be no clearer statement of the adapter's intention of
presenting Richard as an exemplary romance-hero rather than
a historical character. This is confirmed by the action of the poem.
Many episodes are taken over more or less unchanged from other
chivalric romances, such as the miracles in connection with the
hero's descent and birth (ll. 35–240); the three-day tournament at
which he appears three times unrecognized, each time in a different
set of armour (ll. 251–590); the somewhat burlesque exchange of
blows (ll. 739–880); or the love of the King's daughter and the
betrayal of the affair (ll. 881–1118). Here, the tendency, to be seen
in other story-cycles, too, of some outstanding figure (like Richard)
to be credited with more and more adventures gleaned from other
romances, can be followed particularly clearly.[55]

In spite of the patchwork character of the novel, its unity of tone
is very striking. While the author of *Kyng Alisaunder* was obviously
more interested in his exotic material than in the person of the
hero, *Richard Coeur de Lion* betrays the narrator's strong sympathy for the hero, an unusually militant Christian spirit and a
brutal hatred of all unbelievers, such as we only find in the English
Charlemagne poems. Richard is not only a daring adventurer and
an intrepid hero in battle, but primarily a resolute champion of
Christianity; his emblematic coats of arms when he joins the
tournament in disguise, announce his intention of proving himself
a defender of the Church and of slaughtering as many heathens as
possible (ll. 275–84, 337–42, 393–6; see also 5713–22). This theme
is elaborated in Richard's great speech calling for a crusade
(ll. 1348–75). Several of the later additions emphasize this aspect
of the story. Thus the French King is presented as a traitor to the
cause of Christianity because he agrees to spare the heathens if
they pay tribute to him (ll. 4781 ff. and 5423 ff.) instead of butcher-

ing all of them like a good Christian. Richard's overwhelming victories are a sign of God's help (e.g. l. 4579) who shows his superiority over all pagan gods by miracles (cf. ll. 5481 ff.) and lets angels appear to comfort his hero or to warn him (cf. ll. 6960 ff.). For all its fantastic trimmings, the poem shows an unmistakable similarity to Saints' legends. The novel obviously does not so much want to present exotic adventures as to demonstrate the conquering power of the Christian faith as embodied in one of its most ferocious champions. The battles, steadily increasing in violence towards the end, assume an almost ritual character. The heathens are no longer seen as human beings, but as personifications of all that is unchristian and of the malice of Satan. Their massacre is an act of Christian duty, approved by God; the savage brutality of this wholesale slaughter is evidently not felt by the author because of its exemplary, almost symbolic quality. Again it would be a mistake to assume that any form of realism was intended here.

There is some reason for assuming that the author of the English romance, and possibly the subsequent adapter, were clerics.[56] It is obvious that he made liberal use of many conventions and clichés of romance. The two lists of romance-heroes which are quoted as a foil to Richard's own, equally glorious deeds (ll. 7–20 and 6725–42), show, in spite of their conventional character, that the author wanted to appeal to an audience that was fond of such stories. The novel seems to be an attempt to fill the well-worn clichés of romance with Christian significance and to combine genuine entertainment with overt edification. The manuscripts suggest that the poem appealed to collectors with quite different interests.[57] Thus, *Richard Coeur de Lion* occurs in the almost entirely homiletic and devotional Thornton Ms. (B.M. Additional 31.042) in which the Charlemagne poems (*The Sege off Melayne* and *Rowlande and Ottuell*) are practically the only 'secular' items; it stands next to *The Romance of the Childhode of Ihesu Christe*. The scribes or redactors of the manuscripts A (College of Arms HDN 58) and H (Harley 4690) seem to have included the poem above all as a chronicle (although in the somewhat toned-down version b), whereas the collections E (Egerton 2862) and C (Gonville & Caius College 175) give evidence of the editor's or collector's particular interest in popular English heroes.

In its use of narrative formulas the poem reveals many similarities with *Kyng Alisaunder* and *Arthour and Merlin*, though in its simple and unambitious use of convention it is rather more like the latter. The adapter evidently did not find it necessary to impose a firm structure on the poem, though its episodic character is often emphasized by the usual calls for attention, short blessings (ll. 5188, 6222–4, 6742), some modest attempts to combine a description of the seasons with an indication of the time of the action (ll. 1783, 4817–18, 6743–4), and, in one place, by an extended 'head-piece' with a lively description of May and its activities (ll. 3759–71). As the passage introduces the most extensive interpolation in the poem, it is quite possible that the later adapter took over the device from the other two novels.[58] In other ways, too, the interpolated passage differs from the older part of the poem because of its somewhat broader narrative style and more frequent use of narrative formulas. On the whole, the rhetorical element is much less marked in this novel than in *Kyng Alisaunder* and one would not necessarily conclude from its style that the two poems were written by the same author. On the other hand, the action is more varied and often related with more gusto and precision than that of *Arthour and Merlin*.

The points which these three novels have in common do not seem sufficient to confirm the theory that they can all be attributed to the same author. Nevertheless, they are, all three, typical examples of a newly developed epic form in English: a biographical novel, addressed to a wide public, episodic in structure, but with a central focus in the person of the hero who gives some unity to the otherwise rather incoherent incidents. *Kyng Alisaunder*, the most ambitious of the three, shows a marked attempt at rhetorical stylization, but the other two also reveal occasional rhetorical flourishes. This type of novel is on the whole far less characteristic of the epic literature of the thirteenth and fourteenth centuries than the shorter romances, but, as the history of the fifteenth century shows, it anticipated some later developments.[59]

### 'WILLIAM OF PALERNE'

*William of Palerne* is in many respects one of the most successful and interesting of the Middle English novels in verse. For one thing, we are told much more about the circumstances of its composition and to whom we owe its adaptation than in the case of any other of the works mentioned in this chapter. The poem, as the author mentions in two places (ll. 161–9 and 5521–33), was commissioned by Humphrey de Bohun, Earl of Hereford.[60] Unfortunately we do not know anything about the author himself, but the style and tone of the poem suggest that he could hardly have been an unlearned minstrel, but that he had a genuine understanding of courtly literature and a thorough knowledge of the native alliterative tradition. It is also evident that the poem is not addressed to an audience of simple people only, because the material has not been 'popularized' to any marked degree, but is only adapted to an English audience without the courtly and ceremonial character of the work being lost. It is apparent that the poet's remark to the effect that he wrote the novel 'for hem þat knowe no frensche ne neuer vnderston' (l. 5533) does by no means refer to the lower classes. It is probable that in this case it means a large part of Humphrey's noble household.

*William of Palerne* is one of those English verse novels which follow a French source (in this instance the French novel *Guillaume de Palerne*, written about 1200) fairly closely and yet develop a very individual style of their own, quite different from that of the original. A detailed comparison between the two, as was undertaken by M. Kaluza, reveals that the English adapter kept, on the one hand, very close to his model, making no drastic changes in the plot, but at the same time adapted it in accordance with the English alliterative tradition and enriched it by many smaller additions.[61] The conscious artistic judgement that must have led to the rearranging of individual scenes, the condensing of lengthy descriptions and the dramatizing of several passages of dialogue, also proves that the poem was composed at the desk and that oral transmission is very unlikely in this case.

The adapter shows his originality also in his choice of metre. The French rhyming couplets are transformed into alliterative long lines and this often forced the poet to extend or freely alter the text. He makes frequent use of conventional formulas from English alliterative poetry, though not always very skilfully or imaginatively. This alone gives the novel a distinctive English flavour; it has to be counted among the poems of the 'alliterative revival' (though these are often more original in their treatment of the sources).[62] It is true that we often come across rather clumsy phrases and that something of the grace and elegance of the French work is lost, but we are hardly justified in making this a reproach of the translator.

*Sir Gawain and the Green Knight* is convincing proof that the alliterative metre was not in itself unsuitable for courtly or fairy-tale material so that the weaknesses of the poem cannot primarily be attributed to the poet's choice of metre.

The author's comparatively faithful adherence to his source stands in striking contrast to most of the shorter romances. In his presentation of the love-story in particular, the English adapter is careful to reproduce the tone of the original. Admittedly, he does coarsen some effects and turns a chiefly spiritual relationship into a frankly sensual love-affair; on the other hand, he describes the beginning of the passion with particular exactness; the symptoms of *amour courtois* are analysed in detail, and Melior's long reflective soliloquy at the beginning is taken over complete, though with some characteristic changes.[63] Here again, as for instance in *Ipomedon*, the secret love is betrayed by meaningful glances, by 'kuntenaunce of kastyng of lokes' (l. 942). Indeed, *William of Palerne* is, in its portrayal of courtly love, almost as close to French courtly literature as the A-version of *Ipomedon*.[64]

In other respects, too, the adapter shows, as did the French poet before him, his preference for elaborate ceremony and long speeches, but he often sacrifices something of the tempo and quick repartee of the French dialogue. Thus, messengers' reports, important communications or the telling of news are almost always reproduced as direct speech, even when this leads to lengthy repetition and to a sometimes ponderous progress of the action. Such ceremonious scenes accumulate especially in the last part of the novel. The last thousand lines (that is to say, a fifth of the whole work) consist almost solely of ceremonial receptions, messages and reunions, because the actual plot has come to an end with the disenchantment of the Werwolf (after l. 4457). It is just this sort of episode that was, as a rule, radically abridged in the more popular romances. The fact that the English translator spends so much time on these static, and on the whole rather undramatic, concluding scenes, is a particularly clear indication of his interest in courtly etiquette and rhetorical ornament. It seems therefore hardly likely that he was a minstrel, as Kaluza supposed. The places in which we are told of the rich rewards given to minstrels (see ll. 5070–3 and 5354–8) must be taken as chiefly rhetorical formulas, not as a direct reflection of the circumstances under which the poem was read, let alone as a begging hint by the author. The generous liberality of the monarch is to his own glory and is a necessary part of the festive occasion which is here described in such detail. It was a literary and well-read artist, not a minstrel in the usual sense of the word, who could write an account like this:

> no tong miȝt telle / þe twentiþe parte
> of þe mede to menstrales / þat mene time was ȝeue,
> of robes wiþ riche pane / & oþer richesse grete,
> sterne stedes & strong / & oþer stoute ȝiftes,
> so þat eche man þer-mide / miȝt hold him a-paied.
>
> (ll. 5354–8)

On the other hand, there can be no doubt that the poem was written for oral delivery. In comparison with his source, the translator has clearly given more prominence to the rôle of the narrator, as can be seen from the large number of transitional formulas, most of them greatly extended in translation.[65] Thus, after line 160 we are explicitly told that this is the end of the first part ('þe first pas'); the audience is asked to listen carefully and to say a paternoster for Humphrey de Bohun. This division into individual sections is not consistently kept up throughout the poem, but there are several attempts to give the listener a clearer idea of the intricate train of events, especially by means of frequent recapitulation and summary.[66] Such recapitulations are often even more detailed in the French poem and are part of the rhetorical embellishment of the story. In the English poem they have been retained as far as they help to connect the various parts of the plot and to explain the somewhat intricate family relationships.

It has sometimes been said reprovingly that *William of Palerne* is rather fantastic and far-fetched, even by medieval standards and that this is the reason why it was apparently never very popular in England,[67] but this is only partly justified. Undoubtedly, the English poet recognized the fairy-tale character of the plot and tried to heighten its effect by his narrative style, above all by his sometimes quite humorous realism. The at first rather absurd disguise of the lovers in bears' skins is made more credible by the fact that it is held up in contrast to the reactions of very normal and ordinary people. The barge-boy has a real shock when he sees the two bears suddenly get up and walk on two feet (ll. 2805 ff.), and the Queen's maid runs away in a fright when the three animals appear at the castle-gate (ll. 3175 ff.). Even the lovers themselves are shocked and occasionally amused by the disguise. They admire each other's new shape and long to see each other's real faces again. When they first put on their bears' skins, Melior asks her friend:

'Leue alisaundrine, for mi loue / how likes þe nowþe?
am i nouʒt a bold best / a bere wel to seme?'      (ll. 1727–8)

Alisaundrine tells her that she looks really frightening, and William, when he is likewise sown up, says 'ful merili':

'sei me, loueli lemman / how likes þe me nowþe?'   (l. 1740)

Later in the poem, he complains that he has not seen her face for such a long time (ll. 3079–81). The scene in which William's mother also disguises herself as a deer in order to be able to approach the two lovers, is particularly humorous. Her reply, when the two become afraid of this animal, 'I am swiche a best as ʒe ben / bi him þat vs wrouʒt' (l. 3133), throws light on a situation whose comical side was evidently seen and relished by the author.[68] There is an unmistakable irony in the way various realistic details of the disguises are portrayed.

It seems that the courtly love-story was only one part of what the English adapter was really interested in. It was evidently the figure of the hero that appealed to him more than anything else. Like Horn and Havelok, William is deprived of his inheritance and grows up in simple surroundings, learning there the essential virtues of justice and loyalty, until at last he comes again into his deserved rank and seizes his inherited power as a particularly worthy ruler. Thus, the first part draws the picture of a happy childhood, full of useful activity (see particularly ll. 170 ff.). His loyalty and gratitude towards the cowherd, his foster-father, comes out clearly at the end, when he sends for him and presents him with a 'tidi erldome' (ll. 5359–97). The considerable extension of the last section of the poem gives particular prominence to William's perfections as an ideal ruler. We are told that good laws are established, robbers punished and flatterers cast out (ll. 5468 ff.). This didactic aspect of the work which almost sounds like a mirror for magistrates towards the end, connects it with other English romances, especially with *Havelok*, where we get a very similar portrait of an ideal King and his just government. It is underlined here by several passages in which young people are admonished and instructed by their elders. Thus, the cowherd who brought up William, gives him a list of useful advice on the proper behaviour in society, reminding us almost of Polonius (ll. 328–44; see also ll. 5114–35, 5204–8, 5437–47).

Thus, the pattern of the disinherited prince who regains his kingdom, saves his mother, proves his superiority as a fighter, and wins the love of a lady equal to his real rank, is the basic theme underlying this poem, and in this respect *William of Palerne* has much in common with several other romances. Of course, the love-story plays a much more important part here and is more elaborated than in *King Horn* or *Havelok*, which leads to a certain lack of unity in the plot. Thematically as well as stylistically, then, the poem is a rather strange mixture of native realistic and French courtly elements, of didactic seriousness and humorous elegance. It is to be regretted that it seems to be the only one of its kind.

# CONCLUSION

Our discussion of the various forms of romance in thirteenth and fourteenth century England has repeatedly shown how difficult it is to find a common formula for such diverse works. Most of the traditional definitions have proved to be inadequate, particularly such that only take the story-material or the form into consideration. In Middle English, 'romance' in its widest sense includes everything that calls itself a tale and cannot strictly be classed as a historical chronicle or a Saint's legend. It has thus been necessary to point out again and again the exceptional diversity of the works in question, the variety of story-material, of form, and of artistic achievement. As far as form is concerned, certain distinctive types can be recognized, such as the tail-rhyme romances or the poems of the alliterative revival, and with regard to the subjects, there are the famous *matières*, but neither of these aspects has proved to be useful as a general principle of classification.

Nevertheless, there are some groups of romances which within themselves have more in common than just some external similarities of form or content, and suggest that there were various model patterns according to which certain definite types developed. The main characteristic types in Middle English are the shorter romances and the homiletic romances, both resulting in many cases from the drastic abridgement of longer novels or from the selection and independent treatment of individual episodes. Undoubtedly, the Breton lays which were so popular in England served partly as models, but the shorter romances differ considerably from them in many respects, as a comparison of *Sir Landevale* and Chestre's *Sir Launfal* showed. The homiletic romances are a particularly typical group. In the case of these poems, the similarity with legends and *exempla*—a characteristic feature of almost all English romances—is so marked that they can only with some reservations be counted among the romances; they could almost equally well be considered as romantically embellished legends.

The group of longer romances (about three thousand lines) is much more difficult to define; these poems can hardly be said to represent a uniform type. The fact that there are comparatively few works of this size allows the conclusion that this was not such a popular form and that generally shorter tales or extensive novels in verse were preferred, probably because of the way these poems were read. All the same, romances such as *Havelok, Ywain and Gawain, Le Morte Arthure* and *Sir Gawain and the Green Knight* are particularly successful attempts, either to abbreviate longer novels by condensing them and making them more unified, or to extend shorter episodes in an epic manner. Thus we find in this group some of the most effective of Middle English romances, although some of them, especially *Sir Gawain and the Green Knight*, have to be considered quite isolated examples as far as literary genre is concerned.

The group of verse-novels is clearly distinguished from these works; there does not seem to have been very many of them, but several of these enjoyed great and lasting popularity. These novels are almost all elaborate biographies; they describe in numerous episodes, usually without any very definite design, the lives of particularly famous heroes from history and saga, partly such internationally celebrated rulers as Alexander the Great or Richard Coeur de Lion, and partly more local celebrities, such as Guy of Warwick. Here again, the resemblance to the legends is often striking, and it is typical that the best loved of these novels, *Guy of Warwick*, portrays the hero almost as a saint who frees Christianity from satanic monsters and at whose corpse miracles take place.

The marked emphasis on the exemplary aspects of the story, although not always as clearly visible as here, seems to be a common characteristic of the Middle English romances. The exemplary and moralizing tendency makes the plot, which at first often appears to be related for the sake of external effects only, in many cases far more coherent and meaningful than is generally admitted. To this tendency many of the individual examples of 'realism', sometimes taken out of their context and acclaimed with enthusiasm by critics, are clearly subordinated. The striking emphasis on the outward action which we have noticed in many romances, does therefore not come merely from a primitive preoccupation with the mechanism of the story, but only proves that the authors did not usually attempt to point the moral by rhetorical flourishes and explicit statement, but rather by means of the concrete visualization of exemplary episodes and characters.

Another characteristic feature of the romances is the way in which nearly all of them centre around prominent heroes; most of them are, in the words of Chaucer, 'romances of prys', whether the central hero is a dashing warrior (*Sir Launfal*), a humble penitent (*Sir Ysumbras*), a bold lover (*Sir Degrevant*), an ideal ruler (*Havelok*), or an innocently persecuted lady (*Le Bone Florence of Rome*). A comparison of such poems with their sources often shows how consciously the English adapter subordinated the plot to the hero. Even such widely different poems as *Sir Perceval of Gales*, *Sir Ysumbras*, *Sir Tristrem*, *Ywain and Gawain* and *Sir Gawain and the Green Knight* have this feature in common; each portrays in its own way a perfect hero, even where, as in the case of *Sir Tristrem*, the plot is open to quite a different interpretation. This concentration on the chief character connects the romances with the Saints' legends which were also, as a rule, mainly biographical.

I have deliberately refrained from including, as many other writers on the subject of romances have done, the works of Chaucer and Gower. For all the points they obviously have in common with the authors of the romances, the fundamental differences in style, form, and even literary types, are so important that a comparison between the romances and the works of those two courtly poets easily leads to wrong or at least very one-sided assessments.[1] This is particularly apparent in the case of Gower, because the individual tales in the *Confessio Amantis*, even when they deal with romance-material, are always intended as *exempla*, illustrating particular virtues and sins of love, and are told accordingly. They all have a definite place within a close-knit and systematically ordered frame-work, and it would therefore be rather misleading to take individual stories out of their context and treat them as separate romances.[2] For similar reasons I have left out of consideration the collection *The Seven Sages of Rome*, although it has been preserved together with romances in some manuscripts.[3] It should also be admitted that Gower, as a conscious artist and a creative literary poet has to be judged by somewhat different standards than the anonymous authors of the romances because he evidently had a different conception of his own work and belongs to a rather different stylistic tradition. This is even more true of Chaucer. Both poets were not only under the influence of native and Old

French literature; they received quite new impulses from the more sophisticated contemporary literature of France and Italy,[4] so that here we have indeed the beginnings of something quite new in English poetry, something that can only to a very limited extent be compared with what went before. The relationships between Chaucer's poetry and the Middle English romances would indeed deserve a more precise examination, but they only concern a comparatively small part of Chaucer's tales and are not immediately relevant to our purpose.

Chaucer's *Canterbury Tales*, though at first sight not as closely knit as the *Confessio Amantis*, are thematically hardly less dependent on each other and only reveal their full meaning in their proper context within the whole design.[5] Here again it would be misleading to consider individual tales in isolation and put them beside the romances. Even if *The Knight's Tale* is admitted to be an exception because it is perhaps less integrated than most of the other tales, the completely different artistic approach must be apparent: the unmistakable, humorously detached and highly conscious literary personality of the poet is expressed in these tales in a way we do not even find in *Sir Gawain and the Green Knight*, perhaps the most 'conscious' of the romances.

This also applies to the question of literary types. The variety of genres in the *Canterbury Tales* has often been commented on. This variety does not only spring from the poet's pleasure in his own narrative art; it is at the same time an expression of his consummate ability in literary parody, in the widest sense of the term. Chaucer did not write romances in the sense that the authors of *Octavian* or even *Kyng Alisaunder* did, he parodied them—not only in *Sir Thopas*, where it seems most obvious, but also in the tales of the Squire, the Franklin, and the Man of Law, parody being here not so much understood as derision, but as exaggerated, brilliantly precise, and detached imitation. The poet seizes on certain characteristic examples from the wealth of formulas and motifs in the romances, such as the miraculous vision, the use of magic or the long-suffering woman, and transforms them by his art, an art that is very different from the spirit of the romances. The most striking, though not the only sign of this artistic detachment is that he never tells romances in his own person, least of all in *Sir Thopas*, but always through the mouth of others. Nothing could be more mistaken, however, than to see in these parodies

Chaucer's general contempt for the romances. Even the irresistible parody of *Sir Thopas*, which, I feel, has been detrimental to a just assessment of the romances up to the present day, much more than can have been the poet's intention, often makes fun of conventions which Chaucer himself used at other times in all seriousness.[6] The real joke probably lies much deeper than the usual interpretations would suggest.[7] *Sir Thopas* shows, however,—and this is true in a similar way of all the other romances among *The Canterbury Tales* —that the world of the romances was for Chaucer only a small, in every respect limited and subordinate section of that large and differentiated cosmos which *The Canterbury Tales* attempt to circumscribe; in it the romance of *Sir Thopas* has its definite (certainly not arbitrary) place by the side of the story of Melibeus, and the sermon of the Parson is an unmistakable commentary on all that has gone before.

I have, throughout this study, tried to show that the Middle English romances are by no means such naive and artless creations as has often been assumed; nevertheless, none of them has any of the sophisticated refinement and literary consciousness which is apparent in every one of *The Canterbury Tales*. I hope that to treat the romances, as I have tried to do, without constant reference to the works of Chaucer and Gower, which by present-day standards are so much more successful, will contribute to a more just evaluation of these poems; because English literature of the Middle Ages, and even Chaucer's own poetry, would have been so much poorer without them.

# APPENDIX

## *A Note on Some Manuscripts of Romances*

A thorough examination of all manuscripts of Middle English romances has not yet been made. Such an examination would, however, be most desirable and could provide much valuable information about the provenance and transmission of the romances. A start has been made in some studies by Karl Brunner, and some reliable descriptions of individual manuscripts can be found in library catalogues and in many critical editions of romances.[1] Since most romances have only been preserved in very few copies, many of them only in a single one, it would be particularly important to learn more about the origins of the individual collections and their affiliations. Here I can only draw attention to some particularly important manuscripts and perhaps make a few additions to previous descriptions.

As Brunner has already pointed out, there are practically no 'secular' manuscripts in Middle English. Thus, the oldest romances are usually preserved in manuscripts of clerical origin, such as Harley 2253, which contains *King Horn*, and Laud Misc. 108, which presumably also comes from a clerical library, although the part containing *Havelok* and *King Horn*, written in a formal *textura*, was probably not bound with the rest of the collection until some time after the production of the manuscript.[2] The majority of later romances are to be found in larger collections which, it seems, were mostly commissioned for private libraries and households, though it must be admitted that we know far from enough about their origins.

The earliest and most important of these collections is the Auchinleck Ms. written about 1330–40. The manuscript was obviously produced on a commercial basis and seems to have been edited with some care.[3] We can therefore assume that the order of the various items in it was not entirely arbitrary. Although no very definite design is apparent (for that, the entire contents of the severely damaged manuscript would have to be known), the scribes appear to have made some attempt to distinguish between religious and secular works. The first part of the collection (Ff. 1–78) contains chiefly legends (among which, characteristically, *The King of Tars* and *Amis and Amiloun* are grouped) as well as didactic and devotional poems. From f. 78b onwards begins a varied mixture of verse-novels, shorter romances, satirical and didactic works. The romances are not completely separated from the rest, but all the same they are grouped together in this second part of the collection in such a way that related stories follow each other. Thus, for instance, *Reinbrun* follows after the two parts of *Guy of Warwick*, and is in turn followed by *Beues of Hamtoun* and *Arthour and Merlin*. *Roland and Vernagu* is next to *Otuel*, and it is certainly not accidental that *Horn Childe* and *Richard Coeur de Lion* are preceded by the *Liber regum Angliae*.[4] Most of these poems seem to be copies from earlier manuscripts, but the redactors of the Auchinleck Ms. undoubtedly had a large share in the literary form of the poems they collected.

In the case of some other collections, the original order of the items cannot be so easily determined. Thus the manuscript Cotton Galba E. IX, from about the middle of the fourteenth century, which has in common with the Auchinleck Ms. a version of *The Seven Sages of Rome*, consists of several parts which may or may not have been originally in the same order as they are now.[5] The manuscript falls into three parts (Ff. 4–51, 52–75, 76–114). At the two joins the usual catchwords are missing; a new gathering and a new item is begun by a new scribe. At the end of each part a few pages were left empty and were later filled up with shorter poems by other scribes. The collection was therefore not necessarily planned as a whole, and there would be little point in drawing any conclusions from the order of the individual items.

One of the few collections containing almost only romances is the manuscript B.M. Egerton 2862 (previously owned by the Duke of Sutherland and known as the 'Trentham Ms.'), dating from about the last part of the fourteenth century.[6] It was written by one scribe and obviously produced with some care. Thus the title of the respective item is quoted at the top of each page, which is comparatively rare in manuscripts of romances. Originally the collection must have contained the complete texts of at least *Richard Coeur de Lion, Beues of Hamtoun, Sire Degarre, Floris and*

*Blauncheflur*, *The Seege or Batayle of Troye*, *Amis and Amiloun*, and *Sir Eglamour*. Five of these poems are also to be found in the Auchinleck Ms. Unfortunately the manuscript is badly damaged and has been exposed to damp. At the beginning, in the middle, and at the end, at least one gathering (eight double-sides in each case) is missing. In the middle, too, the numbering of the pages has got muddled. Thus, the beginning of *Richard Coeur de Lion*, about one page of *Beues of Hamtoun*, the larger part of *Sire Degarre*, the beginning (probably not very long) of *Floris and Blauncheflur*, and the end of *Sir Eglamour* are all lacking.[7] This is apparently a careful collection of popular romances, possibly made by a professional scribe for some patron or wealthy customer. It is quite possible that a larger number of such manuscripts existed which, if they had been preserved, would have considerably modified our idea of the Middle English romances.

The two Thornton Mss. represent a very different type of collection.[8] Both were possibly commissioned by well-to-do families of the East Midlands, and both are mainly didactic and devotional in character. The famous Lincoln Ms. (Lincoln Cathedral Library A. 5.2) contains in the first part a number of romances (mainly Northern in origin) together with legends, the prophecies of Thomas of Erceldoune and popular medical works. The romances are not consistently kept separate from the other works in the collection, and the whole volume gives the impression of a more casually produced anthology; this, however, applies less to the second part which contains above all religious and devotional works by Richard Rolle and the *Liber de diversis medicinis*. It was probably a collection for practical use in the home. It contains none of the works found in the Auchinleck Ms. The romances preserved here are *Morte Arthure*, *Octavian* (Northern version), *Sir Ysumbras*, *The Erl of Tolous*, *Sir Degrevant*, *Sir Eglamour*, *The Awntyrs off Arthure* and *Sir Perceval of Gales*. The alliterative *Morte Arthure* and *Sir Perceval of Gales* are only preserved in this manuscript which was written about 1440.

The taste of the collector or sponsor of the second Thornton Ms. (B.M. Additional 31.042) is still more clearly apparent. It is more religious in content and contains mainly devotional poems and meditations. The few romances it includes are chiefly works of a decidedly militant Christian character, above all *The Sege off Melayne*, *Rowlande and Ottuell*, and *Richard Coeur de Lion*, as well as the poem *The Siege of Jerusalem* which can hardly be called a romance at all. It is clear that the romances in this collection were chosen mainly for their homiletic and religious qualities and do not stand in any contrast to the purely religious poems. The order of the items seems rather casual and does not reveal any significant design. The various gatherings of the manuscript are not usually connected by catchwords and in several places the ending of a poem is squashed on to the last side of a gathering or even written vertically in the margin, as if the scribe wanted to avoid starting a new gathering or as if the new gathering had already been started before the preceding one was finished (see, for example, ff. 81b, 101b, 119b, 124b). It therefore appears as if the manuscript was not written continuously, but at different times, perhaps as the scribe had access to the poems he wanted to include. New items often begin on a new page. Only a few sections of the manuscript (e.g. ff. 125–63) seem to have been written continuously. This is an anthology of a clearly religious and devotional character, produced over a longer period of time and completed in stages.

The manuscript B.M. Cotton Caligula A.II was probably also written in this way. Here again, the catchwords are usually missing and the original composition of the volume as well as its division into gatherings can only be established approximately.[9] It is, however, a rather more careful collection, giving the titles of the items at the top of each page and revealing a certain consistency in the order of poems. Thus, most romances—*Sir Eglamour, Octavian* (Southern version), *Sir Launfal,* and *Libeaus Desconus*—are to be found in the first part of the manuscript, the last three obviously copied continuously. On the other hand, *Emaré, The Siege of Jerusalem, Cheuelere Assigne* and *Sir Ysumbras* were placed, certainly with deliberation, in the second part of the collection among moral and religious works. It is therefore quite possible that the collection which, like the Thornton Mss. was written during the first half of the fifteenth century in a fairly regular court-hand, was planned as a whole and the items arranged in a previously determined order.

One manuscript which is particularly important for the preservation and transmission of the romances, is the collection Ff. II. 38 in the Cambridge University Library.[10] Its contents partly agree with those of the Auchinleck Ms. and partly with those of the Thornton Mss. and Cotton Caligula A. II. On the whole, the manuscript is also mainly didactic and religious in content. The rather massive paper-volume (it must have contained well over two hundred and fifty leaves) dates back to about the middle of the fifteenth century and was perhaps written in stages, but hardly any poem begins on a new page and the contents are generally arranged in a meaningful order. Various religious and devotional poems are followed by a series of legends, poems on more specific moral questions and exemplary tales (for instance, *How a merchant did his wife betray*). In the last part, we find ten quite different romances: a Breton lay (*Sire Degarre*), shorter romances (*Sir Eglamour, The Erl of Tolous, Sir Triamour, Octavian*, Northern version), homiletic romances (*Le Bone Florence of Rome, Robert of Sicily*), novels in verse (*Beues of Hamtoun, Guy of Warwick*), and the collection of tales, *The Seven Sages of Rome*, for the most part works which have also been preserved in other manuscripts. This is a particularly comprehensive and interesting collection which indicates that the compilers must have had access to a large number of texts. It is therefore all the more regrettable that we know so little about the origin of this important anthology.

A much less elaborate collection is Ashmole 61 (Bodleian 6922), obviously written by an amateur and embellished with primitive drawings. It was probably produced during the second half of the fifteenth century.[11] Once again its contents overlap with a few of the collections mentioned here. The romances it contains are *Sir Ysumbras, The Erl of Tolous, Libeaus Desconus, Sir Orfeo* and *Sir Cleges*. There are only a few catchwords in this manuscript; it is possible that it was composed in the course of a longer period of time, according to what happened to be available to the collector. The size of the little volume is rather striking (ca. 42 × 14.5 cm, that is, about three times as high as wide). This is usually considered to be evidence that the manuscript belonged to a minstrel, but it might equally well be a portable collection of tales to be read aloud in a less well-to-do household. We can only say with certainty that the manuscript could easily have been carried from place to place, but apart from that there is nothing to suggest that it was a minstrel's collection and it is possible to think of a number of very different reasons for its peculiar size.

Even more simple is the manuscript B.M. Harley 2252, a sixteenth century commonplace book to which we owe two important romances, *Ipomedon B* and *Le Morte Arthur*.[12] The two poems are, however, in no way connected with the other, highly varied and rather arbitrarily assembled items in this interesting collection. It probably belonged to John Colyn, a mercer of London, and gives a valuable indication of the literary interests of a London citizen during the reign of Henry VIII.

Apart from these particularly important manuscripts of romances, which are obviously connected with each other by some common ancestors, there are a considerable number of other remarkable collections whose origins and affiliations have hardly been examined and clarified as yet.[13] It is, however, significant that hardly any romances have been preserved in the 'Aureate Collections', together with the works of Chaucer, Gower, and Lydgate. The large majority of them are to be found in very mixed, usually not very pretentious or elaborate collections, often in the midst of religious and didactic works. This, too, confirms what I have tried to say about the close connection between the romances and other genres of Middle English literature, as well as about their bookish and exemplary character.

# NOTES

## CHAPTER 1

[1] The full title is: *Specimens of Early English Metrical Romances, chiefly written during the early part of the Fourteenth Century; to which is prefixed an Historical Introduction, intended to illustrate the rise and progress of romantic composition in France and England. In Three Volumes* (London, 1805). There is a good account of early romance-scholarship in A. Johnston, *Enchanted Ground: the Study of Medieval Romance in the Eighteenth Century* (London, 1964).

[2] See Chapter 2, below.

[3] Such comparisons can be found in most of the older editions of romances. See especially the thorough editions of Eugen Kölbing, e.g. *Amis and Amiloun* (Heilbronn, 1884); *Arthour and Merlin* (Leipzig, 1890); *Ipomedon* (Breslau, 1889); *Die nordische und die englische Version der Tristan-Sage*, 2 vols. (Heilbronn, 1878 and 1882).

[4] Most books on Chaucer mention this variety of literary genres in the *Canterbury Tales*; cf. also *The Works of Geoffrey Chaucer*, ed. F. N. Robinson, 2nd edn. (New York, 1957), p. 4.

[5] See H. R. Patch, 'Chaucer and Medieval Romance', *Essays in Memory of Barrett Wendell by His Assistants* (Cambridge, Mass., 1926), pp. 93–108; reprinted in *On Rereading Chaucer* (Cambridge, Mass., 1939), pp. 195 ff.

[6] What I mean is that no literary type was so predominant in Middle English, and so comparatively uniform, as the courtly novel in French and German.

[7] On the history of knighthood in England see D. Sandberger, *Studien über das Rittertum in England vornehmlich während des 14. Jahrhunderts*, Historische Studien, 310 (Berlin, 1937). On ideals of knighthood in Middle English literature, see K. Lippmann, *Das ritterliche Persönlichkeitsideal in der mittelenglischen Literatur des 13. und 14. Jahrhunderts* (Diss. Leipzig, 1933). Cf. also the relevant volumes of *The Cambridge Medieval History*, *The Oxford History of England* and (shorter, but very good on the social and economic aspects) of *The Pelican History of England*. See also the excellent account by J. Bumke, *Studien zum Ritterbegriff im 12. und 13. Jahrhundert* (Stuttgart, 1963).

[8] See W. F. Schirmer and U. Broich, *Studien zum literarischen Patronat im England des 12. Jahrhunderts* (Köln and Opladen, 1962); also, C. H. Haskins, 'Henry II as a Patron of Literature', *Essays in Medieval History Presented to T. F. Tout* (Manchester, 1925), pp. 71–7; T. F. Tout, 'Literature and Learning in the English Civil Service in the Fourteenth Century', *Speculum*, IV (1929), 365–89.

[9] See M. D. Legge, *Anglo-Norman Literature and its Background* (Oxford, 1963), pp. 85–96, and C. B. West, *Courtoisie in Anglo-Norman Literature* (Oxford, 1938), pp. 80–97.

[10] On the history of the tournament in England see N. Denholm-Young, 'The Tournament in the Thirteenth Century', *Studies in Medieval History Presented to F. M. Powicke* (Oxford, 1948), pp. 240–68; D. Sandberger, pp. 15 ff.;

D. M. Stenton, *English Society in the Early Middle Ages*, The Pelican History of England, 3 (Harmondsworth, 1952), pp. 78 ff. On possible influences of the romances on tournaments, see R. H. Cline, 'The Influence of Romances on Tournaments of the Middle Ages', *Speculum*, XX (1945), 204–11. Another useful study on the relationship of reality and romance is R. W. Ackerman, 'The Knighting Ceremonies in the Middle English Romances', *Speculum*, XIX (1944), 285–313.

[11] See the classic account of J. Huizinga, *The Waning of the Middle Ages* (Harmondsworth, 1955; first English edition, 1924).

[12] See Chapter 6, below.

[13] For instance, *King Edward and the Shepherd* and *The Taill of Rauf Coilȝear*. On the closer connection between town and country, see A. R. Myers, *England in the Late Middle Ages*, The Pelican History of England, 4 (Harmondsworth, 1952), pp. 40 ff.

[14] See especially A. C. Baugh, *A History of the English Language*, 2nd edn. (London, 1957), pp. 150 ff., and H. Käsmann, *Studien zum kirchlichen Wortschatz des Mittelenglischen 1100–1350. Ein Beitrag zum Problem der Sprachmischung*, Buchreihe der Anglia, 9 (Tübingen, 1961), pp. 3 ff.

[15] Such passages can be found, for example, in *Richard Coeur de Lion*, *Kyng Alisaunder*, *A Stanzaic Life of Christ* (9 ff.), and *The Castle of Love* (19 ff.).

[16] See M. D. Legge, pp. 362 ff.

[17] See the introduction by R. H. Robbins to his anthology *Secular Lyrics of the XIVth and XVth Centuries*, 2nd edn. (Oxford, 1955).

[18] It is still instructive (and entertaining) to read the vigorous argument about minstrels between Bishop Percy and Ritson. See T. Percy, *Reliques of Ancient English Poetry*, ed. H. B. Wheatley (London, 1891), pp. xiii ff. and 345 ff., and J. Ritson, *Ancient Engleish Metrical Romanceës* (London, 1802), vol. I, pp. v ff.; also, W. Scott, *Minstrelsy of the Scottish Border*, ed. T. Henderson (London, 1931), pp. 501 ff. On the French minstrels, which probably played a much more important part than the English, see E. Faral, *Les Jongleurs en France au Moyen Age* (Paris, 1910); on the English minstrels, see the still very useful account by J. J. Jusserand, *English Wayfaring Life in the Middle Ages*, University Paperbacks (London, 1961; 1st edn., 1889).

[19] See E. K. Chambers, *The Mediaeval Stage* (London, 1903), vol. I, pp. 42–86, and vol. II, pp. 230–62; C. C. Olson, 'The Minstrels at the Court of Edward III', *PMLA*, LVI (1941), 601–12, and the passages cited by H. H. Carter, *A Dictionary of Middle English Musical Terms* (Bloomington, 1961), under *Menestral*, *Menestralcie*, *Gestour*, *Iogelour* and others. On the later development of the minstrels, see J. Stevens, *Music and Poetry in the Early Tudor Court* (London, 1961), pp. 296 ff.

[20] See the discussions by A. C. Baugh, 'The Authorship of the Middle English Romances', *Annual Bulletin of the Modern Humanities Research Association*, 22 (1950), 13–28, and 'The Middle English Romance: Some Questions of Creation, Presentation, and Preservation', *Speculum*, XLII (1967), 1–31. Baugh's conclusions differ from mine in some points. See also the remarks by R. L. Greene, *A Selection of English Carols* (Oxford, 1962), pp. 18–20. Greene denies that carols were sung by minstrels.

[21] See G. P. Wilson, 'Chaucer and Oral Reading', *The South Atlantic Quarterly*, XXV (1926), 283–99; R. Crosby, 'Oral Delivery in the Middle Ages', *Speculum*, XI (1936), 88–110, and 'Chaucer and the Custom of Oral Delivery', *Speculum*, XIII (1938), 413–32. On the oral character of most medieval literature, see the excellent study by H. J. Chaytor, *From Script to Print: an Introduction to Medieval Literature* (Cambridge, 1945), and the brief, but valuable

remarks by A. C. Spearing, *Criticism and Medieval Poetry* (London, 1964), pp. 16–25.

[22] See the collections in E. Kölbing's editions of *Amis and Amiloun* and *Sir Beues of Hamtoun*, EETS, ES, 46 (1885), pp. xlv ff., and particularly A. C. Baugh, 'Improvisation in the Middle English Romance', *Proceedings of the American Philosophical Society*, 103 (1959), 418–54. There is also an excellent collection of clichés in *Sources and Analogues of Chaucer's Canterbury Tales*, ed. W. F. Bryan and G. Dempster (Chicago, 1941), pp. 486–559.

[23] For example, *The Index of Middle English Verse*, by C. Brown and R. H. Robbins (New York, 1943), lists about eighty poems beginning with some formula 'Listen, lords, and I shall you tell . . .'

[24] See, for instance, the beginning of Book II of Chaucer's *House of Fame*. Chaucer's use of conventional tags has not been adequately dealt with so far. It is, of course, not surprising that *The Canterbury Tales* contain many formulas typical of oral poetry because the relationship between the story-teller and his audience is of central importance there.

[25] *Sir Beues of Hamtoun* contains a number of examples; on its source, the Anglo-Norman *Boeve de Haumtone*, see M. D. Legge, pp. 156–61.

[26] See ll. 637 ff. in the edition by E. Faral, *Les Arts Poétiques du XII^e et du XIII^e Siècle* (Paris, 1924), and H. Brinkmann, *Zu Wesen und Form mittelalterlicher Dichtung* (Halle, 1928), pp. 132, 181 ff., and *passim*.

[27] See L. A. Hibbard, *Mediæval Romance in England*, new edn. (New York, 1959), p. 106 (Ms. Laud Misc. 108), and R. H. Robbins, *Secular Lyrics*, pp. xxvi f. The assumption of a minstrel collection is rather more probable in the case of Ms. Lincoln's Inn 150. See *The Seege or Batayle of Troye*, ed. M. E. Barnicle, EETS, 172 (1927), pp. x ff., and *Kyng Alisaunder*, ed. G. V. Smithers, EETS, 237 (1957), pp. 11–12. Other possible minstrel collections are Ashmole 61 and Douce 228. On Ashmole 61 see *Sir Orfeo*, ed. A. Bliss, 2nd edn. (Oxford, 1966), pp. xi f., on Douce 228 see *Richard Coeur de Lion*, ed. K. Brunner (Wien-Leipzig, 1913), p. 7.

[28] See the important article by L. H. Loomis, 'The Auchinleck Manuscript and a Possible London Bookshop of 1330–1340', *PMLA*, LVII (1942), 595–627; also: L. H. Loomis, 'The Auchinleck *Roland and Vernagu* and the *Short Chronicle*', *MLN*, LX (1945), 94–7; R. N. Walpole, 'The Source Ms. of *Charlemagne and Roland* and the Auchinleck Bookshop', *MLN*, LX (1945), 22–5; H. M. Smyser, '*Charlemagne and Roland* and the Auchinleck MS.', *Speculum*, XXI (1946), 275–88.

[29] See the articles by K. Brunner, 'Der Inhalt der ME. Handschriften und die Literaturgeschichte', *Anglia*, 65 (1941), 81–6; 'Die Überlieferung der Mittelenglischen Versromanzen', *Anglia*, 76 (1958), 64–73; 'Middle English Metrical Romances and their Audience', *Studies in Medieval Literature in Honor of Professor Albert Croll Baugh*, ed. MacE. Leach (Philadelphia, 1961), pp. 219–27. There are a few relevant remarks in the excellent survey by D. Pearsall, 'The Development of Middle English Romance', *Mediaeval Studies*, 27 (1965), 91–116. See also 'A Note on Some Manuscripts of Romances', below.

[30] See H. S. Bennett, 'The Production and Dissemination of Vernacular Manuscripts in the Fifteenth Century', *The Library*, 5th series, 1 (1946/7), 167–78, and M. Deanesly, 'Vernacular Books in England in the Fourteenth and Fifteenth Centuries', *MLR*, XV (1920), 349–58.

[31] See Brunner, 'Middle English Metrical Romances and their Audience'. This is, of course, only guesswork and can hardly be proved.

[32] See W. Clemen, *Chaucer's Early Poetry* (London, 1963), *passim*. It becomes

quite clear from this study that Chaucer's individual style reveals itself even in his earliest poems which are often described as purely conventional.

[33] See the stimulating article 'The Genesis of a Medieval Book' by C. S. Lewis, in *Studies in Medieval and Renaissance Literature*, ed. W. Hooper (Cambridge, 1966), pp. 18–40.

[34] See Chapter 6, below.

[35] *The Canterbury Tales*, VI, 437.

[36] See Trevisa's translation of R. Higden's *Polychronicon*, I, 59, ed. C. Babington and J. R. Lumby, Rolls Series, 41 (1865/86), vol. II.

[37] See N. Griffin, 'The Definition of Romance', *PMLA*, XXXVIII (1923), 50–70; Dorothy Everett, 'A Characterization of the English Medieval Romances', *Essays on Middle English Literature*, ed. P. Kean (Oxford, 1955), pp. 1–22; and the brief comments by G. Kane, *Middle English Literature* (London, 1951), pp. 1 ff.; cf. also the older article by W. W. Comfort, 'The Essential Difference between a "Chanson de Geste" and a "Roman d'Aventure" ', *PMLA*, XIX (1904), 64–74.

[38] W. P. Ker, *Epic and Romance. Essays on Medieval Literature* (London, 1897). There are some highly stimulating remarks in E. Auerbach, *Mimesis*, translated by W. Trask (Princeton, 1953), Chapters V and VI, and in D. M. Hill, 'Romance as Epic', *English Studies*, 44 (1963), 95–107.

[39] See C. Muscatine, *Chaucer and the French Tradition* (Berkeley and Los Angeles, 1957), pp. 166 ff.; on *Troilus*, see especially K. Young, 'Chaucer's "Troilus and Criseyde" as Romance', *PMLA*, LIII (1938), 38–63. Much has been written about the differences between French and English romances. Particularly useful are: J. Wilcox, 'French Courtly Love in English Composite Romances', *Papers of the Michigan Academy of Science, Arts & Letters*, XIII (1933), 575–90, and M. A. Gist, *Love and War in the Middle English Romances* (Philadelphia, 1947).

[40] See R. Hoops, *Der Begriff 'Romance' in der mittelenglischen und frühneuenglischen Literatur*, Anglistische Forschungen, 68 (Heidelberg, 1929).

[41] See Hoops, pp. 34–7.

[42] Referred to by Hoops, pp. 56–7.

[43] Thus in the manuscript B.M. Additional 31.042 we read on f. 163b: 'Here Bigynnys the Romance of the childhode of Ihesu Criste þat clerkes callys Ipokrephum' (not mentioned by Hoops). See the edition of the poem by C. Horstmann. *Archiv*, 74 (1885), 327–39. The term 'romance' may be due to the fact that the poem *Richard Coeur de Lion*, which ends on the same page, is also called 'romance'.

[44] See T. Wolpers, *Die englische Heiligenlegende des Mittelalters. Eine Formgeschichte des Legendenerzählens von der spätantiken lateinischen Tradition bis zur Mitte des 16. Jahrhunderts*, Buchreihe der Anglia, 10 (Tübingen, 1964), pp. 259 ff. and *passim*.

[45] Such a rough separation can be seen in the Auchinleck-manuscript and, I think, in Cambridge University Library Ff.II.38. See also the articles by Brunner quoted in note 29, above.

[46] See *The South English Legendary*, ed. C. D'Evelyn and A. J. Mill, EETS, 235 (1951), Prologue, 59–66.

[47] The manuscript B.M. Additional 31.042 is an example. It contains mainly devotional literature and some homiletic romances. See 'A Note on Some Manuscripts of Romances', below.

[48] See *The Index of Middle English Verse*, p. x. The extensive *Supplement to the Index of Middle English Verse* by R. H. Robbins and J. L. Cutler (Lexington, 1965) has some additional material, but the conclusions remain the same. See

also the list of texts that appear in more than eight manuscripts, *Index*, pp. 737–9, and the slightly corrected list in the *Supplement*, pp. 521–4.

[49] Cf. R. M. Wilson, *The Lost Literature of Medieval England* (London, 1952), pp. 114 ff.

[50] See H. Sparnaay, *Verschmelzung legendarischer und weltlicher Motive in der Poesie des Mittelalters* (Groningen, 1922); also I. P. McKeehan, 'Some Relationships between the Legends of British Saints and Medieval Romance', *University of Chicago Abstracts of Theses, Humanistic Series*, II (1923–4), 383–91: 'it is practically impossible to draw a clear line between saints' legends and romances. A difference in atmosphere, in style, in method of treatment, is usually, though not always, apparent, but the story-stuff is identical' (p. 391). Similar remarks are made by G. H. Gerould, *Saints' Legends* (Boston and New York, 1916), pp. 48 ff., 133 ff., 157 ff., and *passim*. A good illustration is also provided by the story of Saint Eustace; see L. Braswell, '*Sir Isumbras* and the Legend of Saint Eustace', *Mediaeval Studies*, 27 (1965), 128–51, and Chapter 5, below.

[51] *Gesammelte Aufsätze zur romanischen Philologie* (Bern, 1960), pp. 98 ff. and *passim*.

[52] *Heiligenlegende*, pp. 22 ff. and *passim*.

[53] See Hugo Kuhn, *Dichtung und Welt im Mittelalter* (Stuttgart, 1959), p. 177.

[54] 'A Characterization of the English Medieval Romances', pp. 15–16. See also the excellent study by H. Schelp, *Exemplarische Romanzen im Mittelenglischen*, Palaestra, 246 (Göttingen, 1967), where the connections between romances and legends are particularly well set out.

[55] See M. D. Legge, *Anglo-Norman Literature*, pp. 139–75. On the English Arthur-poems see K. H. Göller, *König Arthur in der englischen Literatur des späten Mittelalters*, Palaestra, 238 (Göttingen, 1963), and R. W. Ackerman, 'The English Rimed and Prose Romances', *Arthurian Literature in the Middle Ages. A Collaborative History*, ed. R. S. Loomis (Oxford, 1959), pp. 480–519.

[56] See the edition by M. E. Barnicle, EETS, 172(1927), pp. ix ff. The two long poems on the history of Troy, *The Laud Troy Book*, ed. J. E. Wülfing, EETS, 121, 122 (1902, 1903), and *The 'Gest Hystoriale' of the Destruction of Troy*, ed. D. Donaldson and G. A. Panton, EETS, 39, 56 (1869, 1874), are rather bookish compilations and cannot properly be described as romances. Undoubtedly their authors thought that they were writing true history. Thus, at the beginning of *The Gest Hystoriale*, the author claims that he is not going to tell any invented stories, but that his account is based on the testimony of eye-witnesses. The exemplary deeds of past generations are presented as a model for the present.

[57] See the edition by E. Zettl, EETS, 196 (1935).

[58] See L. H. Loomis, 'The Auchinleck *Roland and Vernagu* and the *Short Chronicle*'.

[59] On Laȝamon, see C. S. Lewis, 'The Genesis of a Medieval Book', and K. H. Göller, *König Arthur*, pp. 19–22. On *Havelok*, see Chapter 6, below.

[60] See C. S. Lewis, *The Discarded Image. An Introduction to Medieval and Renaissance Literature* (Cambridge, 1964), pp. 178 ff.; useful surveys also in E. M. W. Tillyard, *Shakespeare's History Plays* (London, 1944), Chapters I and II, and I. Ribner, *The English History Play in the Age of Shakespeare*, 2nd edn. (London, 1965), pp. 7 ff. and *passim*.

[61] See my article ' "Point of View" in mittelenglischen Romanzen', *GRM*, NF 14 (1964), 35–46; K. H. Göller, 'Stab und Formel im Alliterierenden Morte Arthure', *Neophilologus*, 49 (1965), 57–67, and L. D. Benson, *Art and Tradition in Sir Gawain and the Green Knight* (New Brunswick, 1965), pp. 110 ff.

[62] See T. Wolpers, *Heiligenlegende*, p. 26.

[63] See Chapter 6, below.

[64] See L. H. Hornstein, 'King Robert of Sicily: Analogues and Origins', PMLA, LXXIX (1964), 13–21, note 2, and T. Wolpers, Heiligenlegende, pp. 30 ff. and passim.

[65] I feel that A. C. Baugh, in his masterly presidential address 'The Middle English Romance: Some Questions of Creation, Presentation, and Preservation', takes some of these formulas too literally and draws some conclusions which do not seem to take into account the conventional and literary character of many clichés.

[66] See Chapter 6, below. See also Chaucer's far more sophisticated use of the narrator in Troilus and Criseyde. Cf. E. T. Donaldson, 'The Ending of Chaucer's Troilus', Early English and Norse Studies Presented to Hugh Smith, ed. A. Brown and P. Foote (London, 1963), pp. 26–45.

[67] See my article, quoted above, and L. D. Benson, Art and Tradition, pp. 185 ff.

[68] D. Pearsall, in his important article 'The Development of Middle English Romance' also arrives at a more pragmatic working definition and, while admitting the vagueness of the term 'romance', sees no reason for discarding it.

## CHAPTER 2

[1] Middle English Literature, p. 9. Admittedly, though, Kane rejects all classifications only for his purpose of evaluation, not in general.

[2] Quoted by W. H. Schofield, English Literature from the Norman Conquest to Chaucer (London, 1906), p. 145, A. C. Baugh, A Literary History of England (New York, 1948), p. 174, and others.

[3] To mention only one or two examples: J. E. Wells, A Manual of the Writings in Middle English, 1050–1400 (New Haven, 1916); The Cambridge Bibliography of English Literature (Cambridge, 1940), vol. I, pp. 130 ff. (this part is also by J. E. Wells); the literary histories by Schofield and Baugh, and many others. The new edition of the Manual, ed. J. B. Severs, fascicule I (New Haven, 1967), has adopted a somewhat different system. On the story-cycles see also the useful survey by J. L. Weston, 'Legendary Cycles of the Middle Ages', The Cambridge Medieval History, vol. VI (Cambridge, 1929), pp. 815–42, and W. Thomas, 'The Epic Cycles of Medieval England and Their Relative Importance', The French Quarterly, X (1928), 193–210.

[4] Cf. H. Kuhn, Dichtung und Welt im Mittelalter, p. 45.

[5] See R. M. Wilson, The Lost Literature of Medieval England, pp. 123–4. Pearsall ('The Development of Middle English Romance', p. 96) also comments on the inadequacy of this classification.

[6] See L. A. Hibbard, Mediæval Romance in England. A Study of the Sources and Analogues of the Non-cyclic Metrical Romances. For the purposes of a source-study like that of L. A. Hibbard, the term 'non-cyclic' is, of course, perfectly justified.

[7] See K. H. Göller, König Arthur, p. 92.

[8] See M. van Duzee, A Medieval Romance of Friendship: Eger and Grime (New York, 1963).

[9] See Amis and Amiloun, ed. MacE. Leach, EETS, 203 (1937), pp. ix ff.

[10] See Chapter 5, below.

[11] See Göller's study and G. Cary, The Medieval Alexander (Cambridge, 1956), for numerous examples. A similar case is the history of Richard Coeur de Lion. See B. B. Broughton, The Legends of King Richard I Coeur de Lion: A Study of Sources and Variations to the Year 1600, Studies in English Literature, XXV (The Hague, 1966).

[12] K. H. Göller, König Arthur, passim.

¹³ See Chapter 3, below.

¹⁴ See Chapter 6, below.

¹⁵ See S. F. Barrow, *The Medieval Society Romances* (New York, 1924). The term is also, though with different connotations, used by M. Schlauch in *Antecedents of the English Novel 1400–1600* (Warsaw and London, 1963), pp. 11 ff.

¹⁶ See *Mediæval Romance in England*. Cf. also the two little volumes of translations by E. Rickert, *Early English Romances in Verse* (London, 1908). E. Rickert distinguishes between 'Romances of Friendship' and 'Romances of Love'.

¹⁷ Professor W. F. Schirmer, who very kindly placed some unpublished notes at my disposal, suggests a grouping together of *Havelok, King Horn, Athelston* and *Gamelyn* as 'germanische Romanzen'. What these four poems have in common, is that order and justice are restored at the end after a period of anarchy or disloyalty.

¹⁸ See the provocative article by J. R. Hulbert, 'A Hypothesis Concerning the Alliterative Revival', *MP*, XXVIII (1931), 405–22. On the alliterative tradition see the indispensable study by J. P. Oakden, *Alliterative Poetry in Middle English*, 2 vols. (Manchester, 1930–35), especially the excellent survey 'The Alliterative School', vol. II, pp. 85–111; also D. Everett, 'The Alliterative Revival', *Essays on Middle English Literature*, pp. 46–96.

¹⁹ See the important articles by A. McI. Trounce, 'The English Tail-rhyme Romances', *Medium Aevum*, I (1932), 87–108, 168–82; II (1933), 34–57, 189–98; III (1934), 30–50.

²⁰ See R. H. Robbins, *Secular Lyrics*, pp. xlviii ff.

²¹ See T. Wolpers, *Heiligenlegende*, pp. 262 and 301 f. on the importance of the metre for the narrative technique. Pearsall, too, attaches some importance to the metrical form of the romances, although his distinction between 'epic romance' (written in rhyming couplets) and 'lyric romance' (written in tail-rhyme stanzas) seems to me somewhat questionable ('The Development of Middle English Romance', p. 96).

²² The differences in length are briefly mentioned in W. P. Ker, *Medieval English Literature* (London, 1912), pp. 83–4, A. B. Taylor, *An Introduction to Medieval Romance* (London, 1930), *passim*, and W. F. Schirmer, *Geschichte der englischen und amerikanischen Literatur*, 4th edn. (Tübingen, 1967), *passim*, and others, but they are usually treated as irrelevant.

²³ See Chapter 3, below.

²⁴ See Chapters 3 and 7, below.

²⁵ See M. D. Legge, *Anglo-Norman Literature*, pp. 3 ff. and *passim*.

²⁶ See Pearsall, 'The Development of Middle English Romance', pp. 97 ff.

²⁷ See Chapter 6, below.

## CHAPTER 3

¹ The authenticity of this division is, however, doubtful. See L. L. Hill, 'Madden's Divisions of *Sir Gawain* and the "Large Initial Capitals" of *Cotton Nero A.X.*', *Speculum*, XXI (1946), 67–71.

² See A. C. Baugh, 'Improvisation in the Middle English Romance', pp. 434–5.

³ Cf. D. Everett, 'A Characterization of the English Medieval Romances', pp. 16–19, and on the Arthur ballads, K. H. Göller, *König Arthur*, pp. 166 ff.

⁴ See the editions of the lays of Marie de France by K. Warnke, 3rd edn. (Halle, 1925), and A. Ewert (Oxford, 1944), and the useful survey by E. Hoepffner, 'The Breton Lays', *Arthurian Literature in the Middle Ages*, pp. 112–21.

⁵ See the excellent article by L. Spitzer, 'Marie de France—Dichterin von

Problem-Märchen', *Zeitschrift für Romanische Philologie*, 1 (1930), 29–67; also, F. Schürr, 'Komposition und Symbolik in den Lais der Marie de France', *ibid.*, 556–82, and S. F. Damon, 'Marie de France: Psychologist of Courtly Love', *PMLA*, XLIV (1929), 968–96; on the stories, see G. V. Smithers, 'Story-Patterns in some Breton Lays', *Medium Aevum*, XXII (1953), 61–92.

⁶ See the interpretation by I. Nolting-Hauff, 'Symbol und Selbstdeutung. Formen der erzählerischen Pointierung bei Marie de France', *Archiv*, 199 (1962–3), 26–33.

⁷ E.g. *Emaré*, *Sir Gowther*, *The Erl of Tolous*. On the English lays see the unpublished dissertation by M. J. Donovan, *The Form and Vogue of the Middle English Breton Lay* (Harvard Dissertation, 1951), which contains much useful material, and the interesting, though hardly commented anthology *The Breton Lays in Middle English*, ed. T. C. Rumble (Detroit, 1965), with a good bibliography. Other romances, too, have occasionally been called lays. Cf. W. H. French, *Essays on King Horn* (Ithaca, 1940), pp. 1 ff., and R. M. Garrett, 'The Lay of Sir Gawayne and the Green Knight', *JEGP*, XXIV (1925), 125–34.

⁸ See the exhaustive essay by W. H. Schofield, 'Chaucer's Franklin's Tale', *PMLA*, XVI (1901), 405–49; L. H. Loomis, 'Chaucer and the Breton Lays of the Auchinleck MS.', *SP*, XXXVIII (1941), 14–33, and the collection of parallels in *Sources and Analogues of Chaucer's Canterbury Tales*, pp. 377–97.

⁹ See T. Stemmler, 'Die mittelenglischen Bearbeitungen zweier Lais der Marie de France', *Anglia*, 80 (1962), 243–63, and the briefer comparison in *Sir Launfal*, ed. A. J. Bliss (London, 1960), pp. 24 ff.

¹⁰ Cf. *Sir Orfeo*, ed. A. J. Bliss, 2nd edn. (Oxford, 1966), pp. xxxi ff.; on the origin and adaptation of some motifs see also D. Allen, 'Orpheus and Orfeo: the Dead and the *Taken*', *Medium Aevum*, XXXIII (1964), 102–11.

¹¹ See the edition by G. Schleich, Englische Textbibliothek, 19 (Heidelberg, 1929), and the studies by G. P. Faust, *Sir Degare: a Study of the Texts and Narrative Structure*, Princeton Studies in English, 11 (Princeton, 1935), and W. C. Stokoe, Jnr., 'The Double Problem of *Sir Degaré*', *PMLA*, LXX (1955), 518–34.

¹² *Sir Orfeo*, pp. xli ff., and J. B. Severs, 'The Antecedents of *Sir Orfeo*', *Studies in Medieval Literature in Honor of Professor Albert Croll Baugh*, ed. MacE. Leach (Philadelphia, 1961), pp. 187–207. On the use of dramatic suspense, see pp. 201–2.

¹³ Cf. *Die mittelenglische Gregoriuslegende*, ed. C. Keller, Alt- und Mittelenglische Texte, 6 (Heidelberg, 1914), 485 ff. (Auchinleck version).

¹⁴ See the good chapter on *Sir Orfeo* in W. Habicht, *Die Gebärde in englischen Dichtungen des Mittlealters* (München, 1959), pp. 141–8.

¹⁵ The unity of the structure and the importance of the last episode are convincingly demonstrated by J. B. Severs.

¹⁶ This point is well made by D. M. Hill in his most stimulating interpretation, 'The Structure of "Sir Orfeo"', *Mediaeval Studies*, 23 (1961), 136–53. Hill thinks that there is a suggestion of madness in Orfeo's isolated wanderings which would give additional force to the central contrast portrayed in this poem. See also K. R. R. Gros Louis, 'The Significance of Sir Orfeo's Self-Exile', *RES*, XVIII (1967), 245–52.

¹⁷ See Stemmler's article, quoted above. On the relationship between *Sir Launfal*, *Libeaus Desconus* and *Octavian* see especially D. Everett, 'The Relationship of Chestre's "Launfal" and "Lybeaus Desconus"', *Medium Aevum*, VII (1938), 29–49, and, with some more convincing arguments, M. Mills, 'The Composition and Style of the "Southern" *Octavian*, *Sir Launfal*, and *Libeaus Desconus*', *Medium Aevum*, XXXI (1962), 88–109.

¹⁸ *Middle English Literature*, pp. 34–5. More sympathetic is the interpretation by B. K. Martin, '*Sir Launfal* and the Folktale', *Medium Aevum*, XXXV (1966), 199–210, where the popular elements of the poem are stressed.

¹⁹ *Sir Launfal*, p. 30.

²⁰ See Stemmler, p. 262.

²¹ See the editions by J. Hall (Oxford, 1901) and J. R. Lumby, re-edited by G. H. McKnight, EETS, 14 (1901). On text and metre, see W. H. French, *Essays on King Horn*; there are some useful comments in H. L. Creek, 'Character in the "Matter of England" Romances', *JEGP*, X (1911), 429–52, 585–609, and Pearsall, pp. 105–7.

²² See M. D. Legge, *Anglo-Norman Literature*, pp. 96–104.

²³ Cf. C, ll. 645, 715, 837, 1301; O, ll. 1124, 1136; brief summary, cf. O, ll. 392–3; short dialogue: O, ll. 95 ff. (I quote from J. Hall's edition).

²⁴ A. C. Baugh ('The Middle English Romance', p. 18) concludes from this beginning that the romance was sung. This seems to me far from certain.

²⁵ See the references to his revenge: C, ll. 107–10, 151–2, 156–8, 205 ff.

²⁶ See also the mention of Rimenhild's ring: C, ll. 563, 613, 873, 1483.

²⁷ See Hall's comment (pp. 128–9). Of course this may be merely an excuse by Horn to put the lady off, but it is still remarkable.

²⁸ 'An Interpretation of "King Horn" ', *Anglia*, 75 (1957), 157–72.

²⁹ Printed as an appendix to Hall's edition of *King Horn*, pp. 179–92. On possible connections with *Sir Tristrem* see Kölbing's edition of *Tristrem*, pp. XXXI–II. There are also some parallels between *Horn Childe* and *Amis and Amiloun* (e.g. *Amis*, ll. 475–7 = *Horn Childe*, ll. 820–2, though the passage is rather formulaic). See also the brief comment by Pearsall, p. 109.

³⁰ See also the use of tail-rhyme stanzas in the *Harley Lyrics*. Cf. T. Stemmler, *Die englischen Liebesgedichte des Ms. Harley 2253* (Diss. Bonn, 1962), pp. 103 ff.

³¹ See *Guy of Warwick*, ed. J. Zupitza, EETS, ES, 59 (1891), pp. 631 ff.

³² See especially L. H. Loomis, 'The Auchinleck Manuscript and a Possible London Bookshop of 1330–1340'.

A similar instance is the shorter version of *Arthour and Merlin*, preserved in four manuscripts (e.g. Lincoln's Inn 150). The first part of the long verse-novel was adapted and made into a short romance. Cf. Kölbing's edition of *Arthour and Merlin*, pp. cliii ff.

³³ See the edition by S. J. Herrtage, EETS, ES, 39 (1882), and the articles quoted in Chapter 1, n. 28.

³⁴ See the edition by M. I. O'Sullivan, EETS, 198 (1935), and H. M. Smyser's useful survey of the whole question in *A Manual of the Writings in Middle English 1050–1500*, ed. J. B. Severs, fascicule 1 (New Haven, 1967), pp. 87–94.

³⁵ On *The Sege off Melayne* see Chapter 5, below. *Roland and Vernagu*, too, belongs of course with the 'Homiletic Romances'. It is only mentioned here because of the characteristic mode of adaptation.

³⁶ See M. D. Legge, *Anglo-Norman Literature*, pp. 85–96; and C. B. West, *Courtoisie in Anglo-Norman Literature*, pp. 80–97 (this is somewhat outdated).

³⁷ See the edition by E. Kölbing (Breslau, 1889), with a detailed comparison between the two versions and their French source, though this is mainly a bare account of the facts without an attempt to interpret the differences between the poems.

³⁸ For this technique of describing reflection see also A, ll. 491 ff.; B, ll. 279 ff., 401 ff.

³⁹ The vow is mentioned again in A, ll. 1568 ff., 2175, 2241 ff.

[40] Cf. the monologues and reflections: ll. 693–728, 797–808, 7346–54.

[41] Cf. l. 1532: 'Thus of love he lernythe the artte'.

[42] See the long discussions in A, ll. 1775–2275, as against B, ll. 559–628.

[43] See the humiliating treatment of the pursuer (ll. 1491 ff.) which is lacking in the A-version, and the scene in which Ipomedon tries to pass off Imayne as his wife (ll. 1777 ff.).

[44] See Imayne's reflections, 6954–89, 7079–96, 7121–65. She falls in love with Ipomedon. The author of the B-version obviously did not quite know what to do with this motif (1809 ff.).

[45] See the studies of J. Wilcox and M. A. Gist quoted in Chapter 1, n. 39.

[46] See 'A Note on Some Manuscripts of Romances', below, and the excellent survey by D. Pearsall.

[47] See H. M. Smyser, 'Charlemagne and Roland and the Auchinleck MS.', and the description of the manuscript by A. J. Bliss, 'Notes on the Auchinleck Manuscript', Speculum, XXVI (1951), 652–8.

[48] See the articles by A. McI. Trounce quoted above (Chapter 2, n. 19).

[49] See H. S. Bennett, 'The Production and Dissemination of Vernacular Manuscripts in the Fifteenth Century'.

## CHAPTER 4

[1] See the edition by M. Kaluza, Altenglische Bibliothek, 5 (Leipzig, 1890).

[2] 'Charlemagne and Roland and the Auchinleck MS.'.

[3] Kaluza lists a great number of parallels, not all of them very significant, with Roland and Vernagu, Sir Tristrem, Sir Beues of Hamtoun, Guy of Warwick, Sire Degarre, and Amis and Amiloun. Cf. pp. cxlv ff. of his edition.

[4] See Kaluza's edition, pp. cl ff.

[5] See R. W. Ackerman, 'The English Rimed and Prose Romances', Arthurian Literature in the Middle Ages, pp. 512–14, and Göller, König Arthur, pp. 86–9, with bibliographical references.

[6] See A. Fierz-Monnier, Initiation und Wandlung. Zur Geschichte des altfranzösischen Romans im zwölften Jahrhundert von Chrétien de Troyes zu Renaut de Beaujeu (Bern, 1951), especially pp. 106 ff. Her thesis, however, sometimes leads her to over-interpret the poems.

[7] See R. R. Bezzola, Le sens de l'aventure et de l'amour (Chrétien de Troyes) (Paris, 1947), passim, and the seminal article 'Erec' by Hugo Kuhn, Dichtung und Welt im Mittelalter, pp. 133–50.

[8] See, however, ll. 208 ff. and Kaluza's note, pp. 141–2.

[9] This is also mentioned by Göller, König Arthur, p. 88.

[10] E.g. ll. 716–17 (the rescue is attributed to God), 817–19 (morning prayer), 883–5, 1857–60, 2151–4 (prayer before the adventure).

[11] E.g. ll. 457–9 (transition) and 460–2 ('listen!').

[12] See the edition by F. E. Richardson, EETS, 256 (1965) which prints two texts (Lincoln and Cotton) and gives specimens of the other versions. There is also a good discussion of the sources and the dialect. See also the review by M. Mills, Medium Aevum, XXXV (1966), 269–73. The older edition by G. Schleich, Palaestra, LIII (Berlin, 1906), is still very useful.

[13] See Hibbard, Mediæval Romance in England, pp. 274–8.

[14] Hibbard, p. 276. See also the rather unfavourable comments by G. Kane, Middle English Literature, pp. 13–14 and 22.

[15] See also L, ll. 1329 (a blessing for the characters of the story), 485–6 (the wild boar has been fed so that he may kill Christians), 873 (the King of the Holy Land accepts the baby as a gift from God).

[16] See ll. 1372–4, where the minstrels are richly rewarded. L. A. Hibbard has noticed some rather colloquial expressions and remarked on 'a certain homely flavor' (p. 274). There is not much that could be described as courtly in the poem (cf. the 'breaking' of the boar (ll. 490 ff.) and the description of the feast (ll. 1099 ff.).

[17] See the account in Richardson's edition, pp. xiv–xx, and Baugh's important article on 'Improvisation in the Middle English Romance'.

[18] See the edition by E. Adam, EETS, ES, 51 (1887).

[19] *Medium Aevum*, III (1934), 30 ff.

[20] Cf. Adam's edition, pp. xxvi ff., and Richardson's edition of *Sir Eglamour*, pp. xlv ff.

[21] See L. A. Hibbard, pp. 279–81.

[22] Trounce rightly calls the poem 'the most developed example of the combination of the religious and the heroic' (p. 35).

[23] Cf. Adam's edition, pp. xx–xxi.

[24] This is also Trounce's judgement. He particularly mentions the irony and sophistication of the poem (p. 35).

[25] See the edition by G. Lüdtke, Sammlung englischer Denkmäler in kritischen Ausgaben, 3 (Berlin, 1881), pp. 61 ff.

[26] See Lüdtke's note on line 1219; also *Sir Eglamour*, 1333 (in G. Schleich's edition) and *Torrent of Portyngale*, 2661, with the notes by Schleich and Adam in their respective editions. See also R. Hoops, *Der Begriff 'Romance'*, pp. 40–3.

[27] See Lüdtke's edition, pp. 72 ff. and 130 ff. Lüdtke thinks that the poem is based on a Breton lay. See also L. A. Hibbard, pp. 35–44, and M. J. Donovan, *The Form and Vogue of the Middle English Breton Lay*, pp. 211–23. Donovan also treats the poem as a lay and mentions its brevity, its aristocratic tone and its preoccupation with courtly love as characteristic features. By these standards, of course, several other shorter romances could be considered to be lays. Donovan's interpretation differs in some points from my own: 'Although it represents love and the courtly qualities, it stresses an external feature of chivalry —the trial by combat presented for its own sake. This, in terms of interest, seems to be the climax of the poem' (223).

[28] On the historical background see Lüdtke, pp. 72 ff., and L. A. Hibbard, pp. 37 ff.

[29] In the Lincoln manuscript the romance is even mentioned as 'The Romance of Dyoclicyane' (f. 114b). Lüdtke calls it 'The Erl of Tolous and the Emperess of Almayn' (see pp. 65–6).

[30] See *The Harley Lyrics*, ed. G. L. Brook, 3rd edn. (Manchester, 1964), No. 7, and Stemmler's interpretation, *Die englischen Liebesgedichte des Ms. Harley 2253*, pp. 176–91.

[31] See also Barnard's prayers, ll. 119 ff., 367 ff., 461 ff.

[32] There are also a few other formulas which emphasize the rôle of the narrator, e.g. the transitions, ll. 163–5, 478–80, 805–7.

[33] See the edition by L. F. Casson, EETS, 221 (1949), pp. ix ff. On the Cambridge manuscript see the interesting article by R. H. Robbins, 'The Findern Anthology', *PMLA*, LXIX (1954), 610–42.

[34] Cf. Casson's edition, pp. xlii ff.

[35] See Casson, pp. xxxi ff., and the useful articles by M. P. Medary, 'Stanza-linking in Middle English Verse', *Romanic Review*, VII (1916), 243–70, and A. C. L. Brown, 'On the Origin of Stanza-linking in English Alliterative Verse', *ibid.*, 271–83.

[36] See ll. 1557–60 and Casson's note.

[37] See Göller, *König Arthur*, p. 92.

[38] Cf. also his prayers, ll. 225–32, 365–6, 1613–16, 1673–6.

[39] See Casson, pp. lxvii–lxix. Cf. also the more general account by M. A. Owings, *The Arts in the Middle English Romances* (New York, 1952).

[40] See the articles quoted above, n. 35, and Kölbing's edition of *Sir Tristrem*, pp. lxxxiv–vi. I quote from the edition of *Sir Perceval of Gales*, by J. Campion and F. Holthausen, Alt- und Mittelenglische Texte, 5 (Heidelberg, 1913).

[41] E.g. in the *Harley Lyrics*. See Stemmler, *Die englischen Liebesgedichte*, pp. 69–91.

[42] See the brief summary by R. W. Ackerman, 'The English Rimed and Prose Romances', pp. 509–11, with further bibliographical references.

[43] See Göller, *König Arthur*, 84–6, with further references.

[44] See my article ' *"Point of View"* in mittelenglischen Romanzen.'

[45] See his edition, EETS, 203 (1937), pp. ix ff. The older edition by E. Kölbing, Altenglische Bibliothek, 2 (Heilbronn, 1884), also contains much useful material.

[46] The poem is printed in Kölbing's edition, pp. 111 ff. See also M. D. Legge, *Anglo-Norman Literature*, pp. 115–21.

[47] The C-version of the Anglo-Norman poem (Cod. Durlac. 38) has a very similar scene at this point (after l. 953), but it is generally more prolix than the other versions. The word 'oþes' in the English text is rather revealing and is an obvious reference to the theme of the poem.

[48] See 'A Note on Some Manuscripts of Romances', below.

[49] See the edition by G. Sarrazin, Altenglische Bibliothek, 3 (Heilbronn, 1885), and L. A. Hibbard, pp. 267–73.

[50] See his edition, pp. xliii–iv.

[51] See lines 921–6 (Lincoln-version):

> That maydene brighte als goldene bey,
> Whene sche þe geaunt heued sey,
> Fulle wele scho it kende
> And sayde: 'He was ay trewe of his hete:
> Whene he þe kynges heuede myght not gete,
> His owene he hase me sende!'

[52] Sarrazin (p. xliv) thought that the poet was a cleric and that the more minstrel-like stanzas were interpolated. See also Trounce, *Medium Aevum*, II (1933), 34–7.

[53] See Sarrazin, pp. xlii–iii. An example is the brief scene in which the impression made on the Emperor by Florent is described (C, ll. 1123 ff.).

[54] Sarrazin, p. xliii.

[55] See the articles by D. Everett and M. Mills quoted above (Chapter 3, n. 17) and the linguistic study by E. Fischer, *Der Lautbestand des südmittelenglischen Octavian, verglichen mit seinen Entsprechungen im Lybeaus Desconus und im Launfal*, Anglistische Forschungen, 63 (Heidelberg, 1929). E. Fischer comes to the conclusion that as far as the language of the three poems is concerned, they may well have been written by the same author (p. 200).

[56] Sarrazin suggested that the Northern version was written by the same author as *Sir Ysumbras* (pp. xliv–v), but this can hardly be proved. Trounce also sees some connection between the two poems (*Medium Aevum*, III, 367).

## CHAPTER 5

[1] W. Matthews uses the term 'penitential romances', but in a different context and without enlarging on this point: see *The Tragedy of Arthur* (Berkeley and Los Angeles, 1960), p. 205, n. 19.

² Printed in *Middle English Metrical Romances*, ed. W. H. French and C. B. Hale (New York, 1930). See the useful account in H. Schelp, *Exemplarische Romanzen im Mittelenglischen*, pp. 93–7.
The lively poem *Sir Amadace* belongs to a similar type. It is an edifying anecdote rather than a romance. Again the noble hero is rewarded by a divine miracle. The message seems to be that it 'pays' to be generous and loyal because the final reward makes up for all previous deprivations and suffering. This comforting moral is clearly formulated at the end:

> Botte quo-so serues God truly,
> And his modur, Mary fre,
> This dar I sauely say;
> Gif hom sumtyme like fulle ille,
> ȝette God will graunte hom alle hor wille,
> Tille heuyn the redy waye.             (lxx, 7 ff.)

See the editions by J. Robson in *Three Early English Metrical Romances*, Camden Series, Old Series, 18 (London, 1842), from which I quote, and G. Stephens, *Ghost-thanks or The Grateful Unburied* (Cheapinghaven, 1860); cf. also L. A. Hibbard, *Mediæval Romance in England*, pp. 73–8, and A. McI. Trounce, *Medium Aevum*, II (1933), 190–4. A new edition of the poem would be very welcome indeed.

³ See the edition by F. Krause, *Englische Studien*, 11 (1888), 1–62; also, L. A. Hibbard, pp. 45–8, R. J. Geist, 'On the Genesis of *The King of Tars*', *JEGP*, XLII (1943), 260–8, and Schelp, pp. 131–3.

⁴ See, for instance, the story of Elijah and the prophets of Baal, *1 Kings*, xviii. 17–40.

⁵ See A. C. Baugh, 'The Authorship of the Middle English Romances', pp. 23 ff.

⁶ See the full quotation, Chapter 1, above.

⁷ Printed in the anthology of W. H. French and C. B. Hale. See L. H. Hornstein, '*King Robert of Sicily*: A New Manuscript, *PMLA*, LXXVIII (1963), 453–8, and '*King Robert of Sicily*: Analogues and Origins', *PMLA*, LXXIX (1964), 13–21. There is a good interpretation of the poem in Schelp, pp. 69–84.

⁸ It is included, though with reservations, by L. A. Hibbard, pp. 58–64, and condemned by G. Kane as 'a crude, sprawling and morally unimpressive story' (*Middle English Literature*, p. 19).

⁹ See the edition by K. Breul (Oppeln, 1886) and the good account by Schelp, pp. 84–93.

¹⁰ See the detailed account in Breul's edition, pp. 45–134, and L. A. Hibbard, pp. 49–57.

¹¹ Smithers, very appropriately, calls *Sir Gowther* an 'ecclesiastical counter-blast to the literary Breton lay' ('Story-Patterns in some Breton Lays', 79).

¹² See L. A. Hibbard, p. 55.

¹³ Thus, in the manuscript B. M. Royal 17 B XLIII, line 732 reads: 'And hatt Seynt Gotlake'.

¹⁴ See the account in the edition of the poem by G. Schleich (based on the work of J. Zupitza), Palaestra, XV (Berlin, 1901), pp. 65–87, and the fragment published by C. Brown, 'A Passage from *Sir Isumbras*', *Englische Studien*, 48 (1914–15), 329.

¹⁵ See L. A. Hibbard, pp. 3–11; G. H. Gerould, 'Forerunners, Congeners, and Derivatives of the Eustace Legend', *PMLA*, XIX (1904), 335–448, and L. Braswell, '*Sir Isumbras* and the Legend of Saint Eustace'.

[16] See also the use made of this motif in Chaucer's *Clerk's Tale*.

[17] See also the excellent interpretation by Schelp, pp. 53–69, which in several points coincides with my own.

[18] This point is also made by Schelp, pp. 67–8.

[19] See D. Everett, 'A Characterization of the English Medieval Romances', p. 16.

[20] L. A. Hibbard, p. 4.

[21] See the edition by E. Rickert, EETS, ES, 99 (1908); the older edition by A. B. Gough, Alt- und Mittelenglische Texte, 2 (Heidelberg, 1901), is rather outdated.

[22] See Rickert, p. xxxii, where several examples are given.

[23] Thus the tail-lines of stanzas 28 and 57 are practically identical. They particularly stress the exemplary character of the story.

[24] E. Rickert mentions numerous examples (pp. xxvi-vii). There are about 80 lines containing verbal repetitions and over 90 lines which very closely resemble some other lines in the poem. It seems clear to me that this is a deliberate technique, not unimaginative clumsiness.

[25] E. Rickert, p. xxviii.

[26] See T. Wolpers, *Die englische Heiligenlegende des Mittelalters*, *passim*, on the narrative technique of the Saints' legends.

[27] See M. Schlauch, *Chaucer's Constance and Accused Queens* (New York, 1927), *Sources and Analogues of Chaucer's Canterbury Tales*, pp. 155–206, and M. Wickert, 'Chaucers Konstanze und die Legende der guten Frauen', *Anglia* 69 (1950), 89–104.

[28] See Wolpers, pp. 22 ff. A good example is the passage 661–72, which, in the opinion of some critics, influenced Chaucer.

[29] See his interpretation of the poem, pp. 97–113, especially his convincing explanation of the symbolism of the robe, pp. 105–13.

[30] See the edition by W. Vietor (Marburg, 1893) and the second part of it (*Untersuchung des Denkmals*) by A. Knobbe (Marburg, 1899), also L. A. Hibbard, pp. 12–22, and Trounce, *Medium Aevum*, III (1934), 43–4.

[31] Edited by A. Wallensköld, Société des anciens textes français (Paris, 1907, 1909); see also A. Wallensköld, 'L'origine et l'évolution du Conte de la femme chaste convoitée par son beau-frère (Légende de Crescentia)', *Neuphilologische Mitteilungen*, 14 (1912), 67–77.

[32] It is difficult to decide whether the author knew *The King of Tars* or whether the author of *The King of Tars* based his poem on an earlier version of *Florence*. See L. A. Hibbard, p. 15, and the interpretation by Schelp, pp. 114–29, in which the literary relationships are also discussed.

[33] The similarity with Chaucer's *Merchant's Tale* does not go very far, of course, but in both cases the satire on the senile lover is particularly cruel.

[34] See also ll. 1010–12 (there is no time for minstrelsy before Emere rushes off in pursuit of Garcy). The poet seems to have been rather interested in animal-devices (see ll. 388–93, 421–9, 598–605). They are used in a similar manner as in *Sir Eglamour* (see Chapter 4, above).

[35] See the good edition of *Athelston* by A. McI. Trounce, EETS, 224 (1951), with a good discussion of possible influences; also Trounce, *Medium Aevum*, II (1933), 189 ff., and the criticism of G. Taylor, 'Notes on *Athelston*', *Leeds Studies in English and Kindred Languages*, III (1934), 20–9, and IV (1935), 47–57.

[36] See also the slightly humorous scene between the treacherous Earl and the messenger (ll. 723–55) and Trounce's note on this passage, p. 133.

[37] See the good account in Trounce's edition, pp. 52–60. A more thorough,

but less critical account is given by J. Zupitza in the 'Epilegomena' to his edition, *Englische Studien*, 14 (1890), 321–44, especially 326 ff.

[38] See Trounce, pp. 31–8.

[39] See Chapter 6, below. Both poems are particularly English, and both are concerned with the restoration of law and order after a period of anarchy or a temporary success of disloyalty.

[40] See also the irony in ll. 232 ff. Egeland does not know of Wimound's treachery and rejoices about the honour the King is going to bestow on him and his sons.

[41] See Trounce, pp. 31–8; cf. also L. A. Hibbard, '*Athelston*, A Westminster Legend', *PMLA*, XXXVI (1921), 223–44, and A. C. Baugh, 'A Source for the Middle English Romance, *Athelston*', *PMLA*, XLIV (1929), 377–82.

[42] Trounce (pp. 41–5) does not want to claim too much for the poem and quotes with disapproval the enthusiastic praise of L. A. Hibbard and A. C. Baugh. See also Kane's favourable verdict, p. 54.

[43] See A. C. Baugh, 'The Authorship of the Middle English Romances', pp. 23 ff.

[44] See the editions by S. J. Herrtage (Ashmole), EETS, ES, 34 (1879), and M. I. O'Sullivan (Fillingham), EETS, 198 (1935), with a very useful introduction. A briefer version of the Firumbras story is contained in the poem *The Sowdone of Babylone*, written in four-line stanzas, probably after 1400; see the edition by E. Hausknecht, EETS, ES, 38 (1881), and the brief account in *A Manual of the Writings in Middle English 1050–1500*, pp. 81–6.

[45] See Chapter 3, above, and the good account by M. I. O'Sullivan, pp. lv ff.

[46] See the edition of the two poems by S. J. Herrtage, EETS, ES, 35 (1880), and Trounce, *Medium Aevum*, III (1934), 45–6.

[47] See Trounce's edition of *Athelston*, pp. 32–8.

[48] See ll. 1262 and 1333; for similar formulas, see ll. 259, 267, 386, 389, 491, 1496, 1519, 1534, and others.

[49] See, for instance, Roland's address to the Sultan, urging him to believe in the Holy Trinity (ll. 406 ff.). There is a rather more lengthy speech by Roland in *Roland and Vernagu* (ll. 668 ff.), where Roland gives an exposition of the Christian faith. Similar homilies can be found in *Joseph of Arimathie*, ed. W. W. Skeat, EETS, 44 (1871), ll. 75–145, and in *Titus and Vespasian or The Destruction of Jerusalem*, ed. J. A. Herbert, Roxburghe Club (London, 1905), ll. 2333 ff.

[50] Very similar in tone is the rather militant poem *The Siege of Jerusalem*, ed. E. Kölbing and M. Day, EETS, 188 (1932), probably written towards the end of the fourteenth century in the North-West of England, a typical product of the alliterative revival. It is preserved in seven manuscripts, among them B.M. Additional 31.042 and Cotton Caligula A.II. It is a romantically embellished legend rather than a romance and it describes a holy war in revenge for the death of Christ. The alliterative poem *Joseph of Arimathie* belongs to a similar type, whereas *Titus and Vespasian*, written in rhyming couplets, is much longer. All these poems are curious mixtures of romantic, legendary and homiletic elements and illustrate a rather crude concept of the Christian faith. This, it seems, is best expressed by slaughtering as many infidels as possible.

[51] See the edition by H. H. Gibbs, EETS, ES, 6 (1868). Kane thinks the poem 'artistically incompetent' (p. 9); J. P. Oakden's verdict is similar, *Alliterative Poetry in Middle English*, II, 40–1.

[52] See Gibbs, pp. xv–xviii, on the dialect of the poem. On the sources of the story see also L. A. Hibbard, pp. 239–51.

[53] There are hardly any 'minstrel-formulas' in the poem. See ll. 92 ff. (transition) and l. 120 (a curse on the wicked Malkedras).

## CHAPTER 6

[1] An exception is *Havelok*, of which, apart from the complete manuscript (Laud Misc. 108), some fragments have survived on four scraps of paper. See the edition by W. W. Skeat, 2nd edn., rev. by K. Sisam (Oxford, 1915), pp. ix–xi.

[2] See B. v. Lindheim, *Studien zur Sprache des Manuskriptes Cotton Galba E.IX*, Wiener Beiträge zur Englischen Philologie, LIX (Wien-Leipzig, 1937), pp. 4 ff., for a description of the manuscript.

[3] See R. H. Robbins, *Secular Lyrics of the XIVth and XVth Centuries*, pp. xxviii–ix, for some relevant remarks on the manuscript.

[4] Brief descriptions of the *Gawain* manuscript can be found in the editions of *Sir Gawain* by J. R. R. Tolkien and E. V. Gordon, 2nd edn., rev. by N. Davis (Oxford, 1967), pp. xi ff., and by I. Gollancz, with introductory essays by M. Day and M. S. Serjeantson, EETS, 210 (1940), pp. ix–x, and of *Pearl*, ed. E. V. Gordon (Oxford, 1953), pp. ix–xi, and *Purity*, ed. R. J. Menner, Yale Studies in English, 61 (New Haven, 1920), pp. vii–x. See also the facsimile-edition of the manuscript, ed. I. Gollancz, EETS, 162 (1922), and the rather specialized study by J. C. McLaughlin, *A Graphemic-Phonemic Study of a Middle English Manuscript* (The Hague, 1963).

[5] See *Le Lai D'Havelok and Gaimar's Haveloc-Episode*, ed. A. Bell (Manchester, 1925), and L. A. Hibbard, pp. 103–14. See also the useful article by H. L. Creek, 'The Author of "Havelok the Dane"', *Englische Studien*, 48 (1914–15), 193–212, and the remarks by Pearsall, pp. 97–9.

[6] See Stemmler, *Die englischen Liebesgedichte*, pp. 59–61 and *passim*.

[7] See also ll. 1838–9, 1967, 2434–40.

[8] C. T. Onions, 'Comments and Speculations on the Texts of "Havelok"', *Philologica: the Malone Anniversary Studies*, ed. T. A. Kirby and H. B. Woolf (Baltimore, 1949), pp. 154–63; cf. also Schelp, p. 33.

[9] See also the specific references to Grim's oath of loyalty to Godard (ll. 578–9, 1423–4) which he breaks for the sake of Havelok.

[10] L. A. Hibbard, p. 104.

[11] See the thorough interpretation by Schelp, pp. 31–53, where the exemplary character of the poem is well treated.

[12] See E. Kölbing's edition (Heilbronn, 1882), pp. xvi ff.

[13] See Kölbing, pp. xxxii ff. The almost identical stanza-form is used by Lawrence Minot in one of his poems on King Edward.

[14] See Chapter 4, n. 35 and 40. I owe some of these observations to an excellent essay on *Sir Tristrem*, written by a member of a seminar of mine, Wolfhard Steppe.

[15] See *Die nordische und die englische Version der Tristan-Sage*, vol. I (Heilbronn, 1878), p. cxlvii.

[16] His name Tristrem is mentioned earlier in the poem when the child is begot (ll. 107–10), but even this does not make the revelation of his later pseudonym quite intelligible or meaningful. See the sympathetic, though perhaps too uncritical defence of the poem by T. C. Rumble, 'The Middle English *Sir Tristrem*: Toward a Reappraisal', *Comparative Literature*, XI (1959), 221–8.

[17] See *Les Fragments du Roman de Tristan, Poème du XII⁰ Siècle par Thomas*, ed. B. H. Wind (Leiden, 1950), and the translation (together with the Norse poem) by R. S. Loomis (New York, 1951); there is also an older translation with a rather facetious introduction by G. Saintsbury (London, 1929).

[18] All the versions are compared in great detail by E. Kölbing, vol. I.

[19] See the edition by A. B. Friedman and N. T. Harrington, EETS, 254

(1964), with a useful account of the relation between the two poems (pp. xvi–xxxiv). The older edition by G. Schleich (Leipzig, 1887) is still indispensable. Cf. also Göller, *König Arthur*, pp. 89–92, with further bibliographical references.

[20] See Lindheim's description of the manuscript. See also the brief account in the EETS edition, pp. ix–xii.

[21] See *ibid.*, pp. xlviii–lvi.

[22] Particularly striking is the cutting down of the reflective passage preceding the duel between Ywain and Gawain. Cf. *Yvain*, ll. 5991–6148, and *Ywain and Gawain*, ll. 3509–48.

[23] See the interpretations by A. Adler, 'Sovereignty in Chrétien's *Yvain*', *PMLA*, LXII (1947), 281–305, J. Harris, 'The Rôle of the Lion in Chrétien de Troyes' *Yvain*', *PMLA*, LXIV (1949), 1143–63, and Bezzola, *Le sens de l'aventure et de l'amour*. Cf. also, on the whole problem, E. Köhler, *Ideal und Wirklichkeit in der höfischen Epik, Studien zur Form der frühen Artus- und Graldichtung* (Tübingen, 1956).

[24] Thus, *Yvain*, ll. 1589–2048, corresponds roughly to ll. 931–1194 in the English poem.

[25] Cf. *Yvain*, ll. 1339–1588, and ll. 870–930 of the English poem.

[26] See the edition by J. D. Bruce, EETS, ES, 88 (1903), and Göller, *König Arthur*, pp. 66–75. Kane also praises the literary qualities of the poem; cf. *Middle English Literature*, pp. 65–9.

[27] It is interesting to note that here, as in *Sir Gawain and the Green Knight*, the poet sees loyalty, not adultery, as the real problem although the story would admit of either interpretation.

[28] This is suggested by Göller, *König Arthur*, p. 73.

[29] This technique, too, points to a certain similarity between *Le Morte Arthur* and *Sir Gawain and the Green Knight*.

[30] See my article ' "*Point of View*" in mittelenglischen Romanzen'.

[31] I do not think that this necessarily refers to Agrawayn, as Göller seems to assume (p. 73). It could just as well refer to the two lovers, but the vagueness of the accusation seems to me the real point of the passage.

[32] See 'in Arthurs tyme but sorow and woo;' (l. 2965) and 'Arthur louyd noght but warynge And suche thynge as hym-selfe soght' (ll. 2975–6). Of course, the author also wants to show the changeableness of the people here, not just their sufferings.

[33] For an excellent survey of scholarship and criticism on *Sir Gawain* down to 1960 see M. W. Bloomfield, '*Sir Gawain and the Green Knight*: an Appraisal', *PMLA*, LXXVI (1961), 7–19. I can only mention those interpretations that are particularly relevant for my purpose and have influenced me most.

[34] See J. P. Oakden, *Alliterative Poetry in Middle English*, I, 153 ff., and the thorough study by M. Borroff, *Sir Gawain and the Green Knight: A Stylistic and Metrical Study*, Yale Studies in English, 152 (New Haven, 1962). There are some very good observations in the chapter on the style of the poem in L. D. Benson, *Art and Tradition in Sir Gawain and the Green Knight* (New Brunswick, 1965), pp. 110–66, especially on the technique of variation within the pattern.

[35] See D. Everett, *Essays on Middle English Literature*, pp. 74–5, and W. Habicht, *Die Gebärde in englischen Dichtungen des Mittelalters*, p. 148.

[36] The importance of the poem's structure is mentioned in most interpretations; see Benson, pp. 158 ff., and the admirable study by J. A. Burrow, *A Reading of Sir Gawain and the Green Knight* (London, 1965), *passim*. Burrow, very appropriately, speaks of the poet's love of 'circular effects' (p. 156). Cf. also the brief summary by S. Barnet, 'A Note on the Structure of Sir Gawain and the Green Knight', *MLN*, LXXI (1956), 319.

[37] I doubt whether we really need Celtic verse-techniques to account for this symmetry. Cf. P. L. Henry, 'A Celtic-English Prosodic Feature', *Zeitschrift für Celtische Philologie*, 29 (1962–4), 91–9.

[38] This only partly agrees with the interpretation of D. F. Hills, 'Gawain's Fault in *Sir Gawain and the Green Knight*', *RES*, XIV (1963), 124–31.

[39] See G. L. Kittredge, *A Study of Gawain and the Green Knight* (Cambridge, 1916), and the sober account by M. Day in the EETS edition of the poem. There is a useful survey of the source-problem in L. D. Benson, pp. 3–55.

[40] The importance of the concept of 'trawþe' is convincingly argued by J. A. Burrow (see p. vii and *passim*). Slightly different interpretations are suggested by G. V. Smithers, 'What *Sir Gawain and the Green Knight* is about', *Medium Aevum*, XXXII (1963), 171–89, and A. C. Spearing, *Criticism and Medieval Poetry* (London, 1964), pp. 26 ff.

[41] See D. E. Baughan, 'The Rôle of Morgan le Fay in *GGK*', *ELH*, XVII (1950), 241–51, and the convincing refutation by A. B. Friedman, 'Morgan le Fay in *Sir Gawain and the Green Knight*', *Speculum*, XXXV (1960), 260–74. On the rôle of magic in the poem see particularly T. McAlindon, 'Magic, Fate and Providence in Medieval Narrative and *Sir Gawain and the Green Knight*', *RES*, XVI (1965), 121–39.

[42] On the symbolism of the hunting-scenes see H. Savage, *The Gawain Poet* (Chapel Hill, 1956), pp. 31 ff., Benson, pp. 160 ff., and Burrow, pp. 86 ff.

[43] See R. Tuve, *Seasons and Months: Studies in a Tradition of Middle English Poetry* (Paris, 1933), pp. 170 ff., and N. E. Enkvist, *The Seasons of the Year: Chapters on a Motif from Beowulf to the Shepherd's Calendar* (Helsingfors, 1957), pp. 85 ff.

[44] See the different interpretations by McAlindon, Benson and Burrow. I largely agree with Burrow (pp. 56 ff.) who convincingly points out the ambiguous characters of Bertilak and of the Green Knight.

[45] See the rather one-sided article by R. G. Cook, 'The Play-Element in *Sir Gawain and the Green Knight*', *Tulane Studies in English*, XIII (1963), 5–31.

[46] Cf. H. Schelp, 'Nurture. Ein mittelenglischer Statusbegriff', *Anglia*, 83 (1965), 253–70.

[47] See my note 'Zu "*Sir Gawain and the Green Knight*"', *GRM*, NF 12 (1962), 414–7, and the very similar explanation by Burrow, pp. 80–2. Benson (p. 49) is an example of the opposite interpretation.

[48] See the particularly helpful and suggestive remarks by Burrow, pp. 160–86, on the problems arising out of the fact that Gawain is a perfect romance-hero and at the same time a fallible human being.

[49] See Burrow's excellent interpretation, pp. 41–51. Many commentators agree that the poem is written as a glorification of the hero. Cf. also A. M. Markman, 'The Meaning of *Sir Gawain and the Green Knight*', *PMLA*, LXXII (1957), 574–86.

[50] See Benson, pp. 240 ff. On this point, too, Burrow's interpretation seems to me preferable (pp. 157–9).

[51] See Burrow, pp. 92–3, and G. M. Shedd, 'Knight in Tarnished Armour: The Meaning of "Sir Gawain and the Green Knight"', *MLR*, LXII (1967), 3–13.

[52] See the studies by Wilcox and Gist, referred to in Chapter I, n. 39, above; also K. Lippmann, *Das ritterliche Persönlichkeitsideal in der mittelenglischen Literatur des 13. und 14. Jahrhunderts*, pp. 64 ff., and G. Mathew, 'Ideals of Knighthood in Late-Fourteenth-Century England', *Studies in Medieval History Presented to F. M. Powicke*, pp. 354–62.

[53] Cf. Burrow, pp. 146–8.

[54] See the interpretations by Spearing, Hills, McAlindon, Smithers and Burrow, to mention only a few.

[55] See the rather extreme and one-sided interpretation by H. Schnyder, *Sir Gawain and the Green Knight: an Essay in Interpretation*, The Cooper Monographs, 6 (Bern, 1961), and the very balanced comment by M. Mills, 'Christian Significance and Romance Tradition in "Sir Gawain and the Green Knight" ', *MLR*, LX (1965), 483–93. Among the more fanciful religious and allegorical interpretations are J. Gardner, *The Complete Works of the Gawain-Poet* (Chicago, 1965), pp. 70–84, and, somewhat more cautious, but still over-stated, D. R. Howard, *The Three Temptations: Medieval Man in Search of the World* (Princeton, 1966), pp. 217–54.

[56] See the useful account by B. J. Whiting, 'Gawain: His Reputation, His Courtesy and His Appearance in Chaucer's *Squire's Tale*', *Mediaeval Studies*, 9 (1947), 189–234. *Sir Gawain and the Green Knight* is, however, only mentioned in passing by Whiting.

[57] See A. Renoir, 'Descriptive Technique in *Sir Gawain and the Green Knight*', *Orbis Litterarum*, 13 (1958), 126–32, M. Borroff, pp. 120 ff., and, particularly, Benson, pp. 167 ff.

[58] See T. McAlindon, pp. 138–9, and Benson, pp. 173–97. Benson's chapter on the narrative technique of the poem is particularly valuable.

[59] See D. Everett, *Essays on Middle English Literature*, pp. 78 ff., and several others.

[60] See ll. 1283–7, and Burrow's note, p. 84. Other critics, as, for instance, Benson (pp. 45–6 and note 46) think that the lines refer to the lady's own reflections, but this would be quite contrary to the poet's usual technique.

[61] At least this is how I would translate line 2008. The word 'steuen' can mean, in this poem, either 'voice' (ll. 242, 2336) or 'contract' (ll. 1060, 2194, 2213, 2238); the latter seems slightly more frequent, although the two meanings may sometimes coincide and cannot always be clearly separated. The line quoted (l. 2008) is taken to be an example of the first meaning by I. Gollancz, whereas Tolkien and Gordon quote it as an example of the second meaning, which in view of the particular importance of the contract seems to me the more likely. B. Stone's translation seems to me the correct one: 'Every cock that crew recalled to him his tryst', *Sir Gawain and the Green Knight*, The Penguin Classics (Harmondsworth, 1959), p. 104, whereas Gardner translates: 'By every cock that crowed he could tell the hour' (p. 303). The different interpretations are even reflected in the choice of the preterite-form. Stone's 'crew' suggests that he was aware of the biblical allusion. See also Burrow, p. 114.

## CHAPTER 7

[1] Good examples are the various versions of *Kyng Alisaunder* and *Richard Coeur de Lion*.

[2] See the chapter on 'The Ancestral Romance' in M. D. Legge, *Anglo-Norman Literature and its Background*, pp. 139–75.

[3] See Chapter 3, above.

[4] See *Partonope of Blois*, ed. A. T. Bödtker, EETS, ES, 109 (1912), and *Generydes*, ed. W. A. Wright, EETS, 55, 70 (1873, 1878).

[5] See also Chapter 1, above

[6] See Chapter 6, above.

[7] See the very thorough edition by E. Kölbing, EETS, ES, 46, 48, 65 (1885, 1886, 1894), pp. vii ff.

[8] See her *Anglo-Norman Literature and its Background*, pp. 156–61, and A. Stimming's edition of *Boeve de Haumtone*, Bibliotheca Normannica, VII (Halle, 1899), especially pp. CXXX ff.

[9] The first twenty-four lines of *Richard Coeur de Lion* are also composed in tail-rhyme stanzas in the Auchinleck-manuscript. See K. Brunner's edition, pp. 25–6.

[10] See Kölbing's introduction, pp. x ff.

[11] See, however, ll. 19 ff.

[12] See Kölbing's stemma, p. xxxviii. We need to know a lot more about the copying of manuscripts and the methods of transmission before we can be very confident about such neat stemmata.

[13] See H. L. Creek, 'Character in the "Matter of England" Romances', *passim.* Creek repeatedly refers to the useful study by W. W. Comfort, 'The Character Types in the Old French *Chansons de Geste*', *PMLA*, XXI (1906), 279–434, which contains much interesting material.

[14] In most versions there is a clear break after line 3962 and again after line 4252. See also the prophetic hint, 4027–8, which connects several episodes.

[15] See Kölbing's edition, p. xxxvii.

[16] See ll. 1006–7 and the scene in which the Emperor tells Beves (whom he does not recognize) his (Beves') own story (ll. 2985 ff.), or the messenger's rough answer (ll. 3105 ff.).

[17] Beves' escape from the prison is a direct answer to his prayer (see ll. 1579 ff., 1645 ff., 1795 ff.).

[18] See also the prophetic hints in ll. 1200, 1204, 1328, 1388, etc.

[19] See ll. 510, 846, 1261–2, 1431–2, 2784, 3286 ff., 3619, 4016, 4352 (prayers for the hero or other characters) and 80–1, 1211 ff., 3458, 4030 (curses).

[20] See also ll. 46–7, 1192, 1215 ff., 3352.

[21] E.g. ll. 737–8, 848, 1068, 1263–4, 1345, 1433, 1527.

[22] *Anglo-Norman Literature*, p. 160.

[23] See also 1483–4 and 4563–8.

[24] See the edition by J. Zupitza, EETS, ES, 42, 49, 59 (1883, 1887, 1891), and his edition of the Cambridge-version, EETS, ES, 25, 26 (1875, 1876); both editions were reprinted in 1966. Copland's version was edited by G. Schleich, Palaestra, 139 (Leipzig, 1923). See also the edition of *Gui de Warewic* by A. Ewert (Paris, 1932–3).

[25] There are many smaller omissions in C which it would be interesting to investigate. The relationship between the various manuscripts, is, however, rather complicated. See M. Weyrauch, *Die mittelenglischen fassungen der sage von Guy of Warwick und ihre altfranzösische vorlage*, Forschungen zur englischen sprache und litteratur, II (Breslau, 1901).

[26] See L. H. Loomis, 'The Auchinleck Manuscript a and Possible London Bookshop of 1330–1340', and Trounce, *Medium Aevum*, II (1933), 45 ff.; also Chapter 3, above.

[27] See *The Minor Poems of John Lydgate*, ed. H. N. MacCracken, Part II, EETS, 192 (1934), pp. 516 ff.

[28] See C, ll. 9776–9805 and ll. 9477–94 of the Cambridge version.

[29] See C, ll. 1801 ff., 2801 ff, 4525 ff., 4939 ff., 7138 ff., 7583 ff. (A 45.3), l. 9040 (A 142.11), l. 10284 (A 233.1).

[30] See R. S. Crane, 'The Vogue of *Guy of Warwick* from the Close of the Middle Ages to the Romantic Revival', *PMLA*, XXX (1915), 125–94. The exemplary and legendary character of the romance is convincingly demonstrated by H. Schelp, *Exemplarische Romanzen*, pp. 133–49. Schelp concentrates mainly on the second part of the poem.

[31] See the edition by G. V. Smithers, EETS, 227 (1952) and 237 (1957), especially II, 40 ff. The problem is also discussed in the introductions to the editions of the other three poems. See also the remarks by D. Pearsall, 'The Development of Middle English Romance', 100–2.

[32] See M. D. Legge, pp. 105–7.

[33] See G. Cary, *The Medieval Alexander*, especially pp. 35–7 and 241–2.

[34] See Smithers, II, 1–2.

[35] Smithers, II, 12.

[36] The way in which manuscripts were copied made it quite possible that errors could arise which seem to be auditory. See H. J. Chaytor, *From Script to Print*, pp. 5 ff.

[37] Smithers says that the lines were omitted 'for no obvious reason' (II, 13). All quotations are from the B-version.

[38] See the excellent survey by Smithers, II, 28–40.

[39] See Smithers, II, 40.

[40] See G. Cary, pp. 220 and 231.

[41] See also ll. 3824 ff., 4365 ff., and the description of the single combat, ll. 7362 ff.

[42] See also ll. 656, 1038, 3577–8, 3584–6, 4843, 5456, 5742–4, 6292–3.

[43] See also the transitions in ll. 3287–8, 3517–8, 4841–2, anticipation (ll. 1038, 1745–6, 4247), curses (ll. 4588, 4717–18), etc.

[44] See Smithers, II, 35–40. There are occasional similar devices in other poems (see *Guy of Warwick*, A and C, ll. 4503–4, *Ipomedon* A, ll. 563–5, 2444–9, *Libeaus Desconus*, ll. 1303–8, *Firumbras*, Fillingham version, ll. 416–17), but nothing like the consistent use of head-pieces in *Kyng Alisaunder*.

[45] In two places, between ll. 2546 and 2567 and between ll. 4061 and 4101, the head-pieces come very near together. In the second instance, the author seems to conclude the section only to start again after a brief introduction.

[46] See also R. Tuve, *Seasons and Months*, pp. 179 ff. An interesting parallel are the little vignettes, showing the signs of the zodiac, with typical human activities, in the beautifully illuminated manuscript of the *Bedford Hours* (B.M. Additional 18.850).

[47] See E. Kölbing's edition, Altenglische Bibliothek, 4 (Leipzig, 1890), and the thorough interpretation of the poem by K. H. Göller, *König Arthur*, pp. 43–57.

[48] Until we have any proof to the contrary, we can assume that the poem was, in fact, never finished. At least it is very unlikely that it was at any time much longer than the version that has come down to us.

[49] See especially the most stimulating discussion by W. Matthews, *The Tragedy of Arthur*, pp. 32–67, particularly pp. 59 ff. *Arthour and Merlin* is, however, not mentioned by Matthews.

[50] See Göller, p. 45, and Kölbing, p. lxxiv.

[51] See Göller, p. 54.

[52] See Smithers, *Kyng Alisaunder*, II, 32 ff.

[53] See Kölbing, pp. lxii ff.

[54] See the edition by K. Brunner, Wiener Beiträge zur englischen Philologie, XLII (Wien–Leipzig, 1913) and L. A. Hibbard, *Mediæval Romance in England*, pp. 147–55.

[55] See the useful survey by Bradford B. Broughton, *The Legends of King Richard I Coeur de Lion: a Study of Sources and Variations to the Year 1600*, Studies in English Literature, XXV (The Hague, 1966). On the English romance see especially pp. 42–5 and *passim*.

[56] See Brunner's edition, p. 70.

[57] See the account by Brunner, pp. 1–24. The Version D (Douce 228) is more minstrel-like than the others. The character of the text and that of the manuscript (it is a portable little volume) suggests that it was written for recitation, not so much as a bookish compilation.

[58] See also L. A. Hibbard, pp. 147–8.

[59] On the history of the verse-novel in the fifteenth century see the brief remarks by D. Pearsall, pp. 91–3. He speaks of a tendency towards 'enhanced sophistication'. We have already seen that not very many novels in verse were written during the fourteenth century, whereas a number of extensive compilations were composed during the fifteenth century, most of them rather more bookish and learned than minstrel-like. It has to be borne in mind, however, that many of the romances discussed here, indeed the majority of them, are preserved in fifteenth-century manuscripts.

[60] See the edition by W. W. Skeat, EETS, ES, 1 (1867).

[61] See M. Kaluza, 'Das mittelenglische Gedicht William of Palerne und seine französische Quelle', Englische Studien, 4 (1881), 197–287. On the French Guillaume de Palerne see also I. P. McKeehan, 'Guillaume de Palerne: a Medieval "Best Seller" ', PMLA, XLI (1926), 785–809.

[62] See D. Everett, Essays on Middle English Literature, pp. 54–5, where the choice of metre is criticized. See also J. P. Oakden, Alliterative Poetry in Middle English, II, 38–40; Oakden, too, thinks the poem a failure.

[63] See Kaluza, pp. 225 ff. It is usually the English authors who present the love-stories in a more innocent way (see, for instance, The Erl of Tolous).

[64] See Chapter 3, above.

[65] E.g. ll. 159–60, 382–3, 794–5, 1634–7, 1762–3, 1784–5, 1836–8, 2447–8, 2707–12, 3528–9, 3577–8, 4805–6, 5167–9, 5232–3, 5395–7, 5465–7. The calls for attention often have a similar function; see ll. 106–8, 161–70, 384, 1929, 2617, 2713.

[66] See, for instance, ll. 415–28, 1354–72, 3133–61, 3493–512, 4069–118, 4204–4265, 4672–703.

[67] See G. Kane, Middle English Literature, p. 51, and L. A. Hibbard, p. 214.

[68] It would, however, be unwise to be too sure about such matters. It is quite possible that our conception of humour is very different from that of the author, but this does not alter the fact that he has a very original way of juxtaposing the homely and the fantastic aspects of the story. See also the scene where the Queen sees the young people's clothes through the hides which the sun had cracked (ll. 3033 ff.) or the conversation of the colliers, overheard by the two from their hiding-place (ll. 2519–57).

## CONCLUSION

[1] George Kane includes Chaucer in his evaluating discussion of the romances (in Middle English Literature), but this seems to lead him sometimes to rather unfair judgements.

[2] On Gower see especially J. H. Fisher, John Gower. Moral Philosopher and Friend of Chaucer (New York, 1964), and Maria Wickert, Studien zu John Gower (Köln, 1953).

[3] See Brunner's edition, EETS, 191 (1933), especially, pp. ix ff., and L. A. Hibbard, Mediæval Romance in England, pp. 174–83. See also the older, but still useful study by K. Campbell, 'A Study of the Romance of the Seven Sages with special reference to the Middle English versions', PMLA, XIV (1899), 1–107. Here, too, the connection of the stories with the framework is so close that there

would be little point in selecting individual stories and compare them with the romances. Apart from that, only the two tales *Inclusa* and *Vaticinium* could at all be described as romances. The other stories are anecdotes, *fabliaux* and *exempla*, mostly with a very definite moral. This is the reason why they are told, and the reaction of the emperor who appears to change his mind after every story, shows that the stories have a very definite moral intention, much more so than most of the romances, though there are, of course, a number of resemblances.

⁴ See especially C. Muscatine, *Chaucer and the French Tradition: a Study in Style and Meaning* (Berkeley and Los Angeles, 1957), and W. Clemen, *Chaucer's Early Poetry, passim.*

⁵ See the somewhat one-sided, but very stimulating interpretation by R. Baldwin, *The Unity of the Canterbury Tales*, Anglistica, V (Copenhagen, 1955), and the remarks by J. H. Fisher, *John Gower*, pp. 251 ff.

⁶ This would make an interesting study. See the material collected in *Sources and Analogues of Chaucer's Canterbury Tales* pp. 486–559. Chaucer's indebtedness to the Middle English romances is admirably demonstrated by D. S. Brewer in his essay 'The Relationship of Chaucer to the English and European Traditions', *Chaucer and Chaucerians: Critical Studies in Middle English Literature*, ed. D. S. Brewer (London and Edinburgh, 1966), pp. 1–38.

⁷ See A. K. Moore, '*Sir Thopas* as Criticism of Fourteenth-Century Minstrelsy', *JEGP*, LIII (1954), 532–45.

## APPENDIX

¹ See above, Chapter 1, notes 28–30, and *passim*. On the history of Medieval English libraries see the excellent survey by H. Gneuss, 'Englands Bibliotheken im Mittelalter und ihr Untergang', *Festschrift für Walther Hübner* (Bielefeld, 1963), pp. 91–121.

² There are brief descriptions of this manuscript in the editions of *King Horn* and *Havelok* quoted in Chapters 3 and 6. I shall only mention the more important descriptions of manuscripts in editions of individual poems.

³ See the description by E. Kölbing in 'Vier romanzen-handschriften', *Englische Studien*, 7 (1884), 177–201, and the useful corrections by A. J. Bliss, 'Notes on the Auchinleck Manuscript', *Speculum*, XXVI (1951), 652–8. Cf. also the articles quoted above, Chapter 1, note 28.

The Auchinleck Ms. contains the more or less complete texts of the following romances: *The King of Tars, Amis and Amiloun, Sire Degarre, The Seven Sages of Rome, Floris and Blauncheflur, Guy of Warwick, Reinbrun, Sir Beues of Hamtoun, Arthour and Merlin, Lai le Freine, Roland and Vernagu, Otuel, Kyng Alisaunder, Sir Tristrem, Sir Orfeo, Horn Childe, Richard Coeur de Lion.* I was unfortunately not able to see the manuscript myself.

⁴ Between *Horn Childe* and *Richard Coeur de Lion* comes, however, the short poem *Praise of Women.*

⁵ See the good descriptions in B. v. Lindheim, *Studien zur Sprache des Manuskriptes Cotton Galba E. IX*, pp. 4 ff., and in the EETS edition of *Ywain and Gawain*. See also the British Museum catalogue of the Cotton Mss. (London, 1802), pp. 363–4.

⁶ See the *Catalogue of Additions to the Manuscripts in the British Museum*, vol. 18 (London, 1912), pp. 238–40, the description by E. Kölbing, 'Vier romanzen-handschriften', pp. 191–3, and the brief descriptions in the editions of the poems, e.g. the EETS edition of *Sir Eglamour of Artois*, pp. ix–x.

[7] With the help of the catchwords and the texts preserved in other manuscripts it is possible to establish that one and a half gatherings are missing from the middle of the volume (twelve leaves) on which the missing parts of *Sir Beues of Hamtoun, Sire Degarre* and *Floris and Blauncheflur* would fit exactly. At the end, the remaining part of *Sir Eglamour* must have taken up another complete gathering. It seems that the volume must have been taken to pieces fairly early. In many places, too, the margin has been cut off, possibly because of the valuable vellum. All the other manuscripts discussed here, except Cotton Galba E. IX, are paper volumes.

[8] I was unable to see the Lincoln Ms. myself. See the descriptions by R. M. Woolley, *Catalogue of the Manuscripts of Lincoln Cathedral Chapter Library* (London, 1927), pp. 51–61, and in M. S. Ogden's edition of the *Liber de Diversis Medicinis*, EETS, 207 (1938), pp. viii ff. On B. M. Additional 31.042 see *Catalogue of Additions to the Manuscripts in the British Museum in the Years 1876–81* (London, 1882), pp. 148–51, and K. Brunner, 'Hs. Brit. Mus. Additional 31042', *Archiv*, 132 (1914), 316–27.

[9] See the description in the catalogue of the Cotton Mss. (London, 1802), pp. 42–3, and the editions of the poems, especially the EETS edition of *Sir Eglamour of Artois*, pp. xi–xii. The manuscript was rebound in 1957 and the leaves mounted on folds so that the original gatherings cannot be ascertained any more with confidence.

[10] See the description in *A Catalogue of the Manuscripts preserved in the Library of the University of Cambridge* (Cambridge, 1857), II, 404–8, and in several editions, most recently in the EETS edition of *Sir Eglamour*, p. xii. A. McI. Trounce, in his discussion of the tail-rhyme romances, also draws attention to the importance of this manuscript; cf. *Medium Aevum*, I (1932), 94 ff.; II (1933), 53–7; III (1934), 33.

[11] See the description in W. H. Black, *Catalogue of the Manuscripts bequeathed unto the University of Oxford by Elias Ashmole* (Oxford, 1845), pp. 106–110, and the brief description in the edition of *Sir Orfeo* by A. J. Bliss, pp. xi–xii.

[12] See the description in the catalogue of the Harley manuscripts, in the editions of *Ipomedon* and *Le Morte Arthur*, and the brief remarks by R. H. Robbins in *Secular Lyrics of the XIVth and XVth Centuries*, pp. xxviii–xxix.

[13] Particularly interesting collections containing romances are Chetham 8009 (containing *Torrent of Portyngale, Sir Beues of Hamtoun* and *Ipomedon A*; described by E. Kölbing, 'Vier romanzen-handschriften', 195–201), Gonville & Caius College, Cambridge, 175 (*Richard Coeur de Lion, Sir Ysumbras, Athelston, Sir Beues of Hamtoun*; see Trounce's edition of *Athelston*, pp. 1–2, and above, Chapter V, on *Athelston*), Lincoln's Inn 150 (*Libeaus Desconus, Arthour and Merlin, Kyng Alisaunder, The Seege or Batayle of Troye*; see Kölbing, 194–5, and Smithers' edition of *Kyng Alisaunder*, II, 3–4), and the manuscript XIII. B. 29 of the Royal Library of Naples (*Sir Beues of Hamtoun, Libeaus Desconus, Sir Ysumbras*). See the description of this manuscript by D. Laing in *Reliquiae Antiquae*, ed. T. Wright and J. O. Halliwell (London, 1841–3), II, 58–70, and the interesting remarks in *The Text of the Canterbury Tales*, ed. J. M. Manly and E. Rickert (Chicago, 1940), I, 376–80, where it is suggested that the manuscript once belonged to Thomas Campanella (1568–1639). Much work on these manuscripts remains still to be done. Studies on individual collections, taking into account all the texts and their transmission, or more thorough studies on individual poems and their possible transmission would be most useful.

# SELECT BIBLIOGRAPHY

## I. EDITIONS OF ROMANCES

All quotations in the text are taken from the editions listed here. Other editions of individual poems and works that are only mentioned in passing will be found in the footnotes. The titles are sometimes abbreviated in accordance with usual practice.

*Sir Amadace*, in *Three Early English Metrical Romances*, ed. J. Robson, Camden Society, London, 1842.

*Amis and Amiloun*, ed. MacE. Leach, EETS, 203 (1937).

*Arthour and Merlin*, ed. E. Kölbing, Altenglische Bibliothek, 4, Leipzig, 1890.

*Athelston*, ed. A. McI. Trounce, EETS, 224 (1951).

*The Awntyrs off Arthure at the Terne Wathelyne*, in *Scottish Alliterative Poems in Riming Stanzas*, ed. F. J. Amours, The Scottish Text Society, Edinburgh, 1897.

*The Avowynge of King Arther, Sir Gawan, Sir Kaye, and Sir Bawdewyn of Bretan*, in *Three Early English Metrical Romances*, ed. J. Robson.

*Sir Beues of Hamtoun*, ed. E. Kölbing, EETS, ES, 46, 48, 65 (1885, 1886, 1894).

*Le Bone Florence of Rome*, ed. W. Vietor, Marburg, 1893.

*Cheuelere Assigne*, ed. H. H. Gibbs, EETS, ES, 6 (1868).

*Sir Cleges*, in *Middle English Metrical Romances*, ed. W. H. French and C. B. Hale, New York, 1930.

*Sire Degarre*, ed. G. Schleich, Englische Textbibliothek, 19, Heidelberg, 1929.

*Sir Degrevant*, ed. L. F. Casson, EETS, 221 (1949).

*The Erl of Tolous*, ed. G. Lüdtke, Sammlung englischer Denkmäler in kritischen Ausgaben, 3, Berlin, 1881.

*Eger and Grime*, in *Middle English Metrical Romances*, ed. W. H. French and C. B. Hale.

*Sir Eglamour of Artois*, ed. F. E. Richardson, EETS, 256 (1965).

*Emaré*, ed. E. Rickert, EETS, ES, 99 (1908).

*Sir Ferumbras* (Ashmole), ed. S. J. Herrtage, EETS, ES, 34 (1879).

*Firumbras* (Fillingham), ed. M. I. O'Sullivan, EETS, 198 (1935).

*Floris and Blauncheflur*, ed. J. R. Lumby, re-ed. G. H. McKnight, EETS, 14 (1901).

*Gamelyn*, in *Middle English Metrical Romances*, ed. W. H. French and C. B. Hale.

*Sir Gawain and the Green Knight*, ed. I. Gollancz, M. Day, M. S. Serjeantson, EETS, 210 (1940).
*Generydes*, ed. W. A. Wright, EETS, 55, 70 (1873, 1878).
*The 'Gest Hystoriale' of the Destruction of Troy*, ed. D. Donaldson and G. A. Panton, EETS, 39, 56 (1869, 1874).
*Sir Gowther*, ed. K. Breul, Oppeln, 1886.
*Guy of Warwick*, ed. J. Zupitza, EETS, ES, 42, 49, 59 (1883, 1887, 1891).
—, Cambridge version, ed. J. Zupitza, EETS, ES, 25, 26 (1875, 1876).
*Havelok*, ed. W. W. Skeat, 2nd ed., revised by K. Sisam, Oxford, 1915.
*Horn Childe and Maiden Rimnild*, in J. Hall's edition of *King Horn*, Oxford, 1901.
*Ipomedon*, ed. E. Kölbing, Breslau, 1889.
*Joseph of Arimathie*, ed. W. W. Skeat, EETS, 44 (1871).
*Kyng Alisaunder*, ed. G. V. Smithers, EETS, 227, 237 (1952, 1957).
*King Edward and the Shepherd*, in *Middle English Metrical Romances*, ed. W. H. French and C. B. Hale.
*King Horn*, ed. J. Hall, Oxford, 1901.
*The King of Tars*, ed. F. Krause, *Englische Studien*, 11 (1888), 1–62.
*The Knight of Curtesy and the Fair Lady of Faynell*, ed. E. McCausland, Smith College Studies in English, IV (1922).
*Lai le Freine*, ed. M. Wattie, Smith College Studies in Modern Languages, X, 3 (1929).
*Sir Landevale*, ed. A. J. Bliss (in his edition of *Sir Launfal*).
*The Laud Troy Book*, ed. J. E. Wülfing, EETS, 121, 122 (1902, 1903).
*Sir Launfal*, by Thomas Chestre, ed. A. J. Bliss, Nelson's Medieval and Renaissance Library, London and Edinburgh, 1960.
*Libeaus Desconus*, ed. M. Kaluza, Altenglische Bibliothek, 5, Leipzig, 1890.
*Le Morte Arthur*, ed. J. D. Bruce, EETS, ES, 88 (1903).
*Morte Arthure*, ed. E. Björkman, Alt- und Mittelenglische Texte, 9, Heidelberg, 1915.
*Octavian*, ed. G. Sarrazin, Altenglische Bibliothek, 3, Heilbronn, 1885.
*Sir Orfeo*, ed. A. J. Bliss, 2nd edn., Oxford, 1966.
*Otuel* (Auchinleck version), ed. S. J. Herrtage, EETS, ES, 39 (1882).
*Otuel and Roland* (Fillingham), ed. M. I. O'Sullivan, EETS, 198 (1935).
*Partonope of Blois*, ed. A. T. Bödtker, EETS, ES, 109 (1912).
*Patience*, ed. H. Bateson, 2nd edn. Manchester, 1918.
*Pearl*, ed. E. V. Gordon, Oxford, 1953.
*Sir Perceval of Gales*, ed. J. Campion and F. Holthausen, Alt- und Mittelenglische Texte, 5, Heidelberg, 1913.
*Purity*, ed. R. J. Menner, Yale Studies in English, 61, New Haven, 1920.
*Reinbrun*, ed. J. Zupitza (in his edition of *Guy of Warwick*).
*Richard Coeur de Lion*, ed. K. Brunner (*Der mittelenglische Versroman über Richard Löwenherz*), Wiener Beiträge zur Englischen Philologie, XLII, Wien-Leipzig, 1913.
*Robert of Sicily*, in *Middle English Metrical Romances*, ed. W. H. French and C. B. Hale.
*Rowlande and Ottuell* (B.M. Additional 31.042), ed. S. J. Herrtage, EETS, ES, 35 (1880).

*Roland and Vernagu*, ed. S. J. Herrtage, EETS, ES, 39 (1882).
*The Seven Sages of Rome*, ed. K. Brunner, EETS, 191 (1933).
*An Anonymous Short English Metrical Chronicle*, ed. E. Zettl, EETS, 196 (1935).
*The Siege of Jerusalem*, ed. E. Kölbing and M. Day, EETS, 188 (1932).
*The Sege off Melayne*, ed. S. J. Herrtage, EETS, ES, 35 (1880).
*The Seege or Batayle of Troye*, ed. M. E. Barnicle, EETS, 172 (1927).
*The Sowdone of Babylone*, ed. E. Hausknecht, EETS, ES, 38 (1881).
*The Squyr of Lowe Degre*, ed. W. E. Mead, Boston, 1904.
*A Stanzaic Life of Christ*, ed. F. A. Foster, EETS, 166 (1926).
*The Taill of Rauf Coilȝear*, ed. S. J. Herrtage, EETS, ES, 39 (1882).
*Titus and Vespasian or The Destruction of Jerusalem*, ed. J. A. Herbert, Roxburghe Club, London, 1905.
*Torrent of Portyngale*, ed. E. Adam, EETS, ES, 51 (1887).
*The Tournament of Tottenham*, in *Middle English Metrical Romances*, ed. W. H. French and C. B. Hale.
*Sir Triamour*, ed. J. O. Halliwell, Percy Society, 16, London, 1846.
*Sir Tristrem*, ed. E. Kölbing. Heilbronn, 1882.
*William of Palerne*, ed. W. W. Skeat, EETS, ES, 1 (1867).
*Sir Ysumbras*, ed. J. Zupitza and G. Schleich, Palaestra, XV, Berlin, 1901.
*Ywain and Gawain*, ed. A. B. Friedman and N. T. Harrington, EETS, 254 (1964).

## II. ANTHOLOGIES

French, W. H. and Hale, C. B., ed. *Middle English Metrical Romances*, New York, 1930.
Gibbs, A. C., ed. *Middle English Romances*, York Medieval Texts, London, 1966.
Rumble, T. C., ed. *The Breton Lays in Middle English*, Detroit, 1965.
Sands, D. B., ed. *Middle English Verse Romances*, New York, 1966.

## III. WORKS OF REFERENCE AND CRITICISM

Articles and books on individual poems are, as a rule, only quoted in the Notes.

BARROW, S. F. *The Medieval Society Romances*, New York, 1924.
BAUGH, A. C., ed. *A Literary History of England*, New York, 1948.
—, 'The Authorship of the Middle English Romances', *Annual Bulletin of the Modern Humanities Research Association*, 22 (1950), 13–28.
—, 'Improvisation in the Middle English Romance', *Proceedings of the American Philosophical Society*, 103 (1959), 418–454.
—, 'The Middle English Romance: Some Questions of Creation, Presentation, and Preservation', *Speculum*, XLII (1967), 1–31.
BENNETT, H. S. *Chaucer and the Fifteenth Century*, Oxford History of English Literature, II, 1, Oxford, 1947.

BENSON, L. D. *Art and Tradition in Sir Gawain and the Green Knight*, New Brunswick, N.J., 1965.

BEZZOLA, R. R. *Le sens de l'aventure et de l'amour (Chrétien de Troyes)*, Paris, 1947.

BILLINGS, A. H. *A Guide to the Middle English Metrical Romances*, Yale Studies in English, 9, New York, 1901.

BORDMAN, G. *Motif-Index of the English Metrical Romances*, FF Communications, vol. LXXIX, No. 190, Helsinki, 1963.

BORROFF, M. *Sir Gawain and the Green Knight. A Stylistic and Metrical Study*, Yale Studies in English, 152, New Haven, 1962.

TEN BRINK, B. *Early English Literature (to Wiclif)*, London, 1887.

BRINKMANN, H. *Zu Wesen und Form mittelalterlicher Dichtung*, Halle, 1928.

BROWN, C. *A Register of Middle English Religious and Didactic Verse*, 2 vols., Oxford, 1916–1920.

BROWN, C. and ROBBINS, R. H. *The Index of Middle English Verse*, New York, 1943 (see also under Robbins).

BRYAN, W. F. and DEMPSTER, G., ed. *Sources and Analogues of Chaucer's Canterbury Tales*, Chicago, 1941.

BURROW, J. A. *A Reading of Sir Gawain and the Green Knight*, London, 1965.

CHAMBERS, E. K. *The Mediæval Stage*, 2 vols., London, 1903.

CHAYTOR, H. J. *From Script to Print. An Introduction to Medieval Literature*, Cambridge, 1945.

DONOVAN, M. J. *The Form and Vogue of the Middle English Breton Lay*, Harvard Dissertation, 1951.

ELLIS, G. *Specimens of Early English Metrical Romances, chiefly written during the early part of the Fourteenth Century*, 3 vols., London, 1805.

ENKVIST, N. E. *The Seasons of the Year: Chapters on a Motif from Beowulf to the Shepherd's Calendar*, Helsingfors, 1957.

EVERETT, D. *Essays on Middle English Literature*, ed. P. Kean, Oxford, 1955.

FARAL, E. *Les Jongleurs en France au Moyen Age*, Paris, 1910.

—. *Les Arts Poétiques du XIIᵉ et du XIIIᵉ Siècle*, Paris, 1924.

FISHER, F. *Narrative Art in Medieval Romances*, Cleveland, 1938.

FRENCH, W. H. *Essays on King Horn*, Cornell Studies in English, 30, Ithaca, 1940.

GARDNER, J. *The Complete Works of the Gawain Poet. In a Modern English Version with a Critical Introduction*, Chicago, 1965.

GIST, M. A. *Love and War in the Middle English Romances*, Philadelphia, 1947.

GÖLLER, K. H. *König Arthur in der englischen Literatur des späten Mittelalters*, Palaestra, 238, Göttingen, 1963.

HABICHT, W. *Die Gebärde in englischen Dichtungen des Mittelalters*, Abhandlungen der Bayerischen Akademie der Wissenschaften, philosoph.-histor. Klasse, N.F., 46, München, 1959.

HIBBARD, L. A., see under Loomis, L. H.

HOOPS, R. *Der Begriff 'Romance' in der mittelenglischen und frühneueng-lischen Literatur*, Anglistische Forschungen, 68, Heidelberg, 1929.

JUSSERAND, J. J. *English Wayfaring Life in the Middle Ages*, University Paperbacks, London, 1961.

KANE, G. *Middle English Literature. A Critical Study of the Romances, the Religious Lyrics, 'Piers Plowman'*, Methuen's Old English Library, London, 1951.

KER, W. P. *Epic and Romance. Essays on Medieval Literature*, Dover Edition, New York, 1957.

—. *Medieval English Literature*, London, 1912.

KUHN, H. *Dichtung und Welt im Mittelalter*, Stuttgart, 1959.

LEGGE, M. D. *Anglo-Norman Literature and its Background*, Oxford, 1963.

LEWIS, C. S. *The Discarded Image. An Introduction to Medieval and Renaissance Literature*, Cambridge, 1964.

LIPPMANN, K. *Das ritterliche Persönlichkeitsideal in der mittelenglischen Literatur des 13. und 14. Jahrhunderts*, Diss. Leipzig, Meerane, 1933.

LOOMIS, L. H. (L. A. Hibbard) *Mediæval Romance in England. A Study of the Sources and Analogues of the Non-cyclic Metrical Romances*, 2nd edn., New York, 1959.

—. *Adventures in the Middle Ages. A Memorial Collection of Essays and Studies*, New York, 1962.

LOOMIS, R. S., ed. *Arthurian Literature in the Middle Ages. A Collaborative History*, Oxford, 1959.

LORD, A. B. *The Singer of Tales*, Harvard Studies in Comparative Literature, 24, Cambridge, Mass., 1960.

OAKDEN, J. P. *Alliterative Poetry in Middle English*, 2 vols., Manchester, 1930–5.

OWINGS, M. A. *The Arts in the Middle English Romances*, New York, 1952.

PEARSALL, D. 'The Development of Middle English Romance', *Mediaeval Studies*, 27 (1965), 91–116.

RITSON, J. *Ancient Engleish Metrical Romanceës*, 3 vols., London, 1802.

ROBBINS, R. H. and CUTLER, J. L. *Supplement to the Index of Middle English Verse*, Lexington, 1965.

SCHELP, H. *Exemplarische Romanzen im Mittelenglischen*, Palaestra, 246, Göttingen, 1967.

SCHLAUCH, M. *Antecedents of the English Novel 1400–1600*, Warsaw and London, 1963.

SCHOFIELD, W. H. *English Literature from the Norman Conquest to Chaucer*, London, 1906.

SEVERS, J. B., ed. *A Manual of the Writings in Middle English 1050–1500*, fascicule 1, New Haven, 1967.

SPEARING, A. C. *Criticism and Medieval Poetry*, London, 1964.

SPEIRS, J. *Medieval English Poetry: the Non-Chaucerian Tradition*, London, 1957.

TAYLOR, A. B. *An Introduction to Medieval Romance*, London, 1930.

TUVE, R. *Seasons and Months: Studies in a Tradition of Middle English Poetry*, Paris, 1933.

WILSON, R. M. *The Lost Literature of Medieval England*, London, 1952.

# INDEX

293